PHOENICIANS AND THE MAKING OF THE MEDITERRANEAN

CAROLINA LÓPEZ-RUIZ

T0326943

HARVARD UNIVERSITY PRESS

CAMBRIDGE, MASSACHUSETTS

LONDON, ENGLAND

First Harvard University Press paperback edition, 2024
First printing

Library of Congress Cataloging-in-Publication Data

Names: López-Ruiz, Carolina, author.
Title: Phoenicians and the making of the Mediterranean /
Carolina López-Ruiz.
Description: Cambridge, Massachusetts : Harvard University Press,
2021. | Includes bibliographical references and index.
Identifiers: LCCN 2021017882 | ISBN 9780674988187 (cloth)
| ISBN 9780674295575 (pbk.)
Subjects: LCSH: Phoenicians. | Phoenician antiquities. |
Mediterranean Region—History—To 476.
Classification: LCC DS81 .L66 2021 | DDC 937.004/926—dc23
LC record available at https://lccn.loc.gov/2021017882

To Antonis, por todo

CONTENTS

PHOENICIANS AND THE
MAKING OF THE MEDITERRANEAN

INTRODUCTION

Orienting the Reader

Think of the year 700 BC or thereabouts. There is much that we do not know about the most advanced societies thriving around the Mediterranean at that time. But we do know this: you could not travel from Tyre to the Straits of Gibraltar or "Pillars of Herakles" without noticing a remarkable interconnectedness among distant communities. And you could not go on this journey without coming across Phoenician harbors, ships, and towns along almost every step of the way. Through technological advancements of a kind unseen since the Neolithic revolution, diverse societies along this axis had joined a pan-Mediterranean "class" of urban, literate, and sophisticated elites, whose affinities were articulated through common visual, cultural, and economic modes. The new shared aesthetics bore the clear imprint of the Near East. This phase, period, or trend of the eighth to seventh centuries BC is commonly called "orientalizing" in modern scholarship. The encounters that produced this shared culture are the subject of this book.

This period is usually seen as an artistic "renaissance" that followed long after the collapse of the Late Bronze Age palatial economies and international cultures in a period between circa 1200–1100 BC. In the subsequent fractured map, lines of communication between the Aegean and the Levant were broken or much more intermittent than before. But as the Iron Age progressed, especially during the eighth century, a burst of economic dynamism produced a global transformation, with the effect of setting the central and western Mediterranean into direct contact with the Levant. Access to cultural assets as well as new markets, with their opportunities and risks, was now within the grasp of local kings, artisans, merchants, farmers, sailors, and soldiers. New forms of writing facilitated a growing and dynamic merchant class. Fast, high-capacity sailing boats transported not just goods but people and new cultural models. And at the helms of those boats were, above all, Phoenician mariners, settlers, traders, and explorers. This book will argue that it was these Phoenicians who set in motion the new connectivity networks and to a great degree created a first, truly interconnected Mediterranean. They paved the way for peoples east and west to join in this very first proto-urban, Mediterranean-wide koine of the Iron Age, and ultimately to stride onto the stage of history, even if in many cases we have lost those groups' testimonies and so cannot easily hear their voices.

We also know that the Phoenicians' commercial and then colonial expansion, reaching as far as the Atlantic coasts of Iberia and Morocco, was not undertaken at random. It was driven and sustained by the city-states of the Levant (especially Tyre). They sought areas rich in metal resources (especially copper, silver, and iron), either in areas that they could directly exploit or where they could tap into local networks and gain access to resources farther afield, such as Atlantic tin or African ivory, but they were also seeking resources such as timber, murex, and salt, and finding good harbors and farmland was crucial for sustaining their long-distance networks. Following in their wake were Greek sailors, especially Euboians, but also Cypriots, Cretans, Rhodians, and others, who made their own contributions to this new emerging koine.

It is only at this point that we can really talk about the first *global* Mediterranean. Despite earlier phases of connectivity among neighboring regions, such as the Aegean and the Near East in the Late Bronze Age, it is not until the eighth to seventh centuries BC that proto-urban cultures around the entire Mediterranean coalesced in an unprecedented way. Coinciding with the end of the so-called Dark Ages and the start of the archaic period in the Greek world, transnational networks formed around the axes of Phoenician and Greek colonial expansion, stimulating the transmission and adaptation of cultural forms, both tangible and intangible, including artistic modes of expression and motifs associated with Near Eastern royal and divine imagery, new technologies, including alphabetic writing, alongside mythological themes and religious ideas and practices. Greeks, Etruscans, Sardinians, and Iberian peoples readily fashioned their own versions of this international culture, referred to as "orientalizing" because it conspicuously followed Near Eastern models, and yet was not itself "Oriental," but a series of local imitations and innovations inflected differently in each context.

Despite increasing interest, the so-called orientalizing phenomenon is rarely treated comparatively on a pan-Mediterranean scale, and even more rarely integrated systematically within the framework of Phoenicians and local commercial and colonial relations across a vast geography. This book takes on that task, and puts the Phoenicians at the center of this development, where they belong. I make the case that their agency, more than that of any other Near Eastern group, explains the rapid spread of new technologies and artistic styles that characterize orientalizing culture. As communities from Cyprus to Iberia emulated the Near Eastern patterns peddled by the Phoenicians, they become visually and economically interconnected in an unprecedented manner. The Phoenicians profited from the export of a modifiable package of orientalizing goods and cultural capital, which I have called an "orientalizing kit." The common denominators of this tool kit span material luxuries and new technologies across regions. I discuss this phenomenon on a case-by-case basis in Part II, and the concept and interpretation of orientalizing materials in Chapter 3. But to give the reader a preliminary sense of it, these are the types of innovations that I consider part of this repertoire:

- symbolic and decorative motifs, most commonly lotus flowers, rosettes, the tree of life, sphinxes/griffins, lionesses, Mistress/Master of Animals figures, and so on
- pottery technologies, shapes, and decoration
- ivory carving and metalwork including jewelry (engraving, filigree, and granulation)
- techniques, motifs, and votive use of terracottas (esp. female Ashtart/Astarte-type figures)
- monumental stone sculpture (e.g., Greek *kouroi-korai*)
- masonry techniques and architectural innovations (quadrangular buildings and urban grid, wall-building measures and technologies, etc.)

- burial forms and rituals (cremation with urns, deposits of Near Eastern, orientalizing, and traditional indigenous items)
- industrial developments (metallurgic, fishing, salting) and farming innovations (domestication and processing of Mediterranean species such as the olive and the vine)
- in some areas, the introduction of wine culture (social and ritual banqueting)
- alphabetic writing
- mythological themes and literary models (where preserved)

Lost Among Disciplines

Growing attention and interest in the Phoenicians are undeniable, ranging from general books and exhibits to a legion of specialized articles and conference proceedings. It might seem strange, then, that the study of the Phoenicians is still extremely fragmented, striving to find a space of its own. This is in part because the Phoenicians are caught between several disciplines and theoretical trends.[1] At the most obvious level, the Phoenicians fall between the geographical and chronological fractures of classics and Near Eastern studies. This divide makes it difficult to attain a coherent, overarching view of the Phoenicians' role in this period. Ancient Near Eastern history and archaeology revolve around different "classical" eras, not aligned with the interests of the classical Greco-Roman world. In the Near East, the early first millennium BC, when the Phoenicians extended their commercial and colonial networks, is the period of the rise of new empires (Neo-Assyrian, 934–610 BC), only at the end of which the Greek poleis really enter the international stage. In other words, the turn of the first millennium is an important historical phase within Near Eastern/Levantine history and archaeology (Iron Age IIA-B: ca.1000–700 BC), and the Phoenicians have their own place in it. They produced written texts and appear in the texts of others (e.g., Assyrian, Egyptian, biblical), and their sites are becoming better known archaeologically.[2] But this phenomenon is only peripheral in Aegean archaeology of the protohistorical "Dark Ages," and the archaeology of Greece does not easily engage with this broader framework. This divide is then built on the artificial dichotomy between the Greek and Near Eastern worlds.

To the degree that we project onto these ancient worlds, imagined as nonconmensurate, our own imagined divisions, between "oriental" and "western," between Indo-European and Semitic, we perpetuate the scheme of a "clash of civilizations." As many have noted before, these dichotomies were created by modern geopolitical circumstances and ideological discourses, but do not explain much about the ancient world dynamics.[3] In this book, we will set the Greeks side by side with other Iron Age and archaic civilizations that responded to similar stimuli when they entered the orbit of the Near Eastern cultures through Phoenician trade. This is the only way to decenter the narrative from an imagined Greek core and gain an integrated view of the early Mediterranean. We can then better appreciate the unique character of each region and the effects of the encounter with the Levantines in their particular cultural trajectories.

The rigid lines imposed by periodization, as well as the idea of the later "Axial Age" also obstruct the study of this cultural-historical phenomenon. The orientalizing trend falls awkwardly between archaeological and historical periods. As J. G. Manning noted, the eighth–seventh centuries BC resist periodization: this key period falls between the "Dark Ages" of the earlier Iron Age and the archaic period in Greece, barely at the dawn of the famed "Axial Age," and far removed from the developments of fifth–fourth century Athens, which constituted the heart of the classics discipline.[4] We can break through this dead end by looking into the earlier first millennium through historically minded (and not only archaeologically minded) lenses, and integrating the history of Phoenician commercial and colonial expansion within the archaeological trail of Levantine exotica and orientalizing local developments. The Phoenicians provide a unique opportunity to escape the pull of this Axial Age schema. They also bridge Aegean (and European) "prehistory" and Near Eastern history, as they interacted with Greeks and others who were just emerging from the isolation of the "Dark Ages" and entering the historical record.

This book pulls together strands from different types of evidence and disciplines: archaeological materials, literature and mythology, art history, and the regional archaeologies of Greeks, Etruscans, Iberians, and others. Although several fields have focused on cultural exchange in this same period, their angles and goals vary and do not often focus on the Phoenicians. In this book, engaging with all these fields, I situate the Phoenicians at the crossroads of ancient Mediterranean encounters, and, in a way, as connectors across disciplines and trends themselves. These are, in broad strokes, the main strands I am referring to:

• **Classics and classical archaeology:** The combination of preserved literature and attractive plastic arts from ancient Greece forms a package that shines more brightly for the broader public than the fragmented legacy of the earlier Iron Age cultures, among them the Phoenicians. The traditionally narrow purview of the "classics" curriculum in turn promotes the old narrative of the "Greek miracle." This view highlights their innate talent for artistic and intellectual excellence, thanks to which the Greeks improved upon Near Eastern art and technologies. It is inconceivable, then, that they would hold any sort of cultural "debt" to others, since so many, such as the Romans and ourselves, are in debt *to them*. The Phoenician agency is instead diffused in vague discussions of "Near Eastern" or "Levantine" models adopted by the Hellenic genius.[5] In a late twentieth-century turn toward a more inclusive model, important works have shifted our attention to the archaic period and the "orientalizing revolution," and helped us to compensate for the dark areas that the blinding "classical" light produces around it.[6] Shifting our lens to the Phoenicians, instead of the Greeks, for the early first millennium (that formative period of "western" culture), not only offers some correctives to the story perpetuated by scholarly and ideological inertias but can result in quite a different story altogether.

• **Studies of ancient colonization:** For similar reasons, these studies tend to prioritize Greek colonization, and double standards are often applied to the treatment of Greek and Phoenician settlements and enterprises. In general, because of the wealth of written sources and the inevitability of our Hellenocentric education, the overwhelming attention to Greek colonization reinforces the impression that therein lies the key to the interconnected Iron Age Mediterranean.[7] Lately, scholars have zoomed in on the colonial relations among Phoenicians, Greeks, and locals, especially in the western Mediterranean.[8] Indeed, when study of ancient colonization moves away from the Hellenocentric framework, it overlaps in scope with Mediterranean archaeology.

• **Study of the western Mediterranean Iron Age:** By contrast, in these accounts, evidence is mostly archaeological and Phoenician colonies are well attested and not overshadowed by Greek colonization. This means that their presence is analyzed more freely from Hellenocentric models; scholars have more easily adopted a postcolonial stance, focusing on the negotia-tion between indigenous peoples and Semitic newcomers in a variety of scenarios.[9] The Phoenicians loom large here, but these contexts of contact are rarely if ever compared directly with those in the eastern Mediterranean, to illuminate the developments we see in Greece in the same period. One of the main goals of this book is to help bridge this gap. If anything, the recognition of the civilizatory role of the Phoenicians in the western end of the Mediterranean has been so overwhelming that it has created internal divides: some local archaeologies verge on denying the existence of rela-tively advanced and organized local cultures at the Phoenicans' arrival (e.g., Tartessians), while others have stressed the native agency and pushed against the "ex oriente lux" narrative limiting the Phoenicians' influence beyond the coasts, if never quite squeezing them out of the picture.

• **National (and nationalistic) narratives:** These accounts have also deter-mined approaches to the Phoenicians. In particular, a strong Hellenocentric pull has shaped national or regional narratives about this period. Whereas in Spain and Sardinia, for instance, there is no particular attachment to the Hellenocentric narrative and the Phoenicians are essential in the discussion about local transformations in the Iron Age, in mainland Italy the term "orientalizing" is used almost exclusively to define a "period," and the cul-tural ramifications of the phenomenon as such are generally avoided.[10] Little agency is ascribed to the foreign participants in the cultural process that oc-curs during this period, that is, until the Greeks enter the scene in the later phase of the archaic period, being the preferred external influence. In Greece itself, the idea of Greek exceptionalism is still quite dominant, and in Cyprus a nativist approach has pushed back against the narrative of Phoenician colo-nization on the island. In other words, the disparity in the treatment of inter-action with these Levantines is determined not only by discipline; it is also determined regionally or nationally. Each country's heritage affects its recep-tion of "classicism" in an age of postcolonial reckoning.

• **Mediterranean studies or "Mediterraneanization":** The twenty-first century has seen a rising interest in the Mediterranean as a transhistorical framework of cultural contact.[11] This historiographical trend makes this book timely, but it also exposes a blind spot when it comes to the Phoeni-cians, as these studies adopt a diachronic perspective and are not usually devoted to the Iron Age or the Phoenicians, with rare exceptions.[12] Recent economic and environmental histories of the Mediterranean have focused on areas and times for which classical sources are available, mainly classical and Hellenistic times,[13] and sometimes they leave out the Near East and North Africa altogether.[14] The Iron Age Mediterranean has also been studied in terms of global theory, which is perhaps the most useful working model for the Phoenician networks, as it highlights the interdependence of global, regional, and local dynamics.[15] Although there are insights to be gained from all these pan-Mediterranean perspectives, "Mediterraneanism" is usually not particularly interested in the role of specific agents, institutions, states, or empires, and avoids historical debates about the "winners and losers" of ancient globalizing movements;[16] this debilitates the framework's capacity to fully engage with underrepresented actors, such as the Phoenicians.

• **Orientalizing art and culture:** The term "orientalizing" is applied to the arts and technologies of this period. It has traditionally been used to describe the appropriation (mostly by the Greeks) of an eclectic set of cultural motifs loosely associated with the Near East. As I discuss in Chapter 3, the label itself has been criticized for vagueness and orientalist connotations. In the end, the phenomenon and the name remain diffuse, its interpretation fragmented across disciplines and regions. Since the early 2000s, there have been valid efforts to pull together the strands that come together under this category.[17] But the output in collections of case studies about different materials and regions is not easy to integrate into an overarching view. Part of our difficulty with the term "orientalizing" is its vagueness. We become frustrated because the category "orientalizing" obscures the diverse origins of the alleged Near Eastern models. If we are to keep using this convention (which seems likely in the absence of a different viable proposition), however, we can find ways to reconstruct its use and meaning. One way to do this is to turn the vagueness in "orientalizing" into an asset. To put it briefly, modern efforts to locate the *origins* of the different oriental models distract us from two facts: first, that Phoenician culture had itself appropriated Canaanite, Assyrian, and Egyptian traits, which formed part of Phoenician art and culture; what we might see as an amalgamated, eclectic art had its own coherence, and lies behind many of the orientalizing adaptations. Second, the recipient cultures did not always need to distinguish among (or care about) the ultimate "original" roots of the new cultural artifacts, since they were getting them largely from one source (whether Phoenicians or others), and soon they created local versions of them anyway.

8

These very different approaches to essentially the same phenomenon, namely, a reaction to contact with the Levantines we call Phoenicians, often reveal our teleological view of the Mediterranean, in which the European idea of "classical history" and the focus on Greeks and Romans tend to overshadow other important historical actors and forces. Pulling together archaeological and historical information, my book offers a way out of the orientalizing conundrum, and proposes a viable reconstruction of this trend of cultural innovation, which fully integrates the Phoenician presence around the Mediterranean. If we look at the orientalizing phenomenon from a distance, a clear pattern emerges: what we see as orientalizing cultures overlap with interaction between Phoenicians and emerging cultures across the Iron Age Mediterranean that strove to "catch up" to the older urban and literate Near Eastern civilizations. This study is driven by a search for those particular interactions and the place of Phoenicians in the making of this first interconnected Mediterranean.

I hope my work shows the Phoenicians not only as "vectors," as they are often qualified, but as active agents, even "makers" of pan-Mediterranean networks and cultural trends. A pan-Mediterranean view of the orientalizing phenomenon with the Phoenician expansion as the working framework accomplishes several goals at once: it shortens the gap caused by poor communication between the various disciplines involved; it contributes to the ongoing dismantling of the clash of civilizations narrative and the ideological (anti-Semitic) exploitation of a linguistic-based dichotomy; and it responds to the recent study of Mediterranean economic and environmental histories that transcend traditional periodizations, modern political boundaries, and European Hellenocentrism.

Finding the Phoenicians

Bringing Egyptian and Assyrian things by way of
merchandise, they [the Phoenicians] arrived,
among other places, to Argos.

(HDT 1.1.1)

This is how the Phoenicians make their entry in Herodotos's *Histories.* They are the third dramatis personae of the work, after the Greeks and Persians. Herodotos begins by saying that according to the Persians, it was the Phoenicians who began the long chain of conflicts that culminated in the Persian Wars. The economic transaction that sets the narrative in motion is rather simple: these Phoenicians "lay out" their cargo by the harbor and sell it to the local women, among them Argive elites. They then kidnap the Argive princess Io, which incites the Greeks to kidnap the Tyrian princess Europa, after which these east–west aggressions expand, including the stealing of Medea from Colchis and Helen from Sparta,[18] leading to the Trojan War, the background of the Persian offensive. Herodotos is careful to note that this Persian tale differed from what the Phoenicians themselves said about Io's kidnapping, which he does not report.

The Phoenicians are central to Herodotos's record of the very first exchange between Near Easterners and Greeks. After this, the Phoenicians appear throughout his unfolding account of how the Persians entered into conflict with the various peoples they conquered. Herodotos provides background on these peoples' earlier history, as far back as he can trace it, usually to the seventh–sixth centuries BC, but not for the Phoenicians. They receive no ethnography or history other than the brief mention that, according to some tradition, they migrated from the "Red Sea" (probably the Persian Gulf) to settle in the coastal land they now inhabit.[19] They are hidden in plain sight. Instead of receiving their own separate history, they are part of nearly everyone else's story, including the Greeks. Phoenicians appear frequently in the *Histories,* whether as a group or by their separate cities (Tyre, Arwad, Sidon, Byblos, Carthage, Gadir/Gadeira, etc.); they are long-distance sailors and merchants, the core force in the Persian navy, literate people whose script the Greeks adopted, founders of cities, sources of religious knowledge and rites, inventors and bringers of new technologies, and engaged in exchange with Greeks, Egyptians, Persians, Anatolians, Iberians, and others.[20]

In short, the ancient Greeks regarded the Phoenicians as integral to the transformations that marked their own early history. But it is more difficult for us to imagine them in that position, and we do not give them the same prominence when we tell the same story. But *who* really were these Phoenicians? And are we allowed to talk about them without quotation marks and "hedging" definitions and caveats?

A general, agreed-upon definition is not difficult to find. Quoting Brett Kaufman, "The Phoenicians [. . .] were essentially seagoing Canaanites from the Lebanese coastal cities such as Tyre, Sidon, and Byblos, distinct from other Northwest Semitic groups . . . mostly because of the gods they worshiped and their maritime, metallurgical, and other technological or craft expertise."[21] The Phoenicians emerged around 1000 BC as a distinct group among those who broke off from the common Syro-Palestinian Canaanite background of the Late Bronze Age. These groups included Phoenicians, Israelites, Moabites, Ammonites, Edomites, and Aramaeans (see Map I.1). They each had distinct languages, distinct scripts that stemmed from the Phoenician one, and distinct cultures and religious systems, functioning as discrete ethnic groups against a shared distant background.[22] The Phoenician group coalesced around several city states along the coastal strip on the outskirts of Mount Lebanon, their main towns reaching from Arwad in the north to Akko in the south, that is, slightly north and south of the modern country of Lebanon, where their settlements concentrated.

The territory of the Phoenician homeland in the Levant was for most of its history structured around four main states that controlled the territory and smaller settlements around them, as documented in Near Eastern and Greek sources. These are (from north to south): Arwad, Byblos, Sidon, and Tyre. Most historical sources from the first millennium BC concentrate on southern Phoenician cities, Sidon and Tyre, which were more active overseas and for most of the ninth–eighth centuries seem to have constituted a joint polity ruled from Tyre.[23] Around the turn of the millennium, Tyre emerged as a maritime commercial powerhouse in the central Levant (see Chapter 9). Over the course of the ninth century, Tyre expanded its economic and political base, controlling areas of northern Israel and establishing its first settlements abroad. The first Phoenician sites overseas are attested on Cyprus, in North Africa (from Morocco to Tunisia), and in southern Iberia, with small settlements from about 800 onward spreading along the coasts of southern and southeastern Iberia and up the Atlantic coast from the Algarve to Lisbon and farther north in today's Portugal. Phoenician sites appear on Sardinia, in western Sicily, and on the Balearic Islands during the eighth–seventh centuries, thus completing a well-connected network in the central western Mediterranean (Map I.1). The reasons for this wave of colonization, its modes of settlement, and level of coordination are not well documented (less so than those of Greek colonization), but this process was not the result of a random disorganized migration. The Phoenicians established a network that gave them sustained access to metal exploitation and trade routes, as they especially looked for

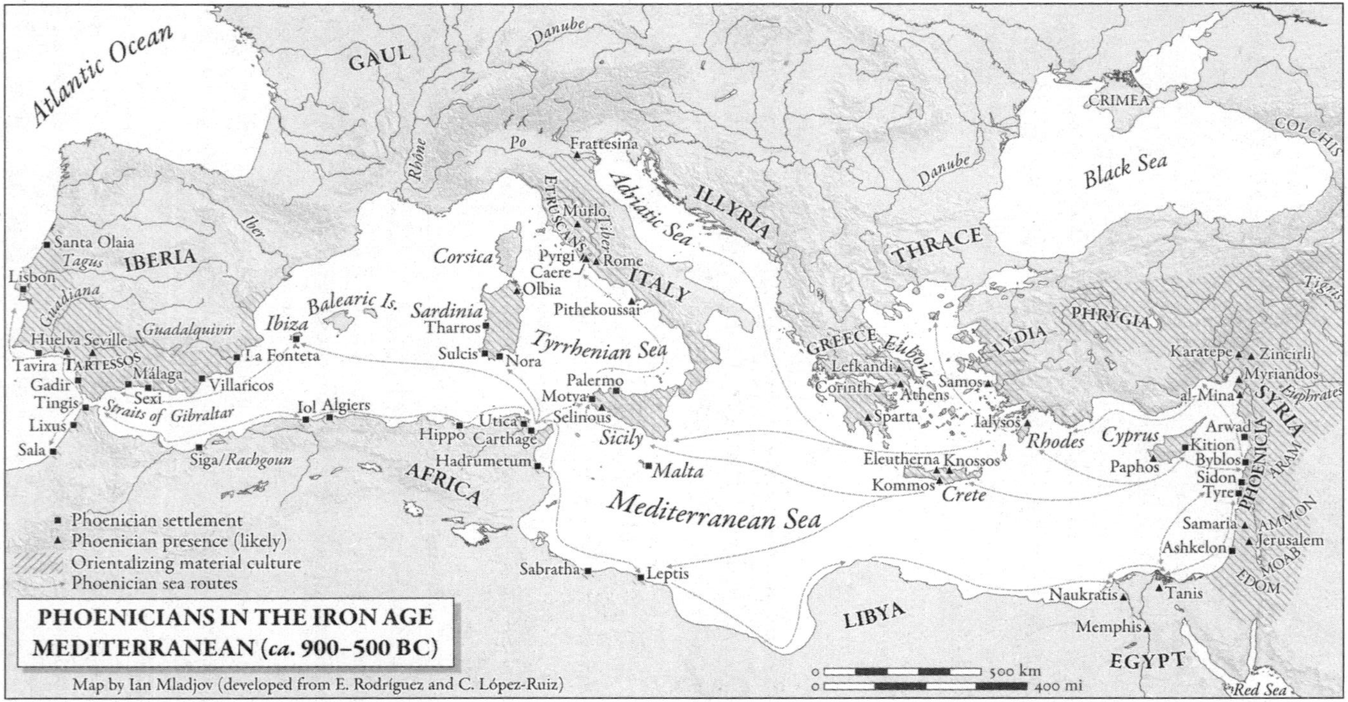
PHOENICIANS IN THE IRON AGE MEDITERRANEAN (*ca.* 900–500 BC)
Map by Ian Mladjov (developed from E. Rodríguez and C. López-Ruiz)
Phoenician settlement
Phoenician presence (likely)
Orientalizing material culture
Phoenician sea routes
Atlantic Ocean
GAUL
IBERIA
Lisbon
Santa Olaia
Tagus
Guadiana
Guadalquivir
Iber
Huelva
Seville
TARTESSOS
Tavira
Gadir
Málaga
Sexi
Villaricos
La Fonteta
Ibiza
Balearic Is.
Tingis
Lixus
Sala
Straits of Gibraltar
Siga/Rachgoun
Iol
Algiers
Hippo
Utica
Carthage
Hadrumetum
AFRICA
Sabratha
Leptis
LIBYA
Rhône
Po
Danube
Frattesina
ETRUSCANS
Murlo
Tiber
Pyrgi
Caere
Rome
ITALY
Pithekoussai
Corsica
Sardinia
Olbia
Tharros
Sulcis
Nora
Tyrrhenian Sea
Palermo
Motya
Selinous
Sicily
Malta
Mediterranean Sea
Adriatic Sea
ILLYRIA
THRACE
CRIMEA
Black Sea
COLCHIS
GREECE
Euboia
Lefkandi
Corinth
Athens
Sparta
Samos
Ialysos
Rhodes
Eleutherna
Knossos
Kommos
Crete
LYDIA
PHRYGIA
Tigris
Euphrates
Karatepe
Zincirli
Myriandos
al-Mina
SYRIA
Cyprus
Arwad
Kition
Paphos
Byblos
Sidon
Tyre
PHOENICIA
ARAM
AMMON
Samaria
Jerusalem
Ashkelon
MOAB
EDOM
Naukratis
Tanis
Memphis
EGYPT
Red Sea
500 km
400 mi

MAP I.1

sources of silver, gold, copper, and Atlantic tin, while also exploiting agricultural and other resources to supplement their own natural resources in the homeland in a densely populated territory. We also know that this program of settlement abroad was not triggered by Assyrian demands or oppression, as had long been thought. Tyre's networks, we now know, well predate the Assyrian domination of the city.

The Phoenicians were organized into city-states, a model they transferred to their colonies, at least the larger ones. Besides the capital cities with their principal harbors (sometimes on islands mirrored by urban centers across in the mainland), there were fortified enclaves to protect agricultural products and key communication passages inland, and smaller villages.[24] Tyre must have become quite dependent on its overseas networks, and promoted strong bonds with its western colonies, as we know from Gadir and Carthage, a relationship articulated through their shared worship of Melqart, the main Tyrian god, as a foundational figure.[25] Tyre thrived as the maritime outlet of the Assyrian overlords for most of this time, and did not receive the same harsh treatment that other Levantine cities did.[26] In the sixth century the "motherland" lost its privileged position when it fell to the Babylonians in 574 BC. Tyre's isolation produced a ripple effect that changed the geopolitical dynamics in the western Mediterranean. The first Carthaginian–Roman treaty dates to 509 BC, marking a time when Rome's military and economic power was growing regionally, its commercial interests partially overlapping with those of the western Phoenicians.[27] The treaty documents that one of Tyre's western colonies, Carthage ("New Town"), had emerged as a maritime powerhouse in the central Mediterranean and also gained control of Phoenician trade from Iberia and hence the Atlantic.

The two expanding forces, Rome and Carthage, clashed in the First and Second Punic Wars during the third century (264–241 and 218–201 BC). By the end of that century, Carthage had lost its grip on the Phoenician territories of Sicily, Sardinia, and Iberia, while for the winner, Rome, these gains were the basis for imperial expansion outside Italy. Only after this point did the Mediterranean become increasingly a Roman sea, their mare nostrum. Rome silenced the "threat" of Carthage when it razed the city to the ground and dispersed its people in 146 BC, the same year that they destroyed Corinth. The history of the Phoenician cities in the Levant followed a different path, outside this Carthaginian–Roman drama. By 323 BC (the year of Alexander's death), Greek power had spread like a blanket over the multiple peoples previously governed by the Persian Empire, triggering lasting transformations. The eastern Phoenicians became Greek speakers and part of the Hellenistic Near East. Still, the Phoenicians preserved features of their religion, language, and cultural identity until they entered the Roman Empire (sometime later), both in the Levant and the western Mediterranean.[28]

The Phoenician language and script span this east–west axis of Phoenician settlement and trade, with over ten thousand inscriptions recovered so far, ranging from the tenth century to the Roman period. In North Africa the language was alive alongside Latin even into the fifth century CE.[29] Phoenician religion is also well attested and is distinct from other religions of the Levant. Even with local and regional variations, the range of Phoenician gods is well-known: versions of the gods Baal and Ashtart tend to dominate the local pantheons—for instance, Baal-Hammon, Baal-Shamem, Baal-Saphon, Melqart, Adonis, Baalat Gubal ("Lady of Byblos"), and Tanit. These share the cult of additional gods such as Eshmoun, Sid, Pumay, the Egyptian Bes, and others. Personal names and funerary formulae are well documented epigraphically and they follow set patterns. These documents convey information about the religious and civic universe of the Phoenicians. Names follow conservative tendencies, as they are mainly theophoric (formed after divine names) and recurrent, and inscriptions also mention religious and civic institutions to which the individual belonged, all of which reflect consistent traditions that lasted for many centuries and tied these communities together culturally.

Phoenician sacred spaces varied in architectural plan, but their cultic installations were held in common, including, among other features, sacrificial altars, lustral basins and other water installations, cult statues and aniconic baetyls, benches for votive deposits, and an array of symbolic decoration tied to their religion.[30] Although there is some variety by period and place, funerary monuments and rituals are also homogeneous and recognizable, and marked by the deposits of Egyptianizing and other types of amulets, banqueting ware, ostrich eggs, oil flasks, and other goods related to funerary practices. The Phoenicians consistently used symbols that denoted a shared belief in the afterlife strongly shaped by Egyptian culture and symbology. More aspects of Phoenician culture will emerge in our survey of their encounters with other groups.

It is important to keep in mind that Phoenician culture is recognizable despite its wide geographical and chronological spectrum. Scholarship of the Levant has increasingly emphasized the continuities between the Late Bronze Age and the Iron Age culture of the region. In turn, in the western Mediterranean, the distinction between Phoenician and Punic is artificial. This is a historiographical, not an ethnocultural convention. *Poenum* (pl. *poeni,* adj. *punicum*) is simply the Latin name for "Phoenician(s)," from the Greek *phoinikes,* and has become the standard term for the Carthaginian realm after around 500, when the Carthaginians became a main concern of the Romans.[31] Hence it is the convention to use "Punic" for the western Mediterranean after the sixth century, with Carthage assumed as dominant, while for the earlier period, the western Phoenician settlements (including Carthage) are still part of the eastern Phoenician network. In reality, "the terms Canaanite, Phoenician and Punic depict aspects of a single nation's historical course, with common ethnic, linguistic and religious roots but differentiate it in terms of chronological and geographical criteria," as Giorgos Bourogiannis remarked.[32] I will use "Phoenician" by default for all periods and areas, unless the distinction is relevant, for instance when referring to specific scholarship on the "Punic world" or to the Carthaginian realm of influence.

In short, a Greek or a Roman could recognize a Phoenician by specific traits, which are backed independently by a convergence of archaeological and epigraphical materials. Still, some modern historians are skeptical that we can treat the Phoenicians as a group, even if ancient onlookers did. It is important to dispel some of these concerns before proceeding with my analysis.

Moving on from Phoenicoskepticism

A recent trend in historiography posits that the Phoenicians cannot be considered an ethnic group or even a valid historiographical category.[33] That trend is most prominently represented by Josephine Quinn's 2018 book *In Search of the Phoenicians,* but it has been explicitly articulated by others as well.[34] This position has created a certain uneasiness when scholars use the category of Phoenicians, even if they are not engaging directly with the issue, perhaps apprehensive to use an allegedly unnuanced category.

The recent Phoenicoskepticism (sometimes even Phoenikodenialism) argues that the Phoenicians did not constitute a coherent group, at least not in the early first millennium BC; that they would not have been distinct from other Levantines, or that in sources that talk about Phoenicians, from Homer or Herodotos to Roman authors, we are dealing with a sheer literary construct. Moreover, the Phoenicoskeptics argue, the ancient construct was overlaid with a modern scholarly construct. Since we do not have proof of an internal ethnonym for the Phoenicians, the Phoenicoskeptics highlight the fact that our subjects identified themselves with their cities (Tyre, Sidon, etc.), and their religious and family groups, but not as part of a larger ethnocultural continuum.[35] An added concern, which does not necessarily deny the Phoenicians' existence as a group, is the way in which the modern study of the Phoenicians was shaped by the Italian school of Phoenician archaeology led by Sabatino Moscati.[36]

These positions are not always expressly stated, but underlie much Hellenocentric and Eurocentric scholarship of the twentieth century. As Nota Kourou has put it, views on the Phoenicians swung from the pre–World War II uncritical assumption of their presence in the Aegean to a point at which "Phoenicia as such was in practice pushed out of focus in the study of interconnections between the Aegean and the Near East and the term Phoenician was kept mostly as a generic definition of Near Eastern people and styles." Phoenician art was considered eclectic and derivative and sources of inspiration for the orientalizing Greek art were sought in the more prestigious realms of Mesopotamia and Egypt. Within this trend, she notes, "contacts between Greeks and Phoenicians in the Early Iron Age were confronted with skepticism and everything about Phoenician presence in the Aegean had to be followed by a question mark."[37] As I discuss in Chapters 1–2, double standards are still often applied to Greek and Phoenician settlement abroad, and the Phoenicians are superficially represented as a vague collective, as "sea peoples" bound, if at all, by commercial interests, their westward expansion as uncoordinated and inconsequential, in implicit or explicit contrast to the Greeks' civilizing agency. The counternarrative has never been absent, of course, and has gained momentum in recent years thanks to the publication of archaeological data for the Phoenician enterprise, and to recent interest in pan-Mediterranean perspectives.[38]

The deconstructionist argument is built ex silentio. The lack of internal narratives for the early period, barring inscriptions, makes it difficult to define the contours of this group in terms of emic ethnic and group identity. But the silence is in fact not that deafening. There is enough internal evidence for an identifiable Phoenician culture, if we combine archaeological and epigraphical materials. The only real problem is that we do not know for sure how our subjects referred to their collective cities and networks, but this is not enough to deny a group identity. At any rate, there is some evidence that they may have used the terms "Canaan/Canaanite" as a self-referent. The name was used by the Canaanites of Phoenician cities (Tyre, Sidon) in the Amarna Letters at least when corresponding with others. *Cnʿ/Cnʿn*, and a derived form *kinahhu* in Akkadian, was a West Semitic name for Syria-Palestine deployed amply since the Bronze Age (we have testimonies in Akkadian, Hittite, Hurrian, Egyptian, and Hebrew), probably meaning "sunset land/west" (like "occident"), the same meaning as the name Amurru/Amorites used for the region too. The term was also tied in Akkadian and other languages to the purple dye/color associated with the specialized technology and with Canaan. The Greek name *phoenix*, in turn, means "purple/red" (and also "palm tree"), and already appears in association with this industry in Mycenaean texts. A likely linguistic hypothesis is that the Greek term either translated the Semitic word for the industry/color, or derived it from a different Semitic root for purple/purple dye extracted from a plant. Then, *phoenix* would have become more narrowly used for the Canaanites they knew best, the Phoenicians.[39] There are a handful of testimonies, scattered through the centuries, of the use of Canaan/Canaanite for their collective or their language (an inscription of third–second century BC North Africa, a New Testament reference, Philo of Byblos's *Phoenician History*, and St. Augustine's testimony).[40] Perhaps more tellingly, from at least the fifth century BC, Phoenician communities and individuals recognized and used the Greek and Roman terms "Phoenicia" and "Phoenician/Punic" to project that collective identity in international or multilingual contexts. The most visual representation of this is in the first Carthaginian coins, issued in the fifth century, which bore the palm tree (in Greek also called *phoenix*) as a symbol of Phoenician self-representation on the international stage.[41] These are small bits from a limited epigraphic corpus and an all-but-vanished literary one, but they are the crumbs we have to work with.

Be that as it may, we can recognize the Phoenicians as a distinct collective by external indicia, and so could the Greeks, Romans, and others. It is difficult to imagine that they themselves did not. We are talking about inhabitants of a set of interconnected cities and settlements, who shared distinct forms of material culture and art, who worshipped the same gods, followed the same rituals, spoke the same language, dressed in the same way (which Plautus made fun of), and specialized in the same occupations. The Phoenicians also sustained ritual bonds and tight commercial networks among their communities and responded to international conflicts as a unit, as when Tyre refused to join Persia's plan to attack its own "sons" at Carthage (τοὺς παῖδας τοὺς ἑωυτῶν [sic]), invoking their oaths and their kinship.[42] The Carthaginians banked on these ancestral bonds as they took over Tyre's leadership in the western Mediterranean, and Hannibal exploited his association with Melqart as a shared Phoenician symbol that connected Tyre and the west. In short, Phoenician identity was not only shaped or defined by the perceptions of others (as all identities are to some extent) but also based on the curation of a collective past strongly marked by a common link to the Tyrian inheritance.

The Phoenoskeptics lean on the fact that there was never a Phoenician "unified state."[43] Indeed, as María Eugenia Aubet put it, we can say that the Phoenicians were "a people without a state, without a territory and without political unity."[44] Aubet's statement rightly acknowledges that peoplehood and statehood are not coterminous concepts or realities (modern examples abound). Phoenicians and Greeks were organized similarly in independent city-states. The Greeks were not politically unified until the Macedonian conquest by Alexander the Great forced them into it in the late fourth century BC. Aristotle reflected on the diversity among the Greeks, and remarked that "the *ethnos* of the Greeks" had "the potential to rule everybody else if only it happened to be a single state."[45] This is not used as an argument to deconstruct Greek culture or ethnic identity, however. As for the idea that the Phoenicians identified themselves by their cities and families or religious institutions, true as that may be, again this is exactly what we find in Greek epigraphical evidence. This individual or small-group identity is not exclusive of broader levels of ethnic or group identity, all of which are culturally construed and articulated.[46] But the argument is applied indiscriminately to the Phoenicians and not to the Greeks. As Herodotos had already noted, the Greeks recognized each other by their "shared kinship and shared language, as well as the common shrines and sacrifices for the gods and our similar customs."[47] And yet, were it not for these rare discursive historiographical reflections (a privilege of the Greco-Roman textual tradition), the sense of shared identity of the Greeks of the archaic or even classical period would remain elusive. In short, the city-state organization and internal fragmentation of the Phoenician cities is not incompatible with a sense of shared cultural heritage and kinship, the basic elements that hold together all ethnic groups. As far as we know, by all reasonable measures, a Tyrian, a Sidonian, or a Carthaginian was no less Phoenician than an Athenian, a Corinthian, or a Syracusan was Greek (while they could recognize each other as both "kin" and enemies, of course). The Phoenicians were also not simply "Levantines," just as the Greeks were not simply an "eastern Mediterranean" crowd. There was no such thing as a monolithic Panphoenicianism, just as there was no monolithic Panhellenism. It is more useful to think of a "practice of being Greek," as Tamar Hodos put it, which was varied and idiosyncratic, but nonetheless sufficient to make the Greeks mutually and externally recognizable.[48] The same applies to the Phoenicians.

There is simply too much evidence that the Phoenicians were both perceived as a distinctive group by others and acted as one. The apparent silence is broken from too many directions and types of materials. With all the nuances and caveats called for by any historical reconstruction, we *can* talk about Phoenicians as much as about other Iron Age groups whose culture we recognize through a critical mass of coherent external and internal evidence.

PART I

BEWARE THE GREEK

◄ 1 ►

PHOENICIANS OVERSEAS

The Gadeirans recall a certain oracle, which, they say,
commanded the Tyrians to send a settlement
to the Pillars of Herakles.

(STR. 3.5.5)

Ancient Colonization and Modern Colonialism

There are various, sometimes competing perspectives on ancient Mediterranean connectivity. They all involve interaction among Greeks, Phoenicians, and other groups, but their interpretation of these relations is tied to different methods and agendas. Before dealing with those perspectives in Chapter 2, we need to understand the nature of Phoenician expansion in the Mediterranean and to dispel some stereotypes that stem from the explicit or implicit comparison of Phoenician and Greek activity abroad.

Our current models for thinking about colonization and cultural exchange are much more refined than they were just a few decades ago. We are aware that one size does not fit all. Sometimes there is contact without meaningful cultural exchange, and when it occurs it may be under colonial or imperial situations, where uneven power relations structure the interaction; at other times circumstances might have allowed for more even, mutually beneficial exchanges. In many cases situations would fall somewhere in between. The Phoenicians, however, have not yet benefited from postcolonial theoretical advances, save within specialists' micro studies. They sit awkwardly in the grand narrative of Mediterranean transformations, as their influence outside their areas of settlement is not always recognized. But archaeological advancements are forcing us to reconsider previous assumptions about Phoenician colonization. In this section I discuss our current understanding of colonial models and I follow recent scholarship in calling attention to the double standards that still underlie views of Phoenician and Greek settlement abroad.

Archaeological interpretation has shifted its attention from colonial to indigenous groups. Postcolonial approaches interrogate the "gray areas" or "third spaces" created by these encounters. Elaborating on the theoretical framework spearheaded by Homi Bhabha, concepts such as "hybridity," "middle ground," and "exchange networks" have become working tools for ancient historians and archaeologists.[1] Scholars have thus distanced themselves from models of center–periphery or World Systems, which revolve around traditional empires and civilizations, and are more interested in reconstructing the perspectives of underrepresented players in world history.[2] The study of the contact among Phoenicians, Greeks, and various local groups has gained new momentum from this trend.[3]

On the other hand, postcolonial ideas do not perfectly match ancient world dynamics, at least to the degree that ancient colonization (its motivations, mechanisms, and dynamics) was not identical to early modern and modern colonialism, which was premised on systematic exploitation, ideological and political domination, and territorial expansion.[4] Concepts such as migration or diasporas can be useful when we want to emphasize lack of expansionist or imperial agendas in the Phoenician and Greek networks.[5] Other scholars have emphasized the idea of selective consumption, and the idea of "hybridity," applied to "hybrid cultures" or "hybrid practices" has become especially useful for addressing ancient intercultural relations.[6] Scholars have found still other ways to challenge traditional colonial models, such as speaking of "cultural colonization" or "colonialism without colonization," and "colonialism within a shared cultural milieu."[7] Attempts to compare ancient and modern colonization processes or situations show the inadequacy of modern categorizations, but also that there is some overlap between ancient and modern hybridization processes and sometimes power relations, even if colonial programs were different.[8]

In the end, the conventional use of the terms "colonization" or "colonial" for ancient settlement abroad remains valid and useful, as long as we do not impose the models of modern colonialism. Ancient settlements abroad, loosely called "colonies," functioned within complex webs or networks that influenced the experiences and identities of all parties involved. This is the core tenet of network theory.[9] We can understand ancient colonization as a subset of the all-encompassing networks of exchange, specifically "the presence of one or more groups of foreign people in a region at some distance from their own place of origin," usually involving "asymmetrical socio-economic relationships between the colonizing and colonized groups."[10] The terms "local" and "indigenous" are used in scholarship roughly interchangeably for those inhabiting a geographical area for a significant period of time (not "forever" or what the Greeks called autochthonously), in contrast to more recently arrived groups like Phoenicians and Greeks. Naturally, after some time, the new settlers become local too, contributing to the hybrid contexts that produce the cultural expressions I discuss in this book.[11]

Decolonizing the Phoenicians

The Phoenicians were a colonizing people. At the same time, Phoenician materials fall outside the Greco-Roman and Near Eastern colonial and imperial narratives traditionally favored by histories. Hence, the Phoenicians provide us with a great opportunity for the study of intercultural relations that are not predetermined by ideas of Hellenization, Romanization, and so forth. This noncanonical position, however, makes the Phoenicians subject to a paradox: because they do not conform to the "classical world" strictly speaking (even though we know much about them through classical sources), they are marginalized. Archaeologists devoted to the Iron Age have denounced the exclusion of the Phoenicians from Europe's preferred pasts, or, as Ian Morris has put it, from "the history that matters."[12] As Peter van Dommelen has remarked, "classicism has dominated western discourse on Phoenician-Punic culture as the effective alter ego of Orientalism," and Greek and Roman cultures continue to be promoted as "the centre and yardstick of development."[13] In other words, the Phoenicians and their colonial movement need to be decolonized themselves from our western, Greco-centric view of the Mediterranean. Martin Bernal famously framed this lopsidedness in terms of early to mid-twentieth-century racist trends in western scholarship.[14] Leaving that aside, this marginalization ultimately derives from the bond between modern European nation-building and the operating assumption that the Greco-Roman past provided the backbone of western culture. As Margarita Díaz-Andreu puts it, during the first half of the nineteenth century, "the past that sustained the ideology of nationalism was classical antiquity. The ideas expressed by the Greco-Roman authors and the art produced by the artists of the period were the canon by which to measure wisdom, knowledge, and civilization."[15] The European view of the past also privileged certain types of materials: temple remains, inscriptions, vases, marble sculptures. When other civilizations were discovered and their texts deciphered, their art and literatures were considered inferior or irrelevant to the foundational classical civilization.[16] Civilizations with states or empires were granted a higher status in academia than those who lacked them, and priority was given to historical periods or cultures, not prehistoric ones (i.e., those without written records), and to the phases when Near Eastern cultures interfaced with Greek and Roman history proper (from the Persian period onward), or to episodes where they illuminated the Hebrew Bible. A group such as the Phoenicians, present in the entire Mediterranean since the turn of the first millennium BC, could be pushed out of the classical narrative from many angles: for not being Greek or Roman, for appearing in the historical record when the Aegean was in its prehistoric or protohistoric phase, and for not representing a single state or an imperial entity (until we have Carthage, which was, ultimately, beaten by Rome).

Moreover, the Phoenician colonial period is not a priority in the past of modern European nation-states, even when Phoenicians were among the most prosperous and influential of their ancient inhabitants, for instance, in Spain, Sicily, and Cyprus. Moreover, they are not central to the national narratives of the countries in which the main Phoenician city-states prospered, Tunisia and Lebanon, not to mention other countries whose territory overlaps almost entirely with a long phase of Phoenician-Punic settlement, such as Malta and Algeria. This is despite enjoying some favor as an alternative narrative to the Christian and Islamic divides and more recently (e.g., in Tunisia) in the booming tourist industry.[17] In the end, the archaeology of these regions is inseparable from their political biography, dominated since their birth as nation-states by European priorities, which inflicted huge loses on the local heritage.[18] The same can be said in general of postcolonial European influence in the Near East.[19]

With this geopolitical framework in mind, the ongoing insistence that the Phoenicians did not generate a unified state is not innocent of ideological bias. Together with other prehistoric and protohistoric stateless and empireless groups, the Phoenicians are kept at arm's length from the "real" western civilizations on which Europe built its identity, Greece and Rome. To the degree that we do not integrate the Phoenician enterprises in our general narratives, our disciplines continue to run in parallel, impervious to each other and (always with exceptions), they tend to perpetuate traditional biases.

From Iberia to Phoenicia: New Evidence and New Perspectives

Our view of Phoenician settlement abroad has changed dramatically in the twenty-first century: we now know the Phoenicians settled farther west than we once thought, along the Atlantic coasts of today's Portugal, and earlier than we thought, in the mid-ninth century BC. By the mid-tenth century, Tyre had already become the main political and economic hub of the Levantine coast and was in a position to revive dormant connections with the Aegean and farther afield. From the Aegean side, Cypriots and Euboians also played crucial roles in the reknitting and expanding of networks, in a phase often called "precolonization."[20] Discussion of these early contacts that followed the Mycenaean period and preceded Greek colonization long revolved around issues of primacy, generally highlighting the Greek materials and Euboian entrepreneurship at sites such as Al-Mina, on the coast of North Syria, or Pithekoussai in the Bay of Naples. This sort of "trade before the flag," as Hans Georg Niemeyer has called it, was framed teleologically, as proof of "trading posts" that preceded and lead to the later process of colonization.[21]

At the other end of the Mediterranean, past the Straits of Gibraltar on the Spanish Atlantic coast, we find a very different picture, in which the Euboians are reduced to second or third place: materials found in an emergency excavation at the Plaza de las Monjas / Calle Méndez Núñez site at Huelva have shown that the Phoenicians were already engaging with native groups this far out in the late tenth century. Small amounts of Aegean, Cypriot, and other eastern materials, probably brought along by Phoenicians westward, suggest a minor Greek participation in long-distance commerce and exploration when the Phoenician enterprise started. These western contacts precede by decades the Tyrian foundations in Gadir and Carthage established in the mid- to late ninth century. The materials reveal that indeed these precolonial transactions happened within a local context, and there is no evidence of permanent foreign settlement yet: in Huelva, local pottery is overwhelmingly dominant, followed by Phoenician pottery corresponding to types attested in the Tyre al-Bass excavations, with a much smaller representation of Greek, Cypriot, and other types (Sardinian, Italic). Besides pottery, the Huelva stash yielded materials connected with luxury products: ivory, wood, murex shells used to produce purple dye, as well as metal scraps and metallic objects, all of which illustrate the interest of the locals in exotic, luxury materials typically carried by Phoenicians and the latter's interest in metal resources.[22]

It is no longer tenable to argue that the Greeks' own renewal of trade with the Levant and their first long-distance ventures westward preceded or overshadowed the Phoenician routes. Greek themselves operated within the opposite assumption. Their historiographical tradition listed Lixus, Gadir, and Utica (in that order) as the earliest Phoenician, specifically Tyrian, colonies.[23] In other words, the Greeks situated these colonies in the post-Mycenaean period of dispersion and migrations, a picture already presented in Thucydides's *Archaeologia*, which included the Phoenicians' role in jump-starting pan-Mediterranean reconnection.[24] While no materials from the twelfth century have supported this ancient Greek reconstruction, its general scheme conforms with our perception of the early nature of the Phoenician enterprise, as archaeological materials and in some cases radiocarbon dating place their earliest activity at Huelva, Gadir, Utica, and Carthage in the mid- to late ninth century.[25]

In the case of Carthage, the Greek tradition was more accurate, giving a date of 814 BC for its foundation, which fits within the current archaeologically documented parameters. This is the date transmitted by the Sicilian Timaios of Tauromenion, generally accepted by others (e.g., Menandros of Ephesos, Josephus) after him. Another view situated Carthage's foundation before the Trojan War (like Gadir's).[26] In the next phase, at the turn of the ninth to the eighth century, a close-knit chain of establishments dotted the coasts of Málaga and the east coast of Iberia. This is also the date of Phoenician materials from Atlantic sites on the Portuguese coasts and Sardinia.[27] In Maria Eugenia Aubet's assessment, these materials reflect "an initial horizon of the recognition and exploitation of metal resources in the Atlantic area in the first half of the ninth century, followed by the founding of the first permanent colonial establishments, starting in the last quarter of the ninth century BC."[28]

In the next phase, during the eighth century, both Phoenician and Greek foundations multiplied exponentially. Phoenician settlements spread through the southern and western coasts of Iberia, the Balearic Islands, western Sicily, west and south Sardinia (the better communicated coasts), and the coasts of North Africa from the Atlantic to Tunisia. As if following a deliberate plan to stay out of each others' way, as implied in Thucydides's narrative about Sicily, Greek colonization geared toward the shores of the Black Sea, some points in southern France and northeastern Iberia (Massalia, Emporion/Empúries), settling also on the Libyan coast (Cyrene), southern Italy and parts of Sicily, and some enclaves in Corsica (see Map I.1).[29]

The new chronologies revealed by the far west materials have considerably reduced the gap between the Greek sources and the independent archaeological sources. Working with the lower chronologies available archaeologically, scholars had long disregarded the historical accounts as unreliable and inconsistent. The view of Phoenician colonization as an eighth-century (even late eighth-century) phenomenon placed it in parallel with or even in response to the Greek movement.[30] On the Near Eastern side, the Phoenicians' enterprise was seen as reactive, not proactive, bound to the Assyrian Empire's demands. In this view, the search for metals and wood was driven by external pressures, and the Phoenicians were but small states operating along the periphery of Assyria, at once victims and profiteers of imperial needs (a clear example of a center–periphery historical framework).[31] A key 1979 article by Susan Frankenstein, "The Phoenicians in the Far West: A Function of Neo-Assyrian Imperialism," provided the basic model for decades to come.[32]

The emerging archaeological picture, matched by Near Eastern written sources, reveals quite a different dynamic: the cities of the Phoenician coast, organized around the states of Arwad, Byblos, Sidon, and Tyre, emerged fairly unscathed from the Late Bronze Age international crisis, and they benefited from the vacuum of powers that ensued. Their rise to prominence in the Levant stems in part from their almost seamless continuity from the Canaanite world, as I discuss in Chapter 9. The Phoenician polities used their networks and status to become indispensable for the Assyrians, a position that forced the Neo-Assyrian Empire to allow them, especially

Tyre, a greater degree of independence than that of other subjects well into the seventh century.[33] In other words, the Phoenicians followed a perfectly programmed and organized strategy, indeed, as Aubet notes, "far removed from the traditional idea that saw the start of the Phoenician expansion as a surge of refugees from the East improvising as they went along."[34] We can speak confidently of a well-organized expansion emerging from the Late Bronze Age "void," preceding (and independent from) both the Assyrian expansion and Greek colonization. In fact it followed "a precise strategy of (inter)action that found its precedents/presumptions in the international policy implemented by the Phoenician cities of the Levant," as Michele Guirguis has recently assessed.[35] The Phoenician movement, like the Greek one, was generated from within the city-states, but with the particularly salient role of one of them, Tyre (with its colonies in turn forming secondary settlements), in contrast to the scenario of the Greek colonies, whose origins were more varied.

The factor of motivation and receptivity or resistance on the side of local elites is equally important, even if more obscure to us than both Greek and Phoenician trade and colonization. Iron Age proto-urban elites were seeking new ways to stand out among their peers and to surpass competing communities, and Greek and Phoenician networks offered priceless economic opportunities. But the "commodities" the Phoenicians were trading (whether with Assyrians, Greeks, or others) had both utility and social value.[36] Where socioeconomic conditions were ripe, then, the Levantine models of art and technology and even political organization brought by Phoenicians (and Greeks in their wake) provided tools for both local differentiation and international enfranchisement. In turn, this does not mean that equal receptivity existed in all areas of contact or that relations were by default peaceful or equanimous.[37] As Ian Morris remarked about the pan-Mediterranean approach, such globalizing processes were not universal or static. It is easy to forget the "human costs of connectedness," including "conflict, inequality, and social dislocations," or that connectedness created winners and losers, all of which concern much of modern globalization literature but are often overlooked as possibilities by studies of ancient Mediterranean networks.[38]

Whatever the economic modes of exchange, these were not only driven by a "free market," akin to the capitalist model, but also involved a range of institutional bonds, documented in the Late Bronze Age Levant, but better attested in later periods for Greeks and Phoenicians alike, as Taco Terpstra has shown. These included ties between city-states and religious and trading organizations as well as public and private "friendships."[39] The local side of the demand and their networks is less frequently explored and still poorly understood, in part because of scarcer information. But it is in those areas that we see the selective appropriation of Levantine art and technologies in this period.[40] Understanding orientalizing adaptations as one of many possible local reactions to the globalizing (Mediterraneanizing) trends of the Iron Age, in particular one associated with Phoenician expansion, provides more clarity about this process.

Recent works have emphasized the economic and institutional bonds among Phoenician colonies. The scarce written sources provide a glimpse into the web of mythological and historical traditions that must have connected the Phoenician communities as well. Not surprisingly, most evidence concerns traditions related to Tyre, Gadir, and Carthage, the most prominent Phoenician cities, which received more attention from ancient historians. The kinship between Tyre and its colonies Gadir and Carthage was transmitted in foundation stories. The quotation from Strabo used as the epigraph to this chapter is part of a longer account about how the Tyrians arrived at Gadir, following an oracle (of Melqart) to find the right spot and only succeeding after several attempts. And the legend about Carthage makes its founder Queen Dido a fleeing member of the Tyrian royal family who successfully fends off native threats.[41] The new city's Tyrian identity is highlighted for the rest of its history, and expressed historically when eastern Phoenicians refused to attack their western kin, as already mentioned, as well as in the fact that Carthage continued to send offerings and delegations to Tyre on a regular basis until at least Hellenistic times. Gadir also strongly identified itself with Tyre: the insular topographies of the two polities closely mirror each other, both organized around two harbors perhaps connected by a channel, with the temples of Melqart, whose cult linked the two ends of the Tyrian "axis," as their most prominent landmarks. Pillars or betyls featured in both temples connected with Tyre's foundational mythology, in turn symbolically transposed to the geographical landmark of the "Pillars of Herakles," under whose Greek name lies the Tyrian Baal and "city-lord," Melqart. We also know that Gadir held the "sacra" of Melqart brought from Tyre, and that the Iberian colony deployed these

31

religious and institutional symbols of authority stemming from Tyre when it founded other subcolonies in Iberia.[42]

The intertwined destinies of Tyre, Carthage, and Gadir lie behind the geopolitical changes that affected southern Iberia in the sixth century BC. Sometime before 500, southern Iberia, deemed the "jewel of the Tyrian maritime commercial network," suffered disruptions in commercial patterns and saw the abandonment of indigenous sites, denoting a crisis that puzzles historians and archaeologists.[43] A recent theory proposes that a maritime cataclysm in the area of Huelva could have disrupted the metallurgic flow from the interior, precipitating or aggravating a crisis in a tight economic system, although this event remains hypothetical.[44] Whatever the case, there must have been some sort of cause-and-effect relationship between this western crisis—the decline of Tyre under the Babylonian grip and its loss of maritime power and control of metal exploitation—and the inversely proportional rise of Carthage's grip in the west, including Iberia. This confluence of circumstances might have affected trade in the Aegean too, as "the Phoenician network lost its eastern terminus with Assyria."[45] Whether or not Carthage's growth played any part in Tyre's increasing isolation to begin with, it certainly benefited from it, and by the end of the sixth century the North African metropolis filled the void as the Phoenician overlord in the western half of the Mediterranean, entering areas already "Phoenicianized" for centuries, and setting itself on a collision course with Rome.[46]

The developments that I sketch here suggest a much tighter network of Phoenician settlement than has previously been appreciated, based not only on cultural and economic ties but also on religious and political bonds promoted over time among the principal colonies. Thanks to archaeology, epigraphy, and written traditions (when we have any), we have begun to reconstruct the axis running from Phoenicia to Iberia, although given where most of the new evidence comes from, perhaps we should say from "Iberia to Phoenicia."

It is also clearer that Greeks and Phoenicians constituted comparable networks of merchants, migrants, and colonists.[47] In turn, the Phoenicians were pioneers in the reopening of trading routes with native groups. The default narrative, however, has not caught up to the new evidence, and double standards and inconsistent treatment are applied to Greek and Phoenician settlement abroad. Brien Garnand has put it most starkly: "When standard textbooks contrast these achievements with those of the Greeks, they reduce the Phoenician alphabet to non-vocalic signs, their trade to the exchange of baubles that seldom penetrated beyond the coastline, and their settlements to trading posts lacking territorial ambition. In this zero-sum equation, they use presumed deficiencies of the Phoenicians to explain Greek superiority."[48] All these issues affect the materials presented in this book. But it is worth discussing three main preconceptions that are brought to descriptions of Phoenician settlement by those outside Phoenician studies proper: first, that Phoenician settlements were not fully urban but mostly "trading posts"; second, that the Phoenicians were associated with harbors and seafaring, not with farming, which implies their limited impact in hinterland areas; and third, that cultural influence outside areas of Phoenician colonies proper was minor, even when we have ample proof of small-scale interaction in other contexts, such as sanctuaries. These axioms lie in explicit or implicit contrast to preconceptions about Greeks abroad and are deeply entangled with each other. I address them in the next three sections.

"Ports of Trade" versus Colonies and Other Asymmetrical Comparisons

The term "*emporion*" means "market" in Greek, and is often used for "trading posts" or "ports of trade." Traditionally, *emporia* were associated in scholarship with the Greeks' commercial activity, at sites where their presence did not amount to colonization (e.g., at Naukratis, Pithekoussai, Al-Mina), and often as a step in the direction of colonization. More recently, the category has provided a useful model for the study of cultural and economic exchange in international or multiethnic contexts, seen as fruitful "spaces of encounter and entanglement" or places of cohabitation and interaction.[49]

On the other hand, "trading post" has been used as a blanket term for Phoenician settlements, not only in the sense considered above, but in place of "colony," whereas the latter is mainly associated with the Greek world and the Greek term for settlement abroad "*apoikia*." The category of "colony" is thus reserved for the Greek world, with few exceptions, such as the better-documented and more consequential case of Carthage.[50] As a result, Phoenician activity abroad is often depicted as limited to small coastal "bubbles" narrowly focused on the manufacture and export of specialized crafts, at most exploiting some resources through their negotiations with natives, mainly metals. The dichotomy between Greek *apoikia* / Phoenician *emporion* presupposes that Greek presence responded to a sort of "civilizing mission" linked to logic and order, "while the Phoenicians offered nothing at best, irregular chaos at worst," as Garnand denounced.[51] Iván Fumadó Ortega articulated similar critiques of the colonial views that for long dominated the discourse about Carthage itself and in general the prejudices affecting Phoenicain-Punic archaeology.[52]

The evolved view is that international trading communities, Greeks or others, did not automatically lead to colonization, and indigenous groups had a decisive role in the outcome. In other words, the forced dichotomy between *apoikia* and *emporion* has been challenged and nuanced.[53] The Greeks themselves used *emporion* in a more flexible way, for commercial activities in various sociopolitical settings. The same place could be interchangeably called *emporion* ("port," "market"), *apoikia* ("settlement abroad"), or *polis* ("city/city-state"), depending on the context and the author's emphasis on civic or mercantile aspects of the community. For instance, both terms appear when Herodotos writes about port towns in the Black Sea and about the multinational community of Naukratis in the Nile Delta.[54] The Greek colony of Emporion in northeast Iberia used that name (Emporion) even when it developed into a polis. An *emporion* can also denote a market inside or outside a city, akin to an agora or the Roman forum. In Latin-Punic inscriptions the Phoenician word "MḤZ" appears as equivalent to *emporion*. This term overlaps with the general semantic field of the Akkadian *karum/karani*, attested since the Bronze Age, which could include harbors, factories, and other points where foreigners found a safe haven for production and transactions. Assyrians called Levantine trade institutions *within* the Assyrian centers *karani*.[55]

More recently, scholars have resorted to another term, *enoikismos* (from the Greek *enoikizo*, "to settle in") to refer to small groups of Greeks integrated within local populations, which need not have been full-fledged trading posts or colonies. It is still difficult to draw a sharp line between *enoikismos* and *emporion* (in its ancient or modern use), but the point is that "pockets" of both Greek and Phoenician resident merchants and their families were integrated in noncolonial areas within trading-oriented communities. The Phoenician materials we will see throughout this book, especially from the Aegean, Cilicia, Etruria, and Iberia reflect such scenarios.

If ancient historians did not draw sharp distinctions between Phoenician and Greek settlement types, modern scholarship often does, implicitly or by omission. To give some examples, the Greek trading post in Naukratis is often discussed, but the similar settlement of Phoenicians at Memphis, also noted by Herodotos, is rarely mentioned. Phoenicians from Tyre lived south of the temple of Hephaistos in an area called "the Tyrian encampment" (*stratopedon*). Their temple to Ashtart must have served a function similar to that of the Greek Hellenion and other temples around which communities of Greeks, Carians, Syrians, and others coalesced at Naukratis and Memphis.[56] Indeed, when Amasis II moved Greek mercenaries and traders to Naukratis in the mid-sixth century BC, the place was probably already inhabited by groups of Greeks and Phoenicians, who continued to coexist there later on. We also know that the Nile Delta was the site for Greek mercenary garrisons at Pelusion and Phoenician ones at Heroönpolis/Pithon (Tell el-Maskhuta).[57] But the presence of Phoenicans in Saite Egypt in such areas, and the role of this context in the contemporary cultural developments, including the orientalizing phenomenon, is still understudied.[58] In northern Syria, coastal "outposts" are ascribed to both Greek and Phoenicians north and south of the Orontes (Myriandos, Al-Mina, Ras-el-Bassit/Poseideion, Tell Sukas), while archaeology suggests that in all instances these groups operated within ethnically mixed settlements dominated by local culture.[59] In other words, when it comes to smaller types of settlements, Phoenicians and Greeks would have functioned in quite similar ways and followed similar strategies.[60]

At the other end of the spectrum, we know that many of the Phoenician foundations were conceived from the start (or very early on) as well-organized towns. The Phoenicians themselves used the word "new city" (QRTḤDŠT, i.e., *qart-hadasht* or the like) for at least three foundations: the famous Carthage in Tunisia, the new "New City" (Carthago Nova) of the Barcids in southwest Iberia, and a Carthage on Cyprus (perhaps Kition) attested in Assyrian and Phoenician inscriptions. The name of Carteia in the Bay of Algeciras has the same root. Carthage, therefore, was a name much like Greek *Neapolis,* "new city" (whence Naples, Nablus, etc.). The name Gadir (in Greek plural *Gadeirai*) may have been frequent too, meaning "fenced territory/enclosure," and it appears in Iberia and in several Gadeirai in the Levant.

Although we have some names and a few stories about Carthage or Gadir, the fact is that very few of the Phoenician colonies were the subjects of preserved narratives and foundation myths, hence also the lack of interest in reconstructing their history. Important but practically "silent" colonies in the historical record include Motya on Sicily, Lixus or Utica in North Africa, Carteia in the Bay of Algeciras, Cerro del Villar in Málaga, to mention a few. We need to rely, therefore, on archaeological recovery to unveil the nature of these settlements. The early layers of settlement documented in Gadir (Cádiz) and along the Málaga coast show urban planning since their inception, structured around harbor installations, fortifications, and an interior market area around which civic activity would cluster, while industrial and artisanal activity was also conducted in houses and peripheral areas.[61] Like the Greeks, Phoenician settlers chose defensible islands or headlands with natural harbors, and an extended area, which the Greeks called *chora* (or *peraia*), that provided access to agricultural or other resources (mining, murex, wood).[62] Phoenician communal spaces were also articulated by intramural and peri-urban (or rural) sanctuaries, a feature most famously emphasized as a sign of territorial organization of the early Greek polis.[63] Thucydides noted this as a typical location in west Sicily (Motya).[64] Other examples include Tyre and Arwad off the Phoenician mainland, Mogador in Morocco, Rachgoun in Algeria, Gadir and Cerro del Villar in southern Iberia, Sulcis on Sardinia, and headlands such as Nora (Sardinia) and Carthage.

A closer look at Gadir is especially revealing. Recent excavations under the Teatro Cómico (Yecimiento Aqueológico Gadir) in downtown Cádiz have confirmed the Phoenician settlement there in the mid- to late ninth century BC (Figure 1.1). Gadir had a regular urban plan from the early stages. Blocks of houses of various sizes built with Levantine techniques and measures rose along narrow angular streets with earth-beaten pavements, following the organization proper of densely populated Near Eastern urban centers.[65] We are not referring to the strict "Hippodamian grid," a form of urban planning and organization that was not in fashion just yet, applied mainly to late classical and Hellenistic cities.[66] Archaic-period townscapes were very different, but no less urban. Greek and Phoenician towns were capable of "regular" (not strictly orthogonal) urban planning and division of plots. This is not only attested in archaic Greek foundations in southern Italy-Sicily, such as Metapontion, Megara Hyblaia, and Kasmenai

FIG. 1.1   Urbanization in Iron Age Gadir.

Reconstruction of the archaeological site of Gadir (Yacimiento Arqueológico Gadir/Teatro Cómico), Period II or Phoenician A (820–760 BC). Courtesy of José María Gener Basallote.

(see Map 5.1), but also at Carthage from its foundation, and rectangular urban layouts had for long been the norm in the Fertile Crescent throughout the Bronze Age (much earlier in some areas).[67] Regarding Carthage, Roald Docter thinks the evidence points to "a central authority that divided the land in regular building plots," following measures roughly corresponding to the Near Eastern sexagesimal system.[68] But Carthage's urban remains (not to mention those of minor colonies) were poorly interpreted during early excavations, and arguments ex silentio emerged about its lack of civilized, classical-style urbanism and monumentality, hence reinforcing predetermined prejudices about the Phoenicians. The recent study of remains from the archaic levels at Carthage (Rue Ibn Chabâat) will do much to correct these misconceptions.[69] The new excavations at Gadir also confirm that builders imported Levantine techniques of construction, including the "Egyptian cubit" as a building measure and the wall-building technique known as "pier and rubble," both typically used by Phoenicians; the *tannurs* (clay kilns) they installed in several of the houses are also identical to those in other Iberian settlements and in the homeland (e.g., kilns at Cerro del Villar and Sarepta in Lebanon).[70]

In short, archaeological evidence supports the view suggested by epigraphical and classical sources, and it is not possible to continue talking about Phoenician and Carthaginian settlements abroad as if we were dealing mainly with small, disorganized, dislocated merchant groups rather than a web of interconnected city-states.[71]

The Plough and the Oar

In the popular imagination, the Phoenicians are merchants and sailors, not farmers. The Greeks and Romans, by contrast, can be both seafaring and land folk. This apparently innocent dichotomy carries with it stereotypes that even today are connected with ethical values: landownership is traditionally connected with economic and military systems that are perceived as stable, noble, and reliable; sea and trading activity is associated with instability, malleability, greediness, change, and independence from official institutions. The dichotomy was exploited by the Romans to characterize the Carthaginians, of course, who were a maritime and commercial force and hence, allegedly, dishonest (the famous *punica fides*).[72] More rarely, modern nation-states have evoked an entrepreneurial free Carthage to represent their "underdog" position vis-à-vis the "new Romes" of the modern world (Britain versus Napoleonic France, the early United States and Ireland versus imperial Britain, Iraq versus the United States).[73] The way in which British and Europeans used and abused stereotypes about the classical world was not random, but of course "reinforced by more widespread acquaintance with classical writers themselves."[74] The representation of the Phoenicians as exclusively maritime people has broader implications. It makes their colonies dependent on others for agricultural produce or easily imagined as living in the margins of others' communities. The "sea–land" contrast (Phoenician vs. Greco-Roman) is born of a combination of assumptions, in part drawn from the lack of literary testimony and the biased nature of the testimonies we have, and in part due to the difficulty of excavating or tracing agricultural and farming activity, especially if you are not looking for it. But new communities were unlikely to survive and organize their economy around trade only. Agricultural landscapes have been studied in few areas, but the agricultural wealth of Carthage's ample *chora* is documented historically, as is its control of the rich agricultural territory of nearby Cape Bon. But agriculture was essential for the dense population up and down the Phoenician strip, which had a narrow but fertile and well-irrigated countryside between the sea and the mountain sides; this is also attested by wine and oil presses, bread ovens, grinding stones, storage jars, and so on.[75] For instance, for most of its history Tyre controlled the mainland across the island (Ushu or Palaiotyre), which gave the city access to agricultural land and freshwater. The island of Gadir had a similar mirror enclave in the Castillo de Doña Blanca (Map 4.1) with access to the deep valley of the Guadalete River and to indigenous channels for other resources. It is remarkable that the most famous agricultural treatise of antiquity was produced by a Carthaginian (Mago's treaty), which the Romans translated and used as a farming and gardening manual for centuries.[76] And indeed the first-century CE Roman expert on agricultural matters, Columella (who cited Mago and others), hailed from Gades and proudly alluded to his Gaditan and Tartessic ancestral land.[77]

Classical archaeologists themselves slowly caught up to the interests of "new archaeology," and turned their attention to the rural landscapes of the Greek poleis and colonies, for instance, on Sicily and in southern Italy.[78] Moreover, Greek historians of the colonial world have criticized the schematic classification of the Greek settlements as agricultural colonies versus trading posts.[79] Still, the idea of the seafaring Semites runs deep, and slips into otherwise sophisticated postcolonial research on Greek colonization, where Phoenician settlements are considered "cities without territories," and not invested in agriculture or land routes, in contrast to Greek settlement in Italy or the Cyrenaica, as noted by Tamar Hodos.[80] The fragmentation of fields and regional studies in many languages is partly to blame. Phoenician archaeology started to adopt these new approaches and scrutinize archaeological evidence for traces of agricultural transformations and domestic and rural life, for which the western Mediterranean provided more ample materials.[81] In the 1980s, the Spanish scholars Jaime Alvar and Carlos González Wagner had already put forward the theory of a Phoenician "agricultural colonization."[82] They proposed that the Phoenicians played a transformative role in the rural landscapes of south and southeastern Iberia and of Ibiza. Although they met with some resistance at first, today it is widely accepted that, at least in Iberia, the Phoenicians did not care for the sea alone. Phoenician enclaves extended there well into the fertile Guadalquivir valley, which was the area of ancient Tartessos and the proverbially bountiful Roman Baetica. In Lebanon itself Phoenician settlement is characterized by access from the coastal harbors to fertile microvalleys that link the sea to the Lebanon mountains, and daily survival relied on small farming and export of inland products. Wood occupies a special place in this economy, including the famous cedarwood exported by Byblos to Egypt since the Middle Bronze Age. It has been noted that the Lebanese settlement pattern closely resembles that along the coast of Málaga, where small settlements ring the coast often at the mouth of rivers leading to and from the mountains, which once provided plenty of wood. The Phoenician presence in Cilicia by the Taurus Mountains has also been explained in part by the propitious access to wood resources.[83]

Another advance on this front comes from bioarchaeology. Archaeologists have recently agreed that the Phoenicians introduced Levantine modes of viticulture and olive farming, those two essential elements of the "Mediterranean diet," at least to Iberia and Italy. This theory is based on DNA analysis of the vine species in the Mediterranean, where the indigenous plant merged with Near Eastern strands.[84] But there might be some archaeological evidence as well for Levantine techniques of cultivation found in Huelva coinciding with the early Phoenician presence.[85] The cultivation of vines is attested in Punic Malta, Ibiza, and Iberia, where similar methods were followed.[86] Finally, the Phoenicians' arrival marked the adoption of other agricultural products and farm animals among locals in Iberia, and the Phoenicians were also strongly linked with the exploitation of marine resources, such as salt and fishing and fish products (the famous Punic *garum* so coveted by Romans is the best known), as well as purple dye for the textile industry, which is first attested in the Atlantic precisely in Gadir.[87]

In the end, like Odysseus, the Phoenicians held both an oar and a plow when they needed to.

Small-scale Presence and the Role of Sanctuaries

Cultural influence is not the sole product of colonization, large-scale migration, invasion, or imperial domination. Some of what Phoenicians and Greeks did corresponded to these schemes. But there are other types of relations through which communities influenced each other, including trade and small-scale migration.[88] The idea of cultural input beyond the colonial realm, however, is more readily accepted or promoted for the Greeks.[89] But evidence is accruing for such Phoenician presence and views are slowly shifting.

Levantine activity is attested at least from the ninth century BC onward in sites such as Lefkandi, Kommos, Knossos, and Athens, with a steep increase in the eighth to seventh century with the boom of the colonial movement of both Greeks and Phoenicians. The Aegean Islands harbored centers of manufacture and trade of specialized Levantine goods, but archaeologists have also proposed that ivory and metalworking workshops in the mainland were most likely attached to permanent or semipermanent communities, such as at Delphi, Perachora, and Sparta.[90] We are still in the process of theorizing this small-scale presence, but modest steps are moving us in the right direction (cf. the mention of *emporia* or *enoikismoi* above). We can see these places at the crossroads of international networks as "transnational hybrid spaces," where Phoenician migrants were active, as indicated by structures, ritual practices, and materials attested at places (for instance, on Crete) where they never established full-blown settlements of their own.[91] Drawing from better-attested contexts later on, we can surmise that the foreign groups were welcome to the degree that they provided a desired workforce or specialized crafts or served as mediators between the locals and long-distance networks, in exchange for which they obtained accommodations such as access to land and permission to conduct their cultic activities, as attested for later foreigners in Greek poleis, such as Piraeus, Athens, and Delos.[92]

Sanctuary areas have left us especially rich evidence for cultural exchange in noncolonial settings, probably because of their accumulation of valuable, durable dedications that survive (and are sought after) archaeologically. For our earlier period, the most cited examples are Kommos, an excavation that produced Levantine-type cultic installations and Levantine pottery; but other sites seem to have been foci of transnational activity humming around workshops and markets *linked* to sanctuaries, especially Eleutherna in Crete, the Heraion at Perachora across the sea from nearby Corinth, the temple of Artemis Ortheia in Sparta, and the Samian Heraion, all of which I discuss in later sections.[93] At the same time, the sort of concentration of international materials we see in these sites is not the norm. Other excavated sanctuaries have produced few foreign votives (e.g., Pherai in Thessaly), which shows a difference in local interest and networks.[94] In turn, Panhellenic sanctuaries developed precisely because of their position as key nodal points for international trade. In other words, religious networks map onto economic ones, which in turn stimulated cultural transfer.[95]

In the eighth century BC, these places were not mere recipients of "trinkets" and exotic valuable votives, they became stages for the performance of prestige and the negotiation of identities as well as "markets" for the exchange of stories and the religious ideas that accompanied ritual artifacts.[96] Communities of Levantines, then, functioned within the satellite economy of sanctuaries for their own benefit. The Phoenicians were present at Greek and Etruscan sanctuaries that functioned as nodal points in trading routes and regional markets, such as the Heraion of Perachora in the Isthmus, and the sanctuary of Ashtart/Uni at Pyrgi. The international fame gained by Gadir's Herakleion (Melqart-Herakles temple) goes hand in hand with the island's strategic position along metal-trade routes from the Atlantic to the Mediterranean. Iron Age sanctuaries themselves were sometimes connected with metallurgy, which reinforced their macroeconomic importance, as best attested on Cyprus since the Bronze Age and suggested by materials at Huelva. But the Phoenician's role as mediators between the Aegean and the Near East also helped bring these sanctuaries into broader international networks, even into the gravitational pull of the Assyrian realm.[97]

There is a further reason that sanctuaries were so frequented by long-distance traders, beyond their being profitable markets. They offered a safe haven for those engaged in this extremely risky endeavor that required large investments of time and resources.[98] In fact, the principal Phoenician deities Baal/Melqart and Ashtart were strongly associated with both seafaring and the protection of mercantile activities.[99] Economic and cultic networks went hand in hand. As Sandra Blakely shows in her study of the Samothracian mystery cult of the Great Gods, documented epigraphically from classical to Roman times, sanctuary networks provided the "face time" that strengthened communications, facilitated the spread of news, and promoted business. By granting special privileges and protections to individuals and groups (*theoroi, proxenoi*), the cult provided what it promised, namely, safety at sea.[100] For sure the mechanisms and modes of operation varied in each case, but the basic link between sanctuaries and trading routes was a constant in all periods.

In addition to the study of Greek and Phoenician colonization proper, there are other subfields of scholarship that look at the same regions, period, and networks that I do, but they highlight different actors. They all have a place in our understanding of the ancient Mediterranean but also have blind spots when it comes to the entanglements between Phoenicians and other groups. In Chapter 2, I take issue with some prevalent inertias within classical archaeology and with an approach to cultural exchange in the Iron Age that overemphasizes Greek (especially Euboian) agency and reveals lingering ideas of Greek exceptionalism. Then I turn to the more recently trending pan-Mediterranean, globalizing approaches, which provide a better model for the Phoenicians even though sometimes, through their focus on broad networks, they can also occlude Phoenician agency.

‹ 2 ›

FROM CLASSICAL TO
MEDITERRANEAN MODELS

Traveling Heroes

The Phoenicians were the Near Easterners closest to Greek culture before Hellenistic times. They stand as a kind of litmus test for how we engage with the Near East as a whole: taking them as seriously as they deserve entails questioning the originality of Greek culture at its roots, shaking at its base a foundational myth that sustains European culture. There are plenty of reasons to be grateful for the survival and promotion of this heritage and its ideals, which need not be listed here. But the deep-rooted admiration for classical Greek culture distorts our understanding of its earlier interactions with other groups in the eighth–seventh centuries BC.

Fortunately, archaeological methods and interests have evolved enormously since the mid-twentieth century, as have interpretive models. To gain some perspective, we can recall how Thomas Dunbabin could open his classical history of the Greek colonies in southern Italy by stating unselfconsciously: "I am inclined to stress the purity of Greek culture in the colonial cities, and find little to suggest that the Greeks mixed much with Sicel or Italian peoples, or learnt much from them."[1] In 1948, words like "purity" and "mixing" and the rhetoric of race were still acceptable. For a whole generation of Commonwealth scholars of Dunbabin's time, the colonialist, imperialist concepts of racial purity and orientalism went hand in hand.[2] Somewhere in the spectrum between the "old school" and the "evolved" postcolonial views of cultural contact lies John Boardman's classic work, *The Greeks Overseas: Their Early Colonies and Trade* (1st ed. 1964, 4th ed. 1999), which has influenced many generations of archaeologists. An art historian by training, the emeritus (and knighted) Oxford professor represents a whole era of archaeology dominated by the one-sided emphasis on Greek primacy in any context of activity "overseas." Even in the fourth edition (1999) of the *Greeks Overseas,* we can still read that "in the west, the Greeks had nothing to learn, much to teach," although Boardman nuanced his views in later publications.[3]

Boardman's positions on orientalizing art and intercultural contact represent a strand of unabashedly Hellenocentric archaeology, according to which the "so-called 'Orientalizing revolution' [. . .] in Greek hands, led inexorably to what have come to be known as 'Classical' forms of realistic art virtually unknown elsewhere in the world."[4] These and other formulations in *The Greeks Overseas* promote Greek exceptionalism, making Greek adaptations into advancements while seeing those of Etruscans, Sicels, Iberians, and others as uninspired copies and gross imitations.[5] All in all, Boardman offers a restrictive interpretation of Greek artifacts abroad: the presence of Greek pottery is assumed to stem from Greek trade and to exclude cultural permeability across these groups. The agency of Levantines or Phoenicians is not considered, and cultural exchange between these groups and the Greeks is deemed "to have been slight, despite the presence of Greek goods in so many Phoenician and Punic settlements."[6]

Gradually adjusting to the accumulating evidence, Boardman later conceded the possibility that Greeks and Semites may have been present in each other's settlements, and imagined the seafarers interacting with a degree of "camaraderie," or similarly involved in piracy and trade.[7] Boardman even settled the old debate over primacy in colonization, stating that "the Phoenicians are the first in the field by a long way."[8] Nonetheless, even in some of the most recent, otherwise theoretically sophisticated works, interactions between Greeks and others are treated in a rather compartmentalized way, and an aura of Greek exceptionalism prevails.[9] S. Rebecca Martin puts it well: "The field's desire to move past the idea of Greece as the birthplace of Western civilization lags behind its ability to let go of or challenge concepts rooted in Greek exceptionalism."[10]

We underestimate how much the lurking influence of Hellenocentrism obscures interpretations of these Iron Age contacts. A great example is the book *Travelling Heroes in the Epic Age of Homer* (2008), in which Robin Lane Fox explores the Mediterranean-wide journeys of Greek merchants and early settlers. In a wonderful survey of archaeological and literary sources, this work traces back to the Near East an array of Greek stories and place names in the archaic period to re-create some of the experience of the exploration of the Mediterranean "in the time of Homer." Lane Fox holds to the "Oxonian" tendency to see Euboians everywhere, coming always first and obtusely closed to other people's ways. He frames Near Eastern input in terms of "creative misunderstandings." The expression provides a perfect formula for maintaining Greek agency and creativity intact and keeping the "other" at arm's length, as if an imagined linguistic and cultural line divided their ultimately incompatible and incommensurable worlds. It is the Euboians who relocate the stories, "siting them" in Greek areas, not due to rubbing shoulders with Levantine peoples, learning and appropriating each other's ideas, but from linguistic and conceptual misunderstanding of each other.

The Greek and Near Eastern cultures portrayed in *Travelling Heroes* meet not to find common ground, but to provide ground for the brilliant adaptations by Greeks of an alien incomprehensible world. This view of the archaic Mediterranean does not bring peoples closer; it serves as a backdrop for Greek exceptionalism. Lane Fox is explicit in stating that "Greeks made little effort nonetheless and generally understood what they saw only in their own Greek terms. The underlying content was 'lost in translation.'"[11] His view echoes the predicament of the "fault of the Greeks," articulated by Arnaldo Momigliano in the 1970s, whereby the Greeks lacked interest and proficiency in other languages and cultures.[12] However, Momigliano was referring to Hellenistic and Roman times, not to the archaic period.[13] While mistranslations fueled the imagination of the helplessly monolingual Greeks, Lane Fox assumes that "informed contact with Near Eastern stories and practice seems suggestively far from their reach."[14] On the other hand, Lane Fox nods toward intermarriage and bilingualism, and proposes that not all was ultimately "lost in translation."[15] A degree of linguistic skill is implied by his thesis that a Euboian learned the alphabet from a Phoenician in order to write Greek.[16] In turn, when Lane Fox discusses Al-Mina, he leans on Boardman's authority to assure the Greek settlement of the place, resorting to rather forced arguments that would never have been used to defend the presence of Levantine merchants in Greek lands, though they can easily be made.[17]

As I discuss in the next sections, double standards are often still applied to similar kinds of evidence, whereby Greek presence and agency are overstated and those of the Phoenicians are sidelined or altogether rejected. To

illustrate these double standards, I discuss briefly three key sites in this debate: Al-Mina in Syria, Lefkandi in Euboia, and Pithekoussai in the Bay of
Naples, three pillars of the idea of a Euboian network that has overshadowed the complex interaction between Greeks and Levantines in this early
period. Thanks to new perspectives and comparable local contexts such
as that of Huelva, the Phoenicians' role alongside Euboians and others is
coming to the fore, as we will also see in the treatment of each region in
this book.

Al-Mina

The most paradigmatic example of these interpretive issues is Al-Mina
(Arabic for "harbor"), a site in coastal North Syria, at the mouth of the
Orontes River, just south of today's Turkish–Syrian border. Sir Leonard
Wooley started excavations there in 1936, but soon lost interest since the
site did not yield the monumental Bronze Age remains he was finding elsewhere. But Al-Mina became a jewel for Iron Age archaeologists, given its
unusual wealth of Greek pottery, an unprecedented finding in the Levant.
The earliest shards were dated between 770 and 750 BC, and this was assumed to be the date for a Greek foundation of this coastal enclave.[18]

At the time, the Levant and Greece were not considered close partners,
and little was known about Iron Age Greece and its commercial networks,
so the presence of Greek pottery in considerable amounts was interpreted
as proof of a Greek colony in northern Syria. Later assessment downgraded
the site as a "trading post," but still a Greek settlement of one sort or another. The pottery assemblages found in the earliest, eighth-century layers
were composed of different sorts of Euboian cups with geometric decoration, besides other styles represented in smaller proportion (Rhodian, Cypriot, and Proto-Corinthian wares). This rapidly triggered a comparison
with materials from Pithekoussai (Ischia) in the Bay of Naples, where Strabo
recorded that Euboians had landed.[19] And voilà, we had the first proof of
Euboian entrepreneurship in the Levant and of a grand Mediterranean-wide
Euboian enterprise. The Euboian "traveling hero" was born.

Upon closer inspection, however, things were far from simple: non-
Euboian materials from other Greek regions predominated after the eighth
century. Moreover, the evidence for a Greek "occupation" (Boardman's term)
is dubious.[20] Architectural remains as well as utensils follow Levantine

traditions and there are no traces of Greek burials.[21] In fact, Phoenician, Cypriot, and local Syrian pottery accompany the Greek materials since the earliest phases, perhaps even in the late ninth century BC, even though the proportion of Greek pottery is still striking for the Levant. In the end, the earliest materials recovered and their sloppy and Greek-biased recording make it difficult to reassess the enclave's foundation and the proportion of "native" versus Greek pottery.[22] From the confluence of ceramics at Al-Mina, the profile of the site that emerges is that of a multiethnic entrepôt integrated into a dominantly local context, as also confirmed by the appearance of Greek, Aramaic, and Phoenician graffiti.[23] The bibliography on Al-Mina, however, still reflects ongoing disagreements and uncertainties about the role of Euboians amid other entrepreneurs at these early stages of international relations, and includes titles framed by question marks and cautious phrasings.[24] My favorite is Niemeyer's "Phoenician or Greek: Is There a Reasonable Way Out of the Al-Mina Debate?" with a follow-up article title answering negatively.[25] Perhaps not.

Lefkandi

If we shift the spotlight to Greece, the double standard becomes even more evident. Wherever possible, this line of scholarship prefers to assume that any Phoenician or Levantine objects found in the Aegean were brought there *by* Greeks. Euboia is central to this argument. The long island east of Attica and Boiotia (6.1) has produced some of the earliest and most dazzling Near Eastern artifacts that reached Greece around the turn of the millennium. The most famous findings come from Lefkandi, where a monumental building from the "Dark Ages" has been excavated, dated to the tenth century. The so-called *Heroon* ("building of the heroes") is an apsidal long structure built of wood and thatch over stone foundations. That the building was of special importance is made clear by the burial of two high-status individuals beneath it, and later burials clustered around the building in what is known as the Toumba cemetery. Grave goods here denote strong ties between this community and the Levant, with an array of luxury items including jewelry and weapons, east Mediterranean faience vessels, and even a set of weights of a Phoenician standard.[26] For many, these materials suggest the presence and perhaps burial of Levantine "resident aliens" on Euboia.[27] Indeed, similarities in the funerary assemblage of a contemporary Phoenician grave at Achziv support the Phoenician link for one of the Euboian graves, Tomb 79, dated around 900 BC.[28]

By contrast, the default assumption by the proponents of the "Euboian-koine" was that the Levantine weights and other artifacts in Tomb 79 at Lefkandi belonged to a Euboian trader (or "warrior trader") actively involved in the Cypro-Levantine world.[29] Similarly, the presence of six Egyptianizing faience vessels in Tomb 39 must belong to a "royal" Near Eastern bride brought to Euboia.[30] Others imagine that the woman had belonged to two worlds, eastern and Greek.[31]

At a minimum, we have to assume that traffic went both ways; that the "traveling heroes" were not only Greek: Euboian Geometric pottery found in Syria (Al-Mina, Tell Sukas, Ras-el-Bassit), even in Lebanon (Tyre) and other Syro-Palestinian sites in the tenth–ninth centuries was at least as likely to have been carried by Levantines going back and forth.[32] After all, the demand for Greek banqueting ware was driven by the local consumer, which explains why Phoenicians and other Levantines were keen to use and trade in Greek banqueting wares.[33] As Roald Docter's study of Greek drinking cups found at Carthage and Toscanos (in Iberia) has shown, in the seventh century the Phoenicians went all out in producing their own copies of Greek *skyphoi* and *kotylai,* using local fabrics and imitating older Euboian characteristic types. In short, Phoenicians liked Greek drinking cups. This pattern shatters previous assumptions and suggests a different range of explanations of the Euboian materials abroad.[34]

As John Papadopoulos notes in his article "Phantom Euboians" and its sequel, we may be dealing with the modern invention of a "Euboian *koine,*" a term used by scholars based on the distribution of a few types of Euboian pottery.[35] A map of pottery styles and common features has turned into a map of shared identity across the communities using these pottery styles.[36] This Euboian koine has even acquired defined contours (according to vase types), and has Lefkandi and nearby Skyros as its "leading members."[37] The disproportionate emphasis on Euboian agency in the Early Iron Age goes hand in hand with the denial of "intrusions" of non-Greek agents, and even contradicts the interpretation of pottery distribution within the Greek world in later periods: no archaic Corinthian settlement is traced by the ample distribution of "Proto-Corinthian" pottery and no ceramic-based cultural koine is based on Athenian red-figure pottery alone, even though they dominate entire cross-regional markets for long periods of time.[38]

In short, the tombs from Lefkandi exemplify the double standards deployed in the identification of artifacts with their users. While the problem of equating "pots and people" in an uncritical way has long been recognized, it is well accepted that social and cultural identities are articulated and performed through objects and their consumption, and material culture is inseparable from a community's shared practices (the concept of habitus).[39] Identifications between materials and social collectives underlie even the most critical interpretations, only disproportionately tilted toward the cultural categories that we feel comfortable with or that support our view of the ancient world.

Pithekoussai

After Al-Mina and Lefkandi, the island of Pithekoussai (modern Ischia) holds a special place in this debate, as it was home to one of the earliest documented Greek trading posts in the west. The volcanic island lies eighteen miles west of Naples. Several sites around the modern town of Lacco Ameno (especially the necropolis of San Montano and the "dump" of the Monte di Vico acropolis) document a settlement that goes back to at least 770 BC. At that time, according to Greek tradition, a group of Euboians from Eretria and Chalkis settled on the island and later founded the colony of Cumae (Kymai) on the mainland, thought to be the oldest colony in Italy.[40] Alongside Greek materials, excavations have demonstrated the presence of people from the Levant. The headlines of the Hellenocentric narrative, however, remain unchanged.

Ancient Greek historians are silent about Phoenician participation in the foundation of or presence on the settlement; but materials on the ground tell a different, more complicated story. Corinthian and (surprisingly fewer) Euboian pots abound at the site. But these appear in combination with local Italian wares and Levantine pottery, such as Phoenician Red-Slip ware and pottery coming from Carthage and other areas, including Iberia and Sardinia. As much as archaeologists seek precision in segregating Egyptian, Sardinian, Iberian, and Rhodian materials, the mix itself is significant, as it corresponds precisely to the types of exotica typically distributed by Phoenicians: faience and steatite scarabs, "lyre-player" stone seals, and Rhodian-made "spaghetti flasks," all of which appear abundantly in graves on Ischia.[41]

The graves on Ischia are exceptional in the geographical range of their contents and reveal that Greeks and Phoenicians lived together on this island.[42] Phoenician amphorae are used in a number of infant burials, and graffiti in Northwest Semitic script is found scratched on various sorts of pots. Due to the similarity of the Phoenician, Aramaic, and even Greek scripts in this early period (which, to be clear, represented different languages) and the sketchy nature of the graffiti (usually three or four letters), it is difficult to classify these inscriptions beyond "Northwest Semitic," and in some cases even to tell apart a Semitic epigraph and a Greek one in the recently adopted alphabet. In one case, a Northwest Semitic inscription and a funerary Tanit symbol mark the Rhodian amphora used to contain a cremated child burial. This burial type is typical in the Phoenician realm and, to further complicate things, even the use of this type of Greek vase is attested in the Phoenician urn fields (tophets) at Sulcis in Sardinia.[43]

The combination of Greek, local (Italic), and Levantine funerary practices at Pithekoussai speaks of a hybrid community where the involvement of Phoenicians or other Levantines is undeniable.[44] As David Ridgway posited, we could consider the grave that contained the celebrated "Nestor cup" as belonging to a mixed family. The cup was found in 1954 among other goods burned and buried in a child grave, and it is most famous for bearing the earliest preserved hexametric inscription, dated to the late eighth century, and perhaps even the earliest Homeric allusion.[45] The question is why a Rhodian *kotyle* was buried with a child in a Semitic-type cremation burial, with an Ionian-style love charm evoking Aphrodite and banqueting.

The site of Pithekoussai shows the complexities of some of these communities "abroad" in the eighth century and highlights Greek and Phoenician entanglements in a context not yet bound by the constraining models of colonization. Indeed, the Phoenicians participated in the intense metal trade that ran from the Etruscan Elban ores down to the Bay of Naples, and Pithekoussai provided a strategic hub at the gates of this route (metalworking is also attested archaeologically in Pithekoussai). The enclave, moreover, corresponds to the preferred type for Phoenician colonies and trading posts: a defensible spot not far from the mainland for access to trade routes.[46] Moreover, although the Euboian foundation of Cumae eventually dominated the colonial landscape of the area, we know that Phoenician activity continued in Etruria and Latium.

All these are but pieces of a largely lost puzzle, and they can go unnoticed in the big-picture reconstruction. From the Hellenocentric and Euboian-centered stance, foreign artifacts are read as "intrusions" or as commodities acquired by the locals (including brides), perhaps part of elite gift exchange or "trinkets," despite calls to consider their cultural and symbolic meaning.[47] Not even the Semitic inscription found near Eretria on a Euboian Middle Geometric cup seems to put a dent in this view.[48] By contrast, few would question that a Euboian "resident alien" was behind the Greek inscription on the above-mentioned "Nestor cup," written not on a Euboian but on an East Greek (probably Rhodian) drinking cup.[49] These objects demonstrate the extent of the Greeks' entrepreneurship, but for some, a similar amount and type of evidence is not enough to prove that Phoenicians were present among Greeks at that time.[50]

Other Greek Horizons

Near Eastern materials from this period also concentrate in other parts of Greece, which complicate the Hellenocentric and Euboian-driven narrative. Evidence comes especially from Crete, from the Gulf of Corinth, and (more recently) from northern Greece. Materials from these sites will appear throughout this book, but I want to call attention to these contexts and their contribution in the current debates.

The site of Eleutherna is becoming better known in the mainstream narrative about this period. The settlement lies on the way between the coast and the foothills of Mount Ida, where the famous Idaean Cave (in which there was a cult to Zeus) has produced one of the richest deposits of Levantine and orientalizing votives. This might explain why Eleutherna became a center for the consumption and most likely production of orientalizing art in the eighth–seventh centuries. At Eleutherna's archaic necropolis of Orthi Petra ("Standing Stone"), three grave markers of typically Phoenician type were found, a type of pointy pillar known as *cippi*, at least one of them dated securely to the eighth–seventh centuries. Two such *cippi* have also appeared at Knossos and have been interpreted as marking Phoenician graves. As Eleutherna's archaeologist, Nikos Stampolidis, has assessed, parallels to these are known only in sites from the culturally Phoenician sites on the Syro-Palestinian coast (Dor, Akko) as well as the western Phoenician colonies (e.g., Carthage, Sicily). Thus, "as the cippi do not seem to have been adopted by the local population, their limited number [. . .], along with the presence of eastern products in those cemeteries, signifies a more long-term stay by easterners, or more specifically Phoenicians there."[51] It has thus been argued that a small Phoenician community of Phoenician craftsmen was involved in the manufacture of precisely the sorts of orientalizing materials abundantly found in the area.[52] But the message has had surprisingly little impact.

The Gulf of Corinth has historically been a crossroads for Greek–Levantine interaction, starting already in the eighth–seventh centuries, and not only later, when the opening of the seven-kilometer-long Diolkos road across the Isthmus (ca. 600 BC) facilitated east–west communications. The deposits at Perachora and the Syro-Phoenician style of Corinthian terracotta plaques are potential traces of this close interaction (Figure 6.1). The "stelae shrines," cultic spaces marked by rectangular stone stelae, have also been potentially related to Phoenician inhabitation; they appear at different locations inside ancient Corinth, including at the "Terracotta Factory" in the Potters' Quarter, which are themselves likely places of Phoenician activity.[53] These "shrines" are still poorly studied and understood, much like the *cippi* found on Crete and Etruria.

The harbor site at Perachora is another puzzling and still underexploited case. Hidden in a cove of a jutting peninsula just north of Corinth, the area has installations from different periods. The sanctuary to Hera included shrines dedicated to Hera Akraia and Limenia, which received an overwhelming amount of Levantine offerings, especially bronzes and amulets. The case is often mentioned in discussions of Near Eastern materials, but in part due to limited publication and in part surely because we are dealing with Levantine artifacts in Greece and not the other way around, the site has not lent itself to the same kind of in-depth analysis that the Greek materials have in places such as Pithekoussai or Lefkandi.[54] A similar international hub with abundant Levantine deposits is the Heraion at Samos, and its materials are often highlighted, but we still lack an interpretive framework for the role of the Levantines in these sanctuary networks. Even more recently, sites excavated in the northern Aegean, such as Methone and Torone, have yielded new contexts for the interactions among Phoenicians, Cypriots, Euboians, and others. The recent materials include a new corpus of early inscriptions that broadens the possible areas of the adoption of the alphabet.[55] These and other ongoing discoveries bring much-needed oxygen to the overcrowded scholarship on a limited number of emblematic sites such as Pithekoussai, Al Mina, and Lefkadi, and expand the contexts where Semitic and other groups interacted closely outside the Levant and the Phoenician colonies proper.

A main problem for the Iron Age and archaic periods (perhaps *the* main problem) is that written testimonies abound only later. On the other hand, the archaeological footprint of any integrated community at these and other sites is bound to remain elusive. Were it not for written sources, for instance, we would not know about the Sidonian, Kitian, and other Phoenician communities living in the Piraeus, Athens, Delos, Rhodes, and other islands in classical and later times, or of any other metics, for that matter.[56] Traces of domestic life are not easily preserved for the Greeks either. Just as invisible were the Greeks living in Carthage in the classical period, whom we know about from a brief mention in written sources.[57] By that point, of course, there were also Carthaginian residents in Syracuse and Rome, and Sidonian residents in Athens, and so forth.[58]

Still, as we move on in time, and material and written testimonies become more durable, we do find Phoenician communities well integrated in Greek city-states, such as those mentioned above, mainly attested in bilingual inscriptions.[59] And yet the Phoenicians' role in the earlier Iron Age and the orientalizing phenomenon is still a thorny problem for classicists, who are generally interested in a more linear, neat Greek trajectory toward classical perfection. In other words, the teleological views and double standards pointed out here hamper our general understanding of the Phoenicians' role. Only looking at the broader Mediterranean networks we can gain a more balanced perspective, as we see next.

Mediterranean Archaeologies

Western Mediterranean Perspectives

When we shift our attention from the Aegean to the central and western Mediterranean, we find a more ample range of contexts for Phoenician interaction with locals and Greeks. The expansion of Phoenician networks, especially Tyrian and then Carthaginian, affected large parts of North Africa, Sardinia, Iberia, Sicily, and even mainland Italy. The view from the far west can be eye-opening, as the archaeological landscapes of small, illiterate communities of Geometric Greece do not differ much from those of the western regions in the ninth–eighth centuries BC. After the collapse of the Bronze Age palace systems, the difference between material culture in the Aegean and the western Mediterranean was less evident.

Scholars studying this same period on the western side are forced into a different perspective than classicists or Near Eastern historians and archaeologists. The massive loss of historiographical sources pertaining to the western groups for the earlier periods (before they entered the Roman world) is frustrating, but it also means freedom from the teleological narratives of the classical tradition, at least to some degree. Western Iron Age archaeologists have been forced to develop more nuanced interpretive frameworks and to build their case from the ground up, leaning mainly on archaeological evidence. Moreover, the locals with whom the Phoenicians interacted in their western enterprise were, for the most part, not Greeks. This fact alone makes room for more flexible and less aseptic interpretations of Phoenician–local interactions. But in other areas, mainly Sicily and Italy, the encounter between Greeks and Phoenicians (including Carthaginians) produces a complicated triangulation of the relationship with native groups. Here, the Phoenicians are awkwardly positioned vis-à-vis the "classical" cultures, and scholarship often highlights the Hellenic heritage, which aligns with Italy's Roman heritage and culture.

In the end, teleological views weigh on us when we interpret the cultural trajectories of Iron Age groups east and west. In the eighth–seventh centuries, local communities in Sardinia, Sicily, and Iberia are at the *end* of a local prehistoric trajectory, moving toward a point in time when they will mingle with better known, more powerful civilizations (Carthaginians, classical Greeks, Romans) and fade away. They do not reach a "classical period" of their own. The Greeks in the eighth century, on the other hand, are for us at the *beginning* of a booming cultural career, marked by no less than the Homeric poems. We cannot easily look at Late Geometric or archaic-period Greece (when orientalizing culture flourishes) without an idea of "Greekness" shaped by classical Greece, the "cradle of western civilization." Put simply, the Greco-oriental encounter is still downplayed as superficial and ultimately inconsequential because complicating Greek culture and identity means shaking the boundaries between "East" and "West" and questioning the immaculate originality of the most valued culture of the ancient world.

Much less is at stake in the far western Mediterranean. Take the case of Tartessos, a culture that did not feature much in Spanish historiography until the early twentieth century.[60] Had Tartessos survived as a cohesive civilization past the sixth century BC, if we had even scraps of its literary traditions and autochthonous narratives, we might be less prompt to emphasize its debt to the Phoenician colonists so much. As an exercise, imagine how strange it seems to even refer to the Greek communities of the "Dark Ages" and the orientalizing period as "indigenous groups" heavily influenced by their contact with the Near Eastern cultures, simply because we see them as the antecessors of the classical Greeks, a view shaped by the preserved literature, and not archaeologically evident. This is the difference between cultures whose "voice" and hence identity are preserved and those without that historical advantage.[61]

Other cultures and areas in the Mediterranean remain even more marginal and unknown for classicists, especially the North African cultures. Their highest points of convergence with the rest of the Mediterranean in antiquity came with the wave of Phoenician expansion, followed by the Roman conquest, until the advent of Islam. Scholarship of this period, however, is devoted to the Phoenician/Punic settlements in North Africa, whereas indigenous developments and adaptations before Hellenistic-Roman times remain almost inexistent or perhaps still undetected.

As van Dommelen has pointed out, the Phoenician past on Sardinia has a certain life in the modern popular perception of identity, although elements of this Punicity (e.g., the popular Punic rebel Hampsicoras/Amsicora) are blurred with the dominant indigenous past, and overall the focus on Nuragic culture dominates local archaeology and overrides "foreign" colonial archaeologies, be they classical or Phoenician. At the same time, much as in Tunisia, Lebanon, and other areas of Phoenician settlement, Roman monumental remains on Sardinia are more visible than those of the Iron Age, hence easier to promote as touristic landmarks, and they overshadow the deep Phoenician past.[62]

By contrast, the archaic culture of Etruria not only benefits from a more impressive archaeological record to attract scholarly attention, but also has the advantage of being perceived as a precursor of Roman culture, and a sort of conveyor of Greek elements. This guarantees a place in "Western history" for the Etruscans.[63] As we draw closer to areas of Greek colonization in our tour from west to east, the Hellenocentric view takes hold and the Phoenicians are sidelined in the general narrative. Sicily is the perfect example of this transition, as it is a hinge between these two colonial worlds, but Hellenization is projected back onto the island's earlier history, even if the Phoenicians also settled there from the eighth to the third centuries BC.

In turn, unlike for Italy, our view of Greek presence in the far west is not so strongly directed by classical sources. Scholars recently emphasize the interaction between Greeks and native Iberians, and between Phoenicians and Greeks, whose settlements and trading stations were distributed along different coastal strips: Greeks in the east and northeast of Iberia, where secondary colonies of Massalia had been established from around 600 BC on, and Phoenicians in the south and west. Overall, the two contingents are treated on an equal footing, focusing on cultural contact and how it affects different areas of life, including commercial transactions, domestic life, industrial production, banqueting, and ritual practices.[64]

At the same time, the concept of "colonialism without colonization" has been used for the Greek input in Iberia, in order to emphasize that cultural influence need not need be exclusively tied to urban colonies and to deal with "non-hegemonic" contact in the periphery of the Greek colonial realm.[65] And yet it is difficult to imagine that Phoenicians would be framed as "colonists without colonies" or as the enactors of a "cultural empire" in the Iron Age Aegean, for instance. I am not arguing for that kind of language either. My point is to highlight the contrast in the treatment both groups are likely to receive. Following the Phoenician trail in publications and museum displays in the various countries involved produces highly inconsistent and confusing results: the "Phoenicians" can equally be championed as the indispensable "culture bringers" (usually in areas without Greeks colonies) or relegated to the role of mere "go-betweens" (in areas with or near Greek colonies), when the Hellenic agency is preferred, depending on disciplinary and national agendas.

Pan-Mediterranean Frameworks

The Mediterranean framework of analysis focuses on connectivity. But here too the Phoenicians are largely overlooked. This is largely because the field has focused more eagerly on the Greco-Roman, medieval, and early modern periods, when historiographical sources abound. After all, the subdiscipline was inspired by the classic work by Fernand Braudel on the early modern period.[66] A good representative of this historiographical subfield is the on-going "Mediterranean Seminar," an international forum "dedicated to the study of Mediterranean societies and cultures and their role in World History and the History of 'the West.'"[67] But here too preconceived ideas are not negligible; they manifest themselves in the assumption that Phoenicians and Carthaginians were lesser players in shaping pan-Mediterranean connectivity. Consider Purcell's assertion:

> The Phoenicians are of course a construction of modern scholarship, and their cultural homogeneity is open to question. [. . .] they are part of the problem, not the answer to it. They are in the net. A Phoenician-writing traveller from Sardinian Nora to Gades in the second half of the 7th century is no cultural ambassador of Tyre, let alone the Orient. And the role of even the cities of Phoenicia in mediating between interior west Asia and Cyprus or the Delta is an ingredient in the network which we are trying to explain, not something which is detachable from it and therefore a possible explanation of it.[68]

Dislocating the Phoenicians from their states, and these states from the networks they created (dissolving them in "the net") makes them easily dismissable as historical agents. The alternative solution is not sought here, namely, accepting them as a complex collective, as historians do with any other culture, and on their own terms. In Peregrine Horden and Nicholas Purcell's *The Corrupting Sea,* the Phoenicians appear as participants in a process leading to Greek colonization, and it is the latter that is celebrated as "one of the most complex manifestations ever of the interactive potential that has been central to Mediterranean maritime history."[69] From this perspective, summed up in yet another Homeric metaphor, "the *Odyssey* has been the creator of the Mediterranean."[70]

By contrast, Syro-Palestinian archaeologists and epigraphists and those who study Phoenician remains across the Mediterranean have no problem with the singling out the Phoenicians amid the networks; they can pinpoint Tyrian pottery or its imitations when they see it, and they regard Phoenician art as distinct as any other even across the broad geographical span of the Phoenician diaspora.[71] From this perspective, it is not controversial, as

Carol Bell puts it, that the Phoenicians were "not only [. . .] the prime-movers in long distance maritime trade of manufactured goods and raw materials in the Early Iron Age but also they transmitted arguably two of the most useful technologies to come out of the Eastern Mediterranean and Levant: an alphabetic script and the knowledge of iron working (even if they did not invent the latter technology)."[72]

Looking at the region from deeper prehistory, Cyprian Broodbank's *The Making of the Middle Sea* shifts the attention to the preclassical past of the region and advocates for those forgotten "Barbarian histories," hence providing a more viable framework for the study of Phoenicians' networks.[73] Broodbank highlights the unique confluence of factors that produced the cultural and economic connectivity of the eighth century BC, the period on which I focus. He qualifies the emerging networks as "one of the most extraordinary creations of its age on the planet."[74] Broodbank emphasizes the process of trial and error, of successful and unsuccessful engagement between native groups and Phoenicians and other easterners, through which proto-urban culture took hold across a good part of the Mediterranean. In his survey, the Iron Age Mediterranean is not an antechamber and "forerunner of the Classical world," but a culminating point of developments long in the making. Thus he explicitly avoids the Euro-centric (Hellenocentric, bible-centric) teleological perspective of most histories of the region.[75] These are all important parameters for my study, as the emphasis falls on the crucial role of merchants "as the ultimate go-betweens," and the "Mediterranean's midwives," who "contributed far beyond their numbers to bringing the Middle Sea into being."[76] Broodbank came closest to pulling the two strands together, the globalizing and the Phoenician, when he states that "by the early 1st millennium BC, the relevance of a pan-Mediterranean perspective is beyond dispute, given the voyaging of people whom we know as Phoenicians between the Levant and the Pillars of Hercules."[77]

With a similar bird's-eye perspective, the Metropolitan Museum of Art exhibit Assyria to Iberia at the Dawn of the Classical Age (2014–2015) offers a refreshing challenge to the classical Mediterranean model.[78] The exhibit and its publications invite viewers into the world of Assyrian power and trade relations, but also to an Odyssean world of far-reaching seafaring connectivity.[79] The exhibit highlights the dynamism and influence of the underdog, epicless Phoenicians, represented through monumental inscriptions and grafitti, bronze and ivory artifacts, and goods from different corners of the Mediterranean. At the same time, Assyria is presented as the prime motor of orientalizing art and the Phoenician expansion, relegating the Phoenicians to a secondary role in their own story. But the Assyria to Iberia exhibit brings attention to the Phoenician networks as the connecting thread, and captures the current spirit of resistance against the rigid "East–West" axiomatic division. It also sets the Near East as the backdrop of the orientalizing-archaic period ("at the Dawn of the Classical Age"), in which thriving entrepreneurship propelled great artistic and technological achievements, thus breaking the mold of European or Greek exceptionalism.[80]

Finally, Hodos's book *The Archaeology of the Mediterranean Iron Age: A Globalising World c. 1100–600 BCE* is the latest and most successful effort to present a new coherent picture of this period's intense connectivity.[81] Hodos surveys the ways in which we see a global culture emerging along the axis of the Phoenician and Greek colonial and commercial exchanges with local peoples. This framework, which stems from social network theory, allows us to explore these encounters without depending on the traditional narratives of colonization and Hellenization. As Hodos shows, the Iron Age networks laid down by Phoenicians and Greeks broadly conform with the tenets of how global cultures are theorized: travel and connectivity allowed the compression of space-time on a Mediterranean scale; the exchange of goods and ideas fostered the perception of an international culture increasingly abstracted from particular territories (deterritorialization); processes of standardization and cultural homogenization emerge in the new middle grounds (or third spaces), while the specific conditions and needs of every area account for a great degree of heterogeneity and unevenness in the particular reactions from those engaged in the networks; and finally, as globalization produces a heightened awareness of similarity and difference among groups, the global networks affect local identities while local cultures also feed into the global networks.[82] It is not difficult to understand the process of orientalization as part and parcel of this first pan-Mediterranean globalizing wave, led by local elites and propelled by booming interconnectivity. Although Hodos's study does not revolve around the Phoenicians in particular, these Levantines appear as much if not more than the Greek settlers and merchants in her narrative and examples, providing a new high ground from which to appreciate the Phoenicians' agency in this process.

The pan-Mediterranean viewpoint that these and other hallmark works are deploying in recent years are the most useful springboard for my own interpretation of the Phoenicians' role in this period. There is a drawback, however, to the recent emphasis on networks, which have become the subject of key monographs and countless conference volumes.[83] This focus creates the impression that the new interconnectedness (the "net" itself) and the markets that supported it took on a life of their own.[84] For all their merits and advantages, the network-based approach in general underestimates Phoenician agency. It is not that scholars overlook the Phoenicians as a key connecting force, like resilient "spiders" forging a wider net. But they are more interested in the net's materials, or its patterns. Here the forest hinders our view of the trees.

Another problem of in studies of Mediterranean connectivity comes precisely from their (otherwise welcome) emphasis on barrierless, institutionless relations, on the "history of" (not "in") the Mediterranean itself, a distinction Horden and Purcell insisted on. As Ian Morris put it, after all, "interconnection did not make institutions, states, and empires cease to matter."[85] On the contrary, "the horror of precise definitions and quantifications that characterizes the new Mediterraneanism is a barrier to understanding."[86] For my purposes, part of the trend shifts attention away from colonial and other political processes and actors, such as the Phoenicians, creating more haziness where in fact the accruing archaeological data allow for more clarity.

In this chapter I have engaged with various disciplinary treatments of the Phoenicians to argue that, in order to understand their historical role in this key period, we need to overcome the sclerotic Mediterranean model of the classics, dominated by Greek and Roman cultures, which allow "others" to enter only as a concession. With no historical sources of their own, no self-generated projection of identity, and no modern nation to advocate for their heritage, the Phoenicians have so far been on the losing side.

Postcolonial, network-based, and pan-Mediterranean perspectives break those tired models. On the other hand, in the next chapters of this book I try to demonstrate ways in which we can be more specific in aligning the pan-Mediterranean narrative for the Iron Age and our knowledge of the Phoenician activity. The Phoenicians were not one among other more illustrious actors in this scenario, but deserve perhaps the most *kleos* for their paramount role among those "midwives" (as Broodbank called them) who brought about the first Mediterranean. The cultural koine that we call "orientalizing" is the most visual expression of that process.

⊰ 3 ⊱

THE ORIENTALIZING KIT

Redefining "Orientalization"

As Sabatino Moscati noted, "orientalizing art appears as a very interesting phenomenon of evolution or interference on the fringe of Phoenician production."[1] The Phoenicians are often recognized as "intermediaries" and transmitters of Near Eastern styles and technologies in the ancient Mediterranean. The precise role of Phoenicians vis-à-vis a pan-Mediterranean cultural trend that we clumsily call "orientalizing," however, is still not fully understood and often treated either superficially or as problematic. The term "orientalizing" was introduced over a century and a half ago (1879) to describe a general type of artistic style of "Near Eastern" outlook, found in Etruria and Greece.[2] The category has a variety of problems, not least because of its lack of a historical-cultural anchor, and also because it has gradually fallen short of our expectations of precision, nuance, and sophistication. I argue in this book that, to the degree that it is a working category in art and archaeology, the Phoenicians provide such a needed "anchor" for this widespread and varied phenomenon. In this chapter I discuss the term and concept of orientalization and repurpose it for a cultural process that had much to do with the Phoenicians' expansion abroad at that precise time and the ensuing interactions with local groups. To do so, I also discuss the disciplinary concerns and limitations that often stand in the way of more fully attaching the "Oriental" side of the *oriental*-izing phenomenon to the Phoenicians.

The most recent effort to offer a critical and pan-Mediterranean view of the orientalizing phenomenon is Corinna Riva and Nicholas Vella's 2006 volume *Debating Orientalization*.[3] The contributions by different experts, but especially the introductory and concluding essays encourage us to pursue a more in-depth and overarching understanding of the phenomenon. Most poignantly, Robin Osborne stresses the need to detach the concept from the dominion of art historians and also from the study of colonization.[4] The chapters, though individually excellent, are geared toward archaeological and art historical approaches and area case studies. The contribution by the art historian Eric Gubel is the only one dedicated to the "Phoenician component" of orientalizing art. While Gubel expressly does not theorize the Phoenician *role* as a whole, he stresses the city-states' participation, especially Sidon, among other "ethnic entities" from the Levant (e.g., Ammonites, Aramaeans, Israelites) who partook in the cultural exchange of the "orientalizing horizon."[5]

Theoretical discussions in *Debating Orientalization* are concerned with flaws and advantages of the concept of "orientalizing" and its relationship to European orientalism and not so much with "the Phoenician problem," which at least Nicholas Purcell considers as much a dead end as the term "orientalizing."[6] Allusions to Phoenicians are otherwise dispersed in the maze of the different case studies. Sarah Morris's paper, which focused on orientalizing materials within Ionian networks, in fact provides the only straightforward position regarding the issue, when she stated that "there was an ancient concept of 'Orientalizing,' called 'Phoenicianizing.'" If we wanted to adopt an ancient term and idea used by the Greeks at least in relation to writing, we should not use "orientalizing" but "Phoenicianizing" (*phoinikizein*).[7] Morris was in turn transmitting the position of Andrew and Susan Sherratt, expressed at the conference from which the volume originated but unpublished. The suggestion, however, is not fully taken up in the theoretical chapters, where the editors wrestle with the question of the Phoenicians' assumed (but not fully explored) "key role" and urge more dialogue among the different disciplines that study them.[8]

To be fair, not a few archaeologists have stressed the role of Phoenicians as cultural agents, as we will see in Part II. But the different areas of scrutiny, which include artistic craft, literature, cosmogony, and magic remain mostly disconnected from each other. Studies that involve these contexts of contact are usually scattered among regional studies (e.g., Sardinia, Iberia, Crete, Cyprus) and separated by disciplinary boundaries. Historians, archaeologists, and philologists have not fully succeeded in putting the pieces together, in order to answer the more general questions: How and why did these "oriental" models meet with such transregional success? What were the mechanisms of contact and adaptation? What kind of cultural capital came along with these models? How do these adaptations map onto colonial relations and trade (or not)? To begin with, we need to understand the parameters of the category "orientalizing," and the effects that this concept has in the discussion about Phoenician culture.

Orientalizing Is Not Orientalism

The first problem, then, is about the vagueness and orientalist overtones of the category of "orientalizing." The term "orientalizing" is tied to a hazy, monolithic idea of the "Near East" (previously "Orient") that discourages the search for specific channels, mechanisms, and groups involved with other Mediterranean cultures. Especially when it comes to the Iron Age, groups not represented in imperial histories (those of the Assyrians, Babylonians, or Persians) or foundational texts (those of the Israelites) are lost in the larger narrative about the "Near East." The category "Indo-European" is no less a reification than the "Near East" or the "Semitic cultures." Even more problematically, the linguistic Indo-European category is upgraded to a cultural, borderline ethnic entity, imagined to hold its end of the dichotomy between "East" and "West." It is easy to get the impression that, while the Indo-European lineage of Greek language asserts the invisible genealogical line between the Greeks and Europe, the accumulating Near Eastern "parallels" simply color Greece superficially with a Mediterranean, lightly exotic character. At the same time, less familiar categories, such as Northwest Semitic, Luwian, Neo-Hittite, and so forth, rarely transcend the titles of dissertations and specialized articles and have less impact on the debate of the orientalizing phenomenon.

We rightly cringe at the lexical proximity with "Orientalism," and the history of the orientalizing category is indeed entangled with modern nationalism, Orientalism, and colonialism.[9] As most recently captured by Jessica Nowlin, by turning "orientalizing" into an art historical category attached to a "period," the East–West encounter was conveniently condensed into a demarcated time span. These parameters enable a "controlled" acceptance of Near Eastern influence, while still allowing scholars to picture the Greeks and Romans as the protagonists of this story and precursors of western culture. As Nowlin puts it, the classical civilizations were propelled by the advances and competition provided by "Oriental" cultures, but only to leave them behind "in a suspended antiquity."[10] Another way in which "orientalizing/orientalization" runs counter to our current sensibilities is that it somewhat parallels early twentieth-century western "fevers" for exotic art styles, such as chinoiserie, japonisme, and turquerie.[11] We can also think of the Mesopotamian, Egyptian, and even Phoenician inflections in art nouveau; or in the classical world the reception of Persian culture in Athens, called by some "Perserie."[12] We can also reflect on the more recent popularity of orientalist Indian, East Asian, and Middle Eastern foods, jewelry, clothes, or practices such as yoga, which can reinforce clichés and veer into the problematic domain of cultural appropriation.

So why is orientalizing still a broadly used category? First, it has become a useful label for a type of material and even a period. We use and depend on many other conventional terms stemming from nineteenth-century scholarship (the list is endless), and that is fine as long as we redefine them according to current theoretical models. How do we do this with "orientalization?" First of all, by recognizing that (lexical resonances aside) we are not necessarily projecting modern orientalist paradigms onto ancient orientalization by using that term. Early Mediterranean reactions to the East (ancient orientalization) and modern Orientalism are fundamentally different: they really stand in inverse relationship to each other, the one denoting a generally positive embrace of Near Eastern culture by up-and-coming Mediterranean groups, the latter a romanticized and demeaning representation of a decadent Near Eastern character standing in opposition to the West's virtues.[13] This is not to deny that the reification of the "Orient" was already at work in antiquity. Stereotypical ideas of "barbarians" existed and could intersect with biases similar to those of Orientalism. But these stereotypes often had more to do with a self-referential discourse of identity than a judgment on the other.[14] Specific ethnic biases existed too, though in forms different from our idea of "racism" based on skin color, which emerged in the early modern west in association with the enslavement of African people.[15] At the same time, ancient orientalisms and the idea of the barbarian had nothing to do with western colonial worldviews, and were part of a mixed bag of perceptions of Near Eastern peoples that also included admiration, imitation, praise, and a long history of intimate relations as also reflected in mythological narratives and historical developments.[16]

In a nutshell, we should avoid projecting modern orientalism directly onto the early Mediterranean context. If anything, "orientalization" captures the complexity of a process of cultural change and emulation of an idealized and prestigious Near East of the imagination. If we worry about the vagueness in "orientalizing," let it be for different reasons. The term still obscures historical actors, and particularly the heaps of evidence that point to Phoenician activity in the Mediterranean, in their role as the main vector for the success of this trend as a whole. The Near East provided the background prestige; the Phoenicians repackaged and distributed the goods; and local societies adapted the goods to their needs.

In the next sections I grapple with the birth and dominant use of "orientalizing" as an art historical category and the various interpretive limitations this poses. But first, I address the expansion of the orientalizing concept beyond art history and the place of Phoenicians in it.

An Expanded "Orientalizing Revolution"

In the post–World War II era, the icebreaking impulse to the study of Northwest Semitic and Greek literatures came from Semitists and comparativists, such as Cyrus Gordon, Michael Astour, and Martin Bernal, as well as from a very few but well-placed classicists such as Martin West.[17] By the 1970s–1980s, even disgruntled classicists had to accept the birth of a field that studied Greece's cultural debt to the Near East. Definitive recognition of an orientalizing phenomenon beyond artistic styles consolidated around Walter Burkert's short but influential book *The Orientalizing Revolution* (1992), based on a series of lectures delivered at Heidelberg in 1984 before an audience of traditional German classicists.[18] Burkert called attention to the Near Eastern traits that inflected the world of Greek religion, especially as reflected in archaic poetry and in the realms of divination, sacrifice, and magic. Although not completely new, Burkert introduced to the international community the attractive idea that itinerant religious figures, such as magicians, diviners, healers, and other "charismatic" leaders were comparable in mobility to the more familiar literary figures of artisans, seers, and doctors. He posited that as part of their religious *techne* they were likely vectors for Near Eastern cosmogonic myths in this period of renewed mobility.[19] He structured his study of the orientalizing revolution around the ancient Greek idea of *demiourgoi* or "public workers," who included not only those who produced orientalizing artifacts but also those involved in healing and magic and those who produced and transmitted epic poetry.[20] Thus Burkert integrated material and literary artifacts within a single orientalizing framework and offered a concrete image of the *who* and *how* of this phenomenon, involving actual people who moved between the Near East and the world of the early Greek communities.[21] Burkert found inspiration in the Homeric worldview itself, where these groups of *technitai* are lumped together: in the words of Eumaios, nobody invites a stranger into a house unless the stranger "is one of the *demiourgoi:* a diviner, or a healer of illnesses, or a wood carver, or a divinely-inspired singer."[22]

Burkert frequently pointed to Ugaritic, Aramaic, Phoenician, and Hebrew literary parallels, loans of words, and writing technology, although their agency remains difficult to trace amid a maze of references to other Near Eastern sources, such as Egyptian, Hittite, and Mesopotamian, whose texts are better preserved.[23] But Burkert suggested that now lost Northwest Semitic versions of Mesopotamian epics may explain their reception in Greece.[24] He also warned us that "there were far more numerous, richer, and denser connections that can be demonstrated by the meager remains available."[25]

The model of the "wandering charismatics" is now somewhat obsolete inasmuch as, upon scrutiny, the evidence for such figures remains too limited to ascribe to them the weight of the orientalizing revolution.[26] Moreover, their representation as "free agents" moving across territories and communities is too lax and assumes a free-market economy completely detached from institutions or political networks, the applicability of which to the post-Mycenaean world is far from obvious.[27] Still, Burkert and others for the first time linked the material and the ideological planes of these contacts, establishing pathways for generations of scholars interested in Greek and Near Eastern religion and mythology, as I discuss in Chapter 7.

The next groundbreaking work in this area came from the ranks of classical archaeology: Sarah Morris's *Daidalos and the Origins of Greek Art* (1992) is a tour de force of orientalizing art and its cultural background.[28] With an ampler scope in material culture than Burkert's work and featuring the Phoenicians more directly, Morris uses the legendary artisan and inventor Daidalos as a thread connecting east and west: this is particularly appropriate as Daidalos is associated with the saga of King Minos of Crete, and his name is used to label Cretan orientalizing sculpture as "Daedalic."

Morris contextualizes artistic developments against the backdrop of Greek and Near Eastern relations, and integrates archaeological materials with historical, linguistic, and mythological sources. She not only challenges the idea of the "Greek miracle," but sets a high bar of multidisciplinarity, which has inspired much later scholarship, including my own. While her work is not only about Greeks and Phoenicians, her explorations overwhelmingly feature the Canaanites and later Phoenicians as likely vectors of Near Eastern models, leaving no doubt as to their key role in these transformative processes, which she has reiterated in other works.[29]

It is rather more difficult to ascertain who is doing what in Martin West's survey of Greek and Near Eastern literary and mythical motifs, *The East Face of Helicon: West Asiatic Elements in Greek Poetry and Myth*.[30] West pushes the opening of "the classics" farther to Near Eastern literatures. He does so from within the ranks of traditional Oxford philologists, hence establishing a prestigious "pedigree" for this line of research. His previous and subsequent studies on early Greek cosmogony, philosophy, and Orphic literature also draw heavily on Near Eastern clues, occasionally zooming in on Phoenician or Levantine traditions.[31] As *The East Face* showcases, however, his method is "agglutinative" or "cumulative," without a clear framework of interpretation of the contact among these cultures or the type of transmission of these literary materials. Answering the "so-what question" that Johannes Haubold poignantly asked was not a priority at that point in the field.[32] Moreover, West's "West Asia" and "Near East" form internally complex blocks that provide comparative materials for his equally blockish Greek counterpart. Ten years later, West published an equivalent and even more catalog-like collection of Indo-European poetic and mythological motifs. In this case he assumes a vertical, genealogical relationship between the multiple Indo-European poetic traditions and the Greek one, as opposed to the historically synchronous (horizontal, nongenealogical) relationship between Greece and the Near Eastern cultures.[33]

For West too, historical context mandated that mythical motifs attested in Hittite or Babylonian epics may have been transmitted by Northwest Semitic intermediaries.[34] However, the gravitational pull exerted by Assyria, which was strong in Burkert's work, is evident in West's only explicit hypothesis about cultural transmission, which he presents rather playfully at the end of the *East Face*: that the Near Eastern input so evident in Greek epic could be explained by "an Assyrian poet 'defecting' to the

West, becoming Hellenized in the course of a few years, and turning into a Greek poet."[35] Even if presented as an exercise of imagination, it is telling that he did not imagine a Phoenician or Aramaic speaker, who would have been historically more likely to live in the midst of Greeks. But we have the works of Babylonian and Assyrian scribes and perhaps composers, even a word for them (*nuru*, "singer"). Their scribal tradition is a known quantity. By contrast, "Phoenician" and "poetry" have practically become oxymorons. A Phoenician can be a merchant, a craftsperson, or a pirate, but not a singer, poet, or writer. This is due not only to our lack of knowledge of Phoenician literature but also to ancient stereotypes peddled by the main antagonists of Carthage, the Romans.[36]

Nonetheless, Burkert, West, Morris, and others introduced the idea that Levantine groups, the Phoenicians among them, played a role not only in the material aspect of the orientalizing revolution but also in the literary and even ritual adaptations that accompanied this cultural wave.[37] Despite all this, as we move through the materials presented below, we should not forget that conceptual barriers still remain, especially the Eurocentric and Hellenocentric equation of language and culture, according to which Greek civilization lies at the other side of an invisible barrier separating Indo-European and Semitic-speaking groups.[38]

The Art Historical Approach

The treatment of orientalizing visual arts has followed a separate track from the study of Greek–Near Eastern interactions in written culture and religion. Despite theoretical efforts, the art historical discipline is still fixated on luxury items, their authorship and origins. The lack of "signature" (actual or stylistically determined) of a specific artist or workshop for this period drives the specialist to disassociate this type of art from Phoenicians or any other specific group of artists. But then again, this is a problem especially for one type of materials, namely, luxury items, and one that particularly troubles art historians for disciplinary reasons. Orientalizing materials can be associated stylistically with "the Levant" and with the impetus of the Assyrian Empire, but ultimately all we have are unnamed agents and vague cultural ascriptions.

Recent art historical works, however, have tried different approaches to endow orientalizing artifacts with more grounded cultural-historical relevance. I focus on three works that I have found particularly insightful and representative of the relevant trends. In *Un art citoyen: recherches sur l'orientalisation des artisanats en Grèce proto-archaïque* (2011), Thomas Brisart analyzes orientalizing material culture in Late Geometric and early Archaic Greece (ca. 750–600 BC).[39] He labels the period "proto-archaic" deliberately to restrict the use of "orientalizing" to a style, not a period. In turn, he includes in his study all sorts of materials, such as decorated pottery, monumental sculpture, and minor arts. As much as the term has been criticized, he concedes that the ancient Greeks developed artistic forms that evoked the cultures east of the Aegean, which justifies the label.[40] Through a series of case studies (Argos, Athens, Crete), Brisart argues that Greek communities used orientalizing culture to facilitate or restrict the body-citizen, that is, as a tool in the process of enfranchisement or exclusion in the emerging states. This study, however, focuses on orientalizing emulation in material culture (not literature, religion, etc.), and is restricted to Greek communities. The role of the Near Eastern cultures, or the Phoenicians more specifically, do not enter his purview. But his model of a cultural trend driven by locally specific goals and internal processes is exemplary and can be applied to other regions, such as the central and western Mediterranean, where a similar phenomenon and set of materials is more clearly linked with Phoenician presence, as we will see in Chapters 4–5.

Two other fundamental art historical works that zero in on orientalizing culture are Ann Gunter's *Greek Art and the Orient* (2009) and Marian Feldman's *Communities of Style: Portable Luxury Arts, Identity, and Collective Memory in the Iron Age Levant* (2014).[41] As a common denominator, both books focus on luxury objects and their circulation in the Levant and (in Gunter especially) in the Aegean. Metal and ivory artwork is particularly key for this analysis: bronze horse blinkers or frontlets, bronze cauldrons with protomes (protruding "heads" decorating the rims), ivory pieces that decorated personal objects or furniture, and other portable objects. These authors confront the challenge of freeing these orientalizing artifacts from the debates about origin and ethnic identification: Gunter embeds the artistic trend within the framework of the Assyrian imperial network; Feldman emphasizes the role of Levantine art and its orientalizing adaptations in creating a regional cultural identity.

The production of Levantine ivories and bronze work was indeed boosted by the demand of the Assyrian elite, who consumed them in parallel with their own Assyrian art (this explains why stashes of Levantine ivories appear mainly in Assyrian centers, such as Nimrud). The Assyrian reception of Levantine art is then imitated by other elites, whether from Israel, Cyprus, or Greece, who also aspire to acquire them. Redistribution spilling from Assyrian circles also accounts for the whole trend, whether from booty or centralized distribution and redistribution to friends and vassals, which in turn produced additional redistribution down the chain. Thus, the Assyrian context is certainly important, and counterbalances the tendency to treat these portable artifacts as decontextualized "trinkets" or luxuries devoid of cultural and social meaning.

An important distinction is in order here. These discussions often involve two sorts of materials: on the one hand, the Near Eastern objects that appear outside the Near East (luxury items often belong in this group); on the other, the local imitations inspired by Near Eastern art. Strictly speaking, the first type are not orientalizing but "oriental," better yet Assyrian, Egyptian, or Levantine, which in turn may be Syrian, Phoenician, Luwian, and so on. In the second category are the objects that form the spectrum of oriental-*izing* art, that is, materials produced by each receiving culture. Both Near Eastern (of whatever origin) and orientalizing versions overlapped in space and time and formed part of the larger network of cultural exchange, which complicates things. The ivories and bronzes studied by Gunter and Feldman, for instance, belong primarily to the first group: they appear in the Levant or in the Aegean, but they are mostly the products of Levantine artisans themselves, whether made in the Levant or in workshops abroad. Another paradigmatic example consists of the decorated bronze horse pieces of Syrian origin, distributed between Eretria and Samos, probably after passing through Assyrian hands as war spoils.[42] In turn, this dislocation distorts our view of the corpus. The bulk of Phoenician/Syro-Phoenician ivories, for instance, are found at the Assyrian courts or outside the Levant in general, that is, at the end point of the artifacts' life, removed from their initial contexts of manufacture, use, and distribution.[43] Moreover, as these studies show, it is not always easy to differentiate between these two sorts of materials. Metal and ivory luxury items are easily portable; their place of manufacture cannot be ascertained materially, unlike for clay or some metals; their cultural or geographical ascription can be ascertained only on stylistic and technical grounds. Imports may also have been carved, or assembled, or modified at their final destination. We will see many such cases throughout this book.[44]

The problem of ascription of Near Eastern artifacts abroad leads to vague classifications, such as "Levantine" or "Oriental," and has made some scholars wary of the assumption that the Phoenicians were responsible for the circulation (let alone manufacture) of such objects, an association that goes back to antiquity and has been traditionally embraced.[45] These critics have their reasons. But here is the problem: once art historians decide, first, that the term "Oriental" (a component in "orientalizing") is inappropriate and inaccurate (which it is), and second, that the Phoenicians of the early first millennium are a difficult category to work with, they often proceed in their analyses without them. There is also a certain circularity in the treatment of luxury items and Phoenicians: as Feldman and Gunter point out, these artifacts represent elite mechanisms of gift exchange, including high-profile votives at sanctuaries and dedications of war booty; they are part of a display of power, control, and dynamics larger than "Phoenician mercantilism."[46] Somehow the role of Phoenicians within those international dynamics is sidelined, precisely because the Phoenicians are blemished by the cliché of mercantilism, not associated with the high culture that these artifacts are presumed to represent. It is this circularity that leaves them out. But in the end, the art historical approach meets with the familiar problem of pinning these artifacts on the Phoenicians.

In my view, our understanding of the mechanisms of cultural exchange that are reflected in orientalizing art is limited when we deal only with luxury items and only with the Levant and the Aegean. In other words, these theoretical discussions of art in the Levant and within the Assyrian realm of influence have the limitation that they leave out the extraordinary extension of Phoenician commercial and colonial networks, not all of which can be understood as offshoots of Assyrian expansion, as discussed in Chapter 1. The way out of this conundrum, if there is one, is precisely to pay more attention to the second type of objects I mentioned, the ones stemming from the "hybrid" cultures created by Iron Age networks, which are typically not the subject of these art historical works. It is there that the cultural exchange between Phoenicians and others is well documented, through materials that include both portable luxury items and a much broader range of Levantine-inflected materials and cultural developments.

As art historians frequently point out, the scarcity of models from Phoenicia itself, obstructs our capacity to pin down the role of Phoenician art in the rest of the Mediterranean.[47] But the problem is again alleviated if we cast our net more widely into the other sorts of materials (not only ivories and metalwork) that are represented all across the Phoenician world (pottery, terracottas, funerary monuments), and if we cover the entire span of Phoenician presence in the Mediterranean, as challenging as that may be.

Phoenicianizing by Any Other Name

When Austin Henry Layard (1817–1894) studied the decorated bronze bowls from the palace of Nimrud, he noticed the similar motifs in Etruscan art of the archaic period, and thought of the Phoenicians as the most likely artists who imitated Egyptian and Assyrian features creating such unique "mixed art."[48] Wolfgang Helbig (1839–1915), an archaeologist at the German Archaeological Institute in Rome, also considered the Phoenicians as the most likely creators of the metallic decorated bowls found in Etruscan Italy, such as those from Praeneste and Palestrina.[49] And still others thought that "Greco-Phoenician" was a more suitable label for this phase of innovation, in which "the untaught instincts of the Hellenic artist were stimulated and developed by the importation of foreign works, the product of a more advanced civilisation."[50]

From Cyprus to Spain, objects of similar formal characteristics were identified during the nineteenth century. The naive diffusionist ideas of the time about how cultures interact account for unnuanced formulations: for Charles Thomas Newton (1816–1894), the keeper of classical antiquities at the British Museum, strongly influenced by Heinrich Schliemann's discoveries at Mycenae in the 1870s, it was clear that "the furthest reaches of the Mediterranean came to be engulfed in the waves of cultural diffusion from the Orient."[51] Archaeologists in Spain suggested Phoenician intermediaries, and sometimes Etruscans and Cypriots, for equivalent artistic developments in their own protohistoric period.[52] Two factors reinforced what was at the time mostly a learned intuition: first, Homer refers to Phoenicians as well-known first-rate international artists (as well as ubiquitous sailors).[53] This was enough of an endorsement to attach the Phoenicians to these precious objects, at a time when textual authority drove archaeological interpretation, whether it came out of the Greco-Roman classics or the

Hebrew Bible. Second, a good number of the metallic bowls that represented this type of style bore Phoenician inscriptions. Perhaps now we know better: a text can be added at a later point in the life of an object, and other Levantine languages are represented on the bowls too.[54] But this established a link between many of these bowls and Phoenician networks.

Before the label "orientalizing" became fossilized in the discipline as a stylistic shortcut and a chronological marker, nineteenth-century art historians dealing with the Near Eastern artifacts and local emulations found in Greece and Etruria played with other labels. These labels, today discarded, reflected this stylistic amalgam while specifically pointing fingers at areas of influence or craftsmanship, such as *phönicisirend, korinthischen, ägyptisirend*, that is, literally, "Phoenicianizing," "Corinthian," and "Egyptianizing" ("Corinthian" being a pottery style we now call "Proto-Corinthian" or orientalizing), and they were all subsumed under the looming Assyrian influence.[55] Instead of an "orientalizing" period, they thought of a "Greco-Phoenician" or "Greco-Oriental" period.[56] Their analysis of the material culture that triggered these categories lacked fine-tuning and was shaped by a limited understanding of the Mediterranean (inflected by Homeric categories). But all the same, we are reminded that "orientalizing" was not an inevitable category and that, short of discarding the terminology all together, we need to revert to a historically contextualized study of the interactions behind these types of materials.

The fact is that many of those initial associations have stood the test of time, and even the "Phoenicoskeptics" have trouble explaining the eclecticism of these bowls and other artifacts without resorting to the Phoenicians. It is evident that whoever designed their different types drew on Near Eastern motifs in a way that is neither strictly Egyptian nor Mesopotamian, but a synthesis seen by ancients and (most) moderns as Phoenician.[57] Still, the initial Phoenician association is in principle suspect, if only because it did stem from flawed nineteenth-century methodologies and biases that need to be questioned. In the nineteenth-century worldview, the Phoenicians provided just the right degree of Oriental exoticism in the incipient discipline of classical archaeology. But there was another aspect to it. Early archaeologists (sometimes amateurs) were usually educated in classics and Hebrew and not harnessed by the later purist ideas of Hellenocentrism or Eurocentrism. For them the Phoenicians were part of the discovery of the great civilizations of the ancient Near East and their texts, which were slowly emerging from mounds throughout the Ottoman Empire. In the case of the Phoenicians, their antiquities could be found at sites scattered all across Mediterranean countries, so they provided an interesting window into the "Orient" beyond the Near East.

The initial romanticized enthusiasm for the "Oriental" was overshadowed by the rise of Indo-European studies and the ideology of cultural exceptionalism and racial superiority that dominated institutional agendas until well after World War II. Renewed interest in Near Eastern intersections with classical cultures had to wait until the 1960s and 1970s, when postcolonial ideas directed European interests toward cross-cultural contact.[58] Consider the orientalizing objects found in the Regolini-Galassi Tomb, in the Etruscan necropolis at Cerveteri. As Maurizio Sannibale summarized, we can follow the interpretation of these same objects from "the immediate recognition of 'Egyptian, Babylonian, and Phoenician' elements by Luigi Grifi in 1836, to the more complex pan-Mediterranean view by Giovanni Pinza in 1915, which itself perpetuated the nineteenth-century appraisal of Wolfgang Helbig, down to the blindly ideological interpretation given in 1947 by Luigi Pareti, who ended up denying any eastern or Semitic links whatsoever."[59]

The pendulum swung similarly in other countries such as Spain, where early twentieth-century archaeologists like the British George Bonsor (1855–1930) were also at a loss about how to categorize the rich metalwork and other sophisticated materials of the Late Bronze Age and Iron Age. Objects were often miscategorized, usually as Celtic or straight-out Punic. Bonsor's rather outlandish neologism "Celto-Punic" captures the self-imposed dilemma between the Indo-European and Semitic categories, both present and assumed to be in tension with each other in pre-Roman Iberia.[60] For decades to come, in Franco's Spain, Tartessos and its orientalizing materials were seen either as the heirs of Greek culture in the West or as purely indigenous, while the Semitic element was unapologetically rejected as a foreign and regrettable influence. Only in the 1950s did a realization emerge that new and previously neglected or misinterpreted materials were part of an orientalizing local culture, that of Tartessos, which developed under influences similar to those of other contemporaneous Mediterranean cultures.[61]

As time passed, an inertia set in according to which Near Eastern–looking artifacts appearing west of the Levant were lumped under the "orientalizing" label. As a result, an entire art historical corpus was placed outside ethnic-national categories. And yet the Phoenicians have remained at the heart of the orientalizing maze, because at the end of the day they remain a constant variable among all the modalities of orientalizing culture. After all, even while Purcell sees them more as a problem than a solution, he admits that the Phoenicians were "the vector of some at least of these changes, a proactive group from the east caught in the act of purveying new ways of thinking, speaking, making and doing to the widest range of other peoples."[62] In short, as I show in this book, there is overwhelming evidence that orientalizing trends overlap with local groups' interaction most of all with Phoenicians, not with Near Easterners in general, and that the history of Phoenician trade and settlement offers a concrete historical framework for this cultural trend and the economic dynamics behind it.

Some may object that the term "Orientalization," which is mostly used as a banal convention for a period, is just as problematic as other essentializing and culturally charged labels, such as Hellenization and Romanization, if in different ways. However, the term can be defended, if it is defined precisely. In this book it denotes the Levantine-inflected cultural traits adopted by many local groups who came into contact with Phoenicians in the Iron Age. "Phoenicianizing" may be an even more precise alternative, but there is in fact an advantage in the allusiveness of "orientalizing," for the Phoenicians themselves, as well as their local customers, were also enthralled by the prestige of eastern culture. Thus, I use the term in two ways: to refer to the broader period and classification of materials, as per scholarly convention, and to signal the emulation and adaptation of Near Eastern cultural capital in general, when we cannot be sure of a Phoenician connection or it is not relevant. In the end, both "orientalizing" and the more specific "Phoenicianizing" emphasize active adaptation.

Marketing the "Oriental"

From a postcolonial stance, the orientalizing phenomenon is a matter of local choice, consumption, and transformation of "foreign" elements. A. Bernard Knapp put his finger on it: "Orientalization is a notion that literally encapsulates and demands local agency, whether eastern or western."[63] At the same time, consumption is not only a culturally and economically transformative process but a sociopolitical one. Recent energies have been directed to interrogating what "orientalizing" meant for the locals, whether in the formative period of the archaic Greek or Etruscan poleis, among the Tartessians in Iberia, or in Iron Age Sardinia, to mention well-studied cases.[64] This type of dynamic is also in play in other periods and geographical areas. To give an example from a different context, that of Iron Age Gaul, Michael Dietler has applied an anthropological lens to the adaptation of artifacts and new practices associated with them, such as banqueting culture, and how they affected both the colonial and local communities and their relations.[65] It is important to define the actors and their relationship in any cultural process (even without rigid definitions).

Ironically, the "eastern" side of the equation in "*oriental*-izing" has, by comparison with the local side, gone undertheorized, with discussions revolving narrowly around art historical issues, as noted. If the local experience does deserve the increased attention, the Near Eastern agency cannot be neglected either if we want to understand this phenomenon. The fresh perspective on orientalization proposed here integrates all these components within a historical framework and gives equal importance to the economic and cultural aspects of the exchange as well as to local and "foreign" agencies. This, in turn, means recalibrating the role of Phoenicians in the story. This was not just their story, but it was a story in which they played a leading role.

Perhaps between the historical specificity of the Phoenician case and the vagueness of "orientalizing" there is a hinge to be found, and we can turn some of the term's weaknesses into interpretive strengths. From a market-oriented perspective, "orientalizing" captures an essential aspect of the exchange between groups, even as it casts a broad net over a wide array of local manifestations of Near Eastern culture. Since branding and stereotypes are not the exclusive by-products of modernity, we can assume a degree of reification of the Near East in the ancient Mediterranean by non–Near Eastern consumers of its products. In other words, the Near Eastern aura would be part of the value of these materials and a stimulant for the local emulations of Levantine culture, through which the Phoenicians and others marketed Near Eastern goods and aesthetics abroad.

In the *Debating Orientalization* volume, Knapp addressed this question in regard to prehistoric Cyprus. By the Late Bronze Age, he observes, "regional or local elites, . . . sought to adopt objects and images of Near Eastern or Aegean kingly authority, icons and exotica that linked them with the distant, mystical civilizations of the ancient Near East."[66] Cyprus was, of course, no stranger to the Near East, lying nearer to the Levant than to any other Aegean island, and Mycenaeans and Minoans themselves had partaken in a sort of Late Bronze Age koine in the eastern Mediterranean. This context offers a near parallel to the later orientalization of the Iron Age, in the sense that the status-seeking aspirations of the local elites met the commercial and ideological aspirations of expanding Phoenician polities. These mutual interests were channeled, among other directions, in the circulation of luxury items and the adoption of a repertoire of shared artistic motifs invested with social and symbolic meaning for the different groups who adopted them.[67] After all, the success of Levantine art in the Near East itself (in this same period) hinged upon its prestige and symbolic meaning, which helped "generate community networks" and "catalyze collective memories" among Iron Age groups in that region.[68] The same value and appreciation lay behind its circulation and consumption in areas of Phoenician activity beyond the Near East, adjusting for idiosyncratic receptions among other emerging societies, such as the Etruscans, Tartessians, and others.

The orientalizing phenomenon is simply the most tangible manifestation of an increasing interconnectedness among cultures across the Mediterranean, a way to signal they were "in the know," part of the international networks. Local groups expressed their participation by inflecting their arts and ways of living in idiosyncratically "oriental" ways. This phenomenon can be seen as a sort of globalization, as Tamar Hodos has proposed, or, put differently, a "Mediterraneanizing" trend articulated through a "flexible, if meaning-laden vocabulary of pan-Mediterranean display," in Cyprian Broodbank's words.[69] But even within the globalizing Iron Age Mediterranean model, something is missing. We have not answered (or perhaps even asked) some questions: Where did the impulse come from? Who was behind this most successful marketing campaign of antiquity? The Phoenicians' commercial and settlement expansion cannot be separated from this cultural and economic phenomenon. Their outposts from east to west thrived precisely because of their ability to provide what their markets coveted, to channel the needs of a growing urban network across the Mediterranean (and beyond) toward what they could trade. With their vast commercial network, which reached north to the Atlantic, east into

Mesopotamia, and south into the African trade routes, they were uniquely positioned to mold and exploit not only exotic raw materials like ivory and metals but, moreover, local perceptions of the new prestige culture.

The Phoenicians were, after all, surviving Canaanite polities of the coastland, and more than anyone else they continued the Canaanite "trademark" as they assimilated artistic and cultural traits from the major Near Eastern civilizations, just as their Late Bronze Age ancestors had done before them. What we see as eclecticism formed part of what was perceived and projected as "Phoenician." Again, this has been argued for later art forms, such as Persian classical period Phoenician sarcophagi, coins, and mosaics.[70] Even in that most eclectic form of art associated with the Phoenicians, the engraved metal bowls, the alleged eclecticism forms a coherent style, whose uniformity in scheme and composition made it "impossible to imagine them to be the product of any other than Phoenician hand," and a similar conclusion can be drawn with regard to the Levantine ivories.[71] Glenn Markoe's in-depth study suggests that Phoenician artisans drew from stock scenes or episodes (perhaps circulating in "sketchbooks"), and the resulting (re)combination and syntax built out of this vocabulary made their craft uniquely Phoenician.[72] (I discuss these below in more detail, since these artforms have become central for the perception of Phoenician culture.)

But the role of the Phoenicians in the orientalizing phenomenon as a whole is not contingent on finding proof of their manufacture of these artifacts, which draw so much of our attention. If it is a historically viable framework for orientalization we are looking for, this framework needs to include a broader range of materials and the archaeology of the western Mediterranean, where local–Phoenician interaction is widespread, as well the historical position of the Phoenicians in the Near Eastern milieu, as revealed by archaeological and written sources. At the heart of this phenomenon is an extremely successful "marketing" operation of "oriental" models by the Phoenicians tailored to the recipient, local groups. The new global culture did not reach every corner with the same intensity, if at all, and perceptions of what it all meant or where it came from would have varied.[73] The technologies and aesthetic innovations had to be synchronically relevant for the locals' own advancement, and their ultimate success lay in the desire to adapt them to local uses and create local versions. The recent emphasis on the "recipient" side, however, should not prevent us from trying to understand the Phoenician "supply" behind the process. Phoenician traders and neighbors became the source for much of the innovative culture, whatever the ultimate origins of the particular artifacts were (which the local merchant elites may or may not have distinguished among or cared about). "Orientalizing," then, can be repurposed to convey appropriately the double-sided dynamics of those cultural contacts: not only the admiration (on the local side) but also the projection (on the Phoenician side) of a general image of the Near East associated with royalty, prestige, sophistication, and remote antiquity, accompanied by a sense of novelty and progress brought on by new technologies and international commerce.

So, we know that there was an Iron-Age Levantine koine, and that it reached farther than the Assyrian Empire's networks ever did and started around the tenth century, well before the Levant was subject to Assyria's imperial grip. We also know that if anyone as a collective represented "the Levant" outside the Levant, it was the Phoenicians, who reached the western Mediterranean in the ninth–eighth centuries. The chain is not so difficult to follow: independently of origins or manufacture of specific items, "orientalizing" denotes the local idiosyncratic emulation of the Near Eastern world. Phoenicians (whether from Tyre, Gadir, or Carthage) were the first and most frequent Near Eastern interlocutors these local groups ever met, and the first and only Levantine group to actually permanently settle in their midst.

Through historical lenses, then, we can see "orientalizing" as the area where the vertical axis of each culture's internal development met the horizontal axis of Phoenician expansion. These two processes are inseparable. Near Eastern historians and archaeologists see the transition into the Iron Age as one of the main revolutionary phases of the ancient Near East, marked by a decentralization of commerce and technological innovation (improved navigation, mining and smelting, agricultural production, and writing systems). In this phase the Phoenician city-states played a key role, by filling a gap in trading and connecting far-off areas of the Mediterranean with the Levant. It was Phoenician traders who "heralded a real turning point in the economic history of the Mediterranean," as broadly recognized.[74] And it is in contexts where Phoenicians and locals met that orientalizing culture (or "*Phoenician*-izing," to be more precise) appears at the exact time that they laid out these networks. Nothing stops us from putting two and two together and systematically studying (not simply occasionally recognizing) the Phoenician impetus.

Despite all the local variations among orientalizing assemblages, there is an impressive overlap in the types of materials and technologies in areas that were in contact with Phoenicians in the eighth–seventh centuries BC. This cannot be explained only on a case-by-case basis and as a result of a local process. The adaptations were responding to the successful marketing of aspects of Levantine culture by the Phoenicians, to the point that they became an integral part of the elite culture of powerful Iron Age groups. We can trace the widespread adoption of a sort of shared "kit" throughout the areas where locals interacted with Phoenicians, always among communities that were ready for international connectedness and eager to project high status. Both the "seller" and the "buyers" could tailor the artistic and technological traits to their communities' means and preferences. In general strokes, as I laid out in the Introduction, this orientalizing kit involved a set of favorite Levantine symbolic and decorative motifs; new technologies of pottery and metalwork; oriental-style monumental sculpture; industries of terracotta figures; ivory work; masonry techniques and architectural innovations; new burial forms and rituals; industrial developments (metallurgy, fishing, salting); farming innovations; banqueting culture (sometimes viticulture itself); the technology of alphabetic writing; and religious-mythological motifs.

It may be helpful to consider how cultural adaptation operates on a global scale in our world. Particular objects may come with a stamp of manufacture that does not correspond to their place of design and marketing (e.g., Spanish clothes made in Indonesia or American electronics made in China). And yet we do not have much difficulty in pinpointing where the cultural trend comes from. In the eighteenth century, French intellectual and cultural dominance (accompanied by imperial expansionism) dictated for generations to come what a bourgeois household looked like, from Portugal to Russia. A type of furniture, mirror, fine tableware, makeup and dress code, and bourgeois recreational activities (we can all think of some) were embraced, with variants and adaptations depending on place and socioeconomic class. But in the end, the trends that marked the global elite's culture for a long period in Europe cannot be detached from the French impetus. The European "bourgeoisie kit" (still latent today) was a pale appropriation of the international aristocratic culture, by which the emerging middle class articulated its status, each family within its means.

In our time, American apparel, pop culture, food, and technology do not lack selective adoption and adaptation. This variation does not annul local character, history, and interpretation. Recall the South African film *The Gods Must Be Crazy* (1980), in which the newly arrived Coca–Cola bottle is interpreted by an unwesternized Botswana villager as a divine present. It is still undeniable that post–World War II American economic dominance has translated into cultural dominance as well and still shapes our way of being "global." Our "Western" elite kit includes tupperware, TV, jeans, Coca–Cola (and its red-and-white icon of Santa Claus), iPhones, fashion, and even rituals and their merchandise represented in North American movies. Whether we prefer a vaguer "western" / "westernizing" or an "Americanizing" referent, we cannot ignore the specific backdrop and promotion of this cultural koine of the second part of the twentieth century (accompanied by its own version of imperial expansionism). Post–World War II American culture had a position on the world stage for expressing what it looked like to participate in the postwar prosperity of the free West. This is just one example of the many ways in which branding, marketing, and ethnicity intersect.[75]

The Phoenicians brought a piece of the prosperity and grandeur of the ancient Near East to Iron Age proto-urban societies at both ends of the Mediterranean. This is not to deny other participants in the process. The interconnected Mediterranean harbored Greeks and other colonial networks that amplified this effect with their own adaptations, and the great Mesopotamian and Egyptian cultures offered a distant backdrop. But the Levant was the immediate façade of what lay farther east, and Phoenician entrepreneurship was what made it accessible from anywhere in the Mediterranean. In Part II of this book, we follow the manifestations of orientalizing culture in a west-to-east itinerary. This direction forces us to consider local contexts where we can appreciate contact with Phoenicians outside the "classical model." As we will see, Phoenician settlement did not have the same effect on all surrounding local groups. Orientalization or Phoenicianization was never inevitable, a matter of inertia.

In Iberia the whole gamut of the orientalizing "kit" is represented, which allows us to explore the relationship between the Phoenician settlers and the locals. On the coasts of North Africa, in turn, the colonial and indigenous realms were less eager to find common ground, or at least there is not enough evidence so far of a local orientalizing culture emerging within the radius of Phoenician contact. Interaction on Sardinia followed a pattern more similar to that of Iberia, where Phoenician settlers negotiated the space with well-defined local cultures with deep roots in the western Bronze Age, producing culturally hybrid situations. A similar scenario played out on Sicily, only with a later wave of orientalization partly mediated by the Greeks, whose massive presence there was roughly contemporary with the Phoenician one. With Etruria and the Aegean we move to the other end of the spectrum, where orientalizing culture was *not* a local response to colonization but to other modes of interaction with Phoenicians and probably other small groups of Levantines, as well as Greeks, who carried their own influential orientalizing "kit" abroad. To close the circle, on Cyprus, a stone's throw away from Syria-Phoenicia, the long presence of Phoenicians and Canaanites before them since the Late Bronze Age left its mark on a local culture with strong Near Eastern flavor. Finally, we will consider the influence of Phoenician culture on the greater Levant and southern Anatolia, where the "purple people" were a strong cultural referent in Cilicia, Syria, Israel, Egypt, and the trans-Jordan region.

But Is It Phoenician Art?

Art historians have recently opened a debate on whether there is such a thing as a Phoenician style in precisely those fine crafts traditionally ascribed to them, or even such a thing as Phoenician art in the early first millennium.[76] This is clearest in discussions about Levantine ivories and engraved metal bowls (Figures 3.1 and 3.2), so I focus on these materials to showcase the problem and its responses.

The traditional classification of Levantine ivories is based on the corpus from the British Museum, found at the Assyrian site of Nimrud but deemed generally "Phoenician." R. D. Barnett distinguished two styles of carved ivories: an Assyrian-inflected "North Syrian" style, hypothetically hailing from northern Syria-Palestine, and a "Phoenician" style proper thought to be from the southern Levant, more Egyptian-looking.[77] This classification was consolidated by Irene Winter, who added a possible "South-Syrian" substyle.[78] This categorization has served as a base to classify ivories found elsewhere. More recently, others have proposed that chronological devel-

FIG. 3.1   Phoenician ivories, ninth–eighth centuries BC.

Left: Falcon-headed figure (Horus/Harakhty), from Nimrud (Iraq) (9.91 × 5.11 × 4.39 cm), with solar disk, downward voluted-palmette flower, and Egyptian kilt. Egyptian hieroglyphs on the top left read "She who is beautiful"; a Phoenician letter *Ḥet* is inscribed on the upper edge as a fitter's mark. The Metropolitan Museum of Art, New York, Rogers Fund, 1964.

Right: "Woman at the Window" motif, probably from Arslan Tash (Syria) (8.15 × 12.3 × 1.1 cm), with volute-capital balustrade. The Metropolitan Museum of Art, New York, Fletcher Fund, 1957.

opments might instead account for the variation in style within Phoeni-cian, Syro-Phoenician, or more general Levantine art, not different regions of production. Thus, an earlier group of ivories would align with Assyrian influence while later ivories gravitated toward Egyptian models.[79] The problem is that both stylistic and chronological divisions are uncertain, as the dates and places of production of these portable artifacts are usually un-known, and North Syrian materials are simply better attested (and compa-rable to preserved Assyrian reliefs) than the Egyptianizing or allegedly more "purely" Phoenician styles.[80] Both classifications are purely stylistic and ulti-mately distance the Phoenicians from the corpus, whether by assuming a north-Syrian and a Phoenician style or by emphasizing different tendencies of this Levantine craft ("Assyrianizing," "Egyptianizing"), none of them "Phoe-nician" proper.

In a recent reevaluation of Levantine styles, based on the Samaria ivo-ries, Claudia Suter concluded that it is likely "we will never attain a com-prehensive stylistic classification of Iron Age Levantine ivories due to too many unknowns and too many blurring boundaries," and that it would be more productive to focus on "the complex interrelations between style and society" rather than on the issues of attribution.[81] Along the same lines, Feldman shows that Levantine art had a supranational value for Iron Age elites as they formed their own cultural identities.[82] From that point of view, the debate about origins or artistic identification is irrelevant. Instead, we should appreciate how particular styles played out within broader networks.[83] Even from this point of view, however, it is hard to deny that the Phoenicians were a historically relevant force behind the successful spread of the Levantine koine to which the ivories and other materials belonged.

The above caveats are a response to the traditional interpretation of certain crafts in Phoenician art. The corpus of engraved metal bowls discovered throughout the eastern Mediterranean (such as the ones in Figure 3.2) has also been traditionally considered "a hallmark par excellence of Phoenician workshops."[84] The Phoenicoskepticism of the past decade has also cast doubt on this association.[85] These bowls are conventionally referred to as "Phoenician metal bowls" (sometimes "Cypro-Phoenician") in most bibliographies, and that is how they will appear in this book. Dating the bowls is difficult. Many come from the antiquities market; some appeared in datable tombs or other archaeological contexts, but even there they could be centuries-old relics by the time they were buried. Overall, most bowls come from contexts ranging from the late ninth century BC to the third quarter of the seventh.[86] Other identifying clues are the inscriptions found on eleven of them. Six of them are Northwest Semitic, with three in Phoenician and three in Aramaic, while five bear Cypro-syllabic inscriptions (including the one in Figure 3.2, left), all of them consisting of proper names. While it is not impossible that some may indicate craftsmanship, they more likely indicate ownership as is frequent in early inscriptions in the Levant and the Aegean (the Semitic names are preceded by *l-* which can indicate "of" or "by").[87]

The metal bowls have subtypes, but they form a fairly coherent and identifiable corpus, with subtle variations marking geographical/cultural preferences on the side of the recipients. The most common type is the shallow bowl or *patera,* with a rounded or flat bottom; the decoration is always on the inside except for a few of the deeper bowls (only one is decorated on both sides), and a few have a central protruding omphalos at the bottom. A few also add a ring base. The so-called shields and *tympana* from Crete

FIG. 3.2 Phoenician engraved metal bowls.

Left: Silver, gold-plated bowl or *patera* from Kourion (Cyprus), ca. 725–675 BC (16.8 cm diam.), with Cypro-syllabic inscriptions of ownership, showing Assyrian-style winged deity and Egyptian-style figures fighting lions and griffins, and other animals and symbols, such as sphinxes and palmettes (Markoe Cy8). The Metropolitan Museum of Art, New York, The Cesnola Collection, Purchased by subscription, 1874–76.

Right: Bronze bowl or *patera* from Olympia, ca. 725 BC (20.4 cm diam.), with star and rosettes in medallion, naked goddess and bearded god inside architectural frame (aedicule or *naiskos*): note winged solar disk and volute-papyrus columns; other ritual scenes include enthroned deities receiving offerings, griffin-slaying figures, and dancers (Markoe G3). National Archaeological Museum, Athens. John Curtis Franklin, *Kinyras: The Divine Lyre.* Hellenic Studies Series 70 (Washington, DC: Center for Hellenic Studies, 2016), figure 34. Courtesy of Glynnis Fawkes.

can be considered offshoots of the bowls.[88] The combination of repoussé and engraving in the same object, which characterizes many of them, is a technique otherwise rare in the early first millennium. This is important to note since choices of technique and material have to be considered together with matters of style, as Gunter insisted.[89] In turn, the decoration follows a simple format and steady pattern (a "skeleton") that allows for expansions and modifications: a central medallion with a scene or rosette with one or more concentric bands with friezes of figurative decoration. This decorative pattern is also by no means common in Near Eastern art.[90] The decoration, in turn, is markedly Phoenician in the preferred selection and modulations of Near Eastern themes that we know from other media.

There are problems of ascription, of course, and probably too much capital is invested in the debate over metal bowls and ivories as examples (or not) of "Phoenician art," as S. Rebecca Martin has noted. But it seems too extreme to give up when tracking Phoenician art in this period, while it is "historically tenable and intellectually responsible" to do this in the later historical periods.[91] We risk falling into a tautological argument and building a negative picture out of silence. The alleged lack of a Phoenician anchor for the portable luxuries in question is used precisely to deny the existence of a Phoenician art in this period before we have written sources to help us out, meaning mainly Greek sources. In turn, the precious source we have that attributes decorated metal crafts and even metal bowls to Phoenicians, that is, the Homeric poems (contemporary to the bowls' production), is dismissed because it is literary, not a historical document:

> Quickly the son of Peleus set out other prices for the speed-race:
> a well-crafted silver mixing bowl, which contained only
> six measures, but much more in beauty across
> all the land, since skilled Sidonian craftsmen had fashioned it well;
> Phoenician men had carried it over the misty sea,
> and once it was set up at a harbour, they gave it to Thoas as a gift.
>
> (*Il.* 23.740–745)

A tradition has developed within the field of art history of breezily dismissing Homer's testimony as being poetic rather than documentary and full of alleged stereotypes and literary tropes, but this approach is not convincing.[92] As Vassos Karageorghis has put it, after all, "Homer was neither a historian nor an archaeologist who could make subtle analysis of social and cultural phenomena in the 9th–8th centuries BC."[93] Even stereotypes can be useful and point to social perceptions. Eighth-century Greeks thought objects like these were made by Phoenicians, and this is significant regardless of whether it was always true. That they did not have much trouble associating this type of metalwork with Phoenician artisans is significant. The silver and gold bowl (called a *krater*) that Menelaos gifts to Telemachos in the *Odyssey* is also presented as the gift of a Sidonian king, again acquired at Sidon but presented as a royal gift (not a purchase) to add prestige to the transaction.[94] It is also likely that the decorative pattern of the metal bowls in concentric bands / friezes inspired Homer's fantastic description of the shield of Achilles in the *Iliad*.[95] The shield's various levels represent scenes of war and peace, of country and city, community rituals, and divine oversight. Other imaginary art depicted in Homer's poems, such as the gold and silver dogs at the entrance to the palace of Alkinoos and Hephaistos's robotic handmaids, also made of gold, denotes a sophistication unlikely to have been seen in contemporary Greek art of the Late Geometric to early archaic period, and more probably fantastically inspired by contemporary Levantine art.[96]

All in all, whether we ascribe them to Phoenicians or to "Phoenicians" in quotation marks, most would agree that we cannot isolate the emblematic bowls and ivories from the general spread of Near Eastern art and the development of orientalizing material cultures around the Mediterranean. As we will see in Part II of this book, their distribution and imitations map precisely onto the networks through which Phoenicians interacted with local elites. Whoever ultimately made them (Levantine artisans or their local disciples), they fit within the parameters of products the Phoenicians marketed. It might be that, as Vella put it, the bowls are at heart "boundary objects," "entangled with multiple agents in a variety of sites." I take up his proposition that "calling the metal bowls 'Phoenician' should *only* serve as shorthand to understand the mobile and mutable world that was the Mediterranean in the Archaic period."[97] In the context of this book, however, I would say not *only* but *also,* as wonderfully mobile and mutable, local and global, is exactly what Phoenicians were.

PART II

✦

FOLLOW THE SPHINX

⊰ 4 ⊱

THE FAR WEST

Iberia: Early Contacts and Colonial Relations

Prehistoric cultures flourished in Iberia in the Chalcolithic and Bronze Ages, some of them leaving behind monumental remains and grave goods. But these peaks of proto-urban civilization are extremely uneven in the western prehistoric record.[1] The long relative isolation ends toward the transition of the first millennium BC, when parts of Iberia, now making up modern Spain and Portugal, were visited by eastern Mediterranean groups. This happens as many as two centuries before Phoenician colonization and the orientalizing phenomenon proper began, perhaps earlier if a sporadic Mycenaean activity in the area can be demonstrated (but for now it is scantly documented).[2] It is in the tenth century, then, that we can trace clearly the trajectories of both indigenous and Phoenician cultures, when trading networks that linked the Atlantic and Mediterranean trade routes finally crossed in this corner of Europe, with a mutually super-charging effect.

The area to watch for is the southwest, between today's Huelva and the Portuguese Algarve, with a large radius of hinterland reaching into the Guadalquivir valley as well as southern Extremadura (see Map 4.1). Here outstanding metal resources could be extracted, including silver and iron, both prized in the Near Eastern economy. Iberia was also a gateway to the routes channeling Atlantic tin, more difficult to obtain in the Mediterranean than copper, both the crucial metals necessary for bronze alloy. The ores from Río Tinto (meaning "tarnished river") lie inland from Huelva, and constitute one of the richest metalliferous areas in the planet, with concentrations of copper, gold, silver, lead, and zinc. Indeed Río Tinto ores have been exploited since prehistory and until modern times. Crossing part of Andalusia,

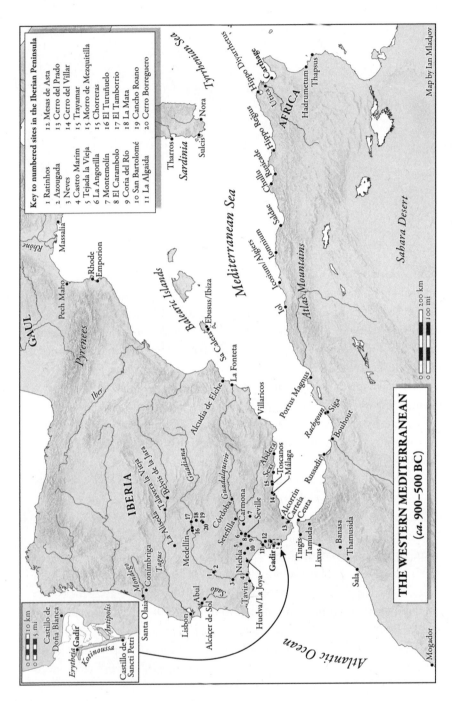

Key to numbered sites in the Iberian Peninsula

1 Ratinhos	12 Mesas de Asta
2 Azougada	13 Cerro del Prado
3 Neves	14 Cerro del Villar
4 Castro Marim	15 Trayamar
5 Tejada la Vieja	15 Morro de Mezquitilla
6 La Angorilla	15 Chorreras
7 Montemolín	16 El Turuñuelo
8 El Carambolo	17 El Tamborrio
9 Coria del Río	18 La Mata
10 San Bartolomé	19 Cancho Roano
11 La Algaida	20 Cerro Borreguero

GAUL

Pyrenees

IBERIA

Balearic Islands

Mediterranean Sea

Sardinia

Tyrrhenian Sea

AFRICA

Atlas Mountains

Sahara Desert

Atlantic Ocean

THE WESTERN MEDITERRANEAN
(ca. 900–500 BC)

MAP 4.1

Map by Ian Mladjov

the Sierra Morena range offered a second vast source of metals, known as the Iberian Pyrite Belt.[3]

This wealth of metals is widely believed to have been the prime motor of Phoenician commerce, but the region was not devoid of pastoral and arable lands either, with fertile valleys along navigable rivers (e.g., Guadalquivir, Guadiana) connecting with the interior and other regions and their resources, including timber and metals. The proximity to the North African coast and its inland routes at the other side of the straits provided access to ivory and other priced goods, which was certainly another advantage of the southern Iberian hubs. The North African and Iberian coasts from Portugal to Alicante were also exploited for fishing and salt pans, indispensable for salted fish and meat products, which leave little archaeological trace other than some installations and the amphorae in which these were traded. We can evoke the famous *garum* that in Roman times was massively exported from Gadir, and how the city featured the tuna on its coins in Republican times, still using Punic characters.[4]

It is no coincidence that the southwest yields the most advanced protohistoric society in Iberia in this period, the backdrop of the civilization that we call Tartessos, after the name given by the Greeks to this region and its main river, the Guadalquivir (meaning "Great River" in Arabic, called Baetis by the Romans). This corner of Iberia acted as a magnet for the Phoenicians at the turn of the millennium. The interaction that ensued changed these landscapes forever, marking the end of the long Bronze Age for the indigenous groups that, in archaeological terms, entered the Iron Age world of international markets and enhanced technologies.

The acceptance of the Phoenician role in this scenario, however, did not come easily. The fixation with the classical past and with racial purity among more powerful European nations in the early twentieth century had an impact in emerging Spanish archaeology, at a time when excavations were often conducted by foreigners such as George Bonsor and Adolf Schulten. Aegean or Celtic (Indo-European) roots were preferred to explain the rich metal objects and sophisticated ceramics emerging from pre-Roman sites in Andalusia (materials that were eventually classified as "orientalizing," as explained in Chapter 3).[5] Views evolved with post–World War II interpretive modes and in reaction to the impressive Tartessic treasure from El Carambolo, discovered in 1958. The steady excavations of Phoenician settlements on the Spanish coasts in the next decades opened new horizons too, spearheaded by the German Institute of Archaeology in Spain, which is still the leading foreign institution in the area. The general consensus has now long been that these protohistoric groups joined international Mediterranean networks through close relationship with Phoenician settlement along the coasts in southern and western Iberia.[6]

In the far western Mediterranean, Hellenocentric tendencies have had a much smaller grip on the interpretation of this period. The near absence of Greek colonization in Iberia (save a small area in the northeast, stemming from Marseille's circle) freed this interpretive space for the Phoenicians. It helped that archaeological discoveries in this region also advanced in an era that favored multicultural, multiethnic, and multinational narratives in Europe. In a country whose heritage is marked by centuries of "convivencia" between non-Semitic and Semitic groups (Jews, Muslims) it is perhaps easier (at least now) to imagine cultural contact with Phoenicians in the pre-Roman period. This narrative has overridden the essentialist views of pre-Roman peoples (as some sort of proto-Spaniards) championed for centuries, as well as the crusading narrative of the Reconquista of Andalusia, a region where so many of the Phoenician hubs lie.[7] Indeed, as Alfredo Mederos points out, it is slowly sinking in that the Phoenician presence in Iberia lasted for almost eight centuries (950–206 BC), which makes it comparable to the long seven centuries of Arab presence, and this in a territory probably larger than that of Phoenician settlement in Lebanon and northern Israel.[8]

If anything, Spanish archaeologists and historians have embraced the Phoenicians' agency with particular enthusiasm. The point of debate is not whether the Phoenicians were part of this picture, but to what degree, and how we can differentiate between the settled Semites and the local culture known as Tartessos. From one reading of the sources, it might seem that the local, Tartessic substratum was with time subsumed under the Phoenician realm altogether.[9] But the archaeological and literary evidence also encourage a more "indigenist" view. Without denying the Phoenician input, the resilience of the Tartessic culture has become increasingly evident, from its Bronze Age roots to the continuities with the later Iberian (Turdetanian) realm in the same region.[10] From this stance, orientalizing elements mark the emergence of Tartessos only to the extent they make it more conspicuous materially, but orientalizing culture (via Phoenician influence) by itself does not account for the culture's roots and identity. Yet acknowledging the native roots of each of these cultures does not exclude acknowledging the role of Phoenicians in their transformations. The reality lies somewhere in the middle, or, rather, probably includes all of the above. The Phoenicians, as this study argues, thrived precisely because they knew how to provide what these markets coveted, selectively exploiting perceptions of what was "international," prestigious, and sophisticated. We have to assume that both groups, Phoenicians and locals, were equally deliberate in the process.

The Findings from Huelva

Beneath the historic center of Huelva, salvage excavations were conducted in 1998 in a parking lot construction site at Plaza de las Monjas/Calle Méndez Núñez; even if recovered in less-than-ideal archaeological conditions, the large bulk of materials found there opened a unique window into early east–west contacts, shocking our traditional chronology. Seventh-century materials were excavated first, before a greater "dump" of muddy dirt from the earlier levels was dug out in haste due to the construction, and archaeologists could then only reverse-excavate the dump, with the earlier materials now lying in disorder on top. A bulk of indigenous, handmade pottery appeared, such as the so-called Huelva type, characteristic of this region during the Atlantic Late Bronze period (ca. 1300–700 BC); these were matched, however, by an equal quantity of Phoenician ceramics, each group making up about four thousand of the eight thousand analyzed fragments. These consisted predominantly of amphorae, the earliest of which matched Tyrian types of the late tenth and early ninth centuries, as well as types reaching down to the eighth. These were infiltrated by small tokens of other "exotic" materials, mainly Sardinian and Greek (Protogeometric Euboian, Attic Middle Geometric), as well as fewer Cypriot and Italian (Villanovan) fragments. But the numbers of these are small: thirty Sardinian fragments, thirty-three Greek, eight Cypriot, and two Italic.[11]

This Huelva deposit speaks of intensive trade between these opposite points, Tyre and Huelva, at least a century before formal Phoenician colonies were established in the late ninth and mostly in the eighth century, a period often classified as a phase of "precolonization."[12] It also confirms the suspected lead of the Tyrians in this commercial expansion, joined by Greeks (perhaps Euboians, after all) and others. Mixed crews are always a possibility, and they were definitely part of the poetic imaginary of the early Mediterranean, as we see in the *Odyssey*'s representation of Phoenicians picking up (or kidnapping) Greeks, or in the mixed crew depicted in the story of Jonah.[13] Archaeological evidence is not lacking, such as in the late fourteenth-century Uluburun shipwreck off the coast of Turkey, which sank with Mycenaean, Canaanite, and Cypriot materials (and presumably a mixed crew) on board.[14] In the case of Huelva, however, the amount of non-Tyrian eastern materials is quite small in proportion and could easily have been part of a Phoenician cargo.[15] Phoenician writing was also found in about eleven inscriptions engraved mostly on previously baked pots, and also on bone and ivory.[16]

The deposit of Huelva showcases the relation between trade and industry on the Atlantic estuary where the rivers Tinto and Odiel meet. The stash concentrates a unique collection of discarded materials and tools that would have been used in Phoenician workshops: pieces of wood from woodwork waste (especially local pine); slag material from copper, silver, and iron; a perforated sheet of tin (used to make bronze alloy); and other implements related to the metalwork industry, such as tuyeres and crucibles used for the manipulation of copper. Among other precious materials, such as a variety of beads and gold earrings, more than eight hundred ivory pieces were also recovered, about 20 percent of them unfinished, as well as other bone and antler pieces used as primary material or tools. The emblematic Phoenician industry of the purple dye was represented too by abundant murex shells. These details paint a lively picture of Phoenicians at work in the types of activities that surrounded a harbor enclave, with workshops of carpentry, smelting, dyeing, and ivory carving, industries that required a somewhat sustained (and sustainable) Levantine presence.[17] Another interesting aspect of the Huelva finds are the traces of cultic activity, registered only in the less disrupted seventh-century layer.[18] These materials suggest a tie between industrial and cultic activity, of the sort attested in other areas of Phoenician settlement such as Carthage and Kition.

Among these early materials from Huelva, little can be classified as "orientalizing." We see indigenous and eastern cultures coexisting and interacting, but not quite fusing. In fact, the archaeological profile of Huelva is that of a primarily indigenous settlement throughout the later orientalizing period of the seventh–sixth centuries. The Phoenician findings there suggest the presence of small "pockets" of foreigners embedded in or around a local community, while in the next phase we find Phoenician establishments and burial grounds west of Huelva (Castro Marim, Ayamonte, etc.), and of course east (Gadir and other), but as far as we know not in Huelva proper.[19] The combination of early contacts driven by the proximity of the Río Tinto mining resources and this strong indigenous character raises the real possibility that the urban center of Huelva was the nucleus of the rich *emporion* that the Greeks knew as Tartessos. That name might also lie beneath the far-off Tarshish of the Hebrew Bible, associated with Tyrian long-distance trade of metals (especially silver) and exotic goods.[20] What we know is that the initial trials of commercial relations were underway from the tenth to ninth centuries BC, although they did not yet penetrate far into the heart of the local society. This process can now even be traced by isotope analysis of the hacksilver hoards found in Israel, especially the Dor hoard, the composition of which reveals the silver trade with Iberia and Sardinia, and in the east with Anatolia and perhaps Cyprus.[21]

Now, the bulk of exogenous materials buried under Huelva (again, dated to the late tenth–early ninth century) are not generally eastern Mediterranean or Near Eastern (let alone "oriental"), but Phoenician. The accumulation of pottery, ivories, and remains of metalwork unambiguously point to Phoenicians, and the pottery particularly to types from Tyre.[22] I emphasize the presence of ivory, since that industry has occupied a prime place in discussions about orientalizing art and its association (or not) with Phoenicians, as I discussed in Chapter 3. These discussions pay little or no attention to the Huelva materials, however, despite the fact that they provide the only clear trace of a Phoenician workshop outside the Levant. Indeed, the ivory workshop at Hama in northern Syria, cited as the only one detected archaeologically in the Levant, was identified thanks to a similar accumulation of the waste materials and unfinished items.[23] (As we will see in Chapter 6, similar evidence might point to a workshop in archaic Sparta.) In turn, since we are dealing with unfinished pieces and fragments, not full pieces, it would be unrealistic to expect the Huelva materials to contribute to our classification of Levantine styles and substyles; this probably explains the lack of interest in them among art historians who have taken on the orientalizing art debate, who build an ex nihilo argument while overlooking a key specimen of it that sets this type of production within the context of Phoenician networks overseas. The Huelva discarded materials prove that here and surely in other points of southern Iberia, Phoenicians opened hubs for this industry, which R. D. Barnett called "secondary centers," places with no elephants but with good access to tusks (from North Africa in this case), via harbors that were well provisioned and connected for subsequent redistribution.[24] Eventually, ivory carving generated a local Iberian production with its own characteristics, which I discuss later in this chapter (cf. Figure 4.3).

Settlements Large and Small

Starting at the end of the ninth century BC and increasingly after that, the southern coast of Iberia is dotted by an almost continuous chain of Phoenician settlements, featuring urban and industrial nuclei, and necropoleis whose graves demonstrate extraordinary wealth compared with other Phoenician areas of occupation at this time. The evidence spans a range of settlement patterns, from larger urban areas, such as the one sprawling throughout the Gadir archipelago (including the island of Cádiz and, on the facing mainland, Mesas de Asta and Castillo de Doña Blanca); nearby villages and industrial and fishing establishments along the coasts of Málaga and Granada (Cerro del Villar, Toscanos, Morro de Mezquitilla, Sexi/Almuñécar, etc.); less concentrated settlements as far east as Almería, Murcia, Alicante, and Ibiza in the Balearic Islands, and along the Atlantic coast, especially in the Algarve area (e.g., Castro Marim, Tavira); also along the mouths of the Sado and Tagus Rivers (Abul, Alcácer do Sal, sites by Lisbon) and as far north as the Mondego River (Santa Olaia, Conímbriga) (see Map 4.1).[25] A full account of the Phoenician presence in Iberia is impractical in this reduced space; such an overview would show that on the coasts of Iberia we have the best-documented contiguous area of Phoenician settlement for the eighth–seventh centuries, especially given how poorly this period is attested in Phoenicia proper.

At the time of the first encounters with native groups (still immersed in the Atlantic Bronze Age), the locals did not have the type of material culture and technologies that would leave traces of urban layouts or even burials. This makes Phoenician settlements stand out easily. Moreover, they settled in locations that followed a usual pattern, as discussed in Chapter 1: near or on the coast, by good water sources, and with access to hills (timber) or good agricultural land. The layout of the settlement, when we can trace it, is of Levantine style, with dense quadrangular constructions and narrow streets, masonry measured by Phoenician standards, flat rooftops, and whitewashed walls. The graves are usually separated from the settlement by a river. The general form of burial is cremation with the remains buried in funerary urns in pits.[26] Richer versions take the form of well-built ashlar chamber tombs (*hypogea*), either built up or carved out of the rock (e.g., Trayamar, Ciudad Jardín, and Puente de Noy), all of which conforms with known Phoenician practices (Tyre al-Bass).[27] In contrast to the context of Huelva, along the coast of Málaga-Granada the Phoenicians established a relationship with the locals we can consider colonial. Even if the settlements along this long coast were of small size, their inhabitants seem to have been both wealthy and strongly invested in maintaining their prestige.[28] Besides Phoenician dinnerware and personal objects, such as jewelry and amulets, some burials contained imported Egyptian pieces, including alabaster jars used as cinerary urns. More than fifty have been found in Iberia (besides fragments), with the tombs from Sexi/Almuñécar alone concentrating over twenty. Some of these jars bore royal emblems, and indeed Phoenician tombs in coastal Iberia have yielded the largest in situ collection of royal Egyptian artifacts outside Egypt, a stark testimony of the well-attested "Egyptomania" of Phoenician elites. In turn, when alabaster jars appear in indigenous, Tartessic contexts, their use as perfume containers for the funerary ritual also fits with Phoenician customs.[29]

During the course of the eighth century BC and especially during the seventh, the effects of generations of cohabitation between Phoenicians and locals become visible. Where there were no burials, now we find native necropoleis with cremations, using a mix of indigenous and Phoenician materials, and in some cases the monumentalization of elite burials too, such as in the tumuli of Huelva. Where there was no local writing, a peculiar form of writing emerges in the southwest, inspired by the Phoenician alphabet but clearly distinct. Where local pottery was handmade, now the potter's wheel is used, although always alongside handmade indigenous pottery. While the Andalusian metal ores had been subject to local metal extraction since prehistory, now new technologies such as cupellation are introduced, and the invisible industries surrounding its maintenance must have expanded as well (timber, ropes, transportation, etc.). Tapping into local resources and species and using new technologies and their own farming traditions, the Phoenicians contributed to the transformation of local landscapes.[30] The domestication and methods of exploitation of the Mediterranean vine and olive are also attributed to the Phoenicians' arrival in Iberia and offer a perfect testimony of the Phoenicians "lubricating cross-cultural encounters" in the Iron Age.[31] However the locals interred their dead before, whatever their domiciles looked like (probably roundish huts made mostly of perishable materials), or whatever they cultivated, by the late eighth century and during the seventh, we can talk about a more visible local culture in all these realms, marked by hybrid ("orientalizing") traits. In the Iberian southwest, this is what the ancient Greeks called Tartessos; a sociocultural (perhaps political) entity whose local character and shared mythical memory was cultivated and evoked by the later inhabitants of Roman Turdetania in the Baetica province.[32]

On the Atlantic coast, in what is now Portugal, similar effects accompanied Phoenician commercial activity and settlement, from as early as the ninth century. Phoenician presence from the Algarve in the south to Lisbon and farther north can be traced through a wide range of areas of culture: these include "domestic and defensive architecture, building techniques, archaeological remains, language, and texts," to quote from Ana Margarida Arruda's recent overview.[33] Here too, the Phoenicians encountered local communities who cultivated continuities with their Bronze Age predecessors and whose local character transcended this period, but who were in time considerably transformed by the entanglement with the western Phoenicians. This is especially clear in areas where no colonies proper were established, such as Huelva, where local elites began to use oriental or orientalizing elements to stand out and signal their status; all the while their use of exotica and new habits, such as ostentatious burials, was highly selective and by no means overshadowed the indigenous character of the community.[34]

In short, the Tartessic artistic output of the eighth–seventh centuries BC that archaeologists characterize as "orientalizing" is the result of a local cultural transformation, of the emergence of hybrid practices and expressions, stimulated by contact with Phoenicians either through direct colonization or other commercial and social relations.

Tartessic Art, or the Iberian Orientalizing

Warrior Stelae

The corpus of "warrior" stelae, also known as "southwestern" or "Tartessic" stelae, has been studied as a sort of fossil marker of the transition from indigenous to orientalizing culture. Many uncertainties surround this corpus of megaliths and their engraved iconography because they appear out of their original archaeological context; their function, therefore, is unknown, although most hypotheses see them as funerary monuments (cenotaphs) or territorial markers. Their systematic displacement and destruction, as well as occasional reuse, suggests they were freestanding visible monuments of importance to the local communities for a chronological span that extends between the eleventh and the seventh centuries BC. Since some appear in datable secondary contexts (which provide a *terminus ante quem*), a relative chronology has been constructed from a few fixed points and the reconstructed evolution of the iconography on the stelae. They appear throughout the Iberian southwest, roughly overlapping with what is considered Tartessic territory and a wide hinterland periphery, concentrated around the Guadalquivir and Guadiana valleys, with a few outliers in other regions.

The iconographical trajectory of the stelae is a great example of both the local resilience and transformation in southwest Iberia, so it is worth summarizing here. The earlier types, which could go back to the eleventh–tenth centuries, are slabs depicting indigenous armor that aligns with Atlantic traditions, such as conical helmets and carp's tongue sword ("lengua de carpa" in Spanish typology). Besides this bronze weaponry, the central feature is a round V-notched shield of the sort probably made of wood and leather, not physically preserved in Iberia but recovered in some European contexts. In the next phase, human figures appear, at first as an addition to the central shield, then increasingly central, representing perhaps gods, heroized humans or ancestors, or deceased elite members; the schematic human figures' position vis-à-vis the objects depicted around them suggests the representation of a horizontal, inhumation burial, but no such inhumations have been found in the Tartessic milieu. The schematic male figures wear no helmet, while female figures brandish diadems, which have been connected with golden diadems and jewelry found in indigenous hoards.[35]

At some point, coinciding with the phase of precolonial contacts in the ninth century, new elements enter the repertoire of objects surrounding the human figure, as further markers of prestige, wealth, and probably human/divine authority. From then on, the compositions become increasingly complex: male warriors appear with horned headgear, and their accoutrement includes chariots and smaller objects such as lyres, mirrors, and combs, presumably evoking imported luxury items made of metals and ivory; occasionally what looks like a group of mourners appears along with the chariots, which suggests a funerary scene. Comparison with Greek and Levantine iconography suggests that these elements were incorporated into the older repertoire at a pace set by local elites as they opened up and embraced Mediterranean modes of representation. Similarities with the roughly contemporary (eighth-century) Greek depictions of heroic-style funerals in Late Geometric funerary *pithoi* and kraters have not gone unnoticed.[36]

Even more striking is the similarity between the horned figures and those in four roughly contemporary (eighth- to seventh-century) stelae from northern Israel and North Syria that appear in a similar stance and with almost identical, diagonally placed short swords. In the case of the Levantine stelae, these are most likely representations of the Storm God Baal, who is likened to a bull in Northwest Semitic lore, and whose crescent-moon horns represent strength and fertility (the rosette that appears in these monuments, associated with Ashtart, adds to this symbology).[37] While the cultic function of those Near Eastern stelae is fairly clear, we cannot say the same of the Tartessic/southwestern stelae. At most, it seems that these monuments, which bridge across Atlantic-indigenous megalithic tradition and Levantine influences, had something to do with the territorial and cultural organization of the indigenous communities that interfaced with Phoenicians and possibly other Levantines in the ninth–eighth centuries. It is still the case that there is no comparable iconography in Phoenician stelae proper (which are carved and of a different tradition, not megalithic), whether in the Levant or Iberia, so the routes of influence are hazy. All we know is that the elites who are represented in or by these stelae adopted eastern Mediterranean markers of prestige only when they fully entered into the Phoenician sphere, adding new elements to their own traditional expressions of socioeconomic status.

Funerary World

During the eighth century BC, burials become visible for the first time in the protohistoric southwestern territory. Cremations in urns become generalized, a practice that arrived with the Phoenician settlers, as did the accompanying mode of funerary ritual; this included the body's preparation (we find perfumed-oil jugs and basinets), banqueting in honor of the dead, and the gathering of dinnerware and personal objects in the grave. In the main Tartessic necropoleis (e.g., in the area of Seville), we find grave goods that were meaningful in the Phoenician funerary realm, such as scarabs, ostrich eggs, and decorated ivory plaques.[38]

At the same time, Tartessic groups clung to their indigenous roots. A well-documented case is the extensive necropolis of Las Cumbres by the Phoenician site of Castillo de Doña Blanca (across from Cádiz), where the grave goods range from typically Phoenician to typically indigenous materials to combinations of the two, much as happens in the radius of other colonial settlements (e.g., Motya on Sicily). In the eighth and seventh centuries, we find some necropoleis that are indeed difficult to classify along this spectrum, which we usually understand as Tartessic: these are found in predominantly indigenous areas, along the Guadalquivir valley and at Huelva, where the wealthier locals created orientalizing but idiosyncratic forms of burial, such as the artificial tumuli in the Huelva area. These mounds were built over cremation burials, in which a mix of indigenous and orientalizing pottery forms were elevated to international status by the company of Phoenician objects, such as ivory palettes, ostrich eggs, Phoenician Red-Slip ware, and even imported decorated Greek vases.[39] In other words, these groups took on the Levantine material language of prestige to articulate their social distinctions, thereby fashioning their own, locally relevant orientalizing code.

Pottery Styles and Techniques

Pottery making is well attested in prehistoric Iberia, which makes it easy to distinguish local from well-known Phoenician types and to track changes. Two main technological innovations are the use of the wheel for ceramic production, and the use of more potent kilns, whose wider range of temperatures allowed for more color variety in the decoration of the pots. This happens in the eighth century, coinciding with the Phoenician settlement on the coasts, so the technologies are assumed to have been adopted from that realm into the indigenous communities. The locals continue to produce many types of indigenous handmade forms, however, such as "à chardon" urns, burnished and geometric vases, while they modify other traditional types through the use of Levantine techniques and decoration.

One of those innovative hybrids is the large globular urn known as "Cruz del Negro," which is wheel-made and has painted decoration in red and black bands and circles. This vase is used as a cinerary urn throughout Tartessic territory for the newly adopted rite of cremation burials. This is considered a local but orientalizing type of vase (as was its use), while a purely indigenous touch is added by the traditional, handmade bowls that cover the funerary urn's mouth.[40] The so-called Carambolo pottery also maps onto Tartessic culture in the eighth century and disappears after that. It is also orientalizing by virtue of its Mediterranean-style decoration, in this case red-painted geometric shapes (resembling the burnished wares), while it remains made by hand, a local trait.[41]

By the seventh century, full-fledged orientalizing decorative style seems to replace the Carambolo decorated wares, deploying unambiguous Levantine motifs such as griffins, rosettes, and lotus flowers on bowls, cups, and large *pithoi,* such as the group found in Carmona (Figure 4.1). The Carmona vases (two taller pithoi and two other slightly smaller vases) were found in the same deposit with indigenous handmade pots, a Red-Slip Phoenician plate, and four ivory spoons of a type paralleled in Carthage. This shows exactly the combination of local and Phoenician culture we are contemplating in Tartessos. The placement of these figurative pots in religious, often funerary contexts, indicates their high value and, what is most important, a seeming understanding of the iconography's symbology, which in the Phoenician realm is expressly associated with Ashtart, regeneration, and the afterlife.[42] These motifs will surface in other plastic arts, for instance in Etruria and the Aegean, and are easily the most obvious testimonies of the use of an international orientalizing language across the Mediterranean.

Metalwork and Ivories

Iberian jewelry and metalwork are rooted in Bronze Age traditions, and, once more, we can be certain of the Phoenician hand in introducing technological and formal innovations around this time. Bronze production and

FIG. 4.1   Tartessic vases with orientalizing decoration.

Two of the large decorated *pithoi* from the Casa-Palacio del Marqués del Saltillo site, Carmona (Seville), dated to the seventh century BC, found together with Red-Slip plates, ivory spoons, and hand-made indigenous pottery. The larger *pithos* (*left*) is decorated with a procession of griffins, one of them with embroidered skirt, and lotus flowers. The other vase (*right*) is decorated with open and closed lotus. Courtesy of Museum of the City of Carmona.

trade had deep roots in the area, as exemplified by the Ría de Huelva hoard of bronze weapons and by the feminine gold diadems mentioned above.[43] Now, however, new bronze objects appear; some are Phoenician, some local with orientalizing traits (that is, Tartessic). The main Phoenician examples are a series of statuettes of the "Resheph" type, a Phoenician priest or god statuette with golden face, and a figurine of a seated Ashtart/Astarte with a Phoenician inscription (see Figure 4.4). From the Tartessic realm come incense burners or *thymiateria,* paralleled by local innovations in Etruria and Cyprus (Figure 4.2) and numerous sets of bronze jugs and basins ("braserillos"), probably of ritual use and deposited in graves. Other objects include oval plates (or small basins with a flat rectangular frame) engraved with Levantine motifs, such as lotus, palmettes, winged lions, and sphinxes. All these have their immediate models in Phoenician metalwork,

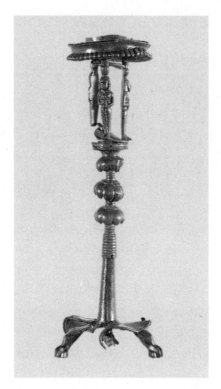

FIG. 4.2   **Bronze perfume burners from Tartessos and Etruria.**

These stands supported receptacles on which incense or other perfume-generating substances were slow-burned, here adorned with anthropomorphic female figures holding lotuses (*left*) and a voluted plant/flower (*right*, receptacle missing).

Left: Incense burner (*thymiaterion*) from Villagarcía de la Torre (Badajoz), seventh century BC. Photo by Vicente Novillo. Courtesy of Museo Arqueológico Provincial de Badajoz.

Right: Incense burner (*thymiaterion*) from Etruria, late sixth century BC. The Metropolitan Museum of Art, New York, Gift of Henry G. Marquand, 1897.

most remarkably perhaps the bronze jugs with palmette handles, versions of which also appear in grave assemblages in Italy, for instance; and yet in small details of style and welding technique they form coherent types of their own. Other bronze artifacts are even more idiosyncratic but still touched by the Levantine traditions, such as the *Potnia Theron* ("Mistress of Animals") that adorned a horse bit known as the "Bronze Carriazo" (from Seville), and the similar "Master of Horses" from Cancho Roano (Badajoz).[44]

Work in gold and silver follows a similar trajectory. Despite the abundance of silver in southern Iberia, silverwork is much more rarely attested than goldsmithing. Thus, indigenous tradition meets with innovation triggered by Levantine styles and technologies: hollow objects, such as earrings, replace the traditional ones made of solid gold; new alloys are adopted; and decorative techniques such as filigree and granulation become the rage. Still, as for other arts, orientalizing jewelry and metalwork coexisted with traditional craftsmanship. What is more, a "hybrid" style of decoration and welding in gold and silver emerges, as attested in several "treasures" (hoards of La Aliseda, El Carambolo, gold candelabra of Lebrija). Local-style large earrings ("arracadas") now appear in both modalities: the indigenous tradition in which they are solid and not engraved, as well as the hollow ones decorated with filigree of floral oriental-style motifs.[45]

It is no surprise, then, that ivory work in southern Iberia also reflects the orientalizing trend, while retaining a local character. The material, technology, and type of objects are themselves part and parcel of Levantine trade and technology. Carved ivories appear in the Tartessic sphere beyond the colonial realm proper, and are recovered in sanctuaries and burials, especially from seventh-century contexts, most famously from the necropoleis of Los Alcores in the province of Seville and Medellín in Extremadura.[46] The forms follow Levantine types (combs, decorative plaques, and circular boxes or *pyxides*), with some outliers, such as the so-called cosmetic palettes (a plaque with a circular receptacle in the middle), whose specific function is unknown.[47]

A particular technique of ivory work takes hold in southern Iberia, however: that of incision, instead of the deeper bas-relief made by carving, common to Phoenician-Levantine ivories (Figures 3.1 and 4.3). The motifs chosen here, in turn, are typically Levantine, including lions, rosettes and lotuses (associated with Ashtart), hybrid creatures, chariots, and hunters. The incision technique as well as some types of objects, such as decorated spoons, have no parallel in the Levant, but seem to be innovations of the western Mediterranean, as they are attested also in Carthage and Sicily. We ignore whether this incision style originated in the Iberian colonies or their periphery and spread from there, or originated elsewhere, at a place such as Carthage. In the later phases, bone and horn objects were also made in the same style, and the orientalizing tradition in ivory carving continued in the

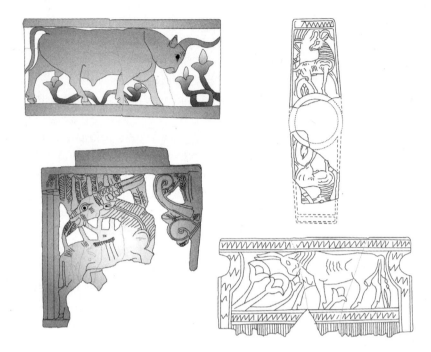

**FIG. 4.3   Ivory plaques from Assyrian and Iberian sites,
eighth-seventh centuries BC.**

Left column: Drawing of ivory plaques from Nimrud carved in relief, with bull and lotus
flowers (British Museum), and (*bottom*) onyx with stylized plants and volute-palmette motif.
The Metropolitan Museum of Art, New York. © Esther Rodríguez.

Right column: Drawing of Tartessic-style ivory palette decorated by incision, with onyx and
stylized plant, from El Acebuchal (Carmona, Seville), and (*bottom*) ivory comb with bull and
lotus flowers, from Carthage (probably Iberian import). © Esther Rodríguez.

interior of Iberia well after the dwindling of the orientalizing period (i.e.,
after ca. 600), until the fourth century BC; remarkable tokens of this tradition come from the Guadiana valley (Cancho Roano, El Turuñuelo).[48]

Whatever the case, the evidence of raw ivory pieces, even tusks from different periods (e.g., from Huelva, Bajo de la Campana wreck, Cancho
Roano sanctuary), shows that southern Iberia was a hub for the manufacture and export of carved ivory objects, possibly of raw ivory redistribution
too, as well as probably ostrich eggs from the North African networks.[49]
For instance, the cargo from the Bajo de la Campana shipwreck, which
sunk off the coast of Cartagena in southeast Spain and dates to the seventh

or early sixth century BC, included more than fifty elephant tusks, seven of them scratched with Phoenician graffiti, as well as decorated ostrich eggs, another "wildlife" exotic good.[50]

Sanctuaries and Religious Symbols

Impressive sanctuary complexes have been excavated in southern Iberia in recent decades, providing an exceptional laboratory for the study of Phoenician–local relations.[51] Absent written evidence about these sites and their communities, it is sometimes difficult to ascribe them to one culture, Phoenician or native, since the groups were so entangled. Some of their materials and features can be interpreted either as Phoenician idiosyncrasies due to indigenous influence or as native orientalizing traits due to the Phoenician input (typically classified as Tartessic), or a hybrid combination in between that evades classification.

The assimilation of Levantine practices and symbols, however, was strong not only in the core Tartessic area of the lower Guadalquivir in the eighth–seventh centuries (El Carambolo, Montemolín, Coria del Río, all around Seville) but also had a firm grip in the Portuguese south and west (Ratinhos, late eighth century), the Málaga coast (Alcorrín, late ninth or early eighth century), and similar complexes. Perhaps simply due to issues of preservation, even more impressive complexes have been unearthed in the Guadiana valley (e.g., Cancho Roano, El Turuñuelo) dating to the fifth and fourth centuries. These constructions denote a secondary wave of orientalizing culture that can still be called "Tartessic," even if it falls outside the archaic parameters usually associated with the term.[52]

The construction of monumental buildings with rectilinear outlines is an innovation that came with the Levantine models brought by Phoenicians. The earliest remains of presumed Tartessic cultic installations are the above-mentioned Huelva site, followed by structures in the area of Seville (El Carambolo, Carmona), discussed below, while the most famous referent for a Phoenician sanctuary in Iberia is the Herakleion or temple of Melqart in Gadir, which remains are not preserved. Although it is traditionally assumed that this temple's plan was similar to the famed temple of Solomon in Jerusalem, it may have been more similar to other more varied plans attested for Phoenician sanctuaries, as we will discuss especially in Chapters 5 and 9.[53] The new structures in the Iberian pericolonial realm, then, are characterized by whitewashed adobe walls on basic rectilinear plans, with rather complex layouts well attested in the seventh century and later. These include court-yards paved with pebbles or seashells, red-clay pavement in the interior, built-in benches around the central rooms where offerings would have been set, and altars used for burned and liquid offerings, all features at-tested for Phoenician sanctuaries and very neatly attested in El Carambolo (near Seville).[54] Different designs of these rooms and their altars sometimes overlay each other in a series of constructions for centuries, while main-taining the central axis. We see this most clearly at Cancho Roano in Badajoz with three consecutive buildings and altars from the early sixth to the early fourth centuries BC.[55]

Some of the sanctuaries were surrounded by fortified precincts and moats (Alcorrín, Ratinhos, Cancho Roano). In turn, these sites bear the mark of continued local traditions: we can mention the local handmade pottery and traditional jewelry found in them alongside orientalizing artifacts, and the reuse of a Tartessic warrior stela as a threshold for the main entrance in Cancho Roano A (sixth century BC). Moreover, the constructions seem to follow peculiar territorial patterns: they are placed on promontories or in open-country sites near rivers or springs, and always oriented toward the rising sun.[56] Finally, a degree of cultic continuity is suggested by the fact that the rectilinear constructions are built on top of previous round or oval huts typical of the local Bronze Age, at least at El Carambolo, Cancho Roano, and Cerro Borreguero.[57]

We can say little about the religion of these communities, but the mark of Phoenician influence at a symbolic level is obvious in the presence of ma-terials such as ostrich eggs, scarabs, stone and bronze vases, the use of seashells in pavements (associated with Ashtart in the Phoenician world), the adoption of symbols associated with Ashtart and Baal, and traces of ritual practices that mirror or adapt eastern ones, such as communal ban-queting (meat skewers, cups, and bowls are often found in situ), perfume burning, and burned animal sacrifice.[58]

Perhaps the most striking shared features of these Tartessic sanctuaries are the "oxhide-shaped" clay altars that appear in the central cultic rooms of many of these buildings (El Carambolo, Coria del Río, Cancho Roano, Neves, El Turuñuelo). Their shape is generally interpreted as a symbol of Canaanite-Phoenician Baal or adopted for a local storm or fertility god identified with Baal; his female counterpart would be a fertility goddess who in turn adopted features and symbols of Ashtart.[59] Such a dual worship is exemplified at El Carambolo (eighth–seventh centuries), where the complex is structured around twin chambers with two separate altars (one of them "oxhide-shaped"), presumably for the cult of Ashtart-Baal or their local version. At Cancho Roano, an "oxhide-shaped" altar was placed in the inner cultic room of the building (Cancho Roano A, fifth century), while the oldest version of the altar underlying it (Cancho Roano C, sixth century) was circular with a triangular receptacle, a shape that may evoke the Tanit symbol (attested only later in Iberia) or perhaps the Egyptian *shen*-symbol associated with the sun (and Horus, Isis), transferred to the Phoenician world as part of the Ashtart repertoire.[60]

Of these sanctuaries, El Carambolo outside Seville has a good chance of being an actual Phoenician cult site, or, at a minimum, a combined local–Phoenician cult site.[61] This is often cited as evidence of the deep reach of the Phoenician presence in the Guadalquivir valley, at a time when the deep estuary of the river directly connected the area with the sea. The devotion to Ashtart in the area is documented by a bronze statuette from Seville representing a seated Ashtart (Figure 4.4, left). The piece was dedicated by a pair of brothers, as we know from the small but neat Phoenician inscription:

[Dedication] which Baalyatan
son of Du'mmilk, and Abdbaal
son of Du'mmilk, son of YŠ'L made for
our mistress Ashtart of Hor, because
she heard the voice of their prayers.[62]

This piece, along with Resheph-type figures (Figure 4.4, right) and some others, are among the few examples of bronze statuary found in the Tartessic realm, and this is one of not many formal Phoenician inscriptions found in Iberia. On the other hand, the sanctuary of El Carambolo may still have functioned mainly in a local context, in which case this dedication may be the visitor's interpretation of a Tartessic cult of a goddess who acquired Ashtart's symbology, as pointed out above (assimilation and identification works both ways). The lack of written sources about the place makes interpretations hypothetical. El Carambolo is a perfect example of the engagement with Phoenician religion beyond the attested Phoenician settlements proper, and of orientalizing material culture as both international (global) and resiliently local.

FIG. 4.4 Phoenician bronze statuettes of divinities.

Left: Votive dedication of Ashtart from the area of El Carambolo (near Seville), eighth century BC, with Phoenician inscription (16.60 cm tall). Photo by José Morón Borrego. Courtesy of Archaeological Museum of Seville.

Right: Statuette of male god (Resheph or Melqart) (24.6 cm tall), from Spain (unknown provenance), eighth–seventh centuries BC. © Hispanic Society Project.

Language and Script

Throughout the Mediterranean, the Phoenician alphabetic script provided a model for developing societies that so far lacked a writing system, while the newly alphabetized locals maintained their language, whether Greek, Phrygian, Etruscan, or Tartessic. In all cases, the adoption of writing was part of the orientalizing process, while clearly a "Phoenicianizing" phenomenon.[63]

In Iberia the earliest native writing appears in the early seventh century BC, more than a century after the Phoenicians settled along the southern and southwestern coasts. It appears precisely in the southwestern corner of the peninsula, the Tartessic realm. This is the earliest systematic script found in the western Mediterranean. The script known as "southwestern" or "Tartessic" is an adaptation of the Semitic alphabet, with modifications and extensions (the system is partly syllabic). The earliest inscriptions come from a corpus of funerary stelae in the Algarve region of Portugal, with later testimonies scattered in graffiti around southern Iberia. The adaptation in Iberia was relatively later than the Greek adaptation in the earlier eighth century, and roughly contemporary with the Etruscan adaptation (presumably from a Greek alphabet ca. 700), although some propose that the Iberian adaptation may have been as early as 825–800, the time of the first Phoenician colonies.[64] The Tartessic script seems not to have been used profusely or monumentally, at least judging by the limited corpus so far, and many questions remain unanswered. For instance, why are there no early inscriptions in the core of Tartessic culture, such as in Huelva or Seville? Whatever the reasons, Tartessic script served as the basis of the writing used for the Iberian languages later on and their southern branch in Turdetania (a Roman name for the same region the Greeks had called Tartessos). Although the Tartessic script is deciphered thanks to the later Iberian and Celtiberian versions, the language (like Iberian) is unintelligible, as it lies outside the Indo-European linguistic family.[65]

Phoenician inscriptions, on the other hand, are attested in Iberia by the hundreds (around four hundred recorded so far), mostly in the form of graffiti on ostraca, although papyri or other perishable materials were used too. It is rare to find formal or monumental inscriptions, however, like the one shown in Figure 4.4, or the funerary slab found in Lisbon.[66] The relative absence of monumental or civic epigraphy in Phoenician means that among Phoenician settlers in these western parts, writing was mostly a private and commercial tool, and neither Phoenician nor local communities used it as an aristocratic medium.[67] As Javier de Hoz suggested, we can think of trade in metals with the indigenous populations as the more likely stimulus for the creation of a local version of the script to record transactions or property in the local language, mainly in perishable materials.[68] In any case, the Tartessians and their Iberian heirs preserved their languages for centuries before Latin became the norm, and in the Phoenician-settled areas proper, Phoenician language and writing also continued in use for centuries.

North Africa: A Different Response?

When the Roman poet Lucan describes the landscapes of the Greater and Lesser Syrtes (the gulfs that form the coast of Libya and Tunisia), he describes one of the native peoples, the Nasamonians, as a "hardy race who inhabit unclad the lands next to the sea and whom the barbarous Syrtes nourish with the shipwrecks of the world."[69] This was one of the groups that Cato the Younger and his men encountered in their journey across the region in 48 BC, according to Lucan.

A long tradition preceded him of evoking arid, inhospitable "Libya" and the challenges it posed for explorers and mythical heroes alike, expressed in the genres of historiography, paradoxography, and epic poetry.[70] For the Roman geographer Pomponius Mela, North Africa was part of an alien world of wonders that contrasted with the *terra cognita* of his native southern Iberia, even if both were marked by centuries of Phoenician-Punic presence and the more recent effects of Romanization.[71] What was the difference? And for our purposes, why is it that we do not find equivalent manifestations of the orientalizing koine in North Africa?

Phoenician settlement along the coasts of North Africa started at the end of the ninth century in Tunisia (Carthage and Utica) and on the Atlantic coast of Morocco (Lixus).[72] Our expectations are frustrated, however, if we look for evidence of widespread cultural hybridization accompanying early contact with the Levantines. It may be that among native groups in North Africa the type of hybridization that we see as orientalization did not happen at all, despite the existence of channels of contact for centuries between the Mediterranean and the North African hinterlands. Tamar Hodos noticed this lack of engagement with Levantine culture in the region.[73] As Cyprian Broodbank's survey also shows, connections and developments do not "just happen" out of inertia. In some cases, conditions are more favorable for them than in others. Despite its long coast, much of North Africa is devoid of good natural harbors, and thus its immediate hinterland remained more inward- and southward looking than we might expect.

The main exception is Egypt, which developed along a different axis and was always oriented southward, drawing irrigation and trade from the Nile, and eastward toward the Levant.[74] Indeed, Egypt produced the only Iron Age large state and imperial culture in Mediterranean North Africa before Carthage, and relations with the Levant and the Phoenicians were particularly fruitful in the Late Bronze Age and the earlier Iron Age, and then during the Saite period in the seventh–sixth centuries.[75] Cultural exchange with its western neighbors, by contrast, was scarce, through a desert route that ran through Siwa to the Fazzan region in the Sahara, where one of the few desert civilizations we know about developed, the Garamantes.[76] Unlike the Nile land, the rest of the North African groups were cut off "from their demographic, cultural, and ideological heartland to the south" once the Sahara turned into a desert during the third millennium BC.[77] North Africa thus became insularly locked between the Mediterranean and the world's largest desert.[78] The north of the continent is itself geographically fragmented between the Cyrenaica and Tripolitana, the Maghrib of Tunis and Algeria, and the Maghrib Al-Aqsa along Morocco, and the local groups lacked sustained contact with the broader Mediterranean before the Phoenician input.[79]

The Phoenicians gradually populated the coasts of North Africa with larger and smaller settlements and industrial-commercial areas. There is a general impression, however, that Carthage and other Phoenician enclaves in North Africa functioned much like islands, pulling from networks that connected themselves and other Mediterranean regions, especially with the Phoenician settlements in Iberia, Sardinia, and Sicily. Some traces of native pottery and other materials, however, intimate contact with locals, sometimes in the early stages, more often as time went by. In a few better documented cases, archaeologists have suggested that the Phoenicians settled initially in small trading groups amid a native community (perhaps one whose material culture was not as durable).[80] In other words, the Phoenician and the local hinterland communities were not always standing back to back, and more thorough archaeological research might shed light on these relations.[81] We also know that Phoenician and Greek settlement influenced native agriculture in some particularly fertile areas adjacent to their colonies (e.g., Cape Bon and the Carthage area, Cyrenaica).[82] Still, there is no trace of culturally orientalizing, proto-urban elites across the regions known in antiquity as Cyrenaica, Tripolitana, Numidia, and Mauretania, whose archaeological and historical record is obscure for this early period. We can perhaps take a clue from mythology, where the foundational story of Carthage emphasizes strained relations with the locals and frustrated alliances.[83] It is on the island of Rachgoun in Algeria where we find the rare instance of a Phoenician site armed to the teeth.[84]

Although we should be alert to the risk of drawing definitive arguments from silence, the historiographical and scant material evidence so far suggests that only when the Romans took over Carthage's territory did groups such as the Numidians coalesce as unified entities. Before that, since the third century BC or so (during the Punic Wars), Numidians and other groups like the Garamantians pivoted slightly toward a Mediterranean façade, as they joined international networks of trade and diplomacy. This trend manifests itself in funerary monuments and in the imagery they deployed on coins and monuments, which combined Punic and Hellenistic prestige markers with indigenous traditions.[85]

This subtle Mediterraneanization, however, is outside the period of our focus. Our evidence so far suggests we have no eighth–seventh century orientalizing cultures to speak of; no middle ground created by eager indigenous receptors of Near Eastern cultural capital; no local version of the Phoenician alphabet; no orientalizing innovation on local pottery or metalwork; and no incipient monumental architecture or urbanization, of the sorts that have been found among other Iron Age communities. In turn, once writing became more widespread in the region, during Roman Imperial times, what transpires is a deeper cultural change. What inscriptions and literary testimonies show is not so much a middle ground but the deep grip of Punic culture, persistent in municipal institutions, such as magistrates named *suffetes* and *rabbim,* local, evolving versions of the tophet sanctuaries, and the spread of the Punic language, attested in several scripts until late antiquity (Punic, Neo-Punic, Latino-Punic, and even Greco-Punic), alongside native languages represented in Libyco-Berber script.[86] The dispersal of the population from Carthage itself, after the capture and abandonment of the metropolis in 146 BC, intensified the penetration of Punic culture in the hinterland, whereas we are in the dark as to the degree of hybridity, the depth, and modalities of these Phoenician-Punic features among native populations.[87]

Why then do we not see a full-fledged hybrid culture emerge in North Africa? Other considerations aside, the answer must lie in the local communities' apparent lack of interest in joining the pan-Mediterranean networks, and perhaps in their failure or refusal to offer local resources in return, such as minerals, timber, or (with some exceptions) agricultural land, which would have led to closer negotiations and collaboration. In the case of Cyrenaica, for instance, as Hodos has pointed out, Greek and Phoenician colonization had little effect on native culture until the local communities decided to adopt foreign elements, by the fourth–third centuries BC (three centuries after the colonists' arrival); only then did they open up to imports and adopt writing. There is no orientalizing culture or middle ground for centuries.[88]

The African and the Iberian cases, then, present a stark contrast. If, as so far suggested, neither Greeks nor Phoenicians met with a North African hinterland ready to revolutionize their culture in the eighth–seventh centuries, this in turn may have affected the function of their North African colonies to begin with, all of which in turn was already determined in part by geographical-environmental conditions: the North African coasts were arid and not so much coveted for their agricultural potential, except in Cyrenaica and the Syrtis Minor and Cape Bon area in Tunisia, or the choras of Carthage and Utica. The generally small enclaves, however, were apt for the extension of a support network along the east–west route all the way to the Atlantic, besides providing fishing harbors, factories (e.g., for salt and salted fish), and commercial outlets.[89]

North African enclaves must have been necessary also to channel and fend off competitors for access to coveted and rare African resources. It is possible that Phoenician engagement was mostly limited to the need for sustaining their access to the African trade channels, especially for exotic products such as ivory, ostrich eggs, and gold.[90] For instance, a recent isotopic analysis shows that the ostrich eggs were preferably procured from wild habitats, which required tapping into highly specialized native trafficking, but not necessarily the type of intense collaboration with natives that was needed for the sustained exploitation of metals, such that led to more complex relations in Iberia, Sardinia, and Cyprus.[91] As a sort of "time capsule," the Bajo de la Campana shipwreck sank off the coast of Iberia with all these sorts of materials, often considered in isolation: raw elephant tusks and raw metals traveled together with finished goods of the type that would be exchanged with local elites, including decorated ostrich eggs, ivory-handled daggers, and bronze adornments for wooden furniture.[92]

The Phoenicians had indeed been the first to explore and engage in trade in the Atlantic both north and south of the straits into Sub-Saharan Africa, as captured in the preserved *periploi* of Hanno and Himilkon (ca. 500 BC), and the first to circumnavigate the continent, under the auspices of the Egyptian pharaoh Necho (610–595 BC).[93] By dotting the North African coast with generally small settlements, the Phoenicians completed their network in the western Mediterranean and guarded their access to the Atlantic routes. As Maria Eugenia Aubet put it, "the Phoenicians built a kind of 'Phoenician triangle' in the west that was practically impregnable and provided naval and commercial traffic with a solid support point and a monopoly of all the access routes to the southwest Mediterranean. This triangle virtually closed the Straits of Gibraltar to Greek competition and would be the foundation of the future Carthaginian maritime strength."[94] In short, North Africa provides a sort of "control case" for appreciating the various degrees in which the Phoenician colonial presence intersected with the specific socioeconomic structure of local groups they interacted with. While there is evidence of contact with local groups in specific sites, proto-urban orientalizing cultures of the consistency and scale seen in Tartessos, the Aegean, or Etruria do not seem to have developed in North Africa in this period. Such cultures do not appear by inertia or passive osmosis, and not all groups responded in the same way to the variables of "risk and opportunity" (in Peregrine Horden and Nicholas Purcell's terms) laid before them by the Phoenicians' arrival.

⊰ 5 ⊱

THE CENTRAL
MEDITERRANEAN

A Hybrid Culture in Iron Age Sardinia

Sardinia is a great example of recent trends in Iron Age scholarship in the western and central Mediterranean (Map 5.1). On this large island, local communities adopted Near Eastern traits from Phoenician colonies, while the island remained largely dominated by indigenous landscapes inherited from the Bronze Age Nuragic culture. Megalithic, towerlike constructions known as *nuraghi* stand tall as the most visible representatives of the prehistoric indigenous communities of Sardinia. Built in the so-called Nuragic Bronze Age (1600–900 BC) as dwellings and strongholds, these megaliths subsequently became foci of new communal activity in the first millennium. This development was accompanied by intensified trading, especially with the Phoenicians. The search for metal resources, especially Atlantic tin and silver, which led Phoenicians to Iberia, also took them early on to Sardinia, supposedly famous for its silver.[1] On Sardinia, orientalizing adaptations were highly selective and strongly local and clearly a by-product of sustained entanglement with Phoenicians, as the result of partnerships and intermingling that lasted for over five centuries, from the eighth century until the onset of Roman control in the late third century BC and in some aspects even after.[2]

Early Networks and Settlement Patterns at the Dawn of the Iron Age

During the Late Bronze Age, Sardinia seems to have remained somewhat in the margins of the routes that brought Mycenaean Greeks to the central Mediterranean, especially to southern Italy and Sicily, thus showing signs

121

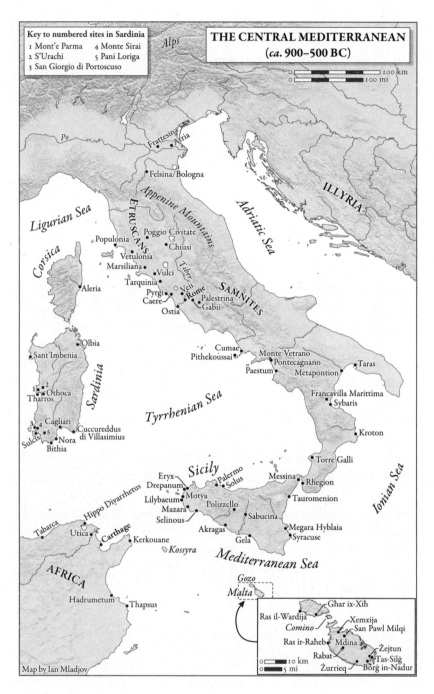

Key to numbered sites in Sardinia
1 Mont'e Parma   4 Monte Sirai
2 S'Urachi   5 Pani Loriga
3 San Giorgio di Portoscuso

THE CENTRAL MEDITERRANEAN
(*ca.* 900–500 BC)

0   200 km
0   100 mi

Alps

Po

Frattesina

Atria

Felsina/Bologna

Appenine Mountains

Adriatic Sea

ILLYRIA

Ligurian Sea

Corsica

ETRUSCANS

Poggio Civitate

Populonia

Chiusi

Vetulonia

Marsiliana

Vulci

Tiber

Tarquinia

Pyrgi   Veii   Rome

Caere   Palestrina

Ostia   Gabii

SAMNITES

Aleria

Olbia

Sant'Imbenia

Sardinia

Cumae

Pithekoussai

Monte Vetrano

Pontecagnano

Paestum

Metapontion

Taras

1 2
   Othoca
Tharros

Francavilla Marittima

Sybaris

Tyrrhenian Sea

Cagliari

3 4

5   Cuccureddus
    di Villasimius

Sulcis Nora
     Bithia

Kroton

Torre Galli

Sicily

Eryx

Drepanum

Palermo

Solus

Messina

Rhegion

Ionian Sea

Lilybaeum

Motya

Mazara   Polizzello

Tauromenion

Selinous

Sabucina

Akragas

Megara Hyblaia

Hippo Diyarrhetus

Tabarca

Utica   **Carthage**

Kerkouane

Gela   Syracuse

Kossyra

Mediterranean Sea

AFRICA

Hadrumetum   Thapsus

Gozo

Malta

Ghar ix-Xih

Ras il-Wardija

Xemxija

Comino

San Pawl Milqi

Ras ir-Raheb   Mdina

Žejtun

Rabat   Tas-Silġ

0   10 km

0   5 mi

Žurrieq   Borġ in-Nadur

Map by Ian Mladjov

MAP 5.1

122

of both connectivity and isolation.[3] After the Mycenaean collapse, the island entered the trade networks of Cypriots, Euboians, and Levantines.
Sardinian materials became part of the new international culture; they are
found in contexts of documented early Phoenician presence east and west,
in Cyprus and Huelva. Perhaps the Sardinians had a role in facilitating the
Phoenicians' access to Tartessos and the Atlantic routes, or perhaps it was
the Phoenicians who directed Sardinian trading goods to these more remote
areas.[4]

For many, these precolonial initiatives were driven by private "merchant-
adventurers" from anywhere in the Levant (North Syrians, Phoenicians,
possibly even Philistines), as well as Cyprus and Euboia, always depending
on networking with native groups.[5] Without excluding these scenarios, however, historical sources and archaeological evidence indicate that the Phoenician city-states and Tyre in particular launched a well-organized commercial expansion during the tenth century BC, paving the way to colonial
settlement in the mid- to late ninth century. It is after this point that the
Phoenicians started dealing more intensely with Sardinian groups, at the
end of the ninth or early eighth century. We can trace those close interactions at Sant'Imbenia, especially in the adoption by the locals of the Phoenician amphora, a new type of artifact inseparable from the new trade networks; epigraphical evidence points to the same horizon, as Sardinia can
boast of having produced the earliest formal Phoenician inscription found
so far in the west, the "Nora stela" (found in Nora/Pula) dated by most to
the ninth century on epigraphic grounds. Although the interpretation of the
monument is far from certain, its very existence implies a strong investment in the area this early on.[6]

Phoenician activity intensified during the eighth century and the first
Phoenician footholds in Sant'Antioco (i.e., Sulcis/Sulky), an island off
the southwest coast, date to the second quarter of this century.[7] During
the seventh century Phoenician settlements proliferated, marking a long-
lasting Phoenician presence on the island, at Monte Sirai, Nora, Bithia, Cagliari, Tharros, Olbia, and other sites. The Phoenicians concentrated their
activity on the western and southern coast, where the Gulf of Oristano and
the Sulcis region provided the most accessible harboring areas and terrain.
The Phoenician foothold at Olbia on the northeast coast was justified by
commerce with Etruria.[8] Olbia also represents the only Greek presence
on the island, associated with the sixth-century Phokaian expansion in the

Tyrrhenian and Sardinian Sea (Massalia, Alalia). But it is clear that Phoenician occupation had dominated Olbia since the late eighth century, before the short-lived Greek phase.[9] In some cases, inland settlements may be secondary Phoenician colonies (e.g., Monte Sirai and Pani Loriga, perhaps from Sulcis).[10] This was only the beginning of a long history of Phoenician presence that lasted up until Roman times and that included subsequent waves of migration or colonists accompanying expansion of Carthage from the fifth century BC onwards. Material evidence indicates that Phoenicians from Carthage, itself a Tyrian colony, were active on the island by the mid-eighth century.[11]

A Carthaginian orientation is also inferred especially by the adoption of the tophet ritual, broadly attested on Sardinia (Tharros, Sant'Antioco, Nora, Bithia). Pending further study and evidence, this seems to have become a cultural marker in the Carthaginian areas of influence in the central Mediterranean, attested on Malta and Sicily too, but not in the Phoenician homeland or the Tyrian-oriented communities of Iberia, western North Africa (Morocco), and Cyprus.[12] Other affinities in burial customs (inhumations, chamber tombs, deposit of ostrich eggs) also point to strong connections with the Phoenician-Punic realm of Ibiza to the west. In a sense, Sardinia was a gateway between the Italic and Iberian Peninsulas, and inevitably was contested between Carthage and Rome, which eventually annexed it after the First Punic War; but the native and Punic heritage was not easily erased.[13]

The Sardinian and Iberian scenarios are comparable in some interesting ways. Bronze Age and Iron groups in both regions formed part of a similar network and followed similar trajectories during the Phoenician and Roman advances. In both areas, indigenous Bronze Age cultures had established their own traditions in ceramics, metalwork, and other artistic forms, such as the Tartessic stelae and the Nuragic megaliths. Artifacts exchanged between the two regions from prehistoric times, such as metallic *fibulae*, demonstrate a preexisting trading relationship by land and sea, into which the Phoenicians inserted themselves.[14] These are the sorts of regional circuits that flourished in the late second millennium BC in the western Mediterranean and "created the maritime preconditions necessary for regular pan-Mediterranean travel."[15] The Phoenicians' skill lay not only in boosting long-distance east–west communications but in "infiltrating" already functioning networks, which required intelligence and collaboration with native traders and mariners as well as sheer logistic and technical capacity.[16] As Marisa Ruiz-Gálvez puts it, we should assume that "when the Phoenicians arrived in the west, they already knew exactly where they were sailing to and what they were looking for, as well as what routes they should follow."[17] This partnership was essential for the success of Phoenician enterprises, but the integration of Sardinia took time. Andrea Roppa posits that in the ninth century BC Sardinia was still not fully integrated in the main sea route of Phoenician expansion toward the West.[18] In other words, although the Sardinian route was previously active, it would seem that the Phoenicians made the open-sea "jump" from Iberia and the Balearic Islands to Sardinia into a viable regular channel.

Unlike in Iberia or North Africa, however, Sardinian indigenous communities had articulated their landscapes in durable ways, through the aforementioned megalithic structures as well as monumental burials, meeting halls, and large sanctuaries. While the *nuraghi* were no longer used as dwellings in the Iron Age, they remained important landmarks, as new settlements often clustered around them, using them for storage, defense, or cultic activity.[19] We can thereby trace the evolving relationship between these communities and the Phoenicians. In an initial phase, the indigenous communities dominated the areas that were later colonized. The presence of Phoenician portable objects, such as bronze artifacts and pottery, demonstrates that the Sardinians developed steady commercial relations with Phoenicians before the latter established permanent settlements of their own. So for a good part of the eighth and seventh centuries, with some exceptions, such as the early colony of Sulcis, the Levantines integrated into native communities, as is best documented at Sant'Imbenia in the northwest.[20] The early partnership between Phoenicians and native Sardinians is also apparent in the distribution of Nuragic materials across nodal points of Phoenician trade, such as at Huelva, Cádiz, along the Málaga coast, and Carthage.[21] This early phase of intensification of trade (often called "precolonial") resembles a phase attested in the Tartessic nucleus of Huelva, where there is evidence of intense trade and cultural influence but no Phoenician settlement proper.[22]

Finally, Iron Age Sardinia is highly regionalized, which affects both internal and international relations and produces infinitely variable modalities of cultural contact.[23] In turn, the presence of Phoenicians in such a variety of contexts on Sardinia dispels the stereotype of their exclusive coastal activity, and supports their interest in agriculture. Indeed, an archaeological survey has found that the Phoenicians transformed Sardinian landscapes in the surrounding hinterland not directly connected to the harbors.[24] This makes Sardinia an ideal laboratory for postcolonial approaches to Iron Age archaeology. The existence of hybrid expressions and practices are but one visible aspect of the internal socioeconomic and cultural development of the indigenous cultures, with links to a deeper past. Moreover, under the general guise of what could be regarded as "orientalizing," lie different modalities of exchange and contact.[25] Sometimes a distinction can be made between the earlier stage of appropriation of particular elements of Phoenician culture (without colonization), especially in the south and southwest of the island, and a more generalized process of hybridization during the centuries of Phoenician-Punic settlement. Crucially, the innovations that we subsume under the rubric of "orientalization" are always articulated "on Sardinian terms," as Peter van Dommelen has emphasized.[26] In the brief overview below, therefore, I pay more attention to these hybrid practices and Sardo-Phoenician relations than to traditional art historical categories and considerations.

Phoenician-Local Interaction and Hybrid Practices in Sardinia

In the Iron Age, native settlements reorganized and clustered around the inherited Bronze Age *nuraghi*. Many of these, such as Nuraghe Sirai and S'Urachi, fell into the middle ground areas of native–Phoenician interaction.[27] These towering structures had become prominent symbols of power for the Iron Age communities and became foci around which cross-cultural relations crystalized. To be clear, these were not the main cultic places on Sardinia (even if cultic materials are also found in or around them); large indigenous sanctuaries were in use through the orientalizing period and later (e.g., S'Arcu 'e Is Forros).[28] What we find at the *nuraghi* are idiosyncratic combinations of local materials with Phoenician-Punic (and occasionally Greek) artifacts, which document a "flexible settlement policy" involving both groups.[29] When possible, archaeologists distinguish between imported Phoenician "trademarks" and subsequent local imitations and idiosyncratic (orientalizing) modifications. The first include, for instance, Phoenician bronze figurines and ritual implements with a strong Cypriot influence (cauldrons, torch holders, tripods), as well as ceramic types, especially Red-Slip dining ware and transport and storage amphorae.[30] These were distributed across indigenous settlements and sanctuaries, with a few preferred types selected for communal dining and ritual activities.[31] The second, hybrid material culture varies by site, as we see in the examples below.

The Nuragic settlement of Sant'Imbenia (Alghero), sheltered on the inner shore of the deep bay of Porto Conte in northwest Sardinia, exemplifies the transition into these hybrid cultural productions. Mutatis mutandis, Sant'Imbenia was the "Huelva" of Sardinia: it was the gateway for the mining resources of the Nurra plain, and the recipient of the earliest Phoenician imports to the island at the end of the ninth and early eighth century. Sant'Imbenia also maintained its native character; no colony was established there, and the Sardinian community stayed connected while remaining out of the area of Phoenician settlement that was concentrated farther south.[32] At Sant'Imbenia we find typical Phoenician pottery and some Aegean imports, but also a local production of amphorae, labeled "Sant'Imbenia-type amphorae," which imitated Phoenician transport amphorae while maintaining indigenous production techniques, shaped by hand or slow wheel.[33] These amphorae were essential to Sardinian trade with Iberia and Carthage, as were Nuragic askoid jugs, likely used for wine or possibly perfumed oil.[34] The amphorae are assumed to have transported wine, or perhaps metal pieces, traces of which have been found in some. Whatever their contents, the use of typological Phoenician amphorae signals more than the start of trade; it signals a commercial strategy by local communities that "wished to convey their products to the transmarine western Mediterranean market at that time managed by the Phoenicians."[35]

From the late seventh century, we see something similar at the *nuraghi* of Sirai and S'Urachi, which remained indigenous settlements in the neighborhood of Phoenician settlements proper, and where Phoenician ceramic types were produced in situ (including domestic wares) using Phoenician-type kilns and the newly introduced wheel. In other words, there is evidence that Phoenicians and locals became integrated "within the social fabric of Nuragic settlements," forming culturally mixed communities.[36] Recent DNA studies (tricky as these may be to interpret) point to this mixed population as well.[37] It is also possible that it was Sardinia-based Phoenicians trading in Sardinian products who commissioned the pottery making from the locals, which would also result in local modifications and uses anyway.[38]

Between Innovation and Resilience

The Nuragic burial site at Mont'e Prama in central-western Sardinia lies just inland from the Phoenician enclave of Tharros. Here a corpus of at least forty-four stone statues known as the "Giants of Mont'e Prama" once marked a long row of pit burials. The monuments are dated to the eighth century (Figure 5.1), which makes them earlier than the anthropomorphic stone sculpture that we will see in the Iron Age Aegean and on Cyprus. These statues exemplify the development of hybrid Sardinian artistic expressions and practices: the warriors, boxers, and archers they represent continue a Nuragic tradition of figurative art, especially known from Nuragic bronze statuettes of warriors, known as *bronzetti*. But their use as tomb markers and their monumentality in both size and stone material were innovations inspired by eastern Mediterranean models, now within reach thanks to the pan-Mediterranean networks brought by Phoenicians to the local back-yard.[39] As summarized by Andrea Roppa, "the context at Mont'e Prama exemplifies the complicated social milieu within Iron Age Nuragic com-munities and their need to re-establish their communal identity through renovated forms of elite self-representation, which were triggered by in-creased interaction with Levantine newcomers."[40]

As in other regions, the presence of hybrid cultural forms and adaptations can be as telling as their absence. In Sardinia, we have plenty of evidence of Levantine adaptations by local artisans in the context of in situ labor and apprenticeship, best exemplified by the Phoenician-type Sant'Imbenia am-phorae. But other typical Phoenician crafts, such as ivory carving, do not take hold in these Sardinian-Phoenician communities. Only glass produc-tion, also new to the island, is attested at Nuraghe Sirai, perhaps manufac-tured at Sulcis too. We may be missing entire areas of artisan production involving perishable materials, however, such as leather products and tex-tiles.[41] Overall, at least on the surface we see a trend of appropriation of in-ternationally successful Phoenician types rather than the creation of local variants of Levantine motifs (which are classified as orientalizing in Tartes-sos, Etruria, or Greece). The abundant production of terracottas, for in-stance, which characterize Phoenician ritual life even into late Punic times, was mostly limited to the colonial realm, although sometimes the votives suggest local practices and cultural syntheses.[42]

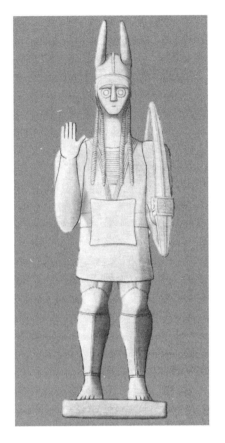

FIG. 5.1   Stone statue from Sardinia.

One of the "Giants of Mont'e Prama," representing an archer, carved in local sandstone (2–2.5 m original height), dated to the eighth century BC. National Archaeological Museum of Cagliari.

Left: Drawing by P. Kruklidis, from A. Bedini, C. Tronchetti, G. Ugas, and R. Zucca, *Giganti di pietra* (Cagliari: Edizioni Fabula, 2012). Courtesy of Carlo Tronchetti.

Right: Funkyfood London–Paul Williams/Alamy Stock Photo.

Another important Phoenician technology not chosen for local consumption is alphabetic writing. Unlike the elites from other areas, Sardinian groups did not deem it necessary or useful to create their own version of the Semitic alphabet to mark their monuments or brand their amphorae in their native language. This is despite the dense Phoenician population along their coasts and valleys and the visual effect that the Phoenician inscriptions must

FIG. 5.2   Phoenician votive stelae from tophet precincts in Sardinia and Sicily.
Left: Stela from Sulcis (Sardinia) in local tuff stone, prob. fifth century BC (height 46.7 cm), with feminine figure holding lotus-flower scepter, framed by *naiskos* with Egyptianizing winged solar disk and cobras (*uraei*) and columns with volute capitals.   Archaeological Museum "Ferruccio Barreca" of Sant'Antioco. Michele Guirguis (ed.), *La Sardegna fenicia e punica. Storia e materiali (Corpora delle Antichità della Sardegna),* Ilisso Editore, Nuoro 2017, p. 424, n. 260. Courtesy of Michele Guirguis.

Right: Votive stela in limestone, from Lilybaeum (Marsala), prob. third century BC (height 40 cm), with Phoenician inscription: "To the lord Baal-Hammon, (what) Hanno dedicated, son of Adonibaal, son of Gerashtart, son of Adonibaal, because he heard his voice, may he bless him!" The stela depicts a male dedicant or priest, incense burner, three aniconic pillars / *cippi,* caduceus-scepter, crescent moon and disk symbol, and "Tanit symbol."   Courtesy of the Antonino Salinas Regional Archaeological Museum of Palermo.

have had in their townscapes: Sardinia is indeed richer in Phoenician-Punic epigraphs than other areas of Phoenician habitation (e.g., Tartessos), and Phoenician writing was displayed especially in cemeteries and sanctuaries (including Tophet precincts) (Figure 5.2). The stelae found at these sites throughout the Punic period show the continuity of Levantine symbolism and institutions, such as the *suffetes.*[43] This epigraphic corpus also attests to the whole array of Phoenician gods, also evidenced in theophoric names: Melqart, Ashtart, Baal-Shamem, and other deities connected the Sardinian religious landscapes to the cults of the Phoenician mainland as well to those most dear to Carthaginian and Cypriot Phoenicians (Tanit, Pumay), and provides a nexus with local religion, as we can see in the assimilation of the figure of Sardus Pater to Phoenician Sid.[44]

⸎⸎⸎

The case of Sardinia, very briefly treated here, confirms the axiom that "to orientalize or not to orientalize" was a matter of choice, as was *how* to do it. This was always an evolving local phenomenon not confined to a fixed period, and the process was permeable to other cultures' input and local interpretations of the Near Eastern elements they were exposed to. With regard to Sardinia, influence from Etruscan culture, noticeably early as well, seems to account for later, secondary orientalizing traits (e.g., scarabs and ivories from fourth-century Tharros), a phenomenon we saw in relation to Tartessic culture in Extremadura in Chapter 4. We will see this again on Sicily, where orientalizing traits are partly mediated through Greek culture. As Sabatino Moscati puts it, orientalizing art is not only the development of Phoenician or other Levantine themes by local cultures but "the secondary action of a return to those themes."[45]

The results of these encounters are always unique and particular to each context, but the meeting of two vectors is a constant: the opportunity provided by a steady Phoenician presence and willingness to establish connections, and the local receptivity and adaptation of technologies and aesthetics to the degree that the latter served local needs and tastes at that particular time. Moreover, here as elsewhere, the cultural influence of local involvement with Phoenicians often went beyond trade and the circulation of luxury items. In other words, the fabulous luxury items that initiated the orientalizing debate cannot be the metric for this complex phenomenon; whatever their ultimate origins, their relevance needs to be calibrated against the broader registers of exchange and reactions to the Phoenician presence.

Sicily: The Triangular Middle Ground

Sicily is the largest island of the Mediterranean, located between the tip of the Italian "boot" and the Tunisian Cape Bon. This triangular island marks the nexus between the world of the western Phoenicians and the extended world of the Greeks. Indeed, before Greek texts start shaping the story, our knowledge of Iron Age Sicily is mainly archaeological, and resists neat ethnic mapping: Greek, Phoenician, and indigenous groups were established throughout the island for centuries (the first two mainly along the coasts), and some cities went back and forth between Greek and Phoenician-Carthaginian dominance. There were Greek colonies farther west, part of the Phokaian enterprise that peaked in the sixth century in southern France, Catalonia, and Corsica; but the trade routes and access to minerals and other resources in the west were, by and large, dominated by the Levantine entrepreneurs, despite occasional Greek attempts to expand their control. This rivalry is exemplified by the reported clash between these realms in the Battle of Alalia off Corsica sometime between 541–535 BC, in which Etruscans and Carthaginians joined forces to confront the expanding Phokaians; while Greek sources reported a draw, the fact is that, after this time, neither Phokaians nor other Greeks extended their networks farther in the west.[46]

The distribution of coastal settlements on Sicily seems to follow a clear division between these two worlds: Phoenicians settled all along the western coast, at Solus (Soluntum), Panormus (Palermo), Drepanum (Trapani), Motya (Mozia), Lilybaeum (Marsala), and Mazara, and Greeks settled on the entire eastern part of the island, from Selinous to Syracuse along the south and spread eastward toward the northwest, up to Himera (see Map 5.1). Dots on a map inevitably simplify a complex and fluctuating reality. Some Greek colonies, such as Selinous, oscillated between Greek and Punic territory throughout their history, as native groups entangled in conflicts and alliances with either side.[47] Both Greeks and Phoenicians encountered native populations, some of which played a crucial role in the conflict between the colonial forces, such as Eryx and Segesta. From the beginning, both sides depended on the locals' cooperation and demographic contribution for the success of the new settlements. Nor were the Greek, Phoenician, or native groups themselves homogeneous. Sicilian communities, according to ancient sources, represented various local groups, with a prehistoric stratum of Sicani (whom some thought originated in Iberia), as well as groups resulting from more recent migrations at the end of the Bronze Age, principally Sicels (probably from Liguria in the mainland) and Elymians (perhaps from the Aegean).[48] Likewise, Levantine or Levantine-style materials can be found in Greek communities, such as, for instance, Egyptianizing faience vessels and scarabs and Cypro-Phoenician pottery that appear in Syracuse, the Greek powerhouse on the island.[49]

Despite this complex multiethnic picture, the approach to early cultural contact on Sicily has been largely Hellenocentric. In the face of Greek presence or its proximity, with colonies on Sicily and the nearby Magna Graecia, Hellenic influence in indigenous communities becomes the preferred interpretive framework, while Phoenicians become a side problem. Studies that place the emphasis on the adaptation and local reinterpretation of Greek culture are still rare, compared with the success of this interpretive mode for Phoenician–local materials. The Greek presence elicits the kind of attention expected of a still dominant classics-centered historiography. As Brien Garnand puts it, "Greek site names are remembered and mapped, the Phoenician forgotten."[50] Disproportionate attention is given to Greek operations in western Sicily, as they encroached on the Phoenician realm, while little attention is paid to the recorded instances of Carthaginians encroaching on Greek-dominated areas during the fifth and fourth centuries, such as Hipponium, Selinous, and Akragas.[51]

With the rise of postcolonial perspectives, Sicily has become a fruitful arena to discuss hybridity and "middle grounds," and a more balanced picture of the plurality of cultural relations there is emerging.[52] In a recent traveling exhibition on *Sicily and the Sea* and its catalog, the Phoenicians were given proper attention within a diachronic treatment of the island's cultural makeup.[53] Sicily is described as "a pluri-ethnic island, with both Phoenicians and Greeks establishing their colonies among [indigenous] populations," and Phoenicians may even be accepted as overall precursors, an idea already floated by Thucydides, who believed they were displaced from areas of the island by Greek incomers.[54] But it is still difficult to shed the general image of Sicily as "proto-Greek" even during centuries when control over the mostly indigenous Sicilian territory was neither Greek nor Phoenician, or for centuries contested by both. A mental line connects Sicilian prehistory with the Greek world that ultimately made Sicily "Western," and our perception of the island's archaic past is colored by literary references from Homer, Pindar, and the classical historians, an aid not available to those reconstructing Phoenician or local cultures.[55]

Phoenician, Greek, and Native Interactions

The Phoenician presence in the west of Sicily reached critical mass in the early eighth century BC. But we cannot really speak of an evident cultural influence on the local population (what one could call "orientalizing" transformations) until much later in the sixth century, when adaptations of Levantine and Greek cultural models become more widespread. If anything, the earlier human and material input seems to come in the other direction, from the native realm into the colonists' world. As far as we can tell, Phoenicians and Greeks followed similar settlement patterns in their colonial networks, privileging coastal enclaves, both islets and peninsulas with good natural bays and harbors with access to an immediately exploitable land (*chora*). Even if Greeks are often presented as more aggressive colonizers in need of fertile territory, both groups equally depended on their deal-making abilities with local groups to prosper and access raw materials. Since our historical sources are Greek, we know more about their encounters with local groups (and, even then, only from a few examples).[56] We can nevertheless assume Greeks and Phoenicians deployed similar strategies in their interactions with local populations, and that both encountered tensions and difficulties, even in areas where the overall context may have been welcoming, as in Iberia.[57]

Early contact with Phoenicians is best documented at Motya, a small, roughly circular island off the northwest tip of the Sicily (today San Pantaleo Island, in the Stagnone Lagoon between Drepanum/Trapani and Lilybaeum/Marsala). Motya was an important stop along the much older route linking the island to the eastern circuits of Syria-Palestine, Cyprus, and Crete and to the western networks of Sardinia, the Balearic Islands, and Iberia.[58] Tyrians or Sidonians settled there with possible input from Phoenicians already on the island, who, according to ancient historians, had been displaced by Greek colonization.[59] Although we talk about the site as a Phoenician-Punic settlement, recent scholarship has not failed to appreciate the complex interaction between Phoenicians and locals attested on the ground, which suggests a hybrid culture in the city: indigenous pottery is abundant since the site's early phases; Levantine architectural and religious traditions adapt to the local landscape and materials; and we can assume a demographic influx from the neighboring Elymian communities of western Sicily, such as Eryx. According to Thucydides, the Phoenicians gravitated toward that side of the island (Motya, Solus, Palermo) in part because of their "alliance" with the Elymians.[60] Locally made Phoenician ceramics, which increase in Motya in the seventh century, show Elymian inflections as well, and some cultic elements, such as the votive dedications of deer antlers stem from the native realm.[61] All in all, Greeks, Phoenicians, and Elymians were particularly involved in "tri-nodal social entanglements."[62] That is, more than a foundation from scratch, Motya might have become predominantly Phoenician in a process of integration and growth that involved other groups, including perhaps a Cypro-Phoenician element.[63]

At the same time, continuities from the local Bronze Age are strong on the island, a pattern we saw also in Iberia and Sardinia. Indigenous indexes of social organization can be traced in central and western Sicily, through settlement structures and public architecture; burial practices, dominated by the multiple burials in rock-cut tombs (e.g., East Necropolis of Polizzello); and through particular shared traditions, for instance, the terracotta models of huts with attached bulls or cows, or the bowls and cups also adorned with bovines.[64] What is more, even when the Phoenicians settle firmly on the island in the eighth century, the local groups do not seem to "take the bait" of the international elite culture that the Phoenicians put within their reach. There is plenty of evidence of interaction and cohabitation, but it is hard to speak of a distinctive hybrid culture emerging in the colonial realm's periphery at this time. The visible cultural transformation comes later in the sixth century, well after other cultures had developed their versions of the orientalizing kit according to their own local and regional styles. Rather, the evidence of indigenous influence on Phoenician and Greek communities exemplifies the other side of these dynamics, how the local element feeds back into regional versions of the "global" culture.

Much of the research that challenges rigid colonial models focuses on Selinous (Selinunte). The site is traditionally presented in maps as a Doric Greek colony (founded by Megara Hyblaia). As the westernmost Greek foundation on Sicily, however, Selinous straddled the geographical and chronological lines dividing Phoenician and Greek Sicily. The city was predominantly Greek until it fell under Carthage's control in 409 BC, where it remained until the end of the First Punic War. We have this sort of political history of the city through the work of Diodorus of Sicily.[65] Culturally and materially, however, it has become difficult to draw neat lines between

"Greek" and "Punic" Selinous or between "classical" (pre-409 BC) and "Hellenistic" periods, the latter of which overlaps with the Punic phase. These efforts are frustrated not only by the city's political mobility between sides but also by the archaeological evidence: Phoenician materials abound in the earlier Greek foundation (neglected in early excavations) as do Greek materials and cultic continuities during the long Punic period.[66] Some specific features of Selinous are discussed below.

All in all, there are strong archaeological signs of coresidence and intermarriage on Sicily, with "pockets" of Greeks and Phoenicians living among local populations, as emerges from epigraphic and historiographical evidence too (the latter mostly about Greeks).[67] But the picture is more complicated than we can even begin to ascertain, as interactions were not unidirectional or necessarily binary. Two examples of the triangular movement of cultural items make the point: one is the case of a drinking cup, which is of indigenous typology but decorated with an orientalizing motif (a winged hybrid creature) and buried in a necropolis of Himera, a Greek city; this artifact provides an example of the adoption of orientalizing motifs by natives, perhaps via Greek models and used in an apparent Greek setting.[68] As a second example, we can cite two archaic Greek amphorae bearing Punic inscriptions, one found at Himera and the other at an indigenous site of Colle Madore. The second vase's inscription reads "servant of the lioness," a likely reference to Ashtart.[69] These and other findings show the complicated trajectories of things, as objects could carry more than one ethnocultural marker and circulate in various directions. In general, it seems that more Greek pottery is channeled toward the Phoenician realm than vice versa.[70] This is hardly surprising since we know Greek drinking cups (*skyphoi, kotylai*) were popular among Phoenicians, as attested in the Levant, Iberia, and Carthage (in the west they created their own imitations).[71] In other words, the Phoenicians themselves exerted the choice over what to import for their own use and what foreign goods to transport and trade within their networks.

We have to wait until later in the sixth century to see what can be considered "orientalizing" adaptations, in this case internal developments that indicate interest in adapting eastern Mediterranean cultural capital on Sicily, not necessarily Phoenician only. This process is most visible through innovations in indigenous settlement layouts, now with rectangular, more complex constructions, and in modifications to native burial practices:

individual graves proliferated and more variety was introduced in burial forms, such as inhumations under terracotta tiles (*cappuccina* burials), small child inhumations in *pithoi* (*enchytrismoi*), fossa graves, and sarcophagus burials. Monumental cultic buildings appear now too, rectangular in shape, the type known as "*oikos/oikoi*" or "*in antis*" which are typically adorned with two columns on the front and clay *akroteria* in archaic Greek style. These new buildings have by default been interpreted not only as a Greek adaptation, but as marking Greek presence inland, overly simplifying their complex local context. As Birgit Öhlinger explains, however, "their usage was very much aligned to the needs of the local indigenous population."[72] In a few cases, old ceremonial huts from traditional hamlet-like compounds were not abandoned but rebuilt in ways that integrated "old world" elements with "new world" architectural models. This is how sites such as Sabucina and Monte Polizzello morphed into monumental cultic magnets for regional synoecism (the clustering of villages around larger urban centers, including city-states), in a dynamic similar to the *nuraghi* in Iron Age Sardinia.[73]

In short, the process of cultural hybridization in archaic Sicily is also highly idiosyncratic and site-specific, and the dynamics and mechanisms were set by the locals more than the newcomers. Moreover, this process falls outside of the orientalizing chronological parameters proper, and both Greek and Phoenician influences are part of it, suggesting a dynamic that complicated the operation of orientalization as studied in the rest of this book.

Monumental Landscapes

When, in the sixth century, Sicilian communities embraced the international style of the "Mediterranean koine," they were also exposed to Near Eastern traits through Greek culture, which had itself undergone an orientalizing transformation. We can see this, for instance, in the *in antis*, quadrangular stone buildings, decorative motifs (gorgons, sphinxes), and the appearance of writing. In other words, the categories "Greek" and "orientalizing" take on different nuances in Sicily.

Discussions of the *oikos* or *in antis* temples tend to create interpretive loops. These are elongated rectangular buildings with columns only at their entrance along a short side. The traditional assumption is that Greek prototypes lie behind these buildings as well as behind the remains of Punic temples on Sicily, such as Temple A at Selinous, which is best known for its cult to Zeus Meilichios, but which hosted a cult to Baal-Hammon in its Punic phase (ca. 500 onward).[74] The *in antis* buildings certainly contrast with the architecture of older Phoenician sanctuaries and their Levantine models, well attested at Motya (Figure 5.3) and even in the previous phase of the Meilichios complex (Temple A) at Selinous.[75] But we should admit that we are far from understanding the development of temple architecture in Punic Sicily, or Punic architecture in general. Moreover, Greek forms of temple architecture, including the *in antis* or *oikos* type, were orientalizing innovations of the seventh century: the rectangular masonry construction with frontal columns was inspired by Levantine prototypes and building techniques. The Greeks also experimented with peripteral rectangular buildings (with columns all around), which became standardized for their larger temples. Finally, Phoenician constructions were varied and complex and used columns (including "Proto-Aeolic capitals) and pillars in entrances or porches as did their Canaanite predecessors.[76]

In short, independent Phoenician-Punic influences on both Greek and native Sicilian architecture should not be discounted. When the *oikoi* temples appear in the Sicel realm, the same layouts were in use in Punic Selinous and perhaps in the Punic phases of other sites on Sicily and beyond, for instance beneath later Roman structures dedicated to Sardus Pater and to Ashtart-Isis/Juno on Sardinia and Malta, respectively.[77] There is a point, after around 500 BC, when Phoenician-Punic communities were assimilating Hellenizing, Persianizing, and other artistic features.[78] Ultimately, there is no reason to think that these constructions were perceived by the Sicilian beholder as more Greek than Phoenician-Punic, especially in a multiethnic place such as Selinous.

The decoration of the metopes of Temple C at Selinous present another example of this sort of circularity of orientalizing art in Sicily, which has to be understood in a particular local context. This is a Doric-style Greek temple built in the mid-sixth century BC. Its reliefs echo orientalizing Greek sculpture both in their Daedalic style and chosen themes, such as the motif of Perseus slaying the Gorgon. The theme is often cited as a Greek adaptation of Mesopotamian imagery of the slaying of Humbaba.[79] The Greek models were themselves, therefore, inspired in Near Eastern forms

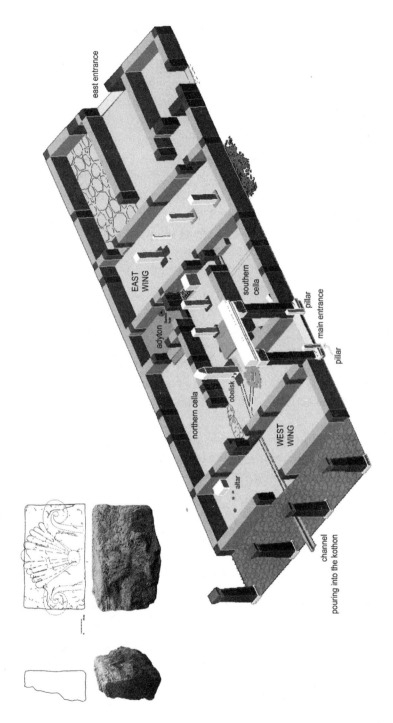

FIG. 5.3   Phoenician Temple of Baal at Motya, Sicily.

Reconstruction of the Baal Temple in the Kothon sacred precinct, Temple C2 (phase 4, 480–397/6 BC), with cultic installations, *cippi* or baetyls, and pillars with volute (Proto-Aeolic) capitals flanking the entrance; the stone capital in the photograph dates to the sixth century level (Temple C1). Courtesy of Lorenzo Nigro.

and motifs, but the same Daedalic style is attested in locally made terra-cottas circulating on the island, which were more directly inspired by Phoenician models.[80] In a hybrid community such as that of Selinous, phys-ically and culturally caught between the Phoenician and Greek spheres, it is difficult to say how the temple's style and mythological references would have been seen by the local onlooker.

The cult of Zeus Meilichios on the Gaggera Hill just outside the center of Selinous presents an even more puzzling case of Phoenician–Greek–Sicilian entanglements. A group of aniconic stelae were found there, some-times twin stelae, bearing Greek dedications and at least one in Punic. All that scholars can agree on is that some Punic cult (perhaps related to the *molch* ritual) and a cult of Hades and Kore or of Demeter and Kore over-lapped there.[81] The cult of Demeter and Kore became popular among the Phoenicians of Sicily, and was officially adopted in Carthage in 396 BC.[82] This cult must have provided yet another ideological and performative meeting space for Greeks, Phoenicians, and native communities on the is-land. As Sarah Morris has explained, emphasizing the continuity of wor-ship at the site, "the Gaggera Hill hosted an unusual fusion of practices surely partly Semitic in inspiration, directed at family, fertility, reproduc-tion, and generations [. . .] and Phoenician or Punic forms of altar and stelae (Meilichios, Triolo) with Greek forms of architecture in the Demeter and Hecate complex."[83]

Another key place of religious overlap was the sanctuary at Eryx, on a mountain overlooking the nearby coast (modern Erice). The goddess of Eryx was worshipped by the Elymians, overlaid with the cult to Ashtart by Phoenicians and adapted to the cult of Venus (hence Venus Erycina) by the Romans in a propagandistic move during the Punic Wars. Even though the temple is buried under a Norman Castle, epigraphical remains confirm the site and the Punic activity there.[84] Moreover, this overlapping cult exem-plifies the religious convergence around female deities associated not only with fertility but with seafaring and trade, which can be traced at other sites of coastal Italy.[85] More generally, epigraphical evidence from Phoeni-cian funerary stelae and votive dedications is abundant on the island and demonstrates that Phoenician religion was resilient and overlapped with the neighboring local and Greek realms (e.g., Figure 5.2 above).[86] The deposit of Phoenician amulets (e.g., scarabs) in local graves points in the same direction.[87] So does the Greek use of inscribed *lamellae* as amulets for the afterlife, which we now think adapted a Semitic ritual technology, to mention other traits that have received recent attention.[88]

Overall, however, Sicilian groups did not produce their own fully fledged local versions of oriental decorative motifs or invest in elaborating orientalizing bronzes or jewelry, perhaps because these were not part of their previous artisan tradition. They did not adopt the Phoenician alphabet either when it became available early on, in the eighth century. Like the Etruscans in mainland Italy, they eventually developed a local script from the Greek alphabet, which they used as much to imitate as to linguistically assert their local identities vis-à-vis the Greeks and others.[89] This brings us again to the issue of social and economic priorities and trajectories: each society would adopt international styles or innovations to the degree that it served their internal and interpolity dynamics and structures of power.

A Note on Malta

With no Hellenic heritage to speak of attested on Malta, for modern scholars the Phoenicians provided a close enough alternative to latch onto as a display of the island's role in early Mediterranean history. Nineteenth-century antiquarians highly prized Phoenician inscriptions and other stumbled-upon artifacts. The pro-Phoenician bias even led to gross misinterpretations: prehistoric megalithic monuments were erroneously associated with the Phoenician past, and the Semitic substratum of the Maltese language was thought to be infused with Phoenician roots rather than Arabic, their real ancestor.[90]

Malta and the smallest islands of Gozo and Comino were important stepping stones in central Mediterranean networks, conveniently placed at the entrance to the sea corridor between Sicily and Tunisia; for Phoenician sailors, they opened the way to their enclaves on Sardinia, the Balearic Islands, Tunisia, and Iberia.[91] Agricultural land and good harbors (not metal resources) also explain why the Phoenicians had frequented the islands since the tenth century, during a period alternatively classified in the scholarship as "orientalizing," "protohistoric," or "precolonial."[92] They settled there extensively and permanently in the eighth century and transformed the island's landscapes and seascapes (see principal sites on Map 5.1), controlling its economy and resources until the Romans took it over after the Second Punic War.[93]

While the archaeology of Malta has been dominated by its impressive megalithic prehistoric remains, Phoenician-Punic culture is extensive on the island and has received increasing attention, with systematic excavation and study of its structures, epigraphic testimonies, tombs (usually rock-cut inhumations) and their materials (including Phoenician/Egyptianizing amulets), cult sites including a tophet, cave shrines, and even traces of Punic viticulture.[94] Moreover, Malta has produced a rare piece of inscribed Phoenician papyrus (see Figure 7.1). Briefly, materials from Malta show that Phoenician settlers smoothly integrated themselves within a local cultural continuum with roots in the local Bronze Age. In the case of Malta, it is difficult to speak of a strong local elite culture or political-territorial organization independent of the Phoenician settlement, but hybridity is evident. For instance, at Tas-Silġ, native and Phoenician cultic activity overlapped: a prehistoric cult site was reused and rebuilt as a shrine to Ashtart, as confirmed by written dedications from the fourth century BC. It was rebuilt by Romans as a temple to Juno and Isis. On the other hand, Phoenician crafts on the island adapted local techniques and forms, and funerary rituals changed over time toward a preference for inhumation over cremation, which was otherwise more popular in the colonial Phoenician realm.

Phoenician Maltese culture was marked by insular idiosyncrasies, covering the spectrum from archaizing Phoenician traits to a strong alignment with the Punic/Carthaginian realm (e.g., Tophet ritual), while the island's material culture displays resilient local traits and even possible affinities with the native North African realm. In short, Malta provides another context in which "orientalizing" is not a particularly useful category in art historical terms, and we cannot clearly point to local adaptations of the orientalizing kit. What we see is a long-term Phoenician (not general "Near Eastern"/"oriental") presence and intense economic activity, which resulted in particular hybrid cultures and practices that implicated and affected both sides, not only the local side.

Levantine Relations in Southern Italy and Etruria

The Etruscans represent in Italy the first local urbanized, wealthy, sophisticated society that could measure up to cultures from the eastern Mediterranean. Like the Tartessians in Iberia and the Iron Age Sardinians, the

Etruscan communities emerged from a continuum rooted in the Bronze Age, coalescing first into what is known as Villanovan culture at the start of the Iron Age (ca. 900–700 BC), as they consolidated their grip over a large coastal and interior territory.

Etruscan contexts have yielded some of the earliest and most emblematic Near Eastern and orientalizing artifacts in Europe, associated with a princely aristocracy entangled with foreign merchants. The birth of the category "orientalizing" itself is inseparable from findings in Etruscan tombs.[95] At the same time, Etruscan antiquities remain trapped between disciplines dedicated to western European prehistory and those devoted to the Greco-Roman tradition, the Near Eastern element somewhat lost in between. The general Etruscan narrative is still teleological and makes the Etruscans into a "preclassical" culture, hence tending to favor Greek agency. Near Eastern artifacts remain decontextualized, studied as "art," and the "orientalizing" label is frozen as a chronological marker in Italic protohistory. The influence of the eastern imports and adaptations are deemphasized in what is seen as the antechamber of the later Greek-infused archaic phase, the cultural influence that matters.[96] The initial retrieval of the artifacts from Etruscan tombs was, in the mid- to late-nineteenth century, determined by the artifact-oriented, treasure-centered way in which Near Eastern materials are discussed and displayed, as the objects were from the start dislocated from their assemblages within the tombs, such as the so-called Isis Tomb, which has produced one of the richest orientalizing assemblages.[97]

In any case, few would deny that Etruscan elite culture was visibly influenced by its interaction with eastern Mediterranean groups moving west. This visibility comes not only through in the quantity of lavish imports found in their graves but also in a new monumental architecture and in the arts: at this time the Etruscans developed a body of anthropomorphic sculpture of Near Eastern style, and an iconography rich in the typical Levantine motifs and symbols also adopted by locals in contemporary Iberia, Cyprus, and the Aegean: sphinxes, griffins, lionesses, and Levantine vegetal motifs, such as rosettes, palmettes, volutes, and lotus flowers. Outside of funerary sculpture, this imaginary is deployed in bronze and terracotta figures, the latter including masks paralleled in the Punic world, figurines of the Levantine Ashtart/Astarte type, and terracotta ornaments on monumental buildings.[98]

In the early first millennium, regional routes of the Late Bronze Age were revived largely by Levantines and Cypriots, who included Sardinia and Sicily in their networks. Judging by the current evidence, engagement with Italic groups intensified in the mid-eighth century in the Gulf of Taranto, the Gulf of Naples, and the large area of Etruria and Latium, and diminished but did not disappear after the mid-seventh century, when Greek influence became stronger.[99] Neither of the eastern newcomers established colonies north of the Bay of Naples (Pithekoussai, Cumae), and yet the transformational influence of both in Etruscan society is undeniable. These transformations were a matter of choice and a loud statement about the Etruscans' international ambitions and wealth vis-à-vis their Iron Age neighbors. Once again, the Phoenicians demonstrated their skill in establishing special relationships with complex societies that had access to metal resources and trading routes, and they did so by "favoring a form of contact between equals rather than wishing to colonize new sites," as Jeremy Hayne puts it.[100]

The changes in funerary display, adoption of artifacts linked to banqueting culture, the incorporation of Levantine artifacts in funerary rituals and deposits, the boom in metalwork and orientalizing-style plastic arts, and even the acquisition of alphabetic writing all denote a relationship with the Levantine culture based on close contact.[101] The challenge, as posed by Corinna Riva in her essay "The Orientalizing Period in Etruria," is to look beyond artifact-oriented and diffusionist models and interrogate the symbolic and political power that these sorts of objects communicated.[102] Part of the meaning and social power of orientalizing artifacts was drawn from their value as traded objects, if we consider trade as one more component "in the aggregate of systems which constitute a culture" as Annette Rathje puts it.[103] While Riva's inquiry was targeted at the artifacts' meaning within Etruscan society, we should also consider just as carefully what/who lay behind the "Near Eastern" component of these sorts of materials. In doing so, recent scholars have addressed Phoenician–Etruscan contact more directly. They have posited, for instance, that some of the artifacts of Syrian-Phoenician style found in central Italy came from Phoenician workshops, whether in the Levant or Cyprus, and that foreign artisans and other transmitters of cultural influences may have settled in Etruria, a view that breaks ground in a rather traditional field.[104] Still, Phoenician agency and the implications of the presence of these "foreign masters" are more often lost amid the general discussions of Etruscan artifacts. Phoenician presence features, if at all, with such caution that the predominant narrative of the Etruscan–Greek nexus remains unmodified, as does the idea of "orientalizing" as a vague category pointing to an indistinct "Near East."

The issue extends to the broader Italian landscape, where there are traces of intensifying Greek, Phoenician, and local interaction since the eighth century BC. As I discussed in Chapter 2, the Bay of Naples, with key sites such as Pithekoussai, has been a key scenario for academic debates in which inertias and biases reveal themselves. Already in 1993 Nicolas Coldstream had advocated for mixed marriages among early Greek settlers and various Italian groups, a view now accepted by many for areas in the Aegean (Crete, Euboia).[105] Nevertheless, and notwithstanding more open interpretation of the materials of particular contexts, the Levantines are still *generally* left out of the grand narrative of Italy's orientalizing phenomenon. "Orientalizing" is sanitized as a mere chronological denomination, a period practically devoid of Near Eastern cultural content.[106] At most, Phoenicians are listed among one of many groups networking in a "composite land."[107]

In short, since Italy was later integrated into the "great Greek world" (Magna Graecia), and given the well-known later Roman bias in favor of Greek culture and hostility to its Punic counterpart, a Hellenocentric view eventually dominated the interpretation of the previous period that concerns us.[108] That earlier phase when the Northwest Semites were influential in the area has until relatively recently remained neglected, the "oriental" element in "orientalizing" unexplained, at most part of a generic "eastern Mediterranean" influx, Phoenician artifacts studied as "art," detached from the question of the vectors or the context that accounted for them.[109] Overall, it was long assumed that Near Eastern imports made their way to Italy by the mediation of Euboians settled in the Gulf of Naples. By now there is ample evidence of earlier commercial contact and of the adoption of Levantine elements in their own right, imbued with the symbology associated with Near Eastern royalty and elite culture.[110] Recent studies and reconsiderations of the material, then, highlight the considerable influence in this process of Phoenicians, some of whom were integrated as craftspeople, wealthy merchants, even farmers, amid Italic communities.

Levantine Imports in Southern Italy

The main reason for tapping into Italian networks may have been the mineral resources in Etruria (Elba, Colline Metallifere). Phoenician activity, however, concentrated in the southern regions of Calabria and Campania, outside of or on the outskirts of Etruria, that is, in regions that provided a springboard for trade with central and northern Italy, as well as human and land resources.[111] As I discussed in Chapter 3, it is important to distinguish (to the degree possible) between Levantine imports and orientalizing materials proper. The first are useful indexes of social-economic patterns and exchange, while the latter reflect deeper cultural developments. I deal first with the Levantine imports, which signal Phoenician activity in central-southern Italy, especially in the eighth century (even since the late ninth). In the rest of the chapter I discuss the full-blown orientalizing culture developed by the Etruscan polities especially during the seventh century.

A good part of the documented Levantine material in Italy consists of what are often referred to as "trinkets," presumed to be what Homer meant by *athyrmata*: beads and pendants, scarabs/seals, and amulets of various sorts. The category itself, as used in Etruscan and Aegean archaeology and art history, diminishes their potential for symbolic and cultural meaning. These scattered artifacts appear already in the late ninth century, pointing to the early contacts between Euboian and Phoenician traders and locals. They often fit into the vague category of *Aigyptiaka* and are difficult to classify by origin, as they could have come from anywhere along the Phoenician trading networks, from Egypt and Cyprus to the western settlements.[112]

Based on materials available before 2007, Richard Fletcher estimated that these small objects made up about 90 percent of the Levantine material imported into Etruria. This contrasts with the small amount of reported Levantine pottery (3.2 percent), not to mention other more spectacular artifacts of the sort already praised by Homer, such as metal jugs, bowls, and cauldrons (1.3 percent), in inverse proportion to the amount of ink dedicated to them. As archaeologists acknowledge, these statistics might be distorted: bronze artifacts are smelted and reused, grave goods are disproportionately represented in the archaeological record in comparison with household and other contexts; large bodies of data remain unpublished; and there is always the chance that materials have been discarded, lost, or mis-classified by earlier antiquarians and archaeologists. In other words, our data set is limited and often heavily skewed.[113]

Eastern Mediterranean and Levantine objects come mostly from funerary contexts, often female graves. These portable objects had previous lives, and were probably used by multiple people and for more than one genera-tion. Materials in late ninth- and eighth-century graves from southern Italy (Campania and Calabria) include Egyptianizing and Egyptian scarabs, ivory sword handles, engraved metal bowls, and glass-paste pendants.[114] The materials also include particular types of vases, such as bronze hemispheri-cal cups of Cypriot or Levantine provenance.[115] Whatever their specific point of origin or route of arrival (separate Phoenician, Cypriot, and Egyptian routes cannot be excluded), many of these artifacts were surely more than "trinkets," just as we argued regarding Lefkandi's grave goods. These items carried ritual meaning appropriate to the funerary context, whether for their protective value, as indicated by the fact that they are often found in children's burials too, or by their function in funerary banqueting and liba-tions: such ritual use has been suggested for the assemblages found in buri-als from Pontecagnano, such as ribbed metal bowls, occasional Red-Slip plates, silver cups (*kotylai*), and bronze wine jugs (*oinochoai*), one of them with fake hieroglyphic inscriptions.[116]

The graves often include local materials alongside Levantine ones: in some cases, the graves likely represent a local elite stratum with access to exotic items. In some sites, Levantine pottery and Sardinian bronzes ap-pear as well. The assemblages of grave goods point to the Levantine com-ponent in some of these communities within a complex local demography and to their possible involvement in activities beyond maritime trade, such as agriculture, local industries, and inland commerce.[117] This is the con-text of the much-discussed grave goods from Pithekoussai. As discussed in Chapter 2, the island was the seat of a Levantine community, a hub for channeling metal resources and smelting metal, with a possible strong con-nection to Carthage.[118] At the San Montano cemetery and the Monte di Vico acropolis dump, we encounter fine Phoenician pottery (Red-Slip ware) as well as transport amphorae used for cremation burials, besides the usual *orientalia,* such as faience and steatite scarabs and "lyre-player" seals. Whatever the ethnicity of the individuals buried here, the existence of a mixed community is well represented in the funerary realm, exemplified in the use of Greek vases as cinerary urn but marked by Northwest Semitic writing and symbols.

It might seem surprising, then, that Levantine pottery proper is not abundant in these sites, though it is not absent, for instance, at Pontecagnano, Pithekoussai, and Francavilla Marittima, sometimes in funerary contexts.[119] This may have to do with the type of presence and activity we are looking at. In contrast to their widespread settlement in southern Iberia, the small groups of Phoenicians living among Italic and Greek communities probably did not have the trading capacity or the need to import large quantities of Levantine pottery. Local wares would have sufficed for daily use. The predominance of Greek vases, moreover, is not necessarily coterminous with the identity of their users: the Levantines highly valued, acquired, and transported Greek banqueting wares, and they even reproduced them for their communities, as we know from the materials found in Al-Mina, Carthage, and Iberia.[120] The small groups of Phoenicians here were more invested in importing portable objects they prized for their personal use, as well as "exotica" for which there was growing demand on the local side: amulets, ivory and fine woodwork, jewelry and engraved metal objects, ostrich eggs, and colorfully dyed textiles. On the other hand, interaction with the Levantines stimulated areas of innovation among the locals, including architectural and shipbuilding techniques, ceramic production, iron metallurgy, bronze work, and viticulture.[121]

It is indeed neither easy nor possible to trace the precise origins, distributors, or consumers of all imports in these regions.[122] Additional excavation and contextualized studies, however, will slowly help us counteract the frequent "catch-all" approach to Near Eastern trade and orientalizing materials in Italy, which leads to the downplaying of Phoenician agency.

The Etruscan "Orientalizing" World: Some Background

Etruscan civilization flourished in central-northern Italy, concentrating in the city-states of Tuscany but exerting its influence from Latium to Umbria on the Adriatic. Phoenician activity can be traced back to the beginning of the eighth century if not slightly earlier. The adaptation of Levantine cultural traits intensified during the second quarter of the seventh century.[123] This stimulated a deeper transformation than what we see in southern Italy.

Once again, the internal developments and trajectories of each society decided the pace and patterns. In Etruria, technological and artistic innovations were incorporated into a cultural continuum originating in the Bronze Age and extending into the Early Iron Age, when the culture traditionally classified as Villanovan is detected (ca. 900–720 BC).[124] On the other hand, the artistic reception of Near Eastern elements would remain part of Etruscan culture in the next centuries (after the end of the orientalizing period proper), further stimulated by sustained relations with the Sardinian, Sicilian, and Carthaginian realms. As in Iberia, Sardinia, and Sicily, it is misleading to confine the engagement with Near Eastern cultures (Phoenician or otherwise) to an "orientalizing period," or limit this process to the powerful Etruscan polities, as recent studies of Italic cultures are showing.[125]

Etruscan culture did not suddenly "start" with an orientalizing outlook; there is no essential break between Villanovan and Etruscan cultures, no more than there was between their Geometric and orientalizing Greek counterparts.[126] Like their contemporaries, Etruscan communities selectively embraced Near Eastern models to project status and elite identity, articulating their own belief system via these new media. Long gone is the idea that they "accepted all they were offered, without discrimination," and "with little understanding" of the Near Eastern models, in contrast to the inspired Greek appropriation of the same, which they in turn passed down to the Etruscans.[127]

It has taken a good deal of archaeological and linguistic work, and even a debate over DNA studies, to dispel the idea that the orientalizing culture in Etruria was responding to a migration from Asia Minor to Umbria, founded on Herodotos's Lydian-origins hypothesis for the Tyrrhenians (i.e., Etruscans).[128] On the one hand, this hypothesis enabled scholars to circumvent the Levant altogether, anchoring Etruscan orientalism in Asia Minor and then within Greek influences. On the other, as scholars rejected the Hellenic migration model, an autochthonist interpretation of Etruscan archaeology took hold for decades to come, which in principle downplayed external influences, whether Greek or eastern. This perspective was introduced after World War II by Massimo Pallottino, the founding father of Etruscan studies, and it still dominates the discipline.[129] The trend was born in part as a reaction to previous racist and colonialist tendencies within Italian historiography, but it also went with the times, accompanying the development of New Archaeology (processual, post-processual) and later of postcolonial theory. Similar autochthonist schools emerged for prehistoric and protohistoric Aegean archaeology in Greece and on Cyprus.[130]

Here is the irony: the Phoenicians were left out of the prewar narratives because of their Semitic affiliation, but they have often been left out of the autochthonist archaeologies as well (born from the rejection of such views), as we will see also on Cyprus. As postcolonial ideas of hybridity were incorporated into Etruscan studies, however, a consensus emerged that Etruscan culture congealed over time out of local roots but in close contact with eastern Mediterranean groups. Despite all the difficulties presented by the scattered materials, the tendency to subsume Phoenicians under a more general Levantine or Near Eastern referent, and the lack of written sources for this early period, not a few specialists have more directly pointed to Phoenicians as the main vectors of cultural change in this process.

Near Eastern and Orientalizing Artifacts in Etruscan Tombs

In general, the north and interior of Etruria remained more traditional, whereas the south and coastal areas were more open to innovations, as they hosted a growing middle class of artisans and traders, including foreigners, who joined or brought Mediterranean networks. Evidence for foreign input comes almost exclusively from funerary contexts, best represented in the necropoleis of Tarquinia and Cerveteri. In Etruscan necropoleis, we see a repertoire of Levantine portable objects similar to the one that marked southern Italic graves: jewelry, ivories, gems, glass, and ostrich eggs, among others (Figure 5.4). These were also conveyers of Levantine iconography, such as sphinxes or griffins and lotus flowers that then proliferate in local adaptations. Just as important, these precious objects appear along the key trade routes frequented by Phoenicians-Carthaginians. Clusters of some of these materials (especially glass, ivory, and ostrich eggs) also appear in sites within the extended Etruscan realm along the Adriatic coast, such as at the key site of Fratesina (by Fratta Polesine), situated between the Adige and Po Rivers, south of Venice (Map 5.1). This area had, since the twelfth century BC, become a center of carving and redistribution of Baltic amber (note that amber was also extracted from the Lebanon mountains and used by Phoenicians).[131] It is possible that these typically Levantine crafts were adopted by the locals as they joined up with international networks.[132] It

FIG. 5.4 Decorated ostrich egg from Etruscan tomb.
One of five ostrich eggs deposited in the "Isis Tomb" at Vulci, seventh–sixth centuries BC, engraved and colorfully painted with griffin/sphinx and lotus motifs.   British Museum (Museum Number 1850,0227.6). © Tamar Hodos, with the permission of the Trustees of the British Museum.

is also likely that Phoenician craftspeople and traders "set up shop" there and blended into the existing artisanal organizations, contributing their skills, techniques, and exotic materials, as they became involved in the distribution of amber jewelry in the eastern Mediterranean.[133]

In turn, Near Eastern artifacts in Etruscan graves dated to the eighth and seventh centuries have fueled long debates over affiliations, origins, and manufacture. While they do not constitute a uniform set, in aggregate it is remarkable that the majority of these artifacts have individually been associated either directly with Phoenician artisan production or with Phoenician distribution, channeling artistic production from North Syria and Cilicia. The materials in question (in no particular hierarchy) include Red-Slip Phoenician pottery, Levantine ivories, the famous decorated metal bowls, glass bowls, decorated ostrich eggs, engraved tridacna shells (only one found so far), *thymiateria* in the Levantine style, and a whole array of Egyptian and Egyptianizing artifacts, including impressive Egyptian vases decorated in relief (e.g., the "Bocchoris vase" from Tarquinia), faience figurines and various faience or stone amulets, such as scarabs/scaraboids (including "lyre-player" seals), as well as Phoenician-style beads, perfume faience flasks in various shapes (e.g., porcupines), alabastra, and jewelry with pendants of common Punic types.[134]

The trade networks in metal and the permanent settlement of Phoenicians on Sardinia and Sicily, and in Carthage provide the immediate background, as Annette Rathje pointed out long ago. The closer interaction of Etruscan groups with these central-western Mediterranean circles might explain why Near Eastern influence in Etruria is more pointed than in Greece, as it penetrates the funerary realm and a wide range of ritualized behaviors. Jodi Magness summarizes it effectively: "Near Eastern influence is evident on almost all aspects of Etruscan life, including art, clothing, chariots, military equipment and warfare, hairstyles, dining habits, religion or cult, and technology (jewelry, glass, hydraulic). This influence is evident not only on aspects of Etruscan life but also in death—that is, on Etruscan tombs, as we shall see. The quantity, nature, and extent of Near Eastern influence on Etruscan culture beg the question: how much Near Eastern influence (and what type of influence) is required to establish a case for transmission via a foreign immigrant element versus trading contacts?"[135] Overall, engagement with the Phoenician-Carthaginian networks and artistic models predominate over and often subsume other Near Eastern or Levantine styles (e.g., Assyrian, Egyptian, Neo-Hittite/North Syrian).[136] While scholarship has certainly advanced, Near Eastern objects scattered across museums are displayed as decontextualized curiosities, and it is difficult to interpret their place in Etruscan culture. At the archaeological museums of Tarquinia and Cerveteri, for instance, these assemblages are labeled as "Oriental," at most

"Egyptian/Nilotic," sometimes pointing to Naukratis and its "Greco-Oriental" milieu, but rarely if ever singling out the Phoenician role behind their appearance in Etruria. The proximity of the harbors of Gravisca and Pyrgi, and parallels of the same sorts of artifacts in Carthage or elsewhere in the Phoenician realm are ignored. This is the more poignant since commercial exchange within a Sardinian–Carthaginian–Etruscan circuit is well documented, whereas there is no evidence of sustained and consequential direct contact with, say, Egypt or Assyria.[137]

What makes these repertoires of *orientalia* relevant is not only that they find parallels in Phoenician-Punic contexts across the Mediterranean but also that they appear in clearly local, Etruscan contexts. And yet there is no general narrative that incorporates Phoenicians into the presentation of these scattered "Levantine/Egyptian/Oriental" elements, or addresses their likely symbolic and religious value, even if specialists are now more frequently insisting on it.[138] Artifacts are often dealt with piecemeal in scholarship and vaguely framed by the grand narrative of Greek influence presented in the videos and panels at these public sites and museums, in guidebooks and virtual tours (e.g., of the necropolis of Cerveteri or the Regolini Galassi Tomb at the Vatican Museum), which might include little more than passing references to trade with "eastern countries" or Egypt, and, more exceptionally, to Phoenician merchants or artisans.

Phoenician models are particularly clear in metalwork and ivories. Ivory items found in Etruria range from direct Levantine imports (e.g., Egyptianizing/Phoenician and Assyrianizing/North-Syrian styles), to what are probably locally made pieces by itinerant artisans operating in Etruria in the first quarter of the seventh century; eventually a "provincial style" of ivories is developed by local apprentices in the second quarter of the century.[139] This local orientalizing style parallels what we see in jewelry after the mid-seventh century, when the Etruscans adopt the technique of granulation and filigree, an innovation that appears in areas of contact with Phoenicians. As Glenn Markoe clarifies, these developments are independent of the often-cited Late Bronze Age Mycenaean influence in Italy.[140] Other new items carried to the grave by Etruscan elites are paralleled in burials in other areas of Phoenician influence, such as bronze and iron weapons, stamped geometric shields, horse trappings, and chariot parts, the latter a funerary habit seen in Iberian and Cypriot wealthy tombs.[141]

The most characteristically Etruscan pots, again found in graves and mass-produced between the seventh and fifth centuries, are the "bucchero" vases, recognizable for their shiny black/gray-slip and elegant forms. Just as Proto-Corinthian pottery adapted the engraving techniques, forms, and decoration of Levantine metal vases to the ceramic medium (see Chapter 6), these bucchero vases were inspired by Levantine ceramic and metal vases, such as Phoenician trefoil-lip and "pear-shaped" jugs (*oinochoai*); the latter were made in bronze and silver and adorned with palmettes under their handle, and are attested with local variants also in Etruria, Cyprus, and Iberia.[142] In Philip Perkins's assessment, the pear-shaped jar or *oinichoe* "blends features of the biconical Etruscan shape with a Phoenician narrow necked jug (Rasmussen *oinochoe* type 2). The artisans must have seen the original jugs made in silver, bronze, ivory/ostrich egg, and ceramic in Phoenicia or Cyprus."[143] A distinct group of bucchero vessels from the late seventh to early sixth century adopt an incised decoration with animal friezes, which "share characteristics particular to Phoenician and Assyrian representations," akin to those adopted in Greek Proto-Corinthian pottery (Figure 5.5).[144] The Etruscans also made bucchero versions of four-stand chalices with female figures as "caryatids," emulating the Levantine types in which the female figure represents an Ashtart-type goddess, a theme that appears also in the Greek stone *perirrhanteria* (Figure 6.5). The models were at hand, it seems, since Levantine ivory chalices of this type are also found in Etruscan tombs.[145]

These artifacts were not markers of status merely because of their exoticism and material value; as Massimo Botto and others have argued, these objects came with built-in associations with Near Eastern royal imagery and elite practices, such as banqueting and libation rituals.[146] The eastern-style jugs and vessels mentioned above, and the practice of reclined banqueting (besides other paraphernalia such as jewelry, hairstyles, and clothing) were part of this package. Also found in the tombs were metal spits (*obeloi*), which were likely used in ritual banqueting and have appeared in similar funerary ritual settings on Crete and Cyprus. Other notable items are the "volute" footstools found in graves from Latium to the Adriatic coast, including the wooden stool at the "Tomb of the Throne" of the Lippi necropolis at Veruccio, which accompanied the rarely preserved and intricately carved wooden throne.[147] Such footstools are found in bronze, stone, ter-

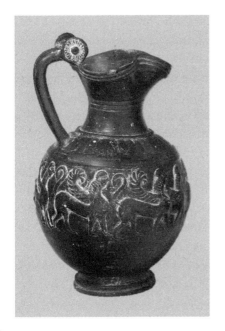

FIG. 5.5   Etruscan Bucchero vases of orientalizing style.

Two jugs in "light bucchero" style (625–600 BC), with relief and incised decoration of sphinxes (*left*) and deer (*right*). The Metropolitan Museum of Art, New York, Rogers Fund, 1921.

racotta, and even wood in Etruria, with one stone example found in Carthage. The footstool imitates the imagery of seated kings, represented in Syro-Phoenician ivories and preserved in relief sculptures from the Syro-Anatolian realm, but already represented on the sarcophagus of King Ahiram of Byblos, dated to around 1000 BC along with other Phoenician royal imagery (Figure 9.1).[148] The footstool represented in an assembly scene in one of the frieze plaques at Poggio Civitate (see below) follows this motif.[149]

One of the earlier and more systematic elements included in this "kit" is a type of ceremonial bowls of great symbolic and ritual connotation in the Near East: the fluted (or ribbed) bronze bowls (*patera baccellatta*), used in the Assyrian court, as depicted in Assyrian reliefs. These bowls were first imported in the late eighth century and were imitated by the hundreds in Etruria in the second quarter of the seventh century, in both metal and ceramic forms.[150] We find an explicit testimony of the association of the bowls with aristocratic values held by elites of different cultures: on Cyprus, a local king marked a bowl of this type with a Cypro-syllabic inscription bearing his name.[151] In another case, a high official or dignitary dedicated two bronze bowls in Phoenician around the eighth century with inscriptions to "Baal of Lebanon, his lord," dedicated by a "governor of Qarthadasht" and "servant of Hiram, king of the Sidonians."[152] A fluted bowl from Kfar Veradim in northern Israel also bears a Phoenician inscription.[153]

The bronze perfume stands or *thymiateria* found in Etruscan tombs, which we have already encountered in Tartessos, are a good example of the ritual baggage carried by some imported objects, even if their local use varied (see Figure 4.2).[154] These are tall stands adorned with downward-looking petals along the stem, and come from an ancient Levantine tradition (the type is already found at Ugarit in tripod form). The Iron Age samples are thought to have been made on Cyprus, where they appear in the eleventh–tenth centuries. These artifacts are not merely decorative pieces but are inseparable from the practice of incense burning, which had been associated with the area of Phoenicia since the Late Bronze Age. This is because incense was extracted from cedar trees mainly from this area (the Greek for "incense" is *libanos,* the name of the Lebanon mountain range and region). Incense was strongly associated with the cult of Ashtart, Ishtar, and in the Greek world with Cypriot Aphrodite and Hera. Material and literary evidence suggests that in the Levant and the Aegean the ritual was connected especially with the goddess's protection of sailors, and indeed these "candelabra" are represented on depictions of Phoenician-type boats, for instance, a ship model from Cyprus (ca. 600 BC) and the painting of a Canaanite ship in Egyptian Thebes (ca. 1427–1400 BC).[155] In other words, this type of artifact, adapted to Etruscan funerary use, encapsulates not only technical but also cultural and ritual transfer; incense burners continued to be made and used in one-foot or tripod form, with decorations evolving during the Etruscan archaic period. They need to be understood as part of the cultic realm of Ashtart/Tanit and her divine counterparts (Uni, Aphrodite, Hera), given the common ground provided by their cults, best demonstrated at Pyrgi. We can see the representation of such incense burners with downward petals in votive stelae and other Phoenician iconography (e.g., Figures 5.2 and 6.6).

About Those Bowls Again...

To grab the bull by the horns, I briefly return to the decorated metal bowls/*paterae,* since they are conspicuous among the goods found in Etruscan-Italic tombs and they epitomize orientalizing art and its problems. These *paterae* are just one component of the orientalizing assemblages found in graves, but they are an important confirmation of the connection between the orientalizing art and Phoenician intermediation. The corpus from Italy comprises thirteen bowls so far, most of silver (once gold-plated), and some of bronze. Their distribution is not restricted to Etruria proper: five were found in Praeneste/Palestrina, four in a single tomb in Caere/Cerveteri, and one in Pontecagnano, besides three unprovenanced. Close comparison of technique, material, design, and iconographic detail reveals a clear affinity with the *paterae* found on Cyprus (e.g., Figure 3.2). The Italian items belong to one group or, at most, two, and were tailored to local clientele, who disliked vegetal decoration and fantastic animals, and preferred military and Nilotic themes. Their homogeneity suggests that they were most likely produced in a single Phoenician workshop, whether in the Levantine homeland or on Cyprus, perhaps by a single master, within a short period of time in the late eighth or early seventh century.[156] This picture is consistent with the recurring Phoenician aspects of other imports and traits of the Etruscan orientalizing milieu, whose Cypriot inflections point to Phoenician networks as well.[157] Most agree that these objects cohere with Phoenician style, which combined "Egyptian tradition and narrative and militaristic Assyrian realism," as Fernando Sciacca put it, or, as Maurizio Sannibale saw it, in which "the Egyptianizing context was interpreted with the lively narrative form of the Neo-Assyrian reliefs," as is characteristic across Phoenician media.[158]

We can imagine the *paterae* as part of the brilliant strategy of giving gifts, which treated Etruscan trading counterparts or their patrons to objects worthy of royal houses. These would include objects we cannot see, such as furniture or textiles, of which only the ivory attachments and *fibulae* remain, with rare exceptions (e.g., the Veruccio throne). These "regalia" would be fundamental in the initial stage of contact aimed at securing trading privileges and access to resources. In this context the gifts signaled special recognition from the part of the Levantine states and agents of the superior status of some Etruscan houses vis-à-vis other members of their community.[159] In other words, the Near Eastern items in the Cerveteri tombs were "given mainly by the agents of Phoenician oligarchies to establish enduring economic relations with the Etruscan elites controlling the local resources."[160] In exchange, the foreigners were presumably granted permission to remain in the area and a privileged access to the networks of metal extraction and trade. Eventually, deeper affiliations developed between the cultures that made these deals. The full integration of Levantine materials in old and new local customs points to the integration of Levantine individuals within Etruscan society and the elite class, through intermarriage and other social bonds.[161]

In short, the case of the engraved bowls confirms what we already know through other media and sources: the Phoenicians were the one group of Levantines who permanently and extensively settled in the central-western Mediterranean; in turn, they were not only familiar with Assyrian and Egyptian royal imagery, they also propagated their own recognizable versions of it. So, if we ask the *who* and *why* of the *paterae,* the answer leads us back to the Phoenicians.

A Monumental Funerary World

Etruscan art is perhaps most popularly identified with the monumental funerary sculpture produced at this time, such as the figures reclining on top of the famous Sarcophagus of the Spouses. This orientalizing style shares some traits with the Greek "Daedalic" style, yet is distinct enough from it, and in Etruria it continues through the early fifth century (ca. 575–480 BC). It is generally said that Etruscan orientalizing sculpture shows affinities with the arts of Asia Minor and from the Syro-Anatolian realm, although Cretan affinities are also suggested.[162] These points of reference are not incompatible with the Phoenician vector, however, as North Syria-Cilicia was in the realm of Phoenician cultural influence in the Iron Age, and scholars also consider "Levantine masters who adopted Syro-Hittite models."[163] In some cases, sculpture is more clearly inspired by North Syrian-Phoenician models, such as the Ishtar-Ashtart-like statues (or "nude standing goddesses"), which appear as decorations on tombs or in cultic contexts.[164] Their nakedness itself and marked genitals align with Levantine tradition and contrast with Greek statuary, even in later versions already influenced by Greek style (e.g., the nude "Cannicella goddess").[165]

Etruscan monumental graves are extraordinary in originality and preservation, and have outlasted the more perishable housing used by the living
in this period. The two typical forms are *hypogea* and *tumuli,* sometimes
combined in the same necropolis. *Hypogea* were dug into the rock, sometimes with well-finished walls decorated with colorful paintings (e.g., Monterozzi necropolis in Tarquinia). The *tumuli,* best known from the necropolis of Banditaccia at Cerveteri, were carved out of soft volcanic rock and
covered by artificial mounds. This necropolis forms a "city of the dead,"
developed between the ninth century (during the Villanovan period) and
the third century BC. The larger *tumuli* are the oldest, and *tumuli* become
more complex from the seventh century onward, when they start replicating
domestic architecture, with triangular roofs, central beams, and pilasters.
Funerary benches with headrests are carved into the rock too, and sometimes a banqueting space is simulated, with carved *triclinia* (the reclining
couches of banqueting halls) and added details such as balconies and cush-
ions, kitchen and dining items sculpted on the walls.

The idea of turning wooden architecture into stone may be a by-product
of the orientalizing current, inspired by Near Eastern monumental masonry,
which accounts for the emergence of sanctuary architecture too (see
Chapter 6). The combination of traditional and innovative traits is stark
here: Etruscan *tumuli* replicate in stone, for eternity, the indigenous huts
made of perishable materials. At the same time, these same *tumuli* have
yielded the Near Eastern and orientalizing assemblages discussed above, but
also rare items such as decorated Egyptian vases, of the sorts we find in the
rich Phoenician elite tombs of the Málaga coast.[166]

Grand burials under *tumuli* are not unseen in the Mediterranean world.
The usual points of comparison are those found in Phrygia, Caria, and
Lydia in Asia Minor, and the monumental chamber tombs on Cyprus, attributed to local royalty and farther afield in Urartu (Van).[167] But the comparison can be expanded in several directions that bring the innovation
closer to trends within the Phoenician realms of influence: Syro-Palestinian
archaeologists have long noted the similarity between Etruscan tombs and
chamber tombs from this same period (eighth–sixth centuries BC) excavated
in Judah, in the areas of Jerusalem and Hebron. Like the Cypriot, Anatolian, and Etruscan tombs, these are carved in the rock, with a dromos
leading to the entrance, flat or gabled ceilings simulating wooden beams,
and carved imitation doors and windows. These chambers also bear stone

benches for the dead with carved headrests. Some of the headrests' shapes evoke Egyptianizing symbology and are only attested in the Etruscan and Judaean tombs. Judging by these parallels, Magness and others have argued that this type of chamber tomb was part of the orientalizing cultural koine.[168] Rock-cut tombs (not necessarily under *tumuli*) with local variations and developments might, after all, be neither inherited from Italic customs nor due to an Anatolian migration, but a result of the adaptation of Levantine ideas and habits. This view is reinforced if we look farther west, at the funerary *tumuli* of the elites of Tartessos (Huelva). These burials display orientalizing adaptations and imports, including banqueting equipment and chariots, which, combined with local practices, produce a unique funerary landscape.[169] In Iberia, this elite culture also developed along the fringes of the Phoenician colonial settlement on Gadir and the Málaga coast, where chamber tombs of the *hypogea* type have been found (for example, at Trayamar).[170]

We know that the Phoenicians used a variety of burial forms in this period, as more recently shown by the necropolis of Tyre al-Bass and the immediate area around Sidon; these included *hypogea* and other chamber tombs, besides simple cremations and other types of burials (e.g., *fossae* or shaft graves, in which a sarcophagus could be placed), although in general Phoenicians themselves did not have a preference for the larger multi-chambered tomb or *tumulus* structure.[171] *Hypogea,* sometimes with a corridor and sometimes with paintings on their walls, are also widespread in other Phoenician-Punic areas later on, such as Ibiza, Sardinia, and Tunisia.[172] More recently, a Phoenician family *hypogeum* was excavated at Achziv in northern Israel.[173] These referents show, at least, that monumental, chamber-tomb building was part of the Phoenician funerary repertoire, and these might be among the wider range of practices and technologies that were adopted on the axis of Phoenician networks, perhaps along with the masons themselves, while local communities elaborated their own, often more bombastic versions.

Another type of burial attested widely throughout Etruria is one marked by a pillar or *cippus* (small pointed pillar). Larger "obelisk-shaped" *cippi* appear too, attested in San Giuliano, Vulci, Castro, Chiusi, and the Viterbo area.[174] The *cippus* monument could accompany cremations or inhumations, although it is difficult to associate them with particular burial materials and it is debated whether their form (triangular or rounded top) corresponded to the gender of the deceased.[175] A few observations about these *cippi* make them relevant regarding the question of Phoenicians in Etruria. First, this innovation is not paralleled in archaic Greek monuments, so the Etruscans did not borrow it from there. In turn, *cippi* and carved stelae are staple burial markers in Phoenician cemeteries of the Levant and the Punic world. Incidentally, stelae and *cippi* appear not only in coastal sites and central Etruria but inland and farther north, in areas where the metal industry proliferated and foreigners might have settled more permanently and been buried. Is it reasonable, then, to link the appearance of *cippi* to Phoenician merchant and artisanal communities integrated in Etruscan society? This exact interpretation has been proposed for the *cippi* found at Eleutherna and Knossos on Crete. Given their large numbers in Etruria, however, they may reflect the adoption of an initially foreign element by local communities. The main specialist in these monuments, Stephan Steingräber, estimates that use of the *cippi* peaked during the archaic period and was related to funerary ancestor cults, as there are signs of ritual libations and offerings around those found in context (e.g., Cima Tumulus, San Giuliano); he also posits that they were not connected to individual burials but to open-air cultic areas near the graves. This type of monument leaves a later trail in funerary urns that represent obelisk-shaped *cippi* in groups of two or three.[176] More clues might emerge as the corpus of Etruscan *cippi* as a whole is systematically studied.

Parallels of these "column-and-tower-like sepulchral monuments" are noted in Lydia, Syria, and Rhodes, and their shape is by default associated with Egypt.[177] Publications strangely bypass the widespread use of stelae and *cippi* of various sorts throughout the Phoenician and Punic realm, including those with obelisk shapes as well as stelae with betyls, cultic/funerary pillars, or *cippi* represented on them (cf. Figure 5.2).[178] In some cases, funerary iconography seems to make the connection even more evident: for instance, in a seventh-century funerary stela from Saletto di Bentivoglio (Bologna), the low relief directly adopted motifs of Phoenician/Syro-Palestinian stock, showing a (rather cowlike) sphinx and a tree of life flanked by climbing goats (Figure 5.6). The group of funerary stelae from Bologna to which it belongs, from the eighth to sixth centuries, is said to show a range of influences "as far apart as western Europe and Northern Syria," but again the Phoenicians are not singled out as the most likely direct channel of these traits.[179] In short, although to date no separate Phoenician necropolis

FIG. 5.6   Etruscan stone stela from Saletto di Bentivoglio, Bologna.

The "Saletto stela" (72 cm height), dated to the second half of the seventh century BC and decorated in low relief, depicting a tree of life flanked by goats and a sphinx above them. Photo Alberto Pascale. Courtesy of Museo Civico Archeologico, Bologna.

has been identified in Etruria, further studies of rock-cut graves and funerary *cippi* should consider the effect that a sustained presence of Levantines among these communities might have had on these funerary landscapes.

In this context we must mention the adoption of the so-called Proto-Aeolic capital in Etruscan funerary architecture, an element I discuss in more detail in Chapter 9. Connected with other orientalizing vegetal forms representing life (Phoenician palmette, lotus, tree of life), this type of capital is emblematic of Phoenician art and it proliferates (with local variations) in the Levant, the Aegean, and Phoenician areas of Cyprus and Iberia. In Etruria, the volute capital has appeared since the sixth century in its full-size version, topping pillars or pilasters in the chamber tombs (perhaps also painted). The earliest ones come from graves at Cerveteri / Caere, but they continue to adorn funerary or votive monuments that replicate the architectural features of small shrines (*naiskoi*), as well as of funerary urns and other artifacts (e.g., footstools, bronze mirrors), sometimes until the second–first century BC.[180]

"Face to Face" in Sanctuaries

Remains of domestic or public buildings are rare in Etruria, often overlaid with later construction, and even the high-class ("princely") homes of those lavishly buried were made of wood and thatched roof, to which tiles and stone foundations were slowly incorporated. Proto-urban or semi-urban settlements developed where the main Etruscan centers stood historically. We can mention Tarquinia, Chiusi, Vetulonia, Volterra, Caere, and Veii, most of them in areas occupied since the Late Bronze Age if not earlier. Early population clusters can only be traced through the appearance of necropoleis and sometimes sanctuaries that articulated the territory, besides the occasional remains of fortifications and houses. At the same time, the specialization of industries evident in Etruscan material culture is also a sign of social organization and stratification.[181] The eventual adoption of quadrangular and more complex structures, entrances or porches with pillars / columns, masonry techniques, and stucco and terracotta decoration, were part of the Levantine-inspired globalizing koine that looked up to the Near Eastern cityscapes.[182] These transformations appear in Iberia, the Aegean, on Cyprus, and other areas and fed into each other to the degree that these societies interacted. In other words, there is no need to assume that Near Eastern patterns of construction and decoration were (only) mediated through Greeks; the emerging Etruscan states had their own direct vectors of exchange with Levantines and with other orientalizing elites.[183]

We know little about early Etruscan sanctuaries. As far as we can tell, their concept of sacred space was flexible, with open-air areas marked by altars and small structures, not necessarily centered around a large building to house the cult statue, that is, a temple. Temple layouts vary greatly. In general, religious architecture is an area where Etruscan tradition resists Greek influences, and maintains idiosyncratic features, such as a high podium, deep porch, tripartite layouts, no peristyle, and so on.[184] Presumably, this flexible, open model allowed for easy transfer of innovative elements, and in this respect the Etruscan sanctuary is closer to the flexible Canaanite-Phoenician model, such as attested, in Sicily (Motya, e.g., Figure 5.3 above), Cyprus (Kition), and Tartessos (El Carambolo).

A direct Levantine influence can be argued with regard to the building known as Edificio Beta at Tarquinia's Monumental complex (early seventh century BC), in which the layout and foundation deposit evokes Levantine practices, and the masonry technique (pier and rubble) is characteristically Phoenician, well attested in western colonies.[185] Another exceptional site for sacred architecture is the hill site at Poggio Civitate site in Murlo, where the archaic building complex from the seventh to sixth century was beautifully adorned by orientalizing decoration. The terracotta friezes of the Upper Building are especially remarkable, as they contain Near Eastern–looking scenes (a procession, banquet, race, and assembly), in which many of the oriental and orientalizing artifacts that are otherwise found in graves appear and are used in specific contexts (chariots, bowls, pitchers, banqueting furniture, cauldrons on stands, fans, footstools with volutes), perhaps representing events enacted in the building itself.[186] The finding of ivories and bronzes at the same site suggests that this complex at Poggio Civitate included a multipurpose workshop or production center, where the industries of metalwork, terracotta molding, and other specialized crafts converged.[187] The case for foreign workers integrated within these local communities and tailoring their production to their tastes and demands is gaining support, not only here but at other sites, such as Caere.[188] In general, Etruscan archaeologists have begun to seriously consider the presence of Near Eastern artisans as earlier than Greek ones.[189]

The legendary story of Demaratus is often evoked in this context: an upper-class trader from Corinth, he was said to have fled political turmoil in the mid-seventh century to settle in Tarquinia, bringing artisans with him, whence he joined the Etruscan aristocracy, and his son Tarquinius Priscus became the fifth king of Rome (and the first of a gens of kings and consuls).[190] The story is often mentioned as a shortcut by modern scholars to evoke the artistic transformation of Etruscan art under Greek auspices, elevated to a legendary level that, once more, leaves out Phoenician artists.[191] Perhaps this is an inherited bias from our Greek and Roman sources, but the fact is that Demaratus has functioned within scholarship as "a literary figure used to reinforce the model of Hellenization."[192] Without written sources like this (and even with them), it is extremely difficult to be sure of the nature or scale of "foreign" elements within a larger community, even when we have archaeological materials. Yet at least we have this one story, even if it is about a Corinthian, not a Phoenician. Demaratus's trajectory invites us to imagine more complex relations and trajectories too, since Corinthians (following on the Euboians' wake) "piggybacked" on the metal trade networks that involved Cypriots, Phoenicians, Sardinians, and Etruscans in the central Mediterranean.[193]

Harbor towns were perfect loci for the encounter of diverse groups and interests. They were the commercial gateways for nearby centers (e.g., Caere-Pyrgi, Tarquinia-Gravisca, Vulci-Regisvilla), and their monumentalization with shrines and temples, especially in the sixth century, responded to the "need for better support structures, formal trade agreements and bureaucratic regulation in which religious authorities played a central role."[194] Some early structures excavated at the port of Tarquinia at Gravisca have been associated with the cults of divinities that would have been easily identified across Greek, Roman, and Semitic worlds: Aphrodite, Hera, Demeter and Kore, and Adonis, whose cult spread from Byblos to Cyprus, Greece, Egypt, and Italy.[195] Ashtart, in turn, was known across the Phoenician networks as a maritime protector, and Melqart as a patron of colonization, metal industry, and trade.

A Phoenician text found at a sanctuary complex at Pyrgi demonstrates an instance of formalized relations with Phoenicians (Figure 5.7). Pyrgi was the most important harbor serving Cerveteri/Caere (just thirteen kilometers, or eight miles inland) and a regional and international hub.[196] The earliest constructions at Pyrgi are poorly attested, buried beneath the later

FIG. 5.7 **Gold tablets with Etruscan and Phoenician inscriptions from Pyrgi.**
Three gold panels inscribed in Phoenician (*left*) and Etruscan (*center* and *right*), dedicated to Ashtart and Uni at the sanctuary complex in Pyrgi, late sixth century BC. Sailko/Wikimedia Commons/CC BY-SA 4.0.

Temples A and B.[197] In an area adjacent to Temple B (called Area C), a set of three gold sheets was found, which contained one Phoenician inscription and two in Etruscan, dated to the late sixth century. The Phoenician text declares that the Etruscan leader Thefarie Velianas, called "king (*melek*) of Caere," had dedicated a space in the sanctuary to the Phoenician goddess Ashtart.[198] What little can be understood of the Etruscan inscription (not a direct translation of the Phoenician text) confirms the king's identity and identifies the Etruscan goddess venerated there as Uni, here a counterpart to Ashtart. Thanks to this text, we know for sure that the Etruscans were not dealing with, for instance, Aramaic or Luwian speakers of the Syro-Anatolian realm, or with Hebrew speakers of Israel/Judah, or other "Levantines" in general; it is the Phoenicians that we find, their language and their gods. Their ritual footprint is revealed only in writing and is elusive archaeologically (as it often happens in the case of migrants and nonpermanent visitors), although the recent finding of five Phoenician oil lamps in situ, probably made in Carthage, can be now added to the picture.[199] With the mutual recognition of the two divine patrons (in such an expensive and permanent medium as gold), the leader of Caere aspired to "participate in international relations, and to be part of the strategic game that the Phoenician institutions had played during their long experience of long-distance trade, coordinating different commercial circuits."[200]

Iconography and Religious Symbolism

The Levantine inflections of much Etruscan iconography of this period has already been discussed above in relation to metalwork, funerary sculpture, reliefs, and other media. Wall paintings, in turn, are preserved in tombs of the later archaic period (they take off in the sixth century), such as those of the chamber tombs at the Monterozzi necropolis of Tarquinia. These frescoes provide us with a wide repertoire of funerary and afterlife iconography, some of which suggest the reception and idiosyncratic adaptations of Near Eastern motifs, outlasting the orientalizing period proper. But Etruscan wall-painting is for the most part difficult to decode, due to the lack of Etruscan literary sources that could shed light on their mythology and religion.[201] If the relationship of Etruscan iconography with themes from Greek and Roman cultures is already opaque, comparison with Phoenician culture is even more challenging, since their own mythology is also scarcely attested. Here I discuss some interesting points of convergence that deserve further study.

The abundant Dionysiac and banqueting themes found there reflect the eastern Mediterranean wine culture, eagerly adopted in all its facets during the Iron Age. Banqueting culture is often presented as part of the "Homeric" world disseminated by Greeks in the west.[202] But vine-cultivation and wine-culture are shared by Greek, Anatolian, and Semitic traditions, and influences would be difficult to disentangle once the Etruscans and other Italic peoples partook in this international *koine*. Moreover, wall paintings and artifacts found in graves show a deep association of banqueting and funerary rituals, which has its closest counterpart and predecessor in the Phoenician world, where funerary banquets and recurring offerings were performed at the grave.[203] The fact that much of the banqueting equipment, especially later on, is of Greek production, obscures independent affinities with the Near East. Within both Etruscan and Greek elite cultures, however, the closest referent was in the type of religious communal feast known as the *marzeah* in the Canaanite and Phoenician-Punic realm, which in turn evoked royal and aristocratic Assyrian practices and paraphernalia also depicted in Phoenician art.[204]

Other underworld motifs deserve further exploration beyond the well-trodden Hellenic and Roman points of comparison. Among the themes that could signal intersections with Egyptianizing or Phoenician-Punic afterlife, but to my knowledge have not been studied in detail from that angle, are the "false doors" (or stepped/recessed windows/doors) in wall carvings and paintings; guardian figures such as the Mistress of Animals and Master of Animals with lions, leopards, deer, and vegetal motifs (including Phoenician-type palmettes); "demons" flanking the entrances of tombs; the motif of afterlife journeys across water; and flying monsters and roosters. Much of this repertoire draws on themes that had previously traveled in other media, such as in terracottas, reliefs in metalwork and bucchero vases, and vase painting.[205]

On safer ground, we can turn to a divinity whose cult and mythology bonded Greek, Phoenician, and Italic cultures: Herakles/Hercules/Heracle. Votives and statues dedicated to him appear in Etruria and some of the earliest cults attested in Rome were devoted to him. Herakles's assimilation to Tyrian Melqart provided a thread along which these collectives intertwined their mythologies and under whose auspices the parties involved sanctioned commercial interactions.[206] The earliest cult of Herakles in Rome is attested in the Forum Boarium (where the Ara Maxima stood later on), a river harbor and commercial area that attracted foreign merchants since at least the eighth century BC.[207] Remains of the Sant'Omobono temple there and materials around it indicate an international meeting point for the Tyrrhenian trading circuit, with a prominent role of Phoenicians-Carthaginians.[208] Is it possible that the intercultural nature of this cult explains the puzzling odd details shared by the Roman cult in later times and the cult of Melqart at Tyre and Gadir (banning of flies and dogs, exclusion of pigs from sacrifices, etc.)?[209] In any case, Phoenician merchants were actively engaged with Italic groups in the same circuits as Euboians and other Greeks, Sardinians, and Sicilians. The standard scholarly narrative, however, tends to associate Herakles's arrival and popularity with Greek merchants only, reinforcing (and determined by) the anti-Phoenician historiography and mythology construed by the Romans themselves after the Punic Wars.

Writing

The adoption of writing by the Etruscans sometime around 700 BC was an integral part of the orientalizing kit. The Northwest Semitic alphabetic system allowed Tartessians, Greeks, and Levantine peoples to boost the formation of their early city-state apparatus. In Etruria, however, the borrowing came not directly from the Phoenicians but from one of the versions of the Greek alphabet, probably the Chalkidian one brought by Euboians.[210] Although the Etruscan language remains largely undeciphered, its cultural influence was enormous on the neighboring Italic peoples. Among the various adaptations of the Etruscan alphabet to Italic dialects was the Latin script, which lies behind our own western alphabets, down to the present.[211] Before this development, however, southern Italy had witnessed early Greek experimentation with the Northwest Semitic script, and Italic groups had been in contact with Greek and Phoenician speakers for a while. As I discuss in Chapter 7, in the bay of Naples some of the earliest Greek alphabetic texts appeared in the mid-eighth century, and they are found in the same contexts and sites as contemporary Northwest Semitic inscriptions of the same type, namely private graffiti.[212]

When the Etruscans adopted writing, a generation or more after the Greeks, they would already have encountered Phoenician writing in the region (Sardinia, Carthage, and Sicily are not far). Like the Greeks, they were adopting a Levantine technology that moved west and became part of the orientalizing "revolution," even if the specific adoption happened through a Greek speaker / writer. Etruscan writing is most visible on funerary monuments and votive objects, but it was not limited to formal inscriptions and the new elite façade; the Etruscans knew Greek literature (Homer was a favorite theme in their imported Greek art), and some Etruscan literature was known to Roman authors. Written documents circulated in perishable materials such as papyrus, parchment, and linen. In fact, the longest Etruscan texts were found in a linen book used to wrap mummies in Alexandria (the third-century BC linen known as the *Liber Linteus Zagrabiensis*, now in Zagreb).[213]

The few preserved texts and literary testimonies show that the Etruscans cultivated a written tradition of ritual and religious texts, including festival calendars and brontoscopic calendars (brontoscopy was divination by thunder).[214] Statues of Etruscan upper-class men posing with scrolls or books on their tombstone are a poignant reminder of the abysmal loss of the literature that circulated in Etruria in various languages, including Greek and Phoenician.[215] Another area where specialized writing and religion met was divination, many types of which are attested in Etruria. One type examined the sacrificial victim's liver (hepatoscopy or haruspicina) and was guided by inscribed liver models: several terracotta exemplars have been found in Etruria, dated to the third–second century BC but reflecting an older tradition.[216] This technique is seen as an orientalizing-period adaptation, long compared to Babylonian practices and liver models transmitted by itinerant specialists in the Iron Age. But, as Walter Burkert notes, such models were used among Hittites and Canaanites since the Bronze Age too, and they appear in Cilicia and Cyprus as well, which makes the Levantines plausible transmitters.[217]

In the Capitoline Museum in Rome lies a precious token of the intercultural mobility of the merchant class: I refer to an ivory piece carved in the form of a lioness belonging to a *tessera hospitalis,* that is, this is one of two identical pieces of a token of hospitality or recognition. The piece dates to the late seventh century, found precisely at the Sant'Omobono sanctuary, and bears the earliest Etruscan inscription found in Rome. Two names are engraved on it: the name of one *silqetenas,* related to Phoenician Sulcis on Sardinia, and the name of his counterpart, *spurianas,* which belongs to a known Etruscan lineage from Tarquinia. Near-identical pieces with Etruscan inscriptions have been found at Carthage and Poggio Civitate.[218] The inscription on the token found in a grave at Carthage (in Etruscan) may bear a self-reference by a Phoenician of this period who crosses the Etruscan and Phoenician realms: *mi puinel karθazie,* that is, "I am a Punic (*puniel*) from Carthage" or "I am Puniel from Carthage" (whether an ethnic self-reference or a proper name, or nickname, like Phoinix in Greek).[219] An ivory *tessera hospitalis* from Lilybaeum on Sicily, shared by men with Greek and Punic names (in handshake shape) also brings these partnerships to life, even if it dates to Roman times (second-first century BC).[220] Whatever their onomastic interpretation, these testimonies push back against a reductionist alignment of the Etruscan world with

Greek and Roman (i.e., "western") cultures, and posit a triangulation between Greeks, Italics, and Phoenicians, which provides a richer and more complex harmony as a backdrop for our understanding of Italy's pre-Roman
culture(s).

꠸꠸꠸

Over a century after the discovery of Etruscan tombs, our understanding
of the social context of the precious objects found in them has advanced
considerably, as has our knowledge of the role of imports and adaptations of Near Eastern cultural capital in Italy. Nonetheless, in the general
discourse and much of the scholarship of the Italic Iron Age, there is a
perception that introducing the Phoenicians forces a "choice" between
the Hellenic and the Near Eastern heritage. Perhaps the fear is a betraying
or diminishing of the classical position of the Etruscans as Rome's fore-
fathers. The apologetic tone used when Phoenicians are postulated in
these lands would never be used by classicists when asserting Greek presence. The idea of networks and "neutral meeting points," especially applied to islands, is popular and solves part of the problem of attaching
hard labels to the groups presumably associated with the materials, particularly when collective ethnic affiliations or political frameworks are not
at all clear. The problem is that we also need to correct an inertia that
tends to leave out some of the elements of that complexity, while keeping others, and that the extra caution and skepticism in the end favors
the groups that are better represented in the later historical record, in
this case the Greeks.

We will never have a detailed history of the Phoenicians' presence in
Italy. While archaeologists and art historians continue to wrestle with the
conundrum of identifying individual objects, a new cultural-historical synthesis should begin to integrate the Phoenicians into the received picture.
Context weighs in their favor as does growing knowledge of materials from
elsewhere in Phoenician areas. In geopolitical terms, it is Phoenician settlement, not Aramaean or Moabite, Assyrian or Egyptian, that is attested archaeologically, historically, and epigraphically, surrounding Italy west
and south, on Sardinia, Sicily, Malta, and in Tunisia (see Map 5.1). Whether
coming from east or west, Phoenicians are the one group of "Near Easterners" or "Levantines" deeply enmeshed in the history of the central and
western Mediterranean. The Italian peninsula was not a colonial area for

them, though its surrounding islands were (Sicily, Sardinia, Malta). Like the Aegean, to which we turn next, the region was integral to their commercial interests. Phoenician agency, however, is often diluted in a sea of uncertainties, technicalities, and granulated analysis of orientalizing art and imports, leaving the Greeks, once again, as the only viable, "reifiable" category and external cultural force acting in early Italy.

← 6 →

THE AEGEAN

*The "miracle of Greece" is not merely the result of a unique
talent. It also owes its existence to the simple phenomenon that
the Greeks are the most easterly of the westerners.*

(WALTER BURKERT)

A Phoenicianizing Revolution

No other area we have treated so far stood as geographically close to West
Asia as the Greek Aegean (Map 6.1) or as close in terms of sustained cultural contact, which Walter Burkert and many others have investigated.
This unique situation has shaped the history of Greece from the second mil-
lennium BC through the Middle Ages and into modern times, as Greece
was periodically enveloped within empires that encompassed parts of both
Europe and Asia. But our story of Greco-Phoenician encounters falls outside the framework of empires and colonization. The entanglements between
Greek speakers and various Near Eastern cultures intensified at a time when
Greek communities were growing and undergoing an all-encompassing
"revolution," which involved more complex and intense relations with
Near Eastern cultures than the label "orientalizing" conveys. The wave of
orientalization was only an intensification of east–west relations within an
uninterrupted continuum of contact going back to the Late Bronze Age.
Along that continuum, as James Whitley remarked, "of all the peoples of
the Levant, the Phoenicians were by far the most important, at least as
far as Greeks were concerned."[1] This proximity (physical and cultural)
worked both ways; as Corinne Bonnet pointed out, in the Phoenician homeland itself the relationship with Greek culture had a lasting effect and far

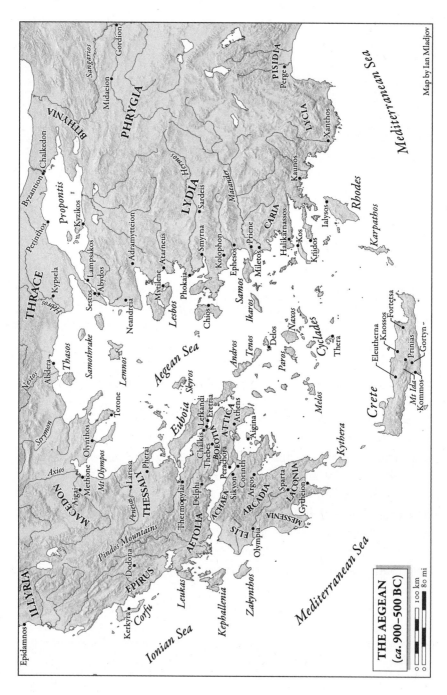

MAP 6.1

**THE AEGEAN
(ca. 900–500 BC)**

Map by Ian Mladjov

174

preceded the wave of Hellenization triggered by Alexander's conquest in the fourth century BC.[2]

The orientalizing phenomenon in Greece was more than an artistic revolution and more than a "period"; and yet it is regularly construed as a phase of art history. This categorization produces an artificial dislocation from the Greeks' long-lasting entanglements with the Near East, turning a process of particularly intense contact into a phase of experimentation in transit to more classically Greek-looking things. The materials we have inevitably force us to engage with the topic through archaeology, with visual culture playing a central role; but in the case of Greece we are lucky enough to have written sources from early times to rely on; these tell us not only that the Greeks adopted the Phoenician alphabet in the eighth century but also that they acknowledged this and other cultural debts to their Levantine neighbors, and even in Greek literature we can see how their two worlds merged through mythical stories. Artistic styles and technologies from this period, therefore, are only the visible tip of the iceberg of a phenomenon for which we have a misleadingly limited body of evidence that is rarely studied comparatively and often interpreted through Athenocentric and teleological viewpoints.[3] As a result, the issue of Greco-Phoenician interaction in this period and the association of Phoenicians with orientalizing art remains elusive, as I discussed in Part I.

To be sure, the task is complicated. Question marks still loom over the relationship between Greek and Near Eastern artistic traditions: What exactly is Greek or Near Eastern within orientalizing Greek art? What were the mechanisms of intercultural transmission? Or, as Ann Gunter put it, what was "the character and chronology of a 'Greco-Phoenician' (now, customarily 'Orientalizing') period?"[4] As she objected, "recognizing that the products of geographically or artistically distinct workshops may not always be neatly separable does not sanction the indiscriminate gathering of foreign-made or foreign-influenced works as 'Levantine' or 'Oriental' or warrant attributing their circulation wholly to Phoenician traders."[5] Nikos Stampolidis stresses the same difficulties in his recent overview of Near Eastern exotica in the Aegean, all of which "could theoretically signify a direct or indirect presence of Phoenicians in the Aegean."[6] Instead of drawing such specific (perhaps for some "radical") conclusions, most scholarship has segregated the "oriental" into its own niche and treated it as its own separate category, rather than as reflecting the main trajectory of Greek culture at this time, shaped to its core by Near Eastern entanglements.

These terms and referents (Near Eastern, Levantine, Syro-Palestinian, Phoenician, and so on) are not interchangeable, however. As archaeologists and art historians continue to refine the analysis of the eastern models behind Greek art, at a macro level there is also a need for refinement and specificity when it comes to explaining orientalization as a phenomenon that transcends the Greek realm. Resorting to vague "Near Eastern" or "Levantine" labels is an unhelpful evasion. Each orientalizing culture has its own idiosyncrasies, yet they all form part of an international koine, marked by various approximations of Levantine aesthetics and technologies, and the lifestyles they represented, which were adopted first and foremost through contact with Phoenicians. This was a specific historical encounter, a "Phoenicianizing" more than simply "orientalizing" revolution, or a vague osmosis of artistic styles, and it happened to the Greeks too, not just the Tartessians and Sardinians.

This does not mean that it is easy, or sometimes possible at all, to determine the origin of particular objects and those who transported them. That is not even the central goal. For over half a century we have been recoiling from oversimplified and racially inflected views of the ancient world. This includes both the unapologetic Eurocentric rhetoric of Greek exceptionalism, and the rushed interpretation of orientalizing art as the product of a "Greco-Phoenician period" among some early archaeologists.[7] The recognition of a Phoenician connection was not necessarily the problem; the intellectual and ideological framework in which it was studied was, at a time when categories of art and language were easily infused with rigid ethnic and national meanings. The influence of Phoenician culture was a given, but so was the emphasis on the absolute originality of the Greek adaptations.[8] We have since then reconceptualized the dynamics of cultural exchange along multicultural, anti-essentialist, postcolonial terms. We do not ask about the *who* so much and, when we do, the point is not to establish supremacy or primacy, but to understand the role of all the historical actors, animate and inanimate: the environment, the objects, the technologies. When we do discuss human agency, however, it is important to integrate all the actors as much as possible, however cautiously, and here is where I argue that we must bring the Phoenicians back into the orientalizing debate.

The timing of the orientalizing phenomenon in Greece speaks volumes about its causes and effects. After the collapse of the Mycenaean palace system, the long-standing contact between centers of power in Greece and the Near Eastern kingdoms was markedly disrupted, and centuries of fragmentation into smaller communities followed. Although the evidence is uneven depending on the region, more complex communities formed and peaked in the eighth century. Renewed prosperity can be detected in the number and wealth of burials, votive dedications, and expansion of rural settlement; trade and communications flourished again too, within and outside the Greek realm, including Greek settlement abroad; political change at home led to synoecism and the enfranchisement of a larger male citizen body.[9] The dynamics behind the orientalizing adaptations are the same that propelled polis formation and stimulated economic growth and elite competition in the early first millennium.

City-states were not a Greek invention. They existed in the Near East and in the Aegean Bronze Age.[10] In the Early Iron Age, independent city-states flourished after the collapse of the regimes of the Late Bronze Age: Neo-Hittite/Aramaean and Phoenician city-states dotted the northern Levant and Cilicia, while various kingdoms were also emerging to the south in Palestine and the Transjordan unifying larger territories (see Map 9.1). The Greeks would have encountered these polities in the Levant but also throughout the Phoenician foundations abroad, which followed this model and were well under way by 800 BC, sprawling from Cyprus to North Africa, Sicily, Sardinia, and Iberia. In Joseph Manning's words, we can say that "the rise of the Greek city state was intimately tied to the Phoenician expansion and to competition for trade routes. Cross-cultural exchange can be found in the 'orientalizing' material culture of early Greece and Etruria."[11] This also emerges from Thomas Brisart's study of orientalizing materials of about 750–600 BC, when orientalizing art appears as one more mechanism of enfranchisement or exclusion; a multipurpose code that could make the elite's status more visible and broaden the socioeconomic gap, or expand the elite culture to a broader citizenry, besides other (personal, religious) functions of these adaptations.[12]

Cultural and economic exchanges were not limited to colonial contexts but also took place in Greece itself. They certainly occurred in places where the Greeks *went* (as per John Boardman's "Greeks overseas") but the Aegean itself became a hub for Phoenicians both in transit and more permanently integrated in the Greek communities. This is exactly what we see when we reach the classical period, when they become epigraphically visible through both private and formal inscriptions, for instance, from Athens, the Piraeus, and Delos.[13] It is much more difficult to detect individuals or small units of Phoenicians and other foreigners who were integrated as *metoikoi* (resident aliens) in earlier periods, before epigraphy became widespread, but the material evidence recovered archaeologically, together with the Greeks' own narratives help us reconstruct these close Greco-Phoenician relations.

Surveying Orientalizing Greek Art

Thematic Selections and Adaptations

The repertoire of iconography in orientalizing Greek art is wide and varied, diversified by regional style and preference. The more widespread themes are those that succeeded in other Mediterranean adaptations: hybrid creatures, animal friezes, animal fight scenes and hunting scenes with lions, and vegetal motifs, especially rosettes, lotuses, and palmettes. This repertoire appears in vase painting, sculpture, terracottas, ivory, and metalwork. We may assume it was also deployed in textiles and other perishable materials.[14] Homer also associated this medium with Phoenicians when he evoked the fine clothing that Paris had acquired for Helen at Sidon, described as "the richly-decorated work of Sidonian women."[15]

Near Eastern motifs such as sphinxes and griffins animated Minoan and Mycenaean art already in the Bronze Age, in the previous iteration of an eastern Mediterranean and international elite koine. But figurative art had been abandoned along with the Mycenaean palaces and their culture, and when it became widespread again during the eighth century, the new wave of contacts with the Levant had an enormous influence on the development of the new repertoire. The inspiration behind Greek orientalizing aesthetics stemmed from the Levant, accented by Assyrian and Egyptian influences that the Phoenicians had already absorbed. In some themes this link is particularly clear: The "Mistress of Animals" or *potnia theron* (less frequently a masculine "Master") had a long Canaanite history and was a popular Levantine adaptation among Tartessians and Etruscans; the suckling calf was a popular motif associated with the fertility goddesses Ishtar, Hathor, and Ashtart in the Levant since the mid-second millennium BC, and had a canonical form in Phoenician art since the eighth century, such as on the ivories.[16] The grazing stags and bovines were also directly borrowed from the repertoire of life-giving and nurturing symbols of Syrian-Phoenician tradition that we find throughout Levantine art and its adaptations (e.g., Figures 4.3 and 5.5).[17] Monsters and demons had also populated Greek and Near Eastern art since the Bronze Age and provided a fertile imaginary realm for crossovers and orientalizing adaptations. Among them was the sphinx, or human-headed lion that became extremely popular in Greek art in a winged version that followed Phoenician prototypes. The griffin, in turn, was a falcon-headed sphinx, which became another staple of Phoenician art by the eighth century (e.g., Figures 3.2, 4.1, 5.4). Griffins appear frequently on seals and gems as guardians or vanquished by a hero and usually with two Egyptian-style hairlocks by way of coiffure.[18]

This is not to say there were no Near Eastern points of reference farther afield, although the associations are often distant and probably mediated through the nearer Levant or Cyprus: for instance, the lion-attack scenes were popular in older Hittite culture, but now followed contemporary Assyrian models, and they often appear with bulls, which are common in Cypriot pottery and Phoenician art.[19] Similarly, the Chimaera resembles creatures from the Hittite bestiary, and the fish-tailed man (akin to the Greek Triton) finds a distant counterpart in Assyrian mythological creatures. The Gorgon, in turn, has been connected with the grimacing frontal face of Humbaba (Mesopotamia), which had a similar apotropaic function, but its grimacing and grotesque frontal face also recalls the protective god Bes, whose figure was highly popular in Phoenician religion and used as an amulet, and comparisons have been made with Phoenician-Punic masks as well.[20]

Orientalizing figures in Greek art are often arranged in friezes or bands, following a principle itself modeled on Near Eastern metalwork, as we can see in the metal bowls (Figure 3.2). Greek craftsmen applied this decorative arrangement mainly to vase painting, as I discuss below. The painted friezes included animals, such as lionesses, deer, goats, and geese or other birds, as well as the floral motifs of the lotus, palmettes, and rosettes. Other recurrent motifs can also be found in Phoenician iconography and its local adaptations. Most notably perhaps, the tree of life appears in various forms, often flanked by animals or sphinxes (cf. Figures 5.6, 8.1, 8.2). Many of these symbols were associated with the goddess Ashtart in the Levant, a goddess of fertility and life, whose protection extended into the afterlife. Her imagery is also behind the above-mentioned Mistress of Animals, holding or standing over lions, and the feminine Naked Goddess, often holding her breasts (e.g., Figures 3.2, 4.4, 6.1, 6.5).[21] The striding "smiting god" posture, in turn, was occasionally adopted to represent Greek gods (e.g., Zeus hurling his thunderbolt at Typhon), following traditions attested in North Syria, Phoenicia, and Anatolia, as can be seen in representations of Baal, Teshub-Tarhuntas, Horus, and Resheph (e.g., Figures 3.1, 3.2, 4.4, 7.1).

Broad as this repertoire might seem, it is in fact quite narrow and intentional. The Greeks too made choices that were tailored to their own local tastes and social needs. To give an example, birds appear in Greek decorative bands since Geometric times, but when they are presented in orientalizing style (e.g., metal bowls, Proto-Corinthian vase painting), the Greeks stayed away from the falcon motif, which was frequent as a representation of Horus in Phoenician art. Other Egyptianizing motifs central to the Phoenicians' repertoire were also left out of the narrower Greek selection, for instance, Horus figures and symbols in general (e.g., Horus and lotus flower, Isis, or Nephthys), representations of Pharaoh, scenes of military procession or ritual procession toward an enthroned goddess, all of which appear on the metal bowls.[22] In other words, we need to assume that the Greeks' selection of Near Eastern adaptations was exactly what these particular emerging elites needed to energize their expression of status, all a local version of the shared language of the Iron Age Mediterranean.[23] At the same time, the choices and use reveal a certain understanding of the background of these symbols even as they translated them to their own culture. For instance, the Greeks showed preference for Near East themes that expressed royal or divine power and protection, so they adapted the imagery of Pharaoh in smiting position to represent the Greek gods, and they enthusiastically appropriated the lion trampling a victim, sphinxes, and griffins (see below).

Figurative art in Greece reappeared before the onset of the orientalizing revolution. Animate figures appeared in the Geometric period in metal and clay objects. Animals appeared first, in the late ninth or early eighth century BC (Middle Geometric), and then human scenes in the mid- and later eighth century (Late Geometric, ca. 775–700 BC), with great regional variation as to the complexity of the scenes and use of the artifacts.[24] On Crete, human figures appear earlier (in Protogeometric B), perhaps owing to exposure to lingering Minoan-Mycenaean art, or to the nearby Levantine and Egyptian realms, or both.[25] In short, the orientalizing trend was uneven and nonlinear, tied to regional histories and preferences. From earlier metalwork, the style spread to vase decoration in the seventh century with new artistic models and techniques, such as the incising of details in black figures. It is possible that some of the pictorial repertoire that appears in the Cypro-Phoenician metal bowls and other Levantine imports also directly influenced the decorative motifs of Late Geometric and Proto-Corinthian Greek vases (ca. 725–635 BC).[26]

Sometimes we can see the rarest experimentation with oriental models, true hapaxes: for instance, we can think of the scene on a Proto-Attic amphora from Eleusis (ca. 640 BC), in which the Gorgon sisters are chasing Perseus after the slaying of Medusa: here the Gorgons' heads are shaped like orientalizing bronze cauldrons with snake protomes (the neck of the vase bears an early representation of Odysseus and his comrades blinding the Cyclops).[27] Often cited too, although later, is the representation of Perseus killing the Gorgon with Athena's help on a metope of Temple C at Selinous, on Sicily, a scene that seems to calque representations of Gilgamesh and Enkidu killing the monster Humbaba, as briefly discussed in Chapter 5. Even more puzzling is the relief on the "Xombourgo *pithos*" from the Cycladic island of Tenos, dated to the early seventh century BC: from the head of a seated "Ashtart-type" goddess with four arms springs a smaller helmeted, winged figure, while winged attendants flank the scene. Not even the resemblance to the birth of Athena from Zeus's head convincingly explains the image, which reminds us of the abysmal loss of local mythological tradition.[28] Another example is the wheeled Trojan Horse depicted on a relief from the "Mykonos *pithos*," dated to around 675 BC, whose artist has adapted depictions of Assyrian or Levantine assault towers to the well-known Homeric theme.[29]

In general terms, an underlying set of shared cultural traits between Greeks and Levantine cultures facilitated the process of mutual identification (*interpretatio*) of gods and symbols, in a process apparently so organic that no ancient author bothered to explain it.[30] Despite the luxury of mythology and literature we have from Greece, it is often difficult to trace the meandering paths of symbols and motifs represented in Greek art, as local

variations creatively modified the prototypes. Independently of the particular cases and the conscious use or appreciation of every item (sometimes
they might have gone unnoticed as fancy decoration), ultimately every cultural trend is driven by deeper and broader dynamics. Greek speakers were
seeking to acquire an aura of internationalism and eastern refinement, and
the Phoenicians were in the right place at the right time to provide just the
appropriate "kit."

"Of Loveliness Surpassing All Others": Orientalizing Metalwork

Metal artifacts show more than other materials that lines of contact between Greece and the Near East never completely ceased after the Mycenaean collapse, even if the finds cluster in a few areas and appear restricted
to small elite units who participated in the exchange of luxury items. In
this section on metalwork, I lean especially on Glenn Markoe's study, which
most systematically contextualizes these findings and their iconography in
relation to Near Eastern and Phoenician art.[31] A general observation about
Near Eastern objects in Greece in this period is that they appear most often
deposited in sanctuaries, and more rarely in burials. This contrasts with
the contexts we have seen for Italy and Iberia, which were more often funerary. These artifacts, then, ended their journey as votive offerings, although in many cases they were likely used for ritual purposes before that.
Although sometimes stratigraphy helps, the votive context has the disad-
vantage that the artifacts do not appear clustered with other datable objects from the same deposit (as they do in burials).

The Phoenician metal bowls exemplify this pattern. Of the findings with
identifiable contexts, very few come from graves, and the rest come from
sanctuaries: at Olympia, Delphi, Athens's Acropolis, Perachora, and on the
islet of Rheneia off Delos.[32] Their occasional funerary use, in turn, is attested in a cremation from the Athenian Kerameikos and several cremations on Crete.[33] Due to the lack of samples from mainland Phoenicia, some
scholars have questioned the classification of the *paterae* as a category of
Phoenician art, while most still acclaim them as "a hallmark *par excellence*
of Phoenician workshops."[34] And we cannot forget that the earliest preserved poems in Greek, those of Homer, allude to decorated silver and gold
mixing bowls as part of Phoenician artisanship and trade.

Some peculiarities characterize the engraved bowls found in Greece: first, they are made of bronze, never silver or gilded silver as in Etruria or Cyprus. Second, as their deposit is more frequently votive, they were likely used as *phialai* or libations and ablution bowls: the bowl shown from Kourion (Cyprus) (Figure 3.2) is one of several "speaking bowls" inscribed in Greek (in Cypro-syllabic script), another of which calls itself a *phiale*.[35] Moreover, in some cases, these items are found grouped with other regular *phialai* or discarded in a *bothros* or sacred pit used for votives and ritual objects. The fact that some of the bowls have holes for suspension on walls further supports the votive use, and the ritual use might be the primary one also for the fewer samples found in funerary contexts, as suggested for the Etruscan bowls. Some metal bowls were also used as lids for cremation vessels (an interesting contrast with the choice of indigenous lids to cover orientalizing cremation urns in Tartessos).[36] Third, the regional clientele had a preference for particular decorative repertoires: symbolic and fantastic motifs predominate, such as the lion attacking a bull, hybrid creatures, winged demons/genii, and ritual processions, in contrast to the Etruscan taste for real-life scenes and vegetal motifs. Fourth, unlike in Italy and on Cyprus, the choice of material (bronze, not gilded silver) and the archaeological contexts (votive or nonextraordinary cremations) suggest that the commissioners or owners of these luxury items were not necessarily leading aristocrats or royalty, but probably well-off merchants or others belonging to an expanding wealthy class, fitting a general pattern in the use of orientalizing art in Greece, as we will see below.[37]

The metal bowls found in Greece span the whole chronological range of production of this corpus: the Kerameikos bronze bowl, dated to the late ninth century, is the first of these bowls attested anywhere west of Cyprus, where the bowl from Idalion belongs to this early period; the Phoenician communities on Cyprus are usually a favorite candidate for the production of these prized objects, and it is not surprising that the expansion of their clientele beyond Cyprus began with Greece. Most of the preserved Greek samples belong to the next phase, the second half of the eighth century (although they might have circulated for some time earlier); finally, few are dated to the first quarter of the seventh century, found on Crete and Rhodes; at this time bowls appear mostly on Cyprus and in Etruria (silver bowls), which seems to have now been the main market.[38]

The technique and iconography of these metal bowls had a secondary influence on pottery decoration (see below), which especially in Greece lingered for a longer period. But on Crete we also find a local adaptation of the engraved bowls/*paterae* in the Cretan "shields." These appear in the same contexts and often in the company of the Cypro-Phoenician bowls, such as in the Idaean Cave and at nearby Eleutherna.[39] The "shields" are larger than the usual metal bowls, and we do not know their function, other than decorative. Unlike the bowls, they are concave, with the decoration on the outer side, and their scenes are not oriented toward the center or navel of the circle, but both halves look "upward," as if meant to be seen in a fixed position. A protruding lion head in the central medallion is the most salient characteristic of these Cretan "shields," while the technique and decorative motifs follow North Syrian and Phoenician models, especially evident in the lion-hunting scenes. Bowls found at Nimrud, Cyprus, and Etruria present close parallels. On the other hand, the famous "Zeus shield" or *tympanon,* from the stash found in Mount Ida, belongs to an Assyrianizing or North Syrian style similar to that of the cauldron supports found at Olympia and Praeneste. Finally, the cable bands decorating the circular friezes and rims of these "shields" are found on Phoenician bowls, and the floral or vegetal friezes and filler motifs are also out of the typical Phoenician repertoire, for instance, lotus flowers, palmettes, rosettes, and papyrus.[40]

Markoe deduced that these Cretan "shields," as well as some of the *paterae,* may have come from local workshops, where Cretan ateliers worked directly from the Phoenician models, since some of the Cretan bronze *paterae* (from Fortetsa and the Idaean Cave) are believed to be imports from Syria or Phoenicia.[41] This would not be a surprising scenario on Crete, as the island renewed contact with the Levant earlier than the rest of Greece, if it was interrupted at all. The earliest Phoenician inscription in Greece comes from Crete, incised on a hemispherical bronze bowl of Cypriot type found near Knossos (the "Tekke bowl"), deposited in a Protogeometric burial dated to the tenth century BC. In fact, this may be the earliest Phoenician inscription outside Phoenicia to date.[42] (Its rival, the Nora stone from Sardinia, probably dates to the ninth century.) The stable presence of Phoenicians on Crete is deduced from religious architecture at Kommos (on the southern coast of the island), and from burial practices (including *cippi*) at places such as Knossos and Eleutherna, a settlement at the foot of Mount

Ida, whose sacred cave has yielded the most impressive stash of oriental and orientalizing artifacts, including bowls, shields, and ivories.[43] In turn, a group of bronze jugs with lotus-shaped handles seems to have reached Crete in the tenth–ninth centuries, while only two were found outside Crete, at Lefkandi.[44] Whether genuinely Egyptian or Phoenician, it is thought that this group of jugs did not reach Crete directly from Egypt but through Levantine (or Euboian-Levantine) networks, as Jane Carter has shown.[45]

Other artifacts that made their way to the Aegean suggest origins in Syria or Cilicia: this is the case with the Neo-Hittite–style bronze relief reworked on bronze statues at Olympia in the earlier part of the seventh century; and the engraved bronze stands and oversized cauldrons on tripod stands, decorated with protruding heads of sirens, griffins, or snakes, soon imitated in local manufacture and found at several sites (e.g., Samos, Olympia, Delphi). In turn, the bronze tripods found at Olympia and other sanctuaries could have been manufactured anywhere in southern Greece, Italy, and the eastern Mediterranean. Plenty of dedicated metal objects belonged to the realm of personal attire, such as pins and *fibulae;* whether orientalizing in style or not, they circulated in contexts similar to those of the artifacts mentioned above and probably drew from the same metal sources.[46]

One of the most famous cases cited in this context is that of the three bronze pieces belonging to horse harness ornaments, found at sanctuaries on Samos and at Eretria in Euboia, associated respectively with the sanctuaries of Hera and Apollo: on Samos, the beautifully preserved frontlet is decorated with a relief of four Ashtart-type naked figures, one in the Mistress of Animals posture (standing on and holding lion heads), the other three holding their breasts, both Levantine themes that recur in terracottas, metal bowls, and other objects. The two pieces from Eretria are side blinkers, with a male figure in the Master of Animals position holding lions. The piece from Samos and one of the Euboian exemplars bear identical Aramaic inscriptions marking the objects as a gift to King Hazael of Damascus, one of the North Syrian Aramaean states, active in the late ninth century, and a similar bronze horse frontlet was found at the palace of Tell Tayinat (ninth century) in the Syrian-Cilician sphere (a third piece from Eretria is nearly identical but without an inscription).[47] The archaeological context at Eretria places the deposit of the piece in the second half of the eighth century, that is, almost a century after it was engraved with the name of the Syrian king, and the Samian piece was found in a sixth-century deposit.[48]

In either case, these dedications provide a glimpse of the long life of such objects and their unpredictable journeys, a destiny shared by ivories and other highly prized portable commodities. The destruction of Damascus around 733 BC by the Assyrians (Tiglath-Pileser III) may have led to the acquisition of the Syrian bronzes and ivories (as war spoils or tribute) by the Assyrian king, since ivories inscribed with Hazael's name have been found at Nimrud and Arslan-Tash. These may have been dispersed over time via exchange between Assyrians and Greek or Phoenician entrepreneurs, and when we find them they are objects that have long been out of circulation, and may have little to do with their original owners or with grand royal donations, whatever the artistic and symbolic value the Near Eastern iconography may have retained for the Greek dedicant.[49]

Some sites have produced extraordinary stashes of Near Eastern metal artifacts, and yet we still lack a full study of what this meant for Greek-Levantine relations. The most interesting case is that of the harbor sanctuary of Hera at Perachora. Situated scenically in the Gulf of Corinth (Map 6.1), this must have been an important stop for travelers from the Levant, Cyprus, and Crete aiming for the western Mediterranean. It is reported that over three-quarters of the metal finds excavated there are of predominantly Levantine origin.[50] These materials consist mostly of small, probably personal dedications, such as jewelry, and objects associated with ritual.[51] Unfortunately, the site's excavation and publication are rather outdated and these foreign materials are not fully studied with the question of Greek-Levantine relations in mind.[52]

The contrast is stark between the types of votives found at Perachora and the more monumental and lavish objects gifted to the gods at Delphi and Olympia, which were often sponsored by a community or given by Greek or foreign aristocrats or even kings. The deposits at Perachora seem the product of personal dedications by travelers concerned with private or commercial matters. There are other peculiarities at Perachora: the site, for instance, does not seem to channel Cretan metalwork, but it receives metal from Italy and the eastern Greek world, pointing to different networks than those that included Delphi (where Cretan metalwork is attributed to Cretans or to intermediaries of nearby Corinth).[53] Besides metal objects, the site has also produced about nine hundred Egyptian and Egyptian-style objects, more than any other mainland Greek site. These are scarabs, seals, and other amulets and figurines, impossible to trace to one point of origin but with parallels in other stashes of *Aigyptiaka* in Greece (e.g., the cave sanctuary of Eileithyia at Inatos on southern Crete). These sorts of portable objects align with the devotion to Egyptian deities associated with fertility, childbirth, and general life protection, hence appropriately dedicated to Hera at Perachora: these include Egyptian Isis, Nephthys, Sekhmet (also Bes and Horus), all of whom were popular among Phoenicians.[54]

Hera was worshipped at Perachora as Hera Limenia, "of the harbor," and Akraia "of the cape/headland," literally evoking the function and situation of the site. As already noted in Chapter 1, the importance of harbor sanctuaries as meeting points cannot be overstated, in particular of the cult of Hera, who was identified, like Aphrodite, with Ashtart and Isis in their roles as mother goddesses and maritime protectors. These places fostered mutual trust and commercial and cultural exchange. These artifacts may have arrived during a longer period of time, or we may be dealing with a deposit stemming from a few cargoes, as some have suggested.[55] What is clear is that the particular amalgam of western and eastern imports, combined with these Egyptian or Egyptianizing religious expressions, make the Phoenicians the main candidates for this particular concentration of imports.

The Heraion at Samos is better documented and more broadly discussed. This is also a site where Near Eastern metal objects concentrated in this period: about two-thirds of nonceramic finds there stem from Egypt, Cyprus, or Syria, according to Sarah Morris, although the site is known especially for its orientalizing ivories.[56] One of the above-mentioned equestrian ornaments comes from this sanctuary, as well as a bronze scepter (or mace head) of Assyrian type that circulated broadly from Iran to the eastern Aegean (Cyprus, Samos, Rhodes), often inscribed with its owner's name in Akkadian or Northwest Semitic languages.[57] Levantine artisanship also left a mark on Greek jewelry, especially goldwork. The rich burials at Geometric Lefkandi (Euboia) and Tekke (Crete) yielded some early Levantine imports, although we have relatively few.[58] More important than imports, however, was the Greek adoption of Levantine iconography and the techniques of granulation and filigree, typical of Phoenician gold and silver work, which was, as we saw, also introduced with the orientalizing kit in other regions studied here.[59]

The Wild and the Precious

Alongside metalwork, ivories constitute the most significant category of exotica and they followed similar routes and destinations. Regardless of chronological or stylistic subdivisions, ivories appear at nodal points where Phoenician and Greek networks intersected, especially sanctuaries and harbors. As in the case of metallic objects, imported ivories trickled into the Aegean already in the mid-ninth century BC and are found in the graves of rich individuals alongside gold objects and local Geometric pottery, as we see in graves from the Areopagos and Kerameikos in Attica.[60] Levantine or Levantine-style ivories in Greece appear more often in sanctuary contexts, from the large networking centers of Delphi and Olympia to the smaller sanctuaries at Perachora, Sparta, Rhodes, Samos, and Crete.[61] At the larger centers, ivories may have arrived in any number of ways and make up a small part of the dedications, increasing in the eighth century (the long list includes terracotta figurines, tripods, bronze cauldrons, pins, stone statues, and armor pieces). At the smaller sanctuaries, however, the impressive quantities of small ivories advocate for production in situ. Such might be the case at Perachora and Samos.

Local production probably also explains the abundance of orientalizing ivory and bone work at the sanctuary of Artemis Ortheia in Sparta, including ivory plaques, combs, seals, and small protomes, which perhaps decorated parts of wooden boxes or furniture, all deposited during the seventh to sixth centuries.[62] The earliest ivory work found in Sparta has, since its discovery, been connected with Phoenician artisanship.[63] It is significant that they appear in the same space and at the same time as the peculiar terracotta masks discussed below. In turn, the presence of unfinished pieces often made of bone, indicates in situ manufacture (more accessible bone replaced ivory when the supply became difficult in the sixth century). There is good reason, therefore, to suppose the presence of a Levantine workshop in or around the sanctuary and the development of "a strong and long-lived genuinely local school."[64]

Ivories in Levantine style have also been found on Crete. The Idaean Cave provides the largest single assemblage in the Aegean, dating to the mid-eighth century. A good number appear also in burials at various sites, among them the usual suspects for Semitic presence, Knossos and Eleutherna.[65] Note that there is an overlap with the contexts in which we found the metal bowls, in the Idaean Cave and at nearby Eleutherna, where a workshop for Levantine metalwork and other crafts is suggested as well by Phoenician burial practices. The bowls and ivories also appear together in funerary contexts in Italy, for instance, the Bernardini Tomb at Praeneste.[66] At a place such as the Samian Heraion, in turn, ivory is accompanied by other "wildlife" exotic dedications, such as ostrich eggs, hippopotamus teeth, antelope horns, crocodile skulls, and other raw materials that were probably brought there to make ivory/bone votives (except for the eggs).[67] Stylistically speaking, ivories found in the Aegean are tentatively subclassified variously with the Phoenician and North Syrian styles or their local imitations.[68] It is likely that these and other types of artifacts that often appear together with ivories circulated in the Aegean mostly through Greco-Phoenician interaction.

An emblematic case of "Levantine exotica" is represented in the delicately engraved tridacna shells. These shells were extracted from the Red Sea *tridacna squamosa* mollusks, although they can also be found in the Persian Gulf and Indian Ocean. Their carved versions were distributed to Cyrene, Egypt, Mesopotamia, Syria, and the Southern Levant, in addition to the Aegean and, less so, Etruria (judging by one specimen found at Vulci). The large shells were engraved and their thickest part (umbo) often sculpted with a human face. They were probably containers for eye cosmetics (kohl), a use attested in antiquity and supported by the fact that the central concave space is left undecorated. These decorated shells came into fashion in the seventh and early sixth centuries, and in the Greek world they appear especially in the eastern Aegean and on the mainland in key centers and harbors, such as Delphi, Olympia, Perachora, and Aegina.[69]

As for their manufacture, according to Markoe, these decorated shells can be "most reasonably assigned to the south Phoenician artistic sphere."[70] Marian Feldman has problematized the ascription of these sculpted shells to Phoenician workshops, on the ground that we lack finds from the Phoenician mainland, and the features of the female faces resemble those on North Syrian ivories and bronzes. At the same time, unfinished pieces and similar features on alabaster grinders and cosmetic palettes from southern inland Palestine and Transjordan point to a possible production in that area.[71] As Annie Caubet points out, however, we also find parallels in the west: for instance, the Vulci *tridacna* shell is probably a local version of Levantine models (by a Greek artisan?), while the facial features carved on the shells closely resemble those of Ashtart in the alabaster *rhyton* from Galera (Granada, Spain) (Figure 6.6).[72] This fine artifact (with Ashtart sitting on a sphinx throne) was produced in a context of local–Phoenician interaction, and is considered by Eric Gubel an "heirloom from the final apogee of Phoenician handicraft."[73] Wherever the shells were carved, the route of these materials from the Red Sea, through the southern Levant, and on to their far-reaching distribution abroad, rather suggests Phoenician involvement, and perhaps a center along the southern Phoenician coast "remains the best guess," as Markoe said.[74]

Ostrich eggs were cherished and traded in the eastern Mediterranean since prehistoric times (for thousands of years in Egypt, Libya, and the Levant), but the circulation of eggs decorated in a Levantine style starts in the eighth century and is seen as a trend "ushered in under Phoenician initiative."[75] Decorated ostrich eggs were, like ivory, made of a raw material that was difficult and dangerous to procure in Africa or Central Asia.[76] In the Aegean they appear in the eighth–seventh centuries in the Cyclades (e.g., Thera, Paros) as well as at the Heraion of Samos and on Cyprus, sometimes in graves but more often in votive contexts.[77] Elsewhere, as we have seen, they appear mostly in funerary contexts (though this might be a result of what has been excavated). In Etruria they are found especially in female "princely" tombs. Best known are the five examples found in the so-called Isis Tomb at Vulci (dated ca. 625–550 BC), now in the British Museum and recently studied for decoration technique and isotope composition (Figure 5.4).[78] But we need to look at the Phoenician-Punic realm to find the use of ostrich eggs as a frequent grave good: they appear at Carthage and Punic North Africa, as well as in the Phoenician-Punic sphere of Iberia, including on Ibiza and in southern Portugal (e.g., Ibiza, Villaricos, Alcácer do Sal).[79] As for the decoration, after a very long process of drying the shell, its surface was either incised or painted in one or more colors; the horizontal bands were combined with vertical friezes of geometric decoration, and framed figurative motifs: the most frequent were plants, such as lotuses, birds and, in the Punic realm, versions of the sign of Tanit.[80]

The eggs' decoration and their appearance in graves along with other religiously charged objects such as scarabs and amulets, throughout the areas of Phoenician diaspora, leave no doubt of their symbolic significance within Phoenician mortuary culture, where themes of life and regeneration are constants.[81] We may surmise that the local cultures that adopted them had some understanding of this dimension. Even as decorated eggs faded out of use in the eastern Mediterranean, their popularity abided in the western Mediterranean during the Punic period, and regional styles of decoration continued to develop. Within these variations, however, the symbolic repertoire maintained a certain coherence, and the style and techniques used (incision) coincide with those of ivories found in Iberia. Raw materials for both industries were channeled through those areas of Phoenicians settlement from North Africa, and it is likely that a center of production remained active in southern Iberia.[82] This crossover between the ivory and eggshell industries deserves further study. The question for now is, what is the likelihood that any other group of Levantine artisans could have taken the leading role in the chain of acquisition, artisan work, and pan-Mediterranean distribution of such exotic artifacts?

Other Portable Items

In the eighth–seventh centuries BC, a broad repertoire of *orientalia* or exotica could be found in Aegean markets, objects similar to what we saw in southern Italy and Iberia, including scarabs, glass pieces, and faience vessels, in addition to the jewelry, ivories, and other items discussed above. As with jewelry, there were occasional earlier finds, for example, in the Lefkandi graves, triggering vague classifications such as "amulet-type ornaments of Syrian and Egyptian style."[83] When they appear more frequently in eighth- to seventh-century contexts, however, they are often framed in terms of Homer's "wonders" and "knickknacks," translating Homer's *daidala* and *athyrmata*. The term is applied by archaeologists to this sort of materials in other areas, especially Etruria, as I discussed in Chapter 5.[84] These small objects may come from diverse areas, from Egypt and Syria to the Dodecanese or Cyprus; their precise origins are difficult to pin down and disentangling Phoenician, Egyptianizing, and Egyptian categories is not always possible.[85] But, once again, the type of assemblages and the networks through which they circulated put them squarely within the Phoenician web, and even the typologies and styles can hardly be disassociated from Phoenician art, as the following will illustrate.

Take faience and glass objects. These were staples of Phoenician production and distribution, part of an industry cultivated in Phoenicia and Egypt since the Bronze Age. Both faience and glass are vitreous pastes made from quartz sand and various combinations of other minerals, but the processes, mixtures, and finished products vary. Faience, for instance, is made of a blue-green paste with a shiny glaze. In the Late Bronze Age, Tyre was a major center of production, as we know from archaeological traces and from the mention in one of the Amarna Letters of a large shipment of raw glass sent to Egypt from Tyre.[86]

Incised faience vessels circulated in Greece, especially small flasks used for perfumed oil, such as pyxides and alabastra, whether with low relief decoration of animals or floral motifs, or in the shape of anthropomorphic perfume flasks. Their decoration fits within the styles rehearsed in ivory and metalwork of this period, discussed above, and their distribution maps onto those other luxury items as well.[87] As for glass vases, beads, and gems, despite the frustrating lack of archaeologically controlled finds from Phoenicia, their style and technique, pattern of distribution, and association with other Levantine imports strongly point to Phoenician networks, perhaps including centers of production among Greek communities. For instance, seventh-century glass juglets and alabastra may have stemmed from a workshop on Rhodes, which found a special market among Etruscan elites, as Markoe suggests also for faience vessels.[88]

Glass beads used in jewelry, on the other hand, are widely distributed in Greece, especially in the shape of Egyptianizing scaraboids in blue and green glass.[89] A more rare and valuable finding is a type of glass bowl made of thick transparent or green glass, which appears rarely, again at Eleutherna and Fortetsa (Crete) and at Ialysos (Rhodes).[90] These circulated in Assyrian markets, as they mostly appear at Nimrud (some also at Gordion in Anatolia). In form, if not material, these glass bowls are most similar to the decorated metal bowls and the fluted bowls discussed above, and sometimes these two types of bowls appear together (e.g., at Fortetsa and Praeneste). While opaque glass paste and faience imitated precious stones such as agate, lapis lazuli, and turquoise, transparent glass imitated rock crystal and was an innovation of the ninth–eighth centuries attributed tentatively to Phoenicians working in Assyria.[91]

In an important subcategory are the abundant Egyptian-style scarabs and scaraboids, sometimes mounted on rings, which Phoenicians used to seal documents (normally papyri rolls), a practice that is also documented by bullae with seal impressions. Scarabs and "scaraboids" (i.e., those with plainer backs and simplified shapes) were also widely used as amulets.[92]

These small objects were made of faience and other materials (steatite, hard stones, soft stones, glass paste), and the role of Tyrian workshops seems essential in their diffusion.[93] Their distribution starts in the mid-eighth century, when they are scattered through southern Iberia, Etruria, southern Italy, Sicily, Greece, and Cyprus. Despite superficial appearances, these scarab seals and scaraboids are not "Egyptian," but a perfect example of the Phoenician synthesis of Canaanite and Egyptian aesthetics and symbolism, which finds no exact parallel in Egyptian glyptic. The Phoenician scarab seals show a preference for symbols of regeneration, such as the birth of Horus from a lotus flower, Isis nursing Horus, or the suckling calf that evokes the same theme, as well as other Phoenician motifs frequent on ivories and metal bowls, for instance, winged deities and genies, sphinxes/griffins, falcons, and palmettes.[94] Scarab seals are sometimes marked by their owners (not necessarily their first owners) in Northwest Semitic languages, usually Phoenician, sometimes Aramaic, which speaks to their distribution in the Levant following Phoenician trade and cultural influence.[95]

In Greece, scarabs and scaraboids appear on Crete, Rhodes, and other islands, and some sites of the mainland. Over seven hundred scarabs were found at Perachora alone, only eleven of them made of steatite (the most common Egyptian material for scarabs) and the rest of glazed paste or faience, the material used by Phoenicians. The publication of these as part of "Egyptian-style objects" occludes their Phoenician affiliation.[96] The excavator at Perachora already corrected earlier misclassifications of Egyptian-style scarabs found in Greece, pointing out that these were not really Egyptian artifacts, nor should they be dated by Egyptian comparisons, but by the archaeological context in which they were found, namely, between 750 and 650. These comparisons need to involve not only similar types found at Naukratis (where Phoenicians and Greeks resided) but also scarabs/seals that appear in Carthaginian graves until the fifth century BC, as they pointed out, as well as throughout the Phoenician-Punic realm (e.g., Figure 6.6).[97]

A peculiar type that became extremely popular among Aegean and Etruscan communities are the so-called lyre-player seals, characterized by their schematic representation of lyre-playing figures alongside birds and other motifs. In contrast to the ones discussed above, these scaraboid seals do not appear in the western Phoenician realm, and their links to Euboian trade are evident by their appearance in great numbers at

Pithekoussai-Cumae. Moreover, they overlap with the distribution of Euboian pendant-semicircle *skyphoi* and plates, the same types that appear in the Levant, for instance at Al-Mina and Cilicia. The current consensus is that this specific type of seal may have come out of North Syria-Cilicia and spread through Euboian channels.[98] By contrast, cylinder seals are less frequent in the Aegean, and make it only to the international sanctuaries of Olympia, Samos, and Delos. Cylinder seals were used in the Mesopotamian world to mark clay tablets, and not used by Phoenicians since the start of the first millennium, when they turned to writing in their own alphabetic script on papyrus scrolls.[99]

As with other crafts discussed above, the affiliation of these objects with Phoenician culture is evident in their continued production in the Punic realm beyond the orientalizing "period," even as they undergo regional adaptations. At the same time, it is not easy to identify their point of departure. It is in the nature of seals and gems to be especially mobile, accompanying individuals along with jewelry and amulets; they could be used over a long period of time before being deposited where we find them. This mobility may also explain the complex artistic trajectories of this evolving corpus, with influences coming from all sorts of directions.[100] As Boardman notes, the initial Egyptianizing patterns were, over time, inflected by Cypriot, Euboian, Persian, Greek, and Etruscan nuances.[101] For instance, the seals produced in fifth-century Tharros (Sardinia) show influences of Etruscan and western Greek art.[102] At the same time, since seals are attested all over the Mediterranean realm, they serve as markers or footprints of Phoenician-Punic activity.[103] Again, this is also shown by clay bullae bearing their impressions, recovered from the Phoenician-Punic west, such as at Gadir and Carthage, and in the Levant during the Persian and Hellenistic periods.[104]

Given the abundance of these objects in the Aegean, Markoe suggests that Rhodes, Aegina, Samos, or Crete might have hosted centers of secondary production and distribution of Levantine exotica such as the scarab seals.[105] Rhodes and Crete seem indeed to have been key stepping-stones on two frequented sea routes from the Levant and Cyprus. One of these routes took sailors via Rhodes and perhaps Samos to the Cyclades and from there to the southeast Peloponnese and the Saronic Gulf (Aegina, Attica); the other route went via Crete to the south and western Peloponnese, leading to Lakonia, Elis/Olympia, and around the peninsula to Delphi and the Corinthian

Gulf (where Perachora is).[106] This lower route is represented by Archaic poets when they imagine Phoenician and Cretan sailors approaching Greece, such as in the *Homeric Hymn to Apollo* and in the *Odyssey*.[107] In short, the seemingly "Egyptianizing" seals that we find in the broader Mediterranean are inseparable from Phoenician culture and its networks, whether the source was in the Levant itself or secondary hubs in places such as Rhodes or Cyprus.

Terracotta Votive Offerings

Greek terracottas receive less attention than the flashier materials discussed above and are rarely treated systematically outside regional studies.[108] Terracottas are, however, perhaps as central for the study of Greek-Phoenician relations. The production of terracotta female figurines and plaques becomes widespread in Greece in the seventh century, with Corinth and Crete as the most important conduits. On Crete, Daedalic-style plaques appear already in the eighth century, marking the beginning of an orientalizing style and technology distinct from the general Greek production of terracottas attested there and in other areas, which continues Geometric traditions (e.g., Olympia, Athens, Samos, and probably Rhodes). The orientalizing style of terracottas, their iconography (all female figures), and method of manufacture by mold suggest a relationship with the Levant, and Syrian or Phoenician referents are often considered, if the exact points or modes of transmission remain elusive.[109] What we know is that the mold-made terracotta figure follows a Levantine type and technique, and, furthermore, that these types of terracotta figures were used profusely by Phoenicians as an important medium of popular religious expression.[110] This is well attested during the entire first millennium not only on the mainland (where Sidon and Tyre were probably production centers) but also on Cyprus and throughout the Punic west, with local inflections. Phoenician-Punic terracottas appear not only in votive contexts but also in domestic and funerary deposits. They represent divinities, miniature shrines, and a variety of ritual scenes, including worshippers and music players.[111]

Greek artisans brought to this material Levantine motifs similar to those found in orientalizing media: most common are sphinxes, the Mistress of Animals theme (sometimes a masculine "nature demon"), and the standing naked goddess, typically holding her breast, which inspired a variety

FIG. 6.1 Terracotta plaque of "Astarte-type" from Corinth.

Plaque made from Syrian mold, with the motif of the naked goddess holding her breasts, found in Corinth, seventh century BC.   Davidson 1952, *Corinth XII*, no. 85, MF-4039, bw-8331. Courtesy of the American School of Classical Studies at Athens, Corinth Excavations.

of versions, including dressed and in different arm positions as well as seated. These are the so-called Astarte plaques or figurines, which appear at Corinth and Perachora and other areas (e.g., Paestum in central Italy) in locally made and imported versions (Figure 6.1). The success of these terracotta female figures illustrates the applicability of Levantine iconography to the domains of Greek goddesses, especially Aphrodite, Hera, and

Demeter.[112] It is generally assumed that the use of molds (and later stamps) was learned from Levantine coroplasts, while the iconography suggests that molds were also made out of ivories or other sculptural work, such as wooden artifacts.[113] In turn, as Susan Langdon makes clear, Greek artifacts acquired a strongly local flavor, as they combined molded products and manual modeling: this allowed them to introduce details or modify the figure after it came out of the mold and experiment with attachments, for instance, adding mold-made lion heads to small vases (e.g., *aryballoi, kalathoi*). In other words, whether initially imported or modeled on Levantine artifacts, a single mold could be the base for an entire series of local figurines, making it more difficult to reconstruct the Near Eastern models beyond ballpark affinities.

Terracotta figures appear mainly at sanctuaries, such as that of Demeter at Akrocorinth, or of Hera at Perachora, in addition to some manufacturing areas, such as the Potters' Quarter at Corinth, but not in domestic or funerary contexts. Langdon, therefore, proposes that these female figurines were initially made for specific cults of these goddesses, which might also explain the older tradition of dedicating jewelry and *fibulae* at these same sites, and the fact that the terracotta figurines there are often represented wearing jewelry.[114] Perhaps wooden figures and clothing were part of this votive landscape as well, which has been suggested for Phoenician votive sculpture.[115] As Langdon puts it, "innovation rarely takes place as an isolated event. In the case of terracotta figurines at Corinth, it would have involved not just the technology of molds but the very notion of figurine use."[116] As mentioned above, these types of *terracottae* appear also in the Potters' Quarter at Corinth. It is here where Punic amphorae from the fifth-century have been found, especially at the so-called Punic Amphora House. Study of these amphorae suggests that they were exported from Gadir and Málaga and especially related to salted fish production, pointing indeed to Phoenician-Punic networks.[117] These data, even if later, add weight to the argument that Phoenician artisans and traders may have not only passed through but "set up shop" in Corinth since earlier on, potentially introducing other crafts, such as the terracottas. This possibility challenges the assumption that foreign pots were carried by Greeks.[118]

Finally, there is a particularly puzzling corpus of terracotta work that provides a direct connection with the Phoenician world: the terracotta masks deposited at the sanctuary of Artemis Ortheia in Sparta. These masks were made and deposited over the course of the seventh and sixth centuries, and exist in different types, mainly falling into the categories of youthlike faces and wrinkled or grimacing faces. Several scholars have proposed they were used for some sorts of ritual impersonation (perhaps in coming-of-age rituals), or possibly in ceremonies similar to those alluded to in various Near Eastern texts. Their material, shape, and size, and the fact that they seemed to have been hung on walls make this idea problematic, unless they were votive, clay versions of wearable masks made of linen or wood.[119]

As many have pointed out, the masks find their only parallels in the Phoenician-Punic world. The use of terracotta masks by Phoenicians spans a thousand years, from the Early Iron Age until the second century BC, and from the Phoenician mainland and the broader Levant to Cyprus and the western Mediterranean, with regional variants at Carthage, Ibiza, the Málaga coast, and Malta. The Phoenician-Punic masks included female types and appear consistently in funerary contexts, although Canaanite precedents in the Levant were found in ritual contexts. This perhaps suggests a primary ritual use before they were placed in graves. The Greek wrinkled masks, in turn, have been associated with terracotta representations of the face of Humbaba, the above-mentioned Mesopotamian monster, whose grimacing face became a protective symbol in the Levant, and whose iconography probably lies behind the appearance of the Greek Gorgon in the early seventh century. Some think that a missing link between Humbaba amulets and the Gorgon is provided by a group of terracotta plaques found in the Archaic sanctuary at Gortyn's acropolis on Crete.[120]

There are two other interesting aspects to the Spartan masks. First, they appear in tandem with a stash of ivory work spanning the same chronological range and with a similar history: both are used as votive objects, and both types of craft start off closely following Phoenician models, then gradually morph into local variants (the existence of a local ivory workshop was signaled by the appearance of unfinished pieces; see above). It is possible that, like the ivories, the terracotta masks also started as a specific Greek adaptation of Phoenician models at local workshops. We should add Sparta, then, to the list of Archaic-period locations where Phoenician artisans were hosted within or in the periphery of Greek communities.[121] Second, their final deposit as sanctuary votives contrasts with the general funerary use of the Phoenician-Punic masks, which reminds us of the different religious universes to which the Spartan adaptations and their models belonged.

Greek Pottery: A New Outlook

Decorated pottery provided a perfect platform for innovation and experimentation. For centuries, Geometric patterns were the norm in Greek vase painting, departing from the earlier taste of Mycenaean and Minoan decoration for vegetal, animal, and human motifs. Only in the early eighth century did artists regularly introduce animal figures, with schematic human scenes following in the Late Geometric phase (ca. 750–700 BC). Before orientalizing vase-painting proper, however, some Geometric-style motifs show a degree of experimentation with Near Eastern models.[122] For instance, the representation of musicians holding rattles and lyres seems inspired by the banquet scenes on Levantine metal bowls and by the lyre-player seals discussed above, signaling the social importance of musical and poetic performance and banqueting in the emerging Greek polities.[123]

By 700 BC, the type of decoration we label "orientalizing" becomes widespread. This style intentionally and systematically adapts themes and techniques drawn from Near Eastern artwork, including ivories, metalwork, and even textiles that had been circulating in the Aegean since the eighth century or earlier. In particular, vase decoration took from metalwork the technique of incising details into the drawn silhouettes, "giving rise to the black figure painting technique, a Greek pottery invention to answer eastern incising in other media."[124] Not surprisingly, this adaptation appears first on Crete, already in the mid-ninth century (Cretan Protogeometric B style), when it is believed that a school of Levantine metalworkers was already active on the island. Following a trajectory similar to the one we saw in the terracottas, it was at Corinth where the orientalizing style that became most widespread appeared around 720 BC, whence it spread to the rest of Greece in the next fifty years.[125] This is known as the Proto-Corinthian style, which inspired the subsequent Proto-Attic style, and other regional variants. Proto-Corinthian wares were widely exported to east and west.[126] This made Corinth again the innovator on the Greek mainland and a nodal point between Crete, the Levant, and the western Mediterranean (Figure 6.2).[127]

FIG. 6.2 **Proto-Corinthian jug with orientalizing motifs.**

Oil jug (*olpe*), with incised and painted decoration, featuring animals, sphinxes, and rosettes, dated to ca. 620 BC. Staatliche Antikensammlungen, München / Bibi Saint-Pol / Wikimedia Commons.

Focusing on vase shapes, Nicolas Coldstream considers exposure to Phoenician art outside of the typical luxury imports as "comparatively slight."[128] On the other hand, a few vase types that became popular on the Aegean islands did have Levantine models, perhaps from the Phoenician sphere on Cyprus: usually cited as exemplifying this connection are the so-called Cypro-Phoenician Red Burnished ware and Black-on-Red ware *lekythoi* (imitated on Crete), but also the Proto-Corinthian *aryballoi* with a wide flat lip (or discoid lip) and the sack-shaped *olpe* (a type of jug/pitcher, Figure 6.2) and similar-shaped alabastra.[129] The perfume containers (*aryballoi*) were the first to be decorated in the new orientalizing style, which intentionally marked them as proper conveyors of a Near Eastern product and promoted their use.[130]

Besides initiating decoration-by-incision, Proto-Corinthian wares also adapted decorative patterns and motifs from metalwork: orientalizing Greek vases are decorated in concentric circles, forming friezes with repeated figures of animals, hybrid creatures, and vegetal motifs such as trees of life, rosettes, and palmettes; they also share with the bowls the interlaced cable (guilloche) decoration, the *potnia theron* motif, processions of worshippers and dancers, and hunting scenes. Markoe points to specific "smoking guns" for Phoenician or at least Levantine influence already in Late Geometric designs: the decorative format in Attic Late Geometric bowls mirrors that of the engraved metal bowls, with the continuous figurative frieze arranged in concentric registers around a central medallion; the specific motif and stylization of the "bull passant" is typical of Phoenician bowls, and some are found in Greece, for instance, in Olympia; the votive-procession theme finds detailed parallels in the "votive-procession [Phoenician] *paterae*," which include the pair of confronted sphinxes, the branch held in the upraised hand of the enthroned deity, who in the Levantine models holds a lotus flower, and other parallels (cf. some of these in Figure 3.2).[131]

Greek adaptations, in turn, are far from formulaic and are almost never exact copies of Levantine models. Orientalizing styles and productions are also fiercely regional and particular in their transitions from previous to later styles.[132] For instance, Anastasia Gadolou stresses the "original, unique" style of Geometric and orientalizing-period pottery from the Argolid, in which "no Near Eastern elements can be discerned."[133] On the other hand, early figurative pottery in the Argolid is poorly attested, and others like Boardman still noted the orientalizing imprint even there.[134] In the case of Corinth, the emergence of its own orientalizing style and its huge marketing success is inseparable from the city's political-economic trajectory, marked both by competition with neighboring Greek polities and by its relations with the Near East, as well as its strong bonds with the colonial world of southern Italy and Sicily, as Angela Ziskowski points out.[135]

The variety and originality of Greek regional styles, then, might give the impression that "what we call the 'Orientalizing revolution' in Greek art was nothing more than a short phase during which certain pottery workshops adopted particular motifs or artistic expressions to suit their own needs."[136] But their encounter with the east is also part of those trajectories; downplaying it only limits our insight into the complexities of Greek cultural transformation at this time. As Gadolou also remarks, in pottery we are not talking about a "revolution" but a stylistic change "brought about mainly by the human interactions that followed the sociopolitical and economic characteristics of the new era."[137] Indeed, we cannot narrow this phenomenon as a purely artistic process, or frame it as the result of some sort of stylistic inevitability triggered by the exhaustion of the Geometric style, just when available *orientalia* provided a fresh sources of inspiration.[138] While undeniably and unapologetically taking on Near Eastern inspiration, Greek orientalizing pottery was a platform for idiosyncratic, local expressions of the broader international koine.

Here are some interesting idiosyncrasies of this adaptation: with the exception of Crete, it took Greek artisans about a century of exposure to richly iconographic portable objects (metals, ivories, textiles) to appropriate these motifs, whether in pottery or other media. Whitley suggests that the aristocratic nature of these objects made the Greeks shy away from using them as models for the humble medium of pottery.[139] But perhaps we look at it the other way around: social conditions in the emerging poleis of the seventh century allowed the international style to become accessible to a much larger portion of the population, once artisans found the formula to convey the orientalizing style through the much more affordable and popular vehicle of clay. As Brisart proposed for the Greek poleis' utilization of the orientalizing koine, we are looking at the adaptation of a "style magnifique" inseparable from the adoption of social practices of Near Eastern cachet, especially banqueting and the use of oil perfume; but the clay perfume containers and the scented oils they carried were part of a

Near Eastern industry that had just become more broadly available and popularized.[140] And something similar can be said about the use of bronze for decorated bowls and shields in Greece, instead of the less affordable silver and gilded silver material privileged by Cypriot and Etruscan royalty or aristocracy.[141] At the same time, Greek artists soon developed a taste for complex decorative, even narrative scenes, in which they departed from the traditions of Levantine and Cypriot vase decoration, whose preference had been, by and large, Geometric and aniconic, or more austerely iconic.

From Wooden to Stone Temples

Greek sanctuaries and temple architecture evolved over centuries, and our understanding of this process is all but clear or unanimous.[142] The main point for our purposes is that "the invention of the Greek temple *does not represent a drastic change in the cult practice, but rather a decision to monumentalize,*" as Nanno Marinatos emphasizes.[143] The shift happened during the course of the Archaic period, first with wooden structures, adding clay entablatures and adornments, and finally with stone buildings, although the initial trajectories that led to the Archaic-classical Doric and Ionic orders are uncertain.[144] What we know is that their available referents were at this point limited to the temple complexes of the Near East. The relationship between Greek and Near Eastern temples, however, is as evident on the surface as it is opaque when it comes to the details. It is agreed that the Greeks were generally "inspired by the monumental stone buildings and masonry practices of the Levant and Egypt," the same inspiration assumed to lie behind the appearance of stone statues.[145] Beyond this, it is difficult to trace the *when, where, who,* and *how* of the relationship.

Upon closer inspection, even the central idea of Egyptian influence becomes hazy. For instance, the technology of the ramp and lever was shared by other Mediterranean cultures that manipulated large stone blocks, including the Mycenaean Greeks, and was not necessarily an Egyptian import; the specific techniques or measures of Greek temples are not Egyptian either, and the same can be said of the main features of the Doric, Ionic, or later Corinthian orders.[146] As Elizabeth Gebhard notes regarding the earliest stone temples at Corinth and Isthmia, with their tiled roofs and "single-skin" walls (i.e., with one course of stones), "Egyptian techniques for quarrying and dressing blocks were widely known and could have been learned from a number of places."[147] Columns or pillars with simple capitals similar to the Doric ones were used in Minoan and Mycenaean architecture, especially in palaces, tombs, and city gates (e.g., the Tomb of Atreus and the Lion Gate at Mycenae).[148] Furthermore, some of the earliest examples of Doric capitals emerged in the Argolid area, pointing to a reformulation of this Mycenaean element by archaic-period architects.[149] In turn, throughout the Geometric period, long buildings of communal and possibly ritual use, of the type best attested by the "Heroon" at Lefkandi, were surrounded by external posts, that is, had a "peristyle" layout, while early shrines were adorned by two frontal columns (*in antis*), as we see in a terracotta models (e.g., from Perachora). These features were later extended to the wooden and stone structures of the larger temples.[150] Finally, the idea of terracotta roof tiles on a sloped roof is clearly a local innovation with no parallel in the Near East.[151]

When pushed to find more specific points of contact, the settlement of Greeks at Naukratis in the mid-sixth century is mentioned as a possible scenario behind the Egyptian stimulus.[152] The Corinthians, however, had already built Doric stone temples by the first half of the seventh century.[153] Therefore, the sixth-century settlement in Egypt cannot have been the impetus behind stone temple-building in general.[154] Perhaps the key lies not so much in stylistic analysis but in contextual and sociocultural clues. Building on the idea of the transfer from wood construction techniques and forms to the stone medium, already posited by Vitruvius, and emphasizing the role of Corinth as an innovator in shipbuilding technology, David Scahill proposes that the same innovations that allowed the manufacture of larger ship hulls also enabled the larger wooden structures of monumental building in which stone elements were eventually incorporated.[155] After all, Scahill notes, at this time "only shipbuilding rivals monumental building projects such as temples."[156] The new technology of mortise-and-tenon jointing, he argues, played a crucial role in large-scale carpentry projects. In other words, it was not exposure to Levantine or Near Eastern architecture in stone (which they had been exposed to since at least the eighth century), but the mastering of woodwork that gave Corinthians the "know-how" to step up their building structures, to which they also applied the limestone masonry skills they had already rehearsed during the Geometric period.[157]

Very few places in Greece would have had the capacity that Corinth had to provide the infrastructure for such projects, which involved entire teams of architects, engineers, and specialized masons, themselves trained in other crafts such as carpentry and metalwork or accompanied by other such specialists. Rather than workshops we are talking about traveling teams hired for large projects across towns, as documented from later periods. This context might also explain the role of Corinth in extending the use of the Doric order throughout its networks in mainland Greece and the colonies.[158] If Scahill's connection between shipbuilding and large wooden architecture is correct, we cannot but postulate a Phoenician involvement: not only was the technology of mortise-and-tenon jointing generally attributed to Phoenician shipbuilders (the Romans even called it *coagmenta punicana*), but their expertise in wood and masonry architecture was recognized in the Near East (Chapter 9). Once again, Corinth may have been the arena for some of the most successful Levantine adaptations.

Returning to the main architectonic orders: unlike the Doric columns, Ionic capitals have no Mycenaean precursors, and are an eastern Aegean innovation. The earliest known monumental Ionic temples are the Archaic iteration of the Samian Heraion, around 570 BC (the hundred-foot-long *hekatompedon*), and the roughly contemporary Artemision at Ephesos. But as early as the seventh century, Ionic capitals appear in the Cyclades, first as self-standing votive offerings in the form of small-scale stands, probably made of stone from the start.[159] Standing over ten meters tall, the votive column with a sphinx dedicated by the Naxians at Delphi (Figure 6.3) follows in this tradition at a grander scale. The volute capital was a flexible type for some time, which explains the coexistence of the "Aeolic" capital, in which the volutes spring upward before curling down, with a central floral element between the volutes, and the type that becomes the standardized "Ionic" capital, in which the volutes are flattened, probably so that they can support a heavier entablature, and hence curved downward (cf. Figures 6.3 and 9.2).[160] The Aeolic type appears in west and northwest Asia Minor, that is, in Aeolia (e.g., Lesbos, Neandreia) and Ionia (e.g., Smyrna). It is clear that both Ionic and Aeolic types are relatives and have precedents in the Near Eastern volute capital, although their specific story of adaptation and symbolic connotations remain elusive.[161] For the Aeolic and Ionic capital, these can be found in "the eclectic arts of Phoenician

FIG. 6.3   **Stone column and sphinx dedicated by the Naxians at Delphi.**
Colossal sphinx (2.2 m) on Ionic style column (only the top preserved, est. 12.5 m original height including sphinx), made in marble from Naxos and dedicated ca. 560 BC. Delphi Archaeological Museum. iStock.com/mofles.

Syria," which in turn traveled east to Assyria.[162] As I discuss in Chapter 9, The "Proto-Aeolic" or volute capital is best attested in stone at sites from Israel (Figure 9.2), but this capital was a feature of Phoenician and Cypriot architecture of the eighth–seventh centuries, and appears throughout the Phoenician colonies and areas of interaction in all sorts of media (e.g., Figures 5.3 and 8.2). Even Syro-Palestinian archaeologists, however, have retained the label "Proto-Aeolic" for this Near Eastern capital, a forced classification that, oddly enough, makes the later Greek order the point of reference for the earlier Levantine capital.

Why the insistence on Egyptian models, then, for early Greek temple architecture? Because they are still standing and remain so impressive (they were already admired by the ancient travelers), it is difficult to see past Egyptian monuments and look elsewhere for comparison. But Greeks encountered Near Eastern stone architecture outside Egypt. Stone temples were built in Early Iron Age Syria, Phoenicia, Cyprus, and Israel, continuing Bronze Age prototypes. Although physical remains from the Early Iron Age are hard to come by in the Phoenician mainland, architectural remains from the broader Levant and the colonies offer a good point of reference (see below), and ancient sources vouch for the Phoenicians' skill as builders, with their temples in Tyre and other places attaining wide recognition in antiquity.[163] The Hebrew Bible most famously acclaims the Phoenicians as skilled timber merchants, masons, architects, and bronze workers in the account of the building of the palace and temple of Solomon in the tenth century. When it came to endowing his capital with a great temple, Solomon's eyes turned to Tyre, a short 167 kilometers to the north: "So Solomon's builders and Hiram's builders and the Gebalites [i.e., men from Byblos] did the stonecutting and prepared the timber and the stone to build the house."[164] The description of that temple conforms to older Canaanite patterns attested in the region.[165] But even if this were a projection of later traditions, the reputation of Phoenicians as experienced builders stands.

Masonry techniques deployed in the Canaanite-Phoenician sites were smaller in scale than the Egyptian ones, and closer to the Greek proportions, as attested in different periods, for instance, at Ugarit and Sarepta.[166] By the eighth century Phoenicians settlers had built stone temples and monumentalized sacred spaces in key harbors around the Mediterranean, from Cyprus to Sicily and in southern Spain.[167] Of course, written sources and archaeology rarely corroborate each other, and early archaeological remains from this period appear mainly in the Phoenician settlements abroad, but they match what we see in the Phoenician homeland in the better-preserved Persian-period remains, such as at Amrit and Bustan esh-Sheikh near Sidon. These religious complexes were conceptually akin to Greek sanctuaries: they included porticoes, sacred groves, pools, and springs or wells, terraced constructions, stelae, and small shrines (*naiskoi*). They did not follow a single pattern, but included various quadrangular shapes and internal partitions, which archaeologists describe in classical terms as *cella, adyton,* and so forth, and their entrances were marked by semi-columns or pillars topped by the above-mentioned "Proto-Aeolic" capitals. The more familiar layout was a long space divided into three wings by internal colonnades and an inner partition two-thirds of the way. The Solomonic temple responded to this type, which in turn was rooted in the Canaanite temple culture of Bronze Age Syria-Palestine. Besides the temple buildings themselves, the Phoenicians typically incorporated altars, obelisks, stelae, small shrines, betyls, and votive offerings into a well-demarcated sacred space, a concept we are familiar with from the Greek *temenos*. Sacred pools were sometimes also part of these spaces, for instance, in the Ashtart complex at Kition (cf. also at Bustan esh-Sheikh sanctuary by Sidon).[168] As a western example, the area articulated around the Kothon (pool collecting fresh water from a spring) and encircled by a *temenos* wall at Motya constitutes one of the largest Phoenician religious complexes excavated so far (see one of its temples in Figure 5.3).[169]

Other models abounded in the Phoenician colonies and were known in the Greco-Roman geographical and ethnographical tradition. Most famously, we know of a cluster of temples at Gadir (Cádiz). The most famous one was known as the Herakleion, dedicated to Melqart, whom the Greeks equated with Herakles, and which mirrored the temple and cult of the founding colony, Tyre.[170] Ancient sources located it on the easternmost tip of the island of Cádiz (probably under the castle of Sancti Petri: Map 4.1), welcoming sailors who approached after crossing the Straits of Gibraltar. Greeks and Romans already remarked on the antiquity of this temple, some version of which stood until Roman times.[171] They also mention other temples in the archipelago and their approximate location: the Kronion (Phoenician Baal-Hammon) and temple of Venus Marina (Ashtart or Tanit), neither of whose remains have been recovered.[172] In short, the Phoenician sacred landscapes and functionality would have been familiar and recognizable to the Greeks along the wide Mediterranean routes in which they interacted, which in turn facilitated the adaptation of models and ideas.

In many respects, the ritual world of the Greeks aligned most closely with that of the Levantine realm, not the Mesopotamian and Egyptian. The idea of a house for the deity and the deity's statue was also familiar across Greek and Near Eastern cultures, as was the sometimes-cited Greek triad of altar–temple–image, neither of which were particularly Egyptian features.[173] The central Greek practice of burned sacrifice, in turn, was attested since Mycenaean times, and shared by Anatolians, Levantines, and Greeks (in a sort of "sacrificial koine"). By contrast, food offering took a different form among the Mesopotamians, and animal sacrifice was altogether alien to the Egyptians. Thus, some have even argued that burned sacrifice (Greek *thysia*) spread from Canaanite culture onto the Aegean in the Late Bronze Age.[174] Whatever the case, these shared ritual practices facilitated the transfer of other aspects of Near Eastern culture to the Aegean, such as in the areas of divination, magic, and healing, to which I return in Chapter 7.

This is a good place to recall that monumental structures did not constitute the only, or perhaps even the main, focus of ritual life, either in the Greek or the Phoenician world: small-scale worship in rustic settings and around natural landmarks is harder to trace, but has been detected in coastal caves accessible to sailors, attested through votives and inscriptions, especially on the islands of Sicily, Ibiza, and Malta.[175] Their locations indicate that "the Phoenician islanders sacralized the headlands and bays that looked out at the worlds beyond."[176] The seafarers' religious experience was an essential part of Phoenician society, and was especially associated with the gods Melqart and Ashtart-Tanit. Votive dedications of anchors and ship models in sanctuaries in southern Spain are expressions of this world.[177] In addition, artifacts recovered from shipwrecks illustrate how sacred space was portable: a good example is the portable stone altar with volute capital found in the Phoenician shipwreck of the Bajo de la Campana, from the late seventh to early sixth century BC.[178] It is no coincidence that Etruscans, Tartessians, and Greeks of this period also adopted the use of frankincense in rituals, a transportable ritual component that came together with the Levantine-style *thymiateria* (incense burners) and *phialai*/libation bowls, and even with the adoption of Semitic words like *myrrha* and *libanos* for myrrh and incense (cf. Chapter 7 for loan words).[179]

In short, monumentalized sacred spaces built by Phoenicians dotted coastal points across the Mediterranean in the eighth–seventh centuries, just when Greeks decided to add masonry structures to their own sacred spaces and when they also poured into them all sorts of Near Eastern and orientalizing ritual implements and votive objects. Phoenician and Greek sanctuaries, in the end, may have had a more similar appearance than we think. More importantly, they functioned similarly to nodal points for economic and cultural exchange and served the same international networks. The evidence is fairly conclusive but rarely assembled in these terms: first, that the standard Greek temple is not a replica of any particular Near Eastern model, and the innovative features or techniques they apply to it are not exclusively found in Egypt; and second, that the Greeks frequented areas where sacred Levantine and particularly Phoenician constructions were visible, for instance, Cyprus and Sicily, and the one clear innovation we can trace, the column with volute capital (Aeolic and Ionic), has a well-established Levantine parallel, which, moreover, was disseminated by Phoenicians throughout the Iron Age Mediterranean.

Monumental Sculpture

Stone statues appear in Greece in the mid-seventh century BC as an integral part of the program of monumentalization of sanctuaries. Before that, small figures in bronze and terracotta were dedicated, showing the rise of activity at Olympia, Delphi, and many cultic hubs in the eighth century, when more ephemeral wooden structures marked the cultic areas. In that phase, animal figurines predominated, as well as weapons, cauldrons, and other valuable objects.[180] In the seventh century, alongside the addition of stone materials, attention shifts toward the human figure, which was incorporated into the architectural decoration of stone buildings. The earliest stone relief sculptures fit right into the orientalizing trend, appearing first on Crete, where they decorated Temple A at Prinias (650–600 BC) in the so-called Daedalic style (Figure 6.5). These reliefs present salient parallels with Syro-Phoenician iconography, especially ivories, but also terracottas and bronze figures (e.g., Figures 3.1, 4.2, 4.4, and 6.1).[181] The idea of the frieze decoration itself, in sculpture as well as pottery, as we saw above, mirrors patterns known to the Greeks from Levantine metalwork circulating much earlier, instead of following stone relief techniques and motifs from contemporary Assyrian, Egyptian, and Syro-Phoenician art.[182]

Near Eastern–looking, moderately large human sculptures, were also made of hammered bronze on Crete, called *sphyrelata* figures. Mostly from literary sources we also know of older revered cult statues called *xoana* by the Greeks, which must have been generally made of wood and likely followed the contemporary orientalizing style familiar from ivory, terracotta, and bronze figures.[183] Next I discuss in some detail early stone sculpture in the round, both female and male. I start with the male statues known as *kouroi,* not only because they are main representatives of Greek orientalizing art, but because their relationship with Egyptian art is taken for granted.

The first stone *kouroi* appeared at the end of the seventh century on the Cyclades (see Map. 6.1), made in marble by Naxians and dedicated at Delos. Their female counterparts or *korai* appeared earlier in the seventh century, following the Daedalic orientalizing style first attested on Crete.[184] When he made his appearance, "the kouros emerged fully formed," as S. Rebecca Martin put it.[185] Despite the absence of a previous tradition, it is remarkable how rapidly the Greeks mastered this specific format and how quickly it spread in the late seventh century.[186] The general impression is that the adaptation from a Near Eastern model occurred at a particular place and point in time, whence the type spread through the Greek world, with subtle variations, in a trajectory parallel to other adaptations of Levantine culture.[187] But the question of how the *kouroi* arrived at their prototypical Greek shape remains open. At first glance, the stance, position of the arms, closed fists, overall proportions, and monumental scale leave little doubt of the ultimate Egyptian model of these male statues (Figure 6.4).[188] The simplest explanation is to assume that Greeks were directly exposed to Egyptian art and created the new style of stone sculpture, with seventh-century Naukratis as the "to-go" context.[189] And yet, after a closer look, art historians often admit that something does not add up. I will argue that introducing a Phoenician element can help us smooth out the wrinkles of the Egyptian–Greek link behind the *kouros.*

Despite appearances, the *kouros* has no exact match in Egyptian statuary, which suggests the adoption may not have been linear: leaving aside the uniquely Greek choice of nakedness, Egyptian stone sculptures are not in the round but in high relief. As for the body's proportions, which are approximately similar among the Greek *kouroi,* there is not an exact canon of proportions to which they can be compared, as male sculptures in Egypt varied across sites and periods. Moreover, the early Greek sculptors were slightly more schematic and conservative in how they approached the

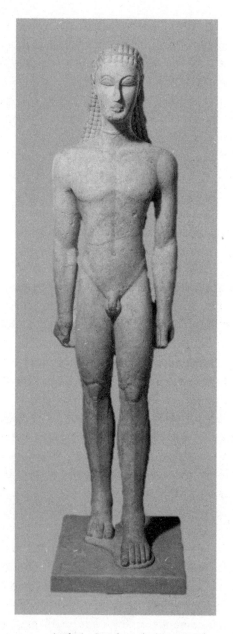

FIG. 6.4   Archaic Greek male statue or *kouros*.

Over-life size statue made from Naxian marble (194.6 cm height), probably from Attica, early sixth century BC. The Metropolitan Museum of Art, New York, Fletcher Fund, 1932.

human body.[190] Some art historians argue that the Greeks borrowed techniques and tools from Egyptian masons.[191] Others think that little in the technology used required innovation.[192] Indeed, Greek artisans had been refining their sculptural skills in other materials and were masters at transferring techniques across different media, as we have seen time and again. Along this line of interpretation, Martin has proposed that the *kouros* statues were the product of one such experiment by Greek bronze workers, perhaps in Egypt, whose main craft was armor, which would account for the cuirass-shaped chest and shins of the *kouroi*.[193] Can we consider the idea of a transfer of techniques and models across media against an ampler context? Egyptianizing male figures circulated in bronze (including amulet cases) and in carved ivory (e.g., Figures 3.1, 4.4, and 7.1); and Egyptian artifacts proper also circulated through Phoenician channels, such as Pharaonic busts as well as Egyptian and Egyptianizing scarabs and alabastra, some decorated with reliefs showing hieratic male figures. I will return to this possibility below.

Where the *kouroi* project a slightly modified image of the Egyptian statues, we cannot say the same of their female counterparts, the *korai*, which seem to predate the male figures in general. The earliest examples (ca. 650–625 BC) appear on the Cyclades and Crete. In their case, the continuity with the so-called Daedalic style associated with Crete is clear (cf. Figure 6.5), as well as with the Syrian-Phoenician female representations in ivories and other media, characterized by Egyptianizing and Assyrianizing features (e.g., Figures 3.1, 4.4). In short, the female statues are more Syrian than Egyptian.[194] We can see a similar patterns in other less-cited artworks, such as the stone basins, known as *perirrhanteria* (Figure 6.5), supported by female statues (caryatids of a sort), which were produced for a few decades in the late seventh century and deposited at the major sanctuaries of Samos, Olympia, Isthmia, and Delphi, with a few specimens also at Rhodes, Corinth, Boiotia, and Lakonia. It is perhaps surprising that the marble for the whole production of these stone basins seems to have come from Lakonia, especially since marble was available in many other areas of Greece.[195] This might indicate that the artifacts themselves were made at a workshop there and exported. Mark Fullerton points to similarities between the *perirrhanteria* and smaller ivory and ceramic chalices found in Greece and Etruria. Fullerton proposes that the larger stone statues, such as

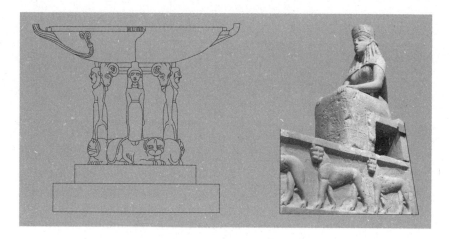

FIG. 6.5　Archaic female sculpture, from Corinth and Crete.

Left: Drawing of a marble cult basin (*perirrhanterion*) with supporting *korai* figures standing over lions (126 cm height without base), from the sanctuary at Isthmia near Corinth, late seventh century BC.　Archaeological Museum of Isthmia. © Esther Rodríguez.

Right: Stone lintel of Temple A at Prinias (Crete), second half of the seventh century BC: one of two seated goddesses at each end of the lintel decorated with a frieze of lionesses; a winged sphinx is engraved on the side of her throne.　Inventory No Γ231, Hellenic Ministry of Culture and Sports, Heraklion Archaeological Museum, Archaeological Resources Fund. Photo by the author.

self-standing *korai* or those used as architectural elements, followed upon smaller types like these stone basins; the smaller figures were not miniaturizations of the monumental ones, as is often assumed, but the other way around.[196] In other words, the stone basins with "caryatids" are another example of the Greek "translation" of Levantine models across different media. This medium-size "enlargement," in turn, translates even into larger sculpture. We can see more distant cousins of this basic model in metalwork, such as the figures on incense bronze stands found in Iberia (Figure 4.2).[197]

Is it possible, then, that the *kouroi* followed in the footsteps of their female predecessors? As with stone temples, our gaze naturally falls on colossal-scale sculpture, which means we focus narrowly on the *kouroi* and on Egyptian art as the sole comparison. But we can, once more, complicate the Egyptian equation by introducing the Phoenician factor. Phoenicians were the masters of Egyptianizing art, as manifest in all sorts of media. Among the few surviving specimens of Phoenician sculpture are a series of striding male bronze statuettes, taken to represent Melqart or Resheph, found from Gadir and Huelva to Selinous on Sicily and Samos (e.g., Figure 4.4).[198] These are difficult to date (they are often found out of context) and are generally placed in the eighth–seventh centuries, although their style is archaizing and looks back to a Canaanite tradition possibly passed down through relics. These bronze statues are, in short, Egyptianizing in a Canaanite way, and are not at all far from the Greek *kouros* concept. Typically, the Phoenician male youth figure is self-standing (unlike the Egyptian), wears an Egyptianizing dress (kilt/shendyt), has one advancing leg (more widely separated than the Egyptian models), and the arms in various positions, whether one arm straight and the other in front, or in smiting pose, or crossed over the torso. The dress style is strikingly close to that in Cypriot sculptures of the Persian period (sixth–fifth centuries), whose conservative features point to Egyptian models of the ninth century (cf. Figure 8.3).[199] The motif of the standing youth, then, spread first in bronze and ivory in portable figurines that could easily travel throughout the Mediterranean. And indeed, Greek artisans also made *kouros*-type statuettes in bronze, in some cases dated earlier than the more famous stone ones.[200]

Phoenician round sculpture in stone is scarce, partly because of the usual archaeological limitations, and also because the Phoenicians poured their iconography more lavishly into specialized portable arts as well as smaller stone monuments, which were also often aniconic.[201] As Gubel summarizes, however, "throughout the first millennium BCE, [Phoenician] stone stelae and statues feature local deities and rulers clad in Egyptian attire as recurring in the iconography of seals and ivories."[202] Evidence of stone sculpture in the round from Phoenician cities has indeed reached sufficient critical mass to be taken into account. We can talk of "a rather homogeneous group of limestone and sandstone statues often compared to Cypriot *kouroi*, but with a stronger emphasis on their Egyptian(izing) paraphernalia."[203] Dated to the late eighth or seventh centuries, these come from the areas of Byblos, Sidon, Sarepta, Amrit, and Tyre, some of them colossal in size. One oversized sample, known as the "Stagnone torso," was found in the waters off Motya in Sicily, made in local stone and dated to the sixth century.[204] These statues were probably dedicated in shrines (even if the shrines have not been preserved or excavated) and are taken to represent deities, officials, or priests.[205] The growing corpus including the Phoenician and Cypriot statues offers a way out of the Greek-Egyptian binary and invites us to consider the Egyptianizing male statue as a "cross-cultural eastern Mediterranean votive type" (see Chapter 8).[206]

So perhaps both male and female orientalizing statues share a Levantine background after all. When the stone *kouroi* emerge, they do so in the Cyclades at Naxos, Paros, and Thera, as well as on Samos, Rhodes, and Crete, places that recur in all discussions of Phoenician-style materials and the distribution of exotica, from scarabs/scaraboids and decorated ostrich eggs to the repertoire of orientalizing ivories and metalwork discussed above. The eastern-Mediterranean Ionic capitals appeared first in this realm too. For the *kouroi*, art historians continue to struggle to find formulations for the Greek–Egyptian axis: we can assume that the eastern Aegeans found inspiration in Egypt as they adapted monumental sculpture to Cycladic stone, or that a place such as Crete, with its prior experience in stone sculpture and frequent relations with Egypt, may have provided the perfect workshop for such innovations.[207] But the Phoenicians rarely if at all enter the various formulations, even if the less well-known Phoenician corpus of Egyptianizing male figures may be our only chance to decode the cultural forces intersecting in the *kouros*.

As Boardman notes, the later Greeks themselves associated archaic sculptures with Egypt, perhaps reacting to their rigid stance, just as we do.[208] It is possible that we have inherited the Greeks' Egyptomania, which was entrenched much earlier among Phoenicians. A closer look at Greek sources also shows that Greeks themselves triangulated Phoenician, Greek, and Egyptian referents in their views of cultural transfer.[209] Places such as Crete and Corinth were part of a circuit where these and other cultures intersected, frequented in the literary imagination (and in reality) by elites, merchants, and pirates, already in Homer's universe.[210] In fact, it is possible that the Egyptianizing mode of representation of Phoenician gods might be precisely what led Herodotos and others to label the Tyrian Melqart as "the Egyptian Herakles," and to posit Egyptian origins for him. But Herodotos's search for the origins of the god led him to Tyre, and to follow the Phoenician trail into the Aegean, where he postulated a Phoenician presence at oddly specific places (Thebes, Thera, and Thasos).[211] At the same time, when he speculated about the origins of Aphrodite, his instinct (and that of his sources) was to look toward Syria-Phoenicia, I think possibly noticing the similarity between Levantine and Archaic Greek female representations of goddesses, including Mistress of Animals representations in different media.[212] This trail cannot be fully explored here, but the relationship between aesthetics and the perception of cultural derivation (then and now) certainly deserves more attention.

Finally, the nakedness of the Greek male figures marks the most evident contrast with both Egyptian and Levantine representations, but also with the Etruscan and Cypriot orientalizing statues, all of which are dressed. Female Greek figures, on the other hand, are dressed (except for later representations of Aphrodite), which breaks with the Near Eastern tradition of the naked fertility goddess (e.g., holding her breasts), but conforms with Levantine representations of female dressed figures in plenty of media. Another difference between the male and female statues is that *kouroi* are usually unnamed, which makes it difficult to know whether they represent individuals or gods or some abstract idea. The male naked standard (so-called heroic nudity) is seen on the abstract plane as a mark of the heroic, divine, or aristocratic nature of the male figure; this innovation, it is often argued, went hand in hand with the function of the *kouroi* within the Greek polis. Robin Osborne searches for a more philosophical (even tragic) interpretation, according to which the unnamed *kouros* represented the place of humankind vis-à-vis the gods ("what it is to be a man"), in contrast to the Egyptian exaltation of the elite individual.[213] More generally, they can be seen as yet another "orientalizing" innovation deployed by the Greeks "to demonstrate the power and privilege of elites."[214] In this sense, as Martin notes, the Greeks are not necessarily setting themselves in opposition to the Egyptians or Levantines, but using stone statuary to express elite ideology within their own sociopolitical parameters.[215] As we saw with other arts, however, the Greek dedications became a mode of expression for an expanding wealthy demographic in evolving civic contexts, and not exclusively an established aristocratic or princely elite.[216]

As Whitley wrote, "there never was a stable or homogeneous 'Oriental' culture, nor was there ever, except in Romantic retrospect, a stable Greek one."[217] We cannot study orientalizing adaptations without considering regional variations and developments, in any art form.[218] This is true of any of the broad regions covered in this book. There was no single uniform response to each group's encounters with the various Near Eastern cultures. Despite all idiosyncrasies, however, the Greeks, shared in the general trends followed by other proto-urban Iron Age communities across the Mediterranean. They were all drawing most eagerly from Phoenician markets, through which flowed a particular stream of Near Eastern cultural synthesis, and the Greeks themselves then propagated their own versions of it. This is exemplified by the sphinx, that ever-present orientalizing motif, made most famous by the Greeks.

Follow the Sphinx

Depicted in all sorts of media, sphinxes mark for us the route of Levantine art's reception among Mediterranean groups, even as the hybrid monster was regionally "domesticated" into local versions. In Greek and other orientalizing-style vase painting they shared friezes with their falcon-headed siblings, the griffins, and in stone they sat atop commemorative columns and funerary stelae. Almost certainly they decorated other socially prominent materials now lost to us, such as textiles, wall paintings, and wooden objects. In these orientalizing repertoires sphinxes shared a distinct common archetype, which was then modulated and given many local faces. The following discussion is meant to show that, while modern popular culture associates the sphinx with Egypt, the pan-Mediterranean winged, human-faced lion, and its variant the griffin, follow the same route as the elite culture exported by Phoenicians and readily adopted by local communities.[219]

A Brief Archaeology of the Sphinx

Whatever their deeper prehistory, sphinxes are eminently associated with Egyptian monuments already dating from the third millennium BC, when the human-headed lion appears as a royal guardian and often represents Egyptian royalty itself. The most emblematic example is the colossal stone sphinx at Giza, part of the funerary complex of Chephren (r. 2570 BC).[220] The name "sphinx" is Greek and has become standard, although Greek writers made some distinctions: there were human-headed sphinxes (*andro-sphinxes*) and other types whose heads were zoomorphic, such as ram-headed lions (*kriosphinxes* / *kriocephalic*), that is, bearing the ram head of Amon, or falcon-headed lions, akin to griffins, associated with Horus (*hierakosphinxes*).[221] Horus represented the archetypal Egyptian king, and the griffin is a variation on this falcon-headed sphinx. Finally, the Egyptian sphinx could also have the head of a youth or "harpocratic" head. These variations that the Greeks noticed appear not only in Egypt but in the Levant, where the sphinx was stylized, usually winged, androcephalic (i.e., with a human head), and more generally feminine (or at least shaven), although in Roman times male and female heads appear.[222]

Perhaps the easiest difference to spot between Egyptian and Greek sphinxes is that the Egyptian sphinx was not winged. Greek sphinxes, by contrast, added wings to the lion's body. In this, the Greeks show that their inspiration came from the Levant, where the sphinx was winged since its Syrian-Canaanite incarnations. This feature became the norm: "Every painter and every sculptor who devotes himself and has been trained in the practice of his art figures the sphinx as winged," as Aelian wrote in his treatise on animals.[223] Also, Egyptian sphinxes were predominantly masculine, perhaps because of their association with the pharaoh, and beardless (except with pharaoh's false beard), although they could also be associated with specific female divinities, such as Hathor, and sometimes with male ones, such as Hauron (a form of Semitic Baal represented as a sphinx or a falcon).[224]

The Greek sphinx, again aligning with the Levantine model, is feminine, typically with the upper body of a breasted woman and sometimes a serpent's tail, and is described along these lines consistently by ancient authors.[225] It is mainly the Levantine-type winged sphinx and griffin, then, that became part of Late Bronze Age, eastern Mediterranean koine. We can see them in the royal contexts of Minoan and Mycenaean palaces, and in the North Syrian and Neo-Hittite world they continue to appear as royal guardians in the early first millennium (for instance at the gates at Karatepe in Cilicia).[226] The sphinx, therefore, is a Near Eastern hybrid, which spread probably from Egypt into the Levant, Anatolia, and Greece. The sphinx's reception was more timid in Mesopotamia, where it was a minor player among an amazing repertoire of hybrid Mesopotamian demons, monsters, and protective entities, set up frequently as gate guardians of cities and palaces. These included horse-men, bull-men, scorpion-men, bird-men, mermen/mermaids, griffins, lion-dragons, snake-dragons, and goat-fish.[227]

As a staple of Canaanite art, the winged sphinx became a typical feature of Phoenician art in the Iron Age, and is ubiquitous throughout the Phoenician-Punic realm. Appearing on luxury artifacts such as ivories and metalwork, but also in stone and other media, sphinxes and griffins are a salient part of the Egyptianizing repertoire that inflected Phoenician religion and culture and its adaptations. The sphinx was accompanied by a range of symbolic connotations, revealed in its iconography. Thus, the Levantine sphinx often appears with palmettes, lotuses, the tree of life, and other motifs associated with Ashtart.[228] This hybrid also conveyed the Egyptian association with kingship and was deployed in royal imagery. We can appreciate this in the first coins minted by Byblos and by Phoenician polities abroad, such as Idalion in Cyprus in the sixth century, which coins display a sphinx on one side and lotus on other.[229] But the clearest expression of the link between sphinxes and royalty is the depiction of sphinxes flanking divine and kingly thrones.[230] For instance, on the sarcophagus of King Ahiram of Byblos (ca. 1000 BC) and on an ivory plaque from Megiddo (thirteenth–twelfth centuries BC) the deceased rulers receive offerings seated on sphinx thrones, a feature absent from similar Mesopotamian scenes. On the Ahiram sarcophagus, moreover, the king holds a lotus flower, another Egyptianizing symbol adapted to Phoenician religion: the withering lotus signals his death (Figure 9.1; cf. Figures 3.1 on ivory, 4.1 with open and closed lotuses in Tartessic vases).[231]

In the Iron Age, the tradition of the sphinx throne is strongly associated with Ashtart and Baal-Hammon. Sometimes this takes the form of an empty throne, which alludes to the divinity, following the aniconic tendencies in Phoenician religion.[232] The empty sphinx throne of Ashtart at the sanctuary of Bustan esh-Sheikh outside Sidon (fourth century BC) is only one of many examples of sphinx thrones (empty or occupied) in different sizes and materials not only found in Phoenicia but along the entire geographical and chronological expanse of Phoenician culture.[233] The throne-guarding sphinx appears in the Phoenician diaspora as part of the repertoire of the gods Ashtart and Baal and their local adaptations, and this is the context in which the Greeks probably encountered it. We already saw examples in the Etruscan realm in Chapter 5.[234] A beautiful example from southern Spain is the seventh/sixth-century alabaster *rhyton* (libation vase) in the shape of a goddess seated on a sphinx throne, known as the "Lady of Galera" (Figure 6.6).[235] But the motif traveled in small portable objects too, such as carved seals from the Persian period, which are scattered along the Mediterranean (Figure 6.6).[236] In fact if we look closely at the seated goddess

FIG. 6.6   Representations of divinities on sphinx thrones.

Left: Alabaster libation vase (*rhyton*) known as the "Lady of Galera"/"Dama de Galera" (18.5 cm height) representing a female goddess (prob. Ashtart), from Iberian necropolis of Tútugi in Galera (Granada), seventh century BC.   National Archaeological Museum, Madrid, Inv. 33438. Photo © Santiago Relanzón. Fundación ITMA.

Right: Phoenician green jasper seals from the Persian period (sixth–fourth centuries BC), depicting male god (prob. Baal/Melqart) on sphinx throne, with scepter, incense burner, winged sun disk (*right*) and moon crescent (*left*) symbols; from Ibiza (*left*) and Nicosia (Cyprus) (*right*).   Drawings by Nora Clair, from Brian R. Doak, *Phoenician Aniconism in Its Mediterranean and Ancient Near Eastern Contexts* (Atlanta: SBL Press, 2015), figure 4.9. Courtesy of Brian Doak.

on the early sculptures from Prinias (Figure 6.5) we can see a sphinx carved on the flank of the figure's throne as well.

The Canaanite sphinx was revitalized by Phoenicians in the Iron Age and easily transferred to emergent neighboring kingdoms: we can see this in the repertoire of Levantine ivories from Samaria, for instance, which include griffins besides the calf–nursing cow motif, the woman at the window, and other Egyptianzing themes that have passed through Phoenician adaptations.[237] Sphinxes were also used as kingly emblems in the young states, as we see on seals from Judah, Israel, and Edom.[238] Scholars have also postulated that hybrids such as the Egyptian griffin or sphinxes lie behind the biblical cherubim, mentioned as divine guardians in various contexts.[239]

As the sphinx became part and parcel of elite aesthetics and as it traveled in portable art, it found new homes and artistic modalities in the Aegean and much farther west.

Pan-Mediterranean Adaptations of the Sphinx

In Greece sphinxes and griffins were not completely new. They were part of the repertoire of the Late Bronze Age koine, with variations. An Egyptian-style sphinx was preferred on Minoan Crete, while the Levantine winged sphinxes and griffins were more frequent in Mycenaean art, where they appear flanking trees, altars, pillars, palace gates (e.g., Pylos fresco), and thrones, such as at Late Bronze Age Knossos and Pylos (though the throne-flanking griffin appears already at Akrotiri, on Thera). The winged sphinx also appears painted on the clay coffins known as *larnakes,* on Crete and Boiotia.[240] But after the post-Mycenaean gap in figurative art, when the sphinx reappears in Greece it follows the Levantine form, which at this time becomes a staple of orientalizing art all across the Mediterranean. In short, the Greek sphinx and other Iron Age adaptations did not emulate the Egyptian guardian but the Levantine winged sphinx.

In Greek art, sphinxes also share space with chimaerae, griffins, centaurs, winged Gorgons, and other fantastic creatures. As we look beyond Greece and into other regions, the use of the Levantine sphinx is consistent and often associated with areas of Phoenician influence. Indigenous crafts adopted the sphinx alongside other Phoenician symbols of royalty, divinity, and protection (lotuses, rosettes, lions, etc.), often used in funerary contexts. Beautiful examples are the griffins and lotuses painted on Tartessic *pithoi* from Carmona (Figure 4.1), quite similar to the ones on the decorated ostrich egg found in the "Isis Tomb" in Etruria (Figure 5.4), evoking Ashtart or a local fertility goddess who adopts her iconography.[241] Sphinxes / griffins indeed also became an integral part of Etruscan art throughout its orientalizing and archaic periods (720–480 BC), appearing in ivories, metalwork, vase painting and frescoes, and sculpture, again often associated with funerary contexts, with similar adaptations on Cyprus.[242]

Despite their iconographic presence across the entire Mediterranean and their importance in Near Eastern art, sphinxes have not been studied systematically. They are usually discussed separately, in purely artistic terms, with some exceptions.[243] Much more extensive interpretive effort has gone into the mythological sphinx in its unique but famous appearance in the Oedipus story, not least thanks to Sigmund Freud. In general, scholars have emphasized the sphinxes' association with funerary culture, as they often appear in funerary artifacts or as grave markers.[244] Thierry Petit has taken this line further to propose that sphinxes and griffins in the Greek world were imagined as underworld guardians.[245] It was their status as terrifying protective creatures, in my view, that easily extended to the funerary realm. Put differently, their symbology applied to the realms of both the living and the dead. The general protective aspect of this and other hybrid beings accords with the Near Eastern function of guardians and demons, and we do see sphinxes placed as protectors of temple areas in Greece. The Naxian dedication shown in Figure 6.3 above is a perfect example, with a sphinx perched on a tall column just before the retaining wall of the temple of Apollo at Delphi. This type of monument (perhaps the very one) probably inspired the representation of Oedipus's sphinx atop an Ionic column in classical times.[246]

Does the recurrence of sphinxes throughout the Mediterranean, then, reveal more than the shallow, passive repetition of a decorative motif? I think it does. Sphinxes in the Levant were associated with royalty and with Ashtart and her symbolism of life and regeneration, a repertoire that conveyed aristocratic or royal cachet (or the aspiration to it). This particular connotation made the sphinx an attractive symbol transferrable across Mediterranean elite cultures. This is not to deny the purely ornamental life of this motif in furniture, which was also part of orientalizing art.[247] But the success of the sphinx denotes a general awareness across cultures of its specific symbolic connotations. Some of these can be inferred from the extant iconography and its contexts alone. The mythology surrounding the sphinx in Greece, however, offers further evidence that the sphinx was understood along the lines of the Canaanite-Phoenician tradition, as a royal-throne guardian.

A Phoenician Throne Guardian?

The story of Oedipus and his accession to the throne at Thebes famously includes his confrontation with the Sphinx. Hesiod called her "the lethal Sphinx, ruin for the Kadmeians."[248] He connected her with a series of hybrids (Echidna, Chimaera, and others) and with Typhon, whom he places "among the Arimoi," probably pointing to the North Syrian Aramaean realm.[249] All versions of the Oedipus myth make the sphinx a guardian of the empty throne of Laius, after he had been killed unknowingly by his own son. Whether she is rationalized as a human daughter of Laius (sometimes leading an army) or remains a demonic hybrid sometimes sent by Hera, posing riddles and cruelly dispensing with passersby, her function is clear: she weeds out the illegitimate heirs to the throne of Laius, which only Oedipus should claim. Sometimes Oedipus is alone, and at other times he is one contestant for the throne among many, who must answer correctly the sphinx's riddle, presented as an oracle delivered to Kadmos or a riddle from the Muses. Only after Oedipus deploys this special knowledge, the "implacable singer" dramatically dies and clears the way to the throne.[250] In other words, the story, taken to its bare bones, which all versions share, mythologizes the sphinx's Near Eastern association with kingship, even evoking its physical attachment to thrones or graves.

But here is the clincher: the Greeks associated the word "sphinx" with the verb *sphingo* (*sphiggo*), "to constrict," "to strangle."[251] Scholars have puzzled about whether this is the real etymology of the name or a popular interpretation tied to the story. Aaron Demsky has recently proposed that the name was the translation of a demon called *honeqet*, meaning "strangler" or "breaker of the neck," which is so named and depicted as a sphinx on amulets from Arslan Tash in North Syria, written in an Aramaic-inflected Phoenician.[252] The two Arslan Tash plaques are dated roughly to the seventh century BC and contain a magic charm destined to protect a house.[253] The Levantine winged sphinx here has a beardless human head and pointy hat/helmet, and the type conforms with sphinxes represented on ivories from Arslan Tash. On this amulet, however, the sphinx and the other demons are the potential threats against whom invoked deities must protect the house. The amulet shows that the Levantine sphinx (like the Greek one) had a "dark side," at least in the realm of incantations. She could serve a double purpose: as a royal emblem and protector of the throne or as a threatening demon, perhaps depending on which side of the "gate" she was on. Her aggressive face as the "strangler" would be part of her protective function, as is the case with other apotropaic monsters, such as the Gorgon. Mentions of other underworld demons in Phoenician amulets and funerary texts (the "devourer," the "hateful lion") support this reading and remind us how little we know of these lost mythologies.[254]

The sphinx's special association with Thebes is telling too. The Theban mythological saga is most explicitly tied to Phoenicia. Greek tradition made Kadmos a prince who arrived at Thebes from Tyre while searching for his sister Europa, and he settled there following an oracle.[255] Meanwhile, the Tyrian princess was stranded on Crete after being kidnapped by Zeus in the form of a white bull (the "rape of Europa" story). Kadmos and Europa provide a mythological bridge between the Phoenician and Greek worlds, even by their names, which seem to be Greek adaptations of Northwest Semitic *qedem* and *'erev* "east" and "west."[256] The label "kadmeians" is used not only for the Thebans and their citadel (*Kedmeis*) but also for the Phoenician script that, according to some traditions, was introduced by Kadmos himself, the *kadmeia grammata*. Although archaeological remains do not support the sort of Phoenician migration in the area that ancient historiographical traditions assumed, the antiquity of Thebes and its kinship with the Near Eastern cultures during the Bronze Age is amply attested archaeologically, and may have provided a backdrop for such traditions in the first place.[257] The royal imagery would, of course, have been read in different keys among different societies, but in each case the sphinx added to the prestige of orientalizing paraphernalia in a world of city-states where, let us not forget, some form of kingship or oligarchy was the norm.

In short, both the saga into which the Greek sphinx was inserted and the name itself bear connections with the Phoenician world, or could have been understood in Phoenician terms in the archaic period. Although this hybrid creature has famous Egyptian precedents, it is through the Phoenician networks that the motif traveled westward. This is the sphinx that followed Kadmos from Tyre, eventually jumping from iconography into the Greek mythology that so stimulated our modern imagination.

◄ 7 ►

INTANGIBLE LEGACIES

Phoenician Letters

If there is an item of undoubted, direct Phoenician origin in Greek culture it is the alphabet. We would have deduced as much independently through epigraphic evidence, but the Greeks tell us about it too. These Phoenician letters traveled far and wide, and versions of them were adopted in various languages by groups in the Aegean, Iberia, and Etruria, as well as in the Levant itself outside Phoenicia in the early first millennium. The ripple effect of orientalization is also felt in the secondary wave of adaptations of the alphabet in the later seventh century and, afterward, via the Greeks (Etruscan), the Etruscans (Latin and other Italic scripts), and the Tartessians (Iberian scripts), mirroring the spread of other artistic models and technologies.

Writing did not develop spontaneously everywhere. It is a learned and transmitted technology. As far as we know, leaving aside isolated or discontinued experiments, writing culture developed in the Near East first (Egypt and Mesopotamia, ca. 3400–3200 BC), and independently in China (2000 BC) and Mesoamerica (650 BC). The technology of writing spread from these societies throughout their areas of influence, and the models that each culture followed are telling of the geopolitical dynamics in which it was immersed. For instance, Hittites, Canaanites, and the Bronze Age Cretans (Minoans) chose clay tablets and archives for their texts, some even adopting the cuneiform shape of letters (Hittites, Ugarit) under the influence of Mesopotamian scribal, administrative, and literary culture. On the fringes of this world, the Mycenaean palace kings adapted the Minoan script to write their language, Greek, keeping the Cretan script's style, technology, and administrative use. Their choice was consistent with their general appropriation of fundamental aspects of Minoan civilization, while the Mycenaeans made no concessions in this adaptation to their own language. On Cyprus, a syllabic form of writing prevailed (Cypro-syllabic/Cypriot Syllabary) descended from Cypro-Minoan, which in turn derived from Linear A (see Chapter 8); this script was in use until the classical period, even when the Phoenician and Greek alphabets were available on the island, showing that writing is an important marker of local identity and that a writing system is not easily or always abandoned in favor of a "simpler" or "more practical" alternative.

Writing choices are tied to broader historical and cultural dynamics. Some cultures had writing and then lost it, as happened to Greek speakers for about five centuries after the collapse of the Mycenaean centers and their archives. When they took up writing again in the mid-eighth century or so, they used the Phoenician alphabet as their model. This was not a chance occurrence, but one tied to the specific dynamics of that historical moment. What changed after the Mycenaean collapse when writing was abandoned and what changed again in the eighth century was the economic framework: the collapse made palace writing (Linear B) redundant, whereas writing became necessary again as transactions intensified and societies grew more complex.[1] This need was now shared by other developing communities throughout Iberia, central Italy, and in the broader Levant, which made writing part of the orientalizing phenomenon in its broadest, socioeconomic scope, and Greece was just one more participant.

When it comes to Greece, more emphasis is generally placed on the technical aspects of the borrowing and less on the cultural dynamics that the borrowing itself illustrates and presupposes. The emphasis falls on Greek innovation, on the "improvement" of the Semitic system (namely, marking vowels), and these discussions often misrepresent the Phoenician script or emphasize the gap between the two systems to highlight Greek originality (see below). This emphasis is not unexpected and is due to one reason only: Greek literature survived and became canonical for the societies that later began to analyze the process of adaptation (namely our own). We do not have Etruscan, Iberian, Phrygian literatures, or much Phoenician-Punic literature. The story that we tell is one of Alexandrian, Roman, and Byzantine scholarship, of the Renaissance and western European reception of Greek art and literature, which eventually produced narratives of the "clash of civilizations" and anti-Semitism.

But against the grain of disciplinary agendas, a subfield has emerged among twentieth- to twenty-first century scholars, who are exploring the points of overlap between Greek and Near Eastern literatures, as texts excavated from the ground have become more available during the past century. Clay tablets from Canaan, Assyria, and Anatolia allow us to appreciate the flow of written culture across languages, including the Aegean, which accompanied other technological, commercial, and political entanglements since the Late Bronze Age. This relationship resumed in the eighth century after an intermediate period of relative isolation of Greek communities. Here I will offer an up-to-date, if brief, overview of the Greek reception of the alphabet and of Near Eastern literature and mythology to show that in the realm of written culture too, helplessly fragmented though our sources are, the Phoenicians left their mark.

Background and Classification

The Phoenician alphabet contained twenty-two phonetic signs. It was used first in Byblos around 1200–1100 BC. Around the turn of the first millennium BC, Tyre standardized the Phoenician script, and this was the basis for its adaptations in the Levant and the Mediterranean.[2] Phoenician is linguistically and epigraphically distinct from other members of the family of Northwest Semitic languages, which includes Aramaic, Hebrew, and other epigraphically attested languages in the region. Moreover, the Phoenician script and language enjoyed notable stability and homogeneity during the entire first millennium: from about 1200 BC to Augustus's time in the Levant and at least until the fifth century AD in North Africa. The script's stability was not hampered by its broad chronological and geographical span across territories that are today within many countries, mapping exactly onto areas of Phoenician settlement and trade from Lebanon and its surrounding areas to the Aegean, southern Italy and Malta, North Africa, Spain, and Portugal.[3]

An important point of classification is necessary. Either intentionally or through inertia, scholarly and popular narratives misrepresent and even misclassify Phoenician writing and language, reproducing a false dichotomy that stems from and reinforces the idea of Greek exceptionalism, and unknowingly rehashing orientalist representations of Arabic and other Semitic languages. Most commonly, the Phoenician alphabet is misleadingly called a "syllabary," even classified with the Cypriot and Mycenaean syllabaries, or it is described as "syllabic-consonantal," even when acknowledging the problem of classification, or vaguely as consonantal and "difficult."[4] One can also find confused or misinformed statements about where the model for the Greek alphabet lay among nonspecialists, usually classicists or art historians.[5] Some works shed doubt on whether the Phoenician language was distinguishable from those of other Levantine groups, or on "whether the Phoenicians shared a language at all."[6] Qualitative evaluations tend to draw an essential difference between the Semitic alphabets and the Greek and Latin adaptations, literally considered more perfect and "essentially different" from previous versions. This is justified in a rather tautological way, considering a "real alphabet" only a system that works like the Greek (or Latin) alphabet, which allegedly "allows one who does not know the language still to pronounce the words."[7] (Needless to say, nonnative English speakers may also struggle to read many of its words in an intelligible way, unless they know how the words sound beforehand.)

Even the broadly disseminated relabeling of Semitic alphabets as *Abjad* instead of *Alphabet* is unnecessary (*a-b-j* refers to the first letters of the Arabic *'abjadī* list, nowadays sometimes called *hijāʾī* based on the shapes; think of Hebrew "aleph-bet-gimmel" or Greek "alpha-beta-gamma"). This formally superficial distinction emerged among linguists precisely to counteract "syllabary" misclassification and create a subclassification for the Semitic alphabets, but it has become widespread on internet sites, producing a consequential dichotomy between "consonantal alphabets" and the allegedly more "complete" and perfect "western" modifications.[8] No alphabet or script ever represents phonetic speech accurately (hence the complex systems of transliteration that linguists use), and different languages eliminated, added, merged, or changed the value of signs as needed to better represent their language, always approximately. For instance, early Northwest Semitic speakers (Phoenician, Hebrew) discarded unnecessary signs used in earlier iterations of the alphabet (e.g., found at Ugarit and recently at Lachish), and Greek speakers in turn rid themselves of some consonants and added or adapted them to vocalic sounds that are essential in Greek. Put simply, in the Semitic languages roots and morphemes are consonantal and vowels basically supportive, so the Indo-European Greek speakers, who did not even have those sounds but whose morphology depended sometimes on single vowels (e.g., including forms of the verb "to be"), reinterpreted as vowels the glottal stops and guttural sounds represented in Phoenician by *'aleph, he, waw,* and *'ayin.* In the end, both alphabets, Phoenician and Greek, initially had twenty-some letters, a stable twenty-two in Phoenician and a more varied number in Greek (twenty-three to twenty-seven) depending on the letter uses in regional dialects and the eventual addition of long vowels.[9]

The real differentiating lines, then, are between alphabetic systems (phonetic, with twenty to twenty-four signs), syllabaries (e.g., Mycenaean, Cypro-syllabic, which also included ideograms), and more complex systems from the Near East and Asia that combine these and other elements. The latter include Sumerian and Akkadian cuneiform syllabaries, Egyptian hieroglyphs, Asian scripts, and many systems that combine logographs, ideograms, syllabic, or alphabetic signs. This is not necessarily a qualitative division: clearly these systems were and are not less usable; neither did the apparent simplicity of the alphabet, by itself, make it immediately transferable, or more "democratic." For our purposes, the main point is that the alphabet learned by the Greeks and others was a particular invention of Canaanites, who departed from other nonalphabetic Near Eastern scripts at a specific time and place.[10] It was also first-millennium Canaanites, particularly Phoenicians, who provided the channels for its dissemination.

The Transmission

To date, our earliest Greek inscriptions are short, individual, nonliterary texts scratched on pottery and dated between 775 and 750 BC.[11] The most cited early examples are scattered around the expanding Greek world of the eighth century: the Dipylon Oinochoe from Athens; graffiti from Pithekoussai, in the Bay of Naples, and Gabii (Osteria dell'Osa), east of Rome; the temple of Apollo Daphnephoros at Eretria (Euboia); Kommos on Crete; and at the Euboian colony of Methone in northern Greece.[12] These early examples of the Greek alphabet are all already slight variants of a single original, and anyplace where early inscriptions appear and where there was close interaction with Phoenicians is a good candidate for this point of origin, the favorites being Cyprus, Euboia, and Crete. It is on Crete that the most archaic, Phoenician-like shapes of the letters are attested as well as the earliest Phoenician inscription in the Aegean (the Tekke bowl); it also seems that, as the recently found graffiti from Methone show, wherever it originated, the Euboians had an important role in the spread of the Greek alphabet.[13]

Most scholars estimate that the Phoenician alphabet was first used to write Greek sometime around 800 BC, certainly no later than 750, although dates might go back earlier to about 850 if new evidence emerges and also depending on the ongoing revision of Geometric pottery dating, with which these texts are associated.[14] Moreover, it is quite possible that the alphabet circulated in perishable materials for some time before it did in the materials that survive (see below).[15] The uncertainty about the exact model is aggravated by the fact that we have few witnesses of the Phoenician script for the key chronological window of the late ninth–early eighth centuries.[16] Some scholars have even proposed that the Greek letter shapes derive from an earlier Semitic model.[17] Barring new evidence, most agree on a Phoenician prototype of 850–750, roughly contemporary to (or slightly earlier than) our first Greek samples.[18] There are, however, fundamental certainties regarding the adaptation, which I summarize here:

- *The shapes* of the first Greek letters mirror those of the Phoenician letters, and follow their corresponding phonetic value, with the expected adaptation to Greek sounds.
- *The order* of the Greek letters follows overall that of the Phoenician alphabet. A fixed order is necessary for learning a script, and has other uses too (e.g., as cardinal numbers).
- *The direction* of writing is also the same in Greek: both directions are used initially (sometimes in the same inscription, which is called *boustrophedon*), always starting right to left, and only later Greek standardizes to a left-to-right direction while Phoenician and other Semitic languages to a right-to-left direction.
- *The name* of the letters is borrowed from the Semitic names, with basic morphological adaptations (i.e., Greek avoids ending words with consonants): *'aleph-alpha, bet-beta, gimmel-gamma, dalet-delta,* and so forth. These names were meaningless in Greek, while at least some of the letters had recognizable meanings for Phoenicians (*'aleph/* "ox," *bet/* "house," *gimmel/* "camel," *mem/* "water," *'ayin/* "eye," etc., following the acrophonic principle of Egyptian and Proto-Canaanite/ Sinaitic writing systems).

The uniformity of these common traits and some nonobvious choices of letter correspondences that are common to all the Greek variants strongly suggest that the adaptation happened at one time and place and diversified from there.[19] A second wave of adaptations then followed and accounts for the changes in value of some letters and the addition of others. Other innovations were made in later centuries and were peculiar to some dialects, such as the modification or adaptation of letters to reflect long /ō/ and /ē/ (*omega* and *eta*), which started in Ionia and the Cyclades and became generalized in the classical period.[20] There are still many unanswered questions regarding how this adoption of the Phoenician alphabet by the Greeks happened. I once heard Walter Burkert remark something along the lines that "the adaptation of the alphabet was part intended, part misunderstanding, part the fruit of genius."[21] Even "narrowing it down" to areas where Greeks and Phoenicians interacted produces a wide spectrum of possible scenarios, from coastal Syria to Euboia, Crete, the northern Aegean, or the Bay of Naples.

The loss of any writing in perishable materials leaves a huge gap in our reconstruction of the early use of the alphabet. But we do know that inscriptions were made on folding wooden tablets (with wax or without it) called *deltos* / *deltoid*. This is the term for "door" in Semitic languages, used already in Ugaritic (*daltu*) and later in Hebrew for the writing tablet (whence the name of the letter *delta*), of the type found at the Uluburun shipwreck and mentioned in Homer (called a *pinax*).[22] The choice of words for writing materials also tells us that the Greeks, like the Phoenicians, used scrolls made from the papyrus plant, which the Greeks called *byblos,* whence *byblos* / *byblion* for "scroll" or "book," also the Greek name for the city of Byblos (Phoenician *gbl* / Gubla / Gebal).[23] Finally, most would agree that the adaptation was the initiative of bilingual (or partially bilingual) speakers who found it practical to use the Phoenician letters to write the Greek language.[24]

The Use

Writing seems to have been used by the Greeks first in the private sphere, not to serve a political or administrative apparatus.[25] The alphabet was used to mark property ("belonging to X," "I am the cup of X"), sometimes in a playful way. Votive inscriptions and grave markers, artisan signatures, and alphabet exercises also appear and belong to the private, individual realm, while we have to wait until the seventh century for unambiguously public inscriptions: written laws, agreements, lists, commemorative inscriptions. Epigraphy also becomes more formal in sanctuaries as these spaces become monumentalized. All these uses are also attested in the Levant (including property markers, alphabets, votives, and funerary inscriptions), with the exception of the private poetic or playful epigraphs, which are a Greek peculiarity. Conversely, we do not find in Greece inscriptions commemorating great deeds and works of monarchs as we do in the Near East.[26]

The pragmatic, commercial use of writing, mostly in perishable materials, must have been important from the start. Looking at the rapid spread of the Phoenician writing system in the eighth–seventh centuries, Eleftheria Pappa has recently argued that it could have been linked to the Phoenicians' use of credit-based trading methods, developed to aid their interaction with various groups outside the Near East.[27] An exceptional document from the western Mediterranean provides us with a glimpse of these complex relations mediated by writing in the fifth century BC. Fourteen or so lines of Greek are preserved on a lead sheet from Pech Maho, an indigenous settlement in the French Languedoc with strong ties to both the Greek and Iberian realms (Map 4.1). Although the details are debated, the recorded names of witnesses indicate that the commercial transaction involved members of three communities: Iberians, indigenous inhabitants, and Greeks. As Greek was the shared international language in that region, it was probably used for both the oral transaction and the written version recorded by one of the individuals on metal.[28] We can imagine a similar situation in areas where Phoenician trade involved various local populations as well as Greeks (e.g., North Syria, Bay of Naples, Cyprus), and where Phoenician language and script would have functioned as a middle ground for communication between two or more linguistic groups.[29]

Not everyone likes the emphasis on an initial prosaic use of the alphabet for trade and status display: Barry Powell revived H. T. Wade-Gery's idea that the main goal of the adoption was to write down the Homeric poems.[30] Even if this may not initially have been the most important use, it certainly became one. The Greeks cultivated epic poetry during their long illiterate centuries, through oral tradition, as we know.[31] Surely the adoption of writing was an aid not only to preserve their orally composed and transmitted epics but probably to compose the first long intricately woven epics of Homer.[32] The newly found "Cup of Acesander" from Methone (ca. 750–735 BC) and the famous "Cup of Nestor" from Pithekoussai illustrate the importance of hexametric poetry for individual "lay" writers, even if the poetic allusion might originally have been subordinate to the individual property marking. Indeed, as Richard Janko notes, "by this time, alphabetic writing could be used to record poetry on more serious occasions and at far greater length."[33]

As for the *how* and *who* of this adaptation, we can imagine a number of more learned or more casual scenarios. While generally scholars see the alphabet as an innovation facilitated by a bilingual environment, others propose a more professional transaction between a Greek-speaking "adapter" and a Semitic-speaking "informant."[34] It is not clear, however, why we must imagine a process in which the two cultures are kept so discrete, except for the sole contact-point enabled by an "informant." The figure inadvertently evokes modern colonial situations and draws a sharp line separating the two societies and their writing cultures. It could all have happened in the mind, or on the writing tablet of one and the same bilingual person.

The Recognition

The Greeks themselves did not see their letters as their own original invention and were the first to acknowledge their cultural debt to the Phoenicians. I close this section with some of this testimony, beginning with a detailed passage by Herodotos, worth quoting in full:

> These Phoenicians who came with Kadmos, among whom were also the Gephyraeans, when they settled in Hellas, brought many other teachings and also the drawn letters [*grammata*], which, as it seems to me, Greeks did not have before. As time passed, the shapes of the letters also evolved with the sounds. Among the Greeks, at this time the Ionians were their neighbors [of the Phoenicians] in most areas, who borrowed them from the Phoenicians and taught the letters and used them, making few changes in shape; and because they [the Ionians] utilized them, and just as it should, since Phoenicians had brought them to Greece, they [the Ionians] claim that they are the ones who named them "Phoenician letters" [*phoinikeia grammata*]. The Ionians, moreover, have long called parchment "*byblos*," since at one point they used hides of goats and sheep because of scarcity of papyrus [*byblos*]. Still, even in my own time, many

foreign peoples write on such hide skins. I have myself seen Kadmeian letters in the temple of Apollo Ismenios in Thebes of the Boiotians [i.e., not Egyptian Thebes], engraved on some tripods and mostly similar to the letters of the Ionians. One of those tripods has the following inscription: "Amphytrion dedicated me from the spoils of Teleboae." This would date to around the time of Laios the son of Labdakos, son of Polydoros, son of Kadmos.[35]

The context of this digression is rarely noted, but it comes in the middle of Herodotos's discussion of the "tyrannicides" Harmodios and Aristogeiton, who killed the autocrat Hipparchos (one of Peisistratos's sons) in 514 BC. According to the historian, the Gephyraeans hailed from those Boiotians of Phoenician origin who traced their background to Kadmos.[36] Independently of the merits of this genealogy, this is a remarkable context in which to bring up the subject of the alphabet: Herodotos makes a point of associating the tyrannicides, famous bringers of political change, with the Phoenicians in their role as "culture heroes."

An amateur epigraphist, Herodotos in fact hits on the main clues that give away the Phoenician origins of the alphabet, mentioned above: he notes the similarity of the early Greek letters, which he saw in several other archaic inscriptions, and he must have compared them to Semitic ones that he would have seen during his travels to Tyre and other harbors of the Levant, perhaps also on Crete, in Egypt, and other places.[37] His autopsy of the Semitic script may not have been limited to stone inscriptions, and of course as a writer himself he is used to the papyrus medium. As he mentions the term "byblos" to explain the imprecise use of the word by Ionians for parchment, rather than papyrus, he offers the name as yet another sign of the Phoenician origins of Greek writing, as that was the name they used for the Phoenician city. Herodotos thus anticipates modern specialists, who have highlighted the important role of Ionians, especially Euboians among them, either as the likely adopters or as distributers of the early alphabet (see above). Herodotos was, however, far from the mark regarding the timeline. By connecting the introduction of the alphabet to Thebes and the time of Laios (the father of Oedipus), that is, before the Trojan War, he weaves the alphabet deep into the Greek "mytho-chronology." He thus reveals that he does not know about Mycenaean writing and considers the alphabet part of Greek "prehistory," which is not altogether inaccurate, inasmuch as its adoption falls outside the parameters of his sources' historical memory, usually limited to the seventh century BC.

The Phoenician origin of the letters was broadly accepted in Greek historiography and ethnography before and after Herodotos: earlier Ionian intellectuals, Hekataios and Anaximander, had already defended an eastern origin, articulated mythologically as an import by Danaos, who came from Egypt, instead of Kadmos.[38] At the same time, a Greek autochthonist tradition brewed in archaic myth and poetry, which associated writing with Palamedes or the default human benefactor Prometheus.[39] The Phoenician link, however, was mainstream after Herodotos.[40] The early Greek letters, after all, were associated with Phoenicians and Kadmos and were variously called "Phoenician letters" (*phonikeia / phoinikika grammata*) and "Kadmean letters" (*kadmeia grammata*), while offices related to writing evoked the same associations, such as the term for "scribe" on Crete (*poinikastas*) and perhaps a title for a priestly office on Mytilene (*phoinikographos*).[41]

The legend of Kadmos, who arrived from Tyre while searching for his sister Europa, captures the east–west movement of people and culture (even in the names of the characters) and the ancient belief in a Phoenician migration or settlement associated with Thebes, correctly perceived as one of the oldest Greek cities.[42] The relevance of mythological stories is shown by their persistence, not necessarily as conveyers of historical reality but of belief systems, customs, and cultural identity vis-à-vis others; in this case, these traditions were construed through deduction from visible cultural affinities and through prolonged interaction between Phoenicians and Greeks.

Literature, Mythology, and More

The Greeks did not surgically extract Phoenician letters from their contexts. They became acquainted with Levantine writing culture, not through a single channel (commerce, poetic performances, religious festivals) but multiple ones, interacting also with popular and learned oral traditions and transmission.[43] But the contribution of Phoenician culture to the written arts is much more difficult to retrieve, given the loss of most of Phoenician literature.[44] Other than epigraphy, the Greek and Roman sources are our

FIG. 7.1 **Papyrus with Phoenician text and Egyptianizing amulet case.**
Small piece of papyrus (*right*) with Phoenician protective text (7.4 cm) and drawing of Isis holding a scepter and an *ankh* symbol (lower-right quadrant); the papyrus was rolled up inside the bronze amulet-case (4.85 cm) (*left*), made in the shape of a falcon-headed figure representing Horus with the solar disk and *uraeus* or sacred cobra; found in a rock-cut tomb at Tal-Virtù outside Rabat, sixth century BC. Courtesy of National Museum of Archaeology, Heritage Malta.

main window into Phoenician sources, Rome being itself partly to blame for the loss. The Phoenicians, like the Greeks, used papyrus (*byblos*) as the main medium for their writings, which is rarely preserved anywhere outside Egypt (see Figure 7.1). And the Phoenicians' legacy (unlike that of Greeks and Jews) did not become the object of a medieval manuscript tradition, so that a curated corpus of it would reach us.

In 146 BC, Rome crushed both Carthage and Corinth, thereby dominating its two military and cultural rivals, the Carthaginians and the Greeks. But the emerging Roman Empire did exactly the opposite with each of them, muffling Carthage's cultural legacy, while elevating and boldly appropriating the Greek one. Rome mythologized its detachment from the Carthaginian world through Aeneas's rejection of Dido, while attaching itself to the Greek epic tradition through his Trojan genealogy, both fictions signaling the bifurcated course that western culture would take. They dismantled the library of Carthage and cherished the Alexandrian scholarly tradition, paving the path for Greek literature to survive.

And yet out of sheer utilitarianism, occasional admiration, and, in Christian times, rejection of "pagan" beliefs, Greeks and Romans sometimes cited and quoted literature written by eastern and western Phoenicians. There were particular genres for which Greeks and Romans resorted to Phoenician lore: mythology, especially cosmogony and foundation stories; city annals and historiography; travel literature (*periploi*); and technical knowledge in the realms of agriculture, philosophy, and law. Doubts expressed by scholars over whether there was a Phoenician and Carthaginian literature stem from a preconceived approach to the rare but precious evidence that we do have, leading to statements like "there is no positive indication that such literature ever in fact existed in Phoenician, and [. . .] a lack of shared identity may even explain why it never developed."[45] Yet past and recent overviews of these sources leave little doubt that this corpus did exist and was lost, not that it never existed.[46]

When Scipio Aemilianus led the conquest and destruction of Carthage, its population was forced to disperse, its temples were razed, and its famous library handed over to Rome's allies, the Numidian kings, whence its records were lost.[47] Still, the historian Sallust, who governed the province of Africa Nova a century later, wrote about the "Punic books" kept by the Numidian king Hiampsal, and still later, Plutarch claimed to know of "a sacred parchment" that had survived the destruction of Carthage.[48] In North Africa at least, Phoenician documents were produced for centuries after the fall of Carthage: Augustine mentions "Phoenician books" (*libri punici*), and we know from epigraphy and other sources that the language survived there until his time.[49] In the east, the archives of Tyre were consulted until the first century AD, and texts transmitting Phoenician lore continued to circulate, as we know from Roman historians and literati, such as Josephus and Philo of Byblos.[50] Even if Plutarch's "sacred parchment" might be a literary trope, it is telling that Phoenician writings were part of a literary legacy that Greeks and Romans fantasized about.

The Needle in the Haystack

The huge loss that we face has caused classical scholars to underestimate the Greek reception of Phoenician culture. At the same time, the neglect and the loss itself are not innocent but inseparable from the Greco-Roman bias against the Phoenicians, intensified by modern ideologies of the nineteenth and first half of the twentieth century. This history was most famously exposed by Martin Bernal in the first volume of his *Black Athena*.[51] Despite criticism for his "black and white" articulation of the issue and the many inaccuracies in his handling of ancient sources, his denunciation of the anti-Semitism and racism underlying the works of classicists at large before and during World War II was necessary, and it had already been more subtly articulated by Michael Astour in the 1960s. In the preface of his *Hellenosemitica*, Astour wrote: "The polemic against admitting any Semitic influence upon Greece was conducted with so much passion that its motivation seemed to be derived from external considerations." He pointed out that "Eastern influences were excluded a priori, but there was a great predilection for seeking northern (or Nordic) influences on Greek religion and culture."[52] Before prejudice erected its walls, nineteenth-century and earlier authors had been able to cross the artificial east–west divide, for instance within trilingual biblical scholarship (Greek-Latin-Hebrew), but it would take generations of textual and archaeological discoveries (including Mesopotamian, Ugaritic, and Hittite texts); the shedding of modern orientalism; the adoption of postcolonial perspectives; the rise of an interest in cross-cultural interaction; and institutional support for interdisciplinary research to fully develop the study of Greek culture within the broader framework of the eastern Mediterranean and Near East.[53]

Part of the revisionism of the "Greek miracle" has involved looking back at the Greeks' views of others, which included both their acknowledgment of the contributions of other cultures and their own baggage of stereotypes and alienations. What Greek impressions tell us is that Phoenicians were not only associated with technology, the alphabet (itself a technology), trade, and craftsmanship already in Homer, but also were deemed among the ancient learned societies that cultivated and transmitted knowledge. This idea is evident in Herodotos's universe but persists until later antiquity. To give a prominent example, Neoplatonic philosophers collected a tradition according to which Pythagoras, one of the most emblematic wisemen in Greek tradition, found wisdom in his travels to Sidon, Byblos, and Tyre, and was initiated by a Phoenician religious specialist led by no less than Thales of Miletus, whom Herodotos thought was of Phoenician stock.[54]

While these sources should not always be taken at face value, they illustrate an idea, counterintuitive for most classicists, that for the ancient Greeks the Phoenicians and other Levantines were prestige sources of written culture and wisdom. This view coexisted with prejudices against them, even forms of orientalism, but as we know one does not preclude the other. In the realm of historical writing, Josephus cites Phoenician antiquarians, Manetho, and Berossus alongside "all those who among the Greeks and the barbarians have compiled antiquities;" and Tertullian, the North African Christian writer, when discussing the early date of Moses, says that for this inquiry "we would have to open up the archives of the oldest peoples also—of the Egyptians, Chaldeans, Phoenicians." As mentioned above, the archives of Tyre long remained in use, and scholars have detected a Phoenician "brand" and even neo-Phoenician cultural identities rehearsed in Greek and Roman works, especially the novel.[55] In Athens we find at least fourteen Phoenician philosophers in residence during the classical and Hellenistic periods, coming from Kition, Carthage, Sidon, and especially Tyre. One of them was Zeno from Kition (fourth-century BC), the founder of Stoicism; another was Kleitomachos/Hasdrubal, who fled Carthage before its destruction and became no other less than the head of the Platonic Academy, after allegedly teaching philosophy at Carthage in his native language.[56]

Instead of brushing off the Phoenician intellectual and literary legacy (in whichever language it was conveyed), we should keep our eyes open for any small shreds of it that we can find in the wreckage. The field of comparative mythology and literature has expanded enormously since the 1980s. It began with a generic task of finding, cataloguing, and presenting parallels between Greek and Near Eastern literatures.[57] This important groundwork established that orientalizing adaptations went beyond artistic styles and paved the way for more focused studies on particular areas, corpora, or genres on the Near Eastern side. The bibliography is by now vast and covers many fronts and approaches.[58] For my part, I have focused on the Northwest Semitic cultural legacy, attested in the Canaanite, Phoeni-

cian, and Hebrew sources. I have argued that motifs related to cosmogonies and theogonies found a specially fruitful reception in Greek tradition,
although that impression might be due to the type of Phoenician references
that happen to be attested.[59]

Mythologies and archaeology rarely align. In places such as Thebes, we
have a mythological saga that involves an explicit connection with the east,
and even historical hypotheses of a migration, but we have no archaeological trail of it for the Iron Age (while there is evidence of a strong connection with the Near East in the Bronze Age). At Corinth, on the contrary,
there is no Phoenician foundation narrative, but we have seen in previous
chapters that plenty of Levantine materials and innovations concentrated
in this area in the eighth–seventh centuries. And, sure enough, historical
(not mythological) sources attribute the city a leading role in material-
technological innovation of the sort that makes it a prime player in the
"orientalizing revolution": according to Herodotos, craftspeople were treated
with particular (unusual) respect there; Pliny gathers the idea that either
Sikyonians or Corinthians introduced ceramic (terracotta) decoration in
buildings; and the Corinthians were reputed to have been innovators in
shipping technology including warships, a prowess otherwise attributed to
Phoenicians-Carthaginians.[60] After all, as Thucydides remarked, "Corinth,
inhabiting a city on the Isthmus, had always had commerce."[61] The story
of Demaratus, the emblematic Corinthian merchant who settled in Tarquinia bringing artisans with him, fits well into the Greek-Phoenician east–
west networks too.[62] The seventh-century Kypselid dynasty at Corinth, in
turn, fostered political connections with Near Eastern royalty, at least from
Egypt, Lydia, and Miletus.[63]

On the other hand, possible connections with Phoenicians are not to-
tally absent from the mythological and cultic landscapes of the Isthmus
area, including the name "Phoinikaios" for a month in Corinth's calendar.
Scholars have, for instance, noticed the very likely Northwest Semitic background of the names and stories of local characters such as Melikertes and
Palaimon (perhaps adaptations of Melqart and Baal-Hammon?).[64] The
motif of Medea's slaughtering of her children at Corinth (an echo of the
trope of Phoenician child sacrifice?); the idea that sacred prostitution was
part of the cult of Aphrodite on the Akrocorinth (often assumed for other
Ashtart, Aphrodite, and Venus temple areas); and the overall prominence

of the cult of the goddess (so frequently overlaid with that of Ashtart in heavily commercial areas), may also suggest mythical-religious overlaps in the Isthmus.[65]

Other mythological clusters represented in ancient Greek literature point in the Phoenician direction. The list includes Myrrha and Adonis, Bellerophon, the Danaans, Danaos and his daughters, Mopsos, and various Phoinix characters, and on Cyprus also the figures of Kinyras, Pygmalion, and Kuthar.[66] The relationship between Greek and other Near Eastern cultures (especially Mesopotamian, and secondarily Hittite), however, has received more attention, not necessarily because these were in more direct contact with the Greeks but because, put simply, these are the texts that are available. This in turn skews our appreciation of Phoenician culture and its role as the direct intermediary. They are often excluded from the list of first-rank Near Eastern cultures. But specialized close-up studies show that the "Near Eastern" motifs detected in Greek literature are not necessarily direct borrowings, but more often the result of a trickling-in of versions of distant themes familiar *to us* from Hittite or Mesopotamian texts (because they happen to survive), whereas we are blind when it comes to the "ghost versions" circulating among closer interlocutors such as the Phoenicians, who may have made these traditions available to Greek lore.

Consider the succession myth. As always noted, the succession of gods (Ouranos, Kronos, Zeus) forms the "backbone" of Hesiod's *Theogony*, the earliest most widely known and revered Greek narrative about the origins of the universe and the gods. The pattern finds ample parallel in the earlier Near Eastern epics, whether as a linear succession (father–son) or in the more general motif of the struggle for power among multigenerational or same-generation gods (the former in Babylonian and Hurro-Hittite versions, the latter in the Canaanite version from Ugarit), in all of which the Storm or Weather god emerges victorious at the end. The most idiosyncratic feature of this struggle in Hesiod is perhaps the castration of the sky (Ouranos), which is attested only in the Greek and Hurro-Hittite epics preserved in the Late Bronze Age ("Song of Kumarbi" or "Song of Birth"). Many other specific parallels have been noted with the Mesopotamian traditions known from the Babylonian *Enuma Elish*, and are also well studied. But the Greek cosmogonies represented by Hesiod and the Greek Orphic texts also converge with Ugaritic and Phoenician traditions in oddly specific ways, the latter preserved in fragments and in the longer narrative of Philo of Byblos. These features include the role of a Time deity and the appearance of a cosmic egg motif, but also a scheme of distribution of powers among the Sky-Sea-Death gods in Homer and Ugarit different from Hesiod's succession myth.[67]

About this conundrum, Martin West argues, "More likely the line of transmission went either directly from Hurrian speakers to Greeks or through north-west Semitic intermediaries. In either case it must have passed through northern Syria or Cilicia."[68] Discussing the "adoption of Semitic idioms in Greek poetic language," he speculates about the "sporadic migration of craftsmen from the Levant from the ninth century on" as the likely vector for the Near Eastern imprint in early Greek poetry.[69] In her study of the transmission of Hittite lore to Homeric tradition, Mary Bachvarova has also noted that "when it is possible to distinguish the source of influence, it is a blended Hurrian-west Semitic tradition," which she points out "would have been at home more in north Syria than in Anatolia," while she also considered Cilicia or Cyprus as the possible loci of these adaptations. All of these were areas where Phoenicians were settled since the ninth century or before.[70] The *Epic of Gilgamesh* also exemplifies this sort of chain of transmission: the most popular epic in the Near East, a "classic" in its own right, we know that versions of the epic were copied, adapted, and "remade" in other languages, including a Hittite version, and that the epic circulated broadly in the Levant, as attested at Ugarit. Even though we do not have attestations of a Northwest Semitic version, the prominent Assyriologist Andrew George is confident that it must have circulated in writing and orally among Aramaeans, Phoenicians, and other Levantines in the Iron Age, perhaps with versions in their own languages.[71]

Finally, when ancient Greeks paid attention to cultural borrowings, they also pointed to the Phoenicians as intermediaries and innovators, as I have already noted. They observed points of convergence particularly in the areas of religion and ritual, which was a main vector for the transfer of mythological traditions. One of the earliest and most explicit such observers was, again, Herodotos, who posited that the cult of Aphrodite came to Greece from Syria via Cyprus, as already mentioned, "for even the temple on Cyprus originated there [i.e., Ashkelon in 'Syria']. As for the one on Kythera, it was Phoenicians who founded it, who came from this same land of Syria."[72] Most famously, the historian provided an excursus about the Egyptian origin of "the names" (perhaps meaning attributes) of the Greek gods. In a sort of Greek-Egyptian-Semitic triangulation that we have seen in other cultural domains, Herodotos posited the Phoenicians as the common factor, most clearly in his inquiry on the cult of Herakles, as mentioned above.[73]

Besides artifacts, technologies, and loanwords (see below), the interaction with Northwest Semites in the harbor, the sanctuary, and the market must have included exchange in the broader realm of ideas. The areas of mythology and religion are somewhat fruitful because of the types of texts we do have, but scholars have suggested influences coming from the Near East in early Greek political models and philosophy, sometimes pointing to the Levant and Asia Minor.[74] Without historical or philosophical narratives from the "other" side, however, further areas of interaction are even more difficult to trace. For instance, commonalities in the political systems of Carthage and the Doric societies of Sparta and Crete have been noted by ancient and modern scholars.[75] This does not mean that their institutions were historically related, nor that there are grounds to suppose the model of the Greek polis lay in the Near Eastern city-states, as some have speculated.[76] Too many internal factors need to converge for states to form, but the Greeks shared in Iron Age developments that underpinned and stimulated the process, there and among other advanced societies, as we have seen in Etruria, Iberia, or Cyprus. Overall, the Greeks would have recognized the schemes of political organization of the independent Phoenician city-states, whether in the Levant or in the colonies abroad, which probably facilitated their interaction at several levels.

A Pattern of Loanwords

The linguistic convergence between the Northwest Semitic and Greek languages still lacks systematic study. In the field of Greek historical linguistics, including the classical etymological dictionaries, Semitic sources are rarely considered, even when Indo-European roots are not viable.[77] But a closer look produces a different picture. West estimated that at the least, more than a hundred loanwords were attested before the fifth century BC "for which [. . .] a good case has been made for a Semitic connection, satisfying the two criteria of a good phonetic correspondence and a good semantic fit." These include names of animals, plants and plant-derived products, minerals, vessels and containers, fabrics and garments, food items, and terms related to commerce and religious life as well as to writing technology.[78] A Phoenician connection can often be hypothesized, even if reconstructed from roots preserved in Akkadian or other Semitic languages better attested than Phoenician (Hebrew, Aramaic, Ugaritic). We depart from the reasonable supposition that we are dealing with a crippled proximate corpus, and that the more intense interaction with Phoenicians may well have accounted for many of the loans, especially when the words were related to specific activities and industries.

Leaving aside a number of roots that seem to have been shared in Semitic and Greek from the deep past (e.g., lion, bull, wine), a quick look at the best-known Greek loanwords from Akkadian and Northwest Semitic languages reveals that they fall within the semantic fields of areas of Phoenician-Greek interaction such as religious ritual, trade, writing, and other technologies.[79] In the realm of ritual, we find loanwords related to purification (*kathairoi, katharos;* cf. Heb. *qatar,* Ugaritic *qtr,* Akkadian *qataru*), all connected with fumigating or smoking, and to praying or cursing, as the Greek verb *araomai* ("to pray, vow," "curse") and *areter* (one who prays or issues an incantation/curse) may be related to the Semitic verb "to curse" (Akkadian *araru,* Hebrew *'arar*).[80] Other items, such as incense (*libanos*), altar (*bomos*), and "assigned land," whence "sacred precinct" (*temenos*) point to interactions in the realm of ritual practices.

Semitic genealogies have been proposed for a group of words connected to mystery cults and the Bacchic and banqueting world, which may go hand in hand with the more general Near Eastern background of banqueting practices and analogies with the Semitic *marzeah* in the Aegean and farther west: the name *Bacchos* for Dionysos and his followers, the *bacchai* (cf. Heb. *bacha*), and the *thyrsus,* which may share the root of "wine" and divinized entities related to it (Ugaritic *trth,* Phoenician *trsh;* cf. *tuwarsa* "vine" in Late Hittite).[81] The war cry *alala* also has similar eastern counterparts.[82] The association of Aphrodite with the Levant is reflected in her names: some think that Aphrodite's name is in fact a muddled version of Ashtart.[83] In turn, her epithets Kythereia, Kypris, and Ourania ("Heavenly") all have Levantine connotations or counterparts, as Ourania is akin to Semitic "Queen of Heaven" and Kythereia might be related to Northwest Semitic Kothar.[84] Ortheia, in turn, a hypostasis of Artemis known from her old *xoanon* at Sparta, meaning "straight up" or the like, may be a direct Greek translation of Asherah.[85]

Accompanying the technology of writing came the names of the letters and the writing tablet, the papyrus roll or "book," and terms for scribes, as mentioned above. Next, the list of trade-related words is impressive, some of them attested since Mycenaean times. Following Burkert's "collection" of well-established terms, we should note the word for frankincense (*libanos*), myrrh (*myrrha*), sesame (*sesamon*), the crocus plant (*krokos*), cinnamon (*kinnamomon/kinnamon*), other plants and spices (*nardos, kasia, kannabis*), and flour (*semidalis*); gold (*chrysos*) and other minerals (*naphtha, nitron*); textile-related vocabulary, such as the word for garment (*chiton*, whence our "cotton") and other fabrics (*sindon, othone, bussos*); types of containers or vases (*kados, sipye, lekane*, perhaps *alabastron*); and coloring terms related to textiles (*calche* for a type of purple and *kuwanos* for blue, from Semitic and Hittite terms, respectively).[86] From the realm of trade came the word for market itself (*makellon*) and a series of other borrowings, such as the "sack" container (*sakkos*) and the main weight unit (*mnea / mna*), attached to the sexagesimal weight system (foreign to the Mycenaean weight system, this was a likely Iron Age adoption linked to the silver trade).[87] Vocabulary related to shipbuilding and masonry construction is also present, with words for the broader trading ship (*gaulos;* perhaps also *naus* has a shared root, cf. Hebr. *'onniyah*), and words attested mainly in Akkadian, such as the verb "to incise" (*charaxai,* cf. Akkadian *haraṣu*), also used for fortified palisades (*charax*), the "rod" / "stave" (*kanon*), and terms for lime (*titanos*) and plaster (*gypson*); even the word for brick (*plinthos*), Burkert proposed, might be related to a basic element of Mesopotamian architecture (Akkadian *libittu < *libintu*).[88]

Whether all these suggestions reflect secure etymologies or not, a pattern emerges loud and clear, and directs our attention to the precise realms of culture that brought together Greek and Near Eastern neighbors, including explicitly Phoenicians, as we know historically and archaeologically, and independently of linguistic criteria. The thread of loanwords and the adoption of Near Eastern artifacts related to cult, which we have frequently encountered among the regional versions of the orientalizing kit, made Burkert think of religious-ritual technicians as conduits for cultural capital, besides the usually posited merchants and storytellers.[89] But we need not limit our reconstruction of contact to people on the move and fleeting path crossings. As argued here and by others cited throughout this book, we can safely consider contexts with bilingual families and resident aliens as some of the most fertile ground for these exchanges and adaptations, which included the alphabet as well as material culture and mythological stories.

The trail of Semitic loanwords in Greek suggests the sorts of intangible legacies left by nonimperial or colonial but lasting and consequential contact. As a comparative exercise, we can think, for instance, of the economic and cultural impact of the Portuguese in the Indian Ocean. These explorations started in the fifteenth century with Vasco de Gama and eventually reached from the Cape of Good Hope in South Africa to China. While the political influence of these traders was rather light and short-lived, their extensive cultural legacy remains to this day and is reflected in linguistic borrowings and adaptations in some fifty different local creole languages. The adopted Portuguese vocabulary coincides precisely with domains of culture particularly influenced by the Portuguese–local exchange: food, flora and fauna, the arts (e.g., music), furniture, architecture, transport and commerce, education, and religion.[90] The Portuguese case in Asia is interesting because, much like the ancient Phoenicians, when the Portuguese entered the Indian Ocean, their intent was not to control its lands and peoples, but to advance their own commercial interests. The Portuguese are presented here as "pioneers of cultural globalization," who enhanced mobility and connectivity among different cultures.[91] Like the Phoenicians, the Portuguese benefited from becoming "cultural brokers," who first introduced western concepts and technologies to "untapped" markets. Thus, by knitting networks of commercial exchange, they effectively turned the Indian Ocean into "a Portuguese lake."[92] Far from their homelands, both Portuguese and Phoenicians acted as spokespeople for larger points of reference (the "West," the "Near East"), and the role of the Portuguese in relation to "Westernization" in the east is perhaps not so different from that of the Phoenicians in the "Orientalizing" transformation.

჻

We are dealing with a fragmentary picture, as we are bereft of literary testimonies from most Iron Age societies save the Greeks and Romans, on whose sources we depend to evaluate the presence and agency of other cultures, which keeps us trapped in a "classical" circle. As Burkert states, "the situation as far as the eighth century B.C. is concerned appears hopeless: Greek documentation is sparse [. . .]. The neighboring languages,

Aramaic and Phoenician, are known mainly through casual inscriptions; the rest of documentation is lost. For a conscientious judge, acquittal by lack of evidence will result again and again—and yet the outcome of minimalism, arrived at in this fashion, must be absolutely false, as a general consideration of probabilities will show."[93] In short, the artistic orientalizing phenomenon had a written counterpart, as hybrid and local and Levantine-inflected as the visual arts, and the Phoenicians were also involved in its making. Given the weight of the evidence that has come to light and been studied from different angles and disciplines, it is absurd, at this point, to imagine the opposite. True, we will never regain a full sense of the live subject we study or know how these channels worked exactly, but, as West puts it, "a corpse suffices to prove a death, even if the inquest is inconclusive."[94] In his 1966 study of Hesiod's *Theogony* he also boldly states that "Greece is part of Asia; Greek literature is a Near Eastern literature."[95]

At the same time, this realization does not annul the character or uniqueness of Greek culture, or of any other cultures discussed in this book, for that matter. As Fritz Graf has said of Greek mythology, while narratives contributed to construct a shared Hellenic identity, they are part and parcel of a Greekness that remained "fiercely local and tied to its kaleidoscopic of individual places."[96] The statements of both West and Graf are true. The elastic tension between tradition and innovation, between the local and global, are part of these cultural transformations. This is true as much of the visual culture discussed in this book (which dominates the preserved evidence for this period), as of the world of stories and ideas, only some of which were captured by those "Phoenician letters."

⊰ 8 ⊱

CYPRUS

An Insular Trajectory

When we reach Cyprus, we arrive at the "ground zero" of Aegean-Levantine relations. Some say that it is possible to see the shores of Syria-Phoenicia from the island's eastern coasts or higher ground (cf. Map 9.1). Here, the term "orientalization" is most artificial or redundant, for two reasons: first, Cyprus was so enmeshed in the Near Eastern world that the cultural distance and abstraction implied in "orientalization" becomes too rarefied. Second, in the period that concerns us, the adoption of Near Eastern cultural capital is overwhelmingly related to the interaction with Canaanites and Phoenicians, so that we should really be talking about "Phoenicianizing," not "orientalizing," adaptations. As it happens, however, neither term is used in Cypriot archaeology.

Overall, the Phoenicians' role on Cyprus is generally overshadowed by the Hellenocentric narrative championed by European scholarship. The idea of an essentially Greek Cyprus projects onto the first millennium BC a combination of European biases we have seen in other areas in addition to modern (Greek and Greek-Cypriot) nationalism. These assumptions still permeate school textbooks and popular literature.[1] More recently, as we shall see, Cypriot archaeologists have championed alternative approaches that provide a more complex view of the island's cultural past.

The Hellenocentric line of interpretation compartmentalizes the Phoenician presence as a limited mercantile and colonial enterprise that did not "Semiticize" the island. In this view, the appearance of Mycenaean materials on Cyprus around the twelfth century is associated with a massive migration of Greek speakers (reflected in the Homeric traditions) who essentially "Hellenized" the island. This view is also called "Mycenaean dogma" or "Achaean theory" and has been vigorously questioned by archaeologists such as Susan Sherratt and others since the 1990s.[2] At the same time, a relatively marginal line of scholarship has stressed the Phoenician legacy in the period of state-formation on Cyprus, linking the development not to Greek influence but to Tyre's expansionism; this has been referred to as the "Phoenician theory."[3] But these are the exception, not the norm, and an "all or nothing" approach has generally been at play, driven by a strong dichotomy between Greek and Phoenician culture, which accounts for statements to the effect that "during their five-hundred-year presence on Cyprus, the Phoenicians did not manage to change the overall character of Cypriot culture," or, more emphatically, they "did not succeed in taking over Cyprus," for, if they had done so, "Cyprus would be speaking Phoenician rather than Greek today."[4] These statements also show the teleological use of linguistic criteria to project a monolithic Greek identity in Hellenocentric, classic-centric terms, a narrative to some degree imposed by the West.[5] The trope of Cyprus as the quintessential "crossroads" between Europe and Asia also implies the island's passive reception of inevitable external forces.[6] This image at least captures the difficult position of Cypriot studies themselves, much like that of the Phoenicians, on the margins of both classics and Near Eastern scholarship, and straddling the fields of Aegean prehistory and Iron Age archaeology.[7]

In reaction to the diffusionist overtones of both Mycenaean/Hellenocentric and Phoenician theories and to the island's long history as a colonial subject, in recent decades a third, "autochthonist" stance has gained terrain among Cypriot archaeologists. This trend partly overlaps with the Hellenocentric national narrative, inasmuch as it highlights the arrival of Greek-speaking groups as providing a thread of cultural (and linguistic) continuity from the end of the Late Bronze Age into the Iron Age. The autochthonist trend, however, stresses the island's extraordinary local character, which pulled in newcomers and assimilated migrants, Greeks included, presenting Cyprus as a culturally hybrid space in the early first millennium BC.[8] The advantages of studying islands on their own terms has also been stressed in recent circles as singular case studies of cultural encounters and hybridity in the Mediterranean.[9]

Where do the Phoenicians stand in all this? The new trend of decoloniz-
ing Cypriot archaeology in the twenty-first century assumes the assimilation of Greek speakers and their culture, but does not assume the similar
effects of absorbing Phoenician speakers or other Near Easterners. On Cyprus there is no "orientalizing period" (as in Etruscan or Greek art); materials with evident Levantine traits are subsumed under the Cypro-Geometric
and Cypro-Archaic labels. While I applaud the emphasis on the local character of these adaptations, the "autochtonous theory" throws the baby
(Phoenicians) out with the bathwater (colonialization, orientalization), but
only *that* baby; the Greeks, even with a reformulated role, still stand at the
center of the island's protohistory. In short, the now dominant narrative
poses a modality of "Cypriot exceptionalism" that does little to help us understand the complex relations between Cypriot and Phoenician culture at
the crucial moment when urban communities evolved on Cyprus.

Recent scholarship has brought the Phoenicians back into the picture,
however, and the pendulum is swinging in the other direction.[10] This is
partly a reaction to the autochthonist trend, and partly due to the impulse
of Mediterranean studies and the mounting archaeological evidence in the
Aegean and Phoenician realms, all of which seem to call for perspectives
that integrate foreign and local input in the cultural history of the island.[11]
In my view, the island can be seen as fiercely local while still partaking in,
even playing a crucial role in Early Iron Age "global" Mediterranean dynamics. As Susan Sherratt puts it: "Confused we may be, [. . .] and baffled
by the superimposition of concepts and their opaque terminologies often
imported from other disciplines, but it seems to me that the question of
cultural contacts is now more exciting than it has ever been."[12]

Greeks and Phoenicians in the Cypriot "Melting Pot"

Into the Iron Age

After the island's relative isolation during the Neolithic period, Cyprus en-
tered the eastern Mediterranean trading circuits in the Middle and Late
Bronze periods, when it appears in Mycenaean texts by its later Greek name
(*Ku-pi-ri-jo / Kypros*) and in a wide range of Near Eastern sources, mainly

under versions of the name "Alashiya" (Ugarit, Amarna Letters, Egyptian and Hittite inscriptions). This was the name used by the Phoenicians, while in first-millennium Assyrian texts it was called *Iadnana*. Trade with the Levant is well attested early on, especially with Ugarit, the large kingdom in northern Syria, and also with Egypt, Anatolia, and the Aegean. The island's natural wealth in copper (necessary to produce bronze) was essential to boost Cyprus's connectivity.[13] Through these contacts, Cypriot communities saw a first wave of orientalization as they engaged in the so-called Late Bronze Age koine to mark their international and urban status.[14] But, inasmuch as Cyprus was in direct or indirect contact with these other Near Eastern cultures, it was first the Canaanites and then their Iron Age heirs the Phoenicians who most frequented and eventually settled the island, leaving their own footprint on its cultural landscape. They left traces of their cults, industries, language, and burials.

After centuries of trading relations, Greek speakers permanently settled on Cyprus during the migrations that followed the collapse of the Mycenaean palace system around 1200–1100 BC. But many have questioned the traditional narrative according to which Cyprus was forever shaped by a Mycenaean "invasion" that "turned Cyprus Greek," so to speak, as represented in Homeric myth, and was then followed by a limited Phoenician colonization in some areas. In recent discussions, the main proponent of the "autochthonist" school, Maria Iacovou, sees the Mycenaeans' arrival as a gradual migration, although a crucial one for the formation of later Cypriot kingdoms in the Iron Age. Whatever their ethnic makeup, she posits, the result was a "pan-Cyprian *koine* culture" that was neither purely Greek nor purely Cypriot, but nonetheless coherent and culturally homogeneous.[15] Others see the twelfth-century culture(s) of the island as not exactly homogeneous but undergoing experimentation and regional variety, for instance, in ceramic production.[16]

The dominant Greek narrative is evident in how some artifacts have been repeatedly highlighted and interpreted while others are occluded. For instance, the bronze *obelos* (spit) found in Tomb 49 at the Palaipaphos-Skales cemetery, which bears a Cypro-Minoan inscription with a Greek personal name (*Opheltas*), is repeatedly cited as evidence for Greek continuity from the Bronze Age into the subsequent period. The unique object appears in an eleventh-century tomb (Cypriot-Geometric I, ca. 1050–950 BC), but many have noted that it is an isolated finding (perhaps an heirloom), and not necessarily evidence for the generalized spread of Greek culture or Greek language in eleventh-century Palaipaphos.[17] The presence of two other *obeloi* in the same tomb with unidentified script, and a bowl with Cypro-Minoan signs (all non-Greek) is understated or ignored, as are the abundant Near Eastern materials from tombs in the same necropolis, which, taken together, coherently present a local culture that is not "Greek" in any meaningful way.[18] These findings are not brandished as evidence of a Semitic migration or colonization, nor is the silver bowl with Ugaritic script from Hala Sultan Tekke (twelfth century BC), near Larnaka, or other early Levantine materials on the island (pottery, ivory, metalwork, architecture, etc.).[19] Thus, singular Greek artifacts point to generalized identity, but Levantine ones are isolated encroachments on the island's culture. The actual complexity of this transition period is also suggested by specific local pottery styles, such as the Proto-White Painted pottery, which synthesize local Cypriot, Aegean, and Levantine traditions in the eleventh century.[20]

Scholars disagree on how the Late Bronze Age collapse affected Cyprus. For some, there is enough evidence that Cyprus did not suffer a collapse of its sociopolitical structures or maritime networks, unlike the Mycenaean palaces or many states to the east. Disruptions on Cyprus's settlement pattern were not devastating, and some communities maintained their political and economic functions intact into the Geometric period.[21] This view relies on the cases of Kition and Palaipaphos (less clearly Idalion), where there are signs of continuous habitation. Even there, however, the abandonment of the large Bronze Age temples raises doubts as to the continuity of institutional and political organization.[22] In the end, it is difficult to escape the fact that most Late Bronze Age settlements on Cyprus were abandoned; some populations shifted (Enkomi to Salamis), entire regions were deserted (e.g., Maroni, Kalavasos), and Iron Age settlements were generally new, with no prehistory. The eleventh- to tenth-century archaeological evidence is ambiguous enough that some see a glass half full and others a glass half empty: the island's copper production continued through the twelfth century, but it seems to have been limited to internal needs, not export; the Cypro-Minoan script was not completely forgotten (e.g., the *obelos* mentioned above, and the circulation of *bullae*), but there is a long writing hiatus before the use of the Cypriot syllabary spread; clear evidence of urban culture and monumentalization has to wait until the second half of the ninth century or later.[23]

The linguistic map of Cyprus when we enter the first millennium was as complicated as its demographic makeup, with very few inscriptions (about twenty) dated to the Geometric period (ca. 1050–750 BC), reflecting three languages in various scripts: Eteocypriot (i.e., "true-Cypriot"), a non–Indo-European language (or languages) as yet undeciphered and best attested in the area of Amathous; Phoenician, especially well-attested in the area of Kition; and Greek, still not dominant on the island and written in Cypro-syllabic and only later in the Greek alphabet.[24] This linguistic configuration, however, does not map onto stark differences in material culture. On Cyprus in particular, the neat labels of Aegean, Phoenician, and Eteo-Cypriot do not correspond to the island's material and linguistic registers, which intersect in complex ways: for A. T. Reyes, by the Cypro-Archaic period we can differentiate only two groups: Cypriots at large (including those originating in the Greek migration) and Phoenicians.[25] For others, the archaeological record and artistic output allow us to talk about a Cypriot-Geometric koine; while regional character can be appreciated within the Cypriot umbrella, whether indicated by ceramic production or the persistence of Eteocypriot language(s) in areas such as Amathous.[26] (I discuss the linguistic situation in the section "A Palette of Languages and Scripts" below.)

Be that as it may, as Vassos Karageorghis conceded, "One cannot deny that the Phoenicians were already active on Cyprus as early as the 11th century BC, trading in timber and copper."[27] He also defended the Phoenicians' partnership with Cypriots in western commercial and colonial enterprises.[28] This view contrasts with that of the predominant view among classical archaeologists, which emphasized the role of Euboians and Cypriots in early contacts with the Levant.[29] Indeed, mounting evidence shows that early Phoenicians, or "proto-Phoenician" Canaanites, were part of the island's demography in this transitional period. The introduction of masonry, for instance, attested in the thirteenth century at Kalavasos (near Larnaka), thus before the Achaean migration, was more likely modeled on contemporary Syro-Anatolian architecture than on Greek models.[30] By the mid- to late ninth century a more permanent Phoenician presence becomes evident at Kition. Excavations on Crete, at sites such as Knossos, Kommos, and Eleutherna, where the presence of Phoenicians is now indisputable, have helped to generally shift scholarly attitudes toward Phoenicians by Aegean archaeologists.[31] The Greek and Phoenician input is roughly contemporary on Cyprus, and both groups adapted to a local substratum. We are dealing, therefore, with a complex scenario that defies the dissecting of territories into neat ethnic and political compartments. That being said, it is clear that Phoenicians too, and not only Greeks, were part of the Cypriot cultural landscape.

Cypriot Phoenicians and the Assyrian Framework

The nature of Phoenician presence at sites such as Kition, Amathous, Palaipaphos, and others is itself not easy to categorize, the question being whether or not we are dealing with colonization, in the sense used by ancient historians (see Chapter 1). Although Cyprus's geographical position and copper resources made it far from "immune to invasions, immigrations and commercial trade," archaeologists have rebelled against the portrayal of the island as a passive "lump of clay" to be molded by different passing cultures.[32] As Susan Sherratt, among others, has remarked, Cyprus has been studied either from a western perspective "as an outpost of western civilization," colonized by various western powers (Greeks, Franks, Genoese, Venetians, British), or from a Near Eastern perspective, as colonized or as a place of interest to Hittites, Phoenicians, Assyrians, Persians, Egyptians, and Ottoman Turks (the Greek–Turkish divide still affects the island today).

In the archaic period, the island was rarely in the grip of foreign powers. There was a phase of alleged Assyrian domination (ca. 707–612 BC) and a shorter one of Egyptian administration (ca. 570–526 BC), while relations with Persia after this were ambiguous.[33] Neither Assyrians nor Egyptians became part of the general population, and their "control" was seemingly mediated through the Phoenician outposts. As far as we can tell, there were no Assyrian governors or garrisons, despite Neo-Assyrian pretensions and propagandistic inclusion of the cities of Iadnana/Cyprus in lists of tribute payers. Notwithstanding any effects that the Assyrian threat may have had as catalyst of synoecism and state formation on the island, there are no traces of Assyrian presence on Cyprus, with the exception of the "Sargon stela."[34] This monumental inscription was erected by Sargon II in 707 at Kition and mentions seven Cypriot kings (without listing them). The Akkadian text glorifies the Assyrian king's conquests in the Near East, instructing the kings on Cyprus to protect this monument, presumably erected there to remind them of his might and as a symbol marking his empire's westernmost border, even though his grip on the island was mediated by Tyre as an Assyrian vassal. But the monument might in fact have represented a recognition by the Assyrian king of the emerging Cypriot kingdoms, and (unintentionally?) strengthened their sense of identity vis-à-vis the Phoenicians.[35] Separately, ten Cypriot kingdoms and their rulers are listed on the prism of King Esarhaddon, a document of around 673–672 BC found at Nineveh. All but two correspond to known historical kingdoms (Idalion, Chytroi, Soloi, Paphos, Salamis, Kourion, Tamassos, and Ledra), leaving the important cities of Kition and Amathous as likely candidates for the other two kingdoms named (but unknown to us): Qarthadasht (another Phoenician "Carthage" or "New City") and Nure[36] (see main locations on Map 9.1).

In other words, Cypriot cities were within the orbit of Assyrian influence and benefited from commercial involvement with it, within a dynamic that most certainly involved Northwest Semites. Besides the Assyrian texts of this period, the island is mentioned in Phoenician inscriptions as Alashiya and in the Hebrew Bible as Elisha or Kittim.[37] Assuming Kition is the Qarthadasht of the Assyrian and Phoenician inscriptions (if it is not, we have to explain the omission of the main Phoenician center on the island), the city was administered by a governor (*skn*), presumably appointed by Tyre, and Kition would have been an Assyrian vassal at least during circa 730–667 BC, which would make it an "overtly political" Tyrian colony.[38] In other words, Cyprus (and especially Kition) was inseparable from Assyrian-Tyrian relations in the Levant. As A. Bernard Knapp puts it, "the role and impact of the Phoenicians on Cyprus [. . .] have perhaps been underestimated, in particular concerning their function as intermediaries, in realms both political (vis-à-vis the Neo-Assyrian Empire) and economic (vis-à-vis other Near Eastern polities)."[39]

According to the evolved view of these historical forces in current scholarship, the edges of Greek and Phoenician cultures softened in the "melting pot" of Cyprus: after Greek speakers settled on Cyprus in the Late Bronze Age, they merged with Eteo-Cypriots, but generalized Hellenic culture is not really manifest until the sixth century (however one would identify and track that). Phoenician culture, which reveals itself much earlier in constructions, iconography, and inscriptions, has also been seen as a stimulus for the revival of Cypriot urban culture since the ninth century.[40] But the emphasis now should also be on how the Phoenicians became integrated into

existing Cypriot communities. In a recent overview, Sabine Fourrier estimates that their presence permeated all Cypriot kingdoms in one way or
another: Phoenician luxury items as well as ceramic shapes entered the local
repertoire, all of which became part of Cypriot elite culture, regardless of
ethnic-linguistic background; Phoenician craftsmen transmitted ceramic
techniques, such as burnishing, and Phoenician traits accented Cypriot Geometric traditions and lay behind evolving features in local pottery forms.
But Phoenicians also absorbed Cypriot artistic traits (see below) and
adopted Cypriot funerary traditions.[41]

Although no Phoenician houses have been excavated or identified so far
from the earlier period of Phoenician activity on Cyprus, their presence is
suggested by burials and the materials in them from at least the mid-ninth
century (e.g., cremations of a Phoenician type in Amathous). Phoenician
pottery itself is well attested on Cyprus in the eleventh century, and Cypriot
influence on Levantine pottery is clear in the tenth (e.g., Cypriot Black-on-
Red pottery at Tel Dor) and Cypriot imitations of Phoenician Red-Slip pottery
were made in the mid-ninth, which suggests early and prolonged contact.
Especially remarkable is the building (or rebuilding) of earlier temples in
honor of Phoenician deities, such as the massive Temple 1 at Kition, which
implies institutional organization.[42]

The main takeaway from recent reassessments of this period is that non–
Greek-speaking locals, Greek speakers, and Phoenician speakers met and
interacted on Cyprus in a variety of scenarios. At one end of the spectrum
we have a Phoenician community somewhat isolated in the peri-urban,
heavily Eteo-Cypriot area of Amathous. The evidence comes from eighth
century burials in cremation urns of Phoenician style, as well as terracottas
of Phoenician-Punic style found in the peri-urban sanctuary areas.[43] At the
other end, we have the thriving compound of Kition (probably Qarthadasht), whether we consider it a colony or an outpost where a Tyrian elite
ruled for some time over a mixed community. Perhaps Kition can be rede-
scribed as a Cypriot-Phoenician state, which emerged from an existing, culturally complex environment.[44] In other communities such as Palaipaphos,
Lapethos, and Salamis, the Greek and Phoenician elements in the early first
millennium were too strongly intertwined for us to uncritically accept the
traditional classifications along ethnic-cultural lines, which lean heavily
on later Greek descriptions, particularly by Pseudo-Skylax's *periplous* in
the fourth-century BC.[45]

Tracing Phoenician Legacies

Pottery Styles

Ceramics are normally used as a baseline to track population movements and cultural-economic change, even though equations between them and peoples are far from direct or simple. Specific types of pottery traditionally classified as "Phoenician" are the most reliable chronological marker of the Phoenician movement across the Mediterranean. Alongside the rich and distinct Cypriot ceramic production of the Geometric and archaic periods, standard Phoenician pottery is also present on Cyprus.[46] Two types stand out: Phoenician Bichrome pottery, which marks the beginning of Phoenician trading activities in Philistia, the northern Negev, Egypt, and Cyprus in the eleventh century BC; and the famous Phoenician Red-Slip ware, starting in the ninth century, when groups of Phoenicians settled on Cyprus and also reached farther out into the central Mediterranean, the coasts of North Africa, and Iberia. At the same time, Cypriot Black-on-Red wares (now dated a bit later than Red-Slip) appear in Phoenician and Palestinian contexts in these early phases, confirming that Cypriots and Phoenicians engaged in joint ventures. Finally, the Canaanite-Phoenician "torpedo-shaped" storage-and-transport jar continued in use throughout the Levant and also on Cyprus with minor morphological changes since the Late Bronze Age.[47]

The technology of the potter's wheel was introduced to Cyprus along with Mycenaean pottery, which was imitated locally in the twelfth century. But handmade Cypriot pottery enjoyed international popularity in the Late Bronze Age, when its hallmark wares, such as Cypriot Base Ring and White Slip wares, appear in the Aegean, Egypt, Syria, and Palestine, at a time when Cypriot potters resided at Ugarit. In fact, ceramic types previously thought to be foreign due to their appearance abroad are now reclassified as Cypriot.[48] In turn, the reappearance of Bichrome ware on Cyprus is attributed to Syro-Palestinian input; but the main changes come at the time of Phoenician settlement in the island in the ninth century, when Cypriots start producing Red-Slip ware locally and even exporting it to the Aegean along with Black-on-Red types (e.g., jugs and perfume flasks). This locally made repertoire imitated both Phoenician shapes and typically Cypriot shapes, usually those traditionally made in Cypriot White Painted and Bichrome fabrics; but now those traditional Cypriot fabrics started to be used to re-create Phoenician shapes. In short, it is difficult to outline precisely how Phoenician pottery influenced Cypriot ceramics and vice versa, as they are so closely intertwined.[49]

Pottery also shows Cyprus's key participation in the renewal of contacts between Greeks and the Levant at the turn of the millennium: Athenian and Euboian pottery started to reach Cyprus around 950 BC, and soon afterward Cypriot imports reached Euboia and Cypriot bronze production was a clear stimulus there too. By the eighth century, Euboians were on their way to Al-Mina and other Syro-Palestinian ports, and they may have carried Cypriot pottery around too, just as Cypriots now made copies of Euboian pottery, and both islands traded with Syria. Crete is another important player in these early Aegean–Levant contacts, as the island had received Cypriot pottery since the ninth century as well as Near Eastern goods. Some of these probably arrived via Cyprus. A steady supply of Cypriot wares reached Crete, Rhodes, and Kos soon after Phoenicians had established themselves in Kition in the mid-ninth century: For instance, Cypriot Black-on-Red perfume jugs had inspired local imitations in those new markets since the eighth century, and they were probably made to hold perfume coming out of workshops set up by Phoenicians from Cyprus on those Aegean islands.[50]

Black-on-Red pottery is especially entangled with Cypriot-Phoenician activity in this crucial phase in the renewal of contacts. This explains the traditional label of this pottery as "Cypro-Phoenician," following Nicolas Coldstream's initial classification, which was later criticized.[51] Antonis Kotsonas has debunked the use of the confusing terms "Creto-Cypriot" and "Cypro-Phoenician" to describe what are really local productions (Cretan and Cypriot, respectively).[52] Giorgos Bourogiannis has pointed out the inconsistent use of the highly ambivalent "Cypro-Phoenician" label, transmitted by decades of scholarly inertia. Bourogiannis sees the term as ultimately driven by Coldstream's firm belief in the "formidable mercantile power of the Phoenicians," a fixation that led him to turn "a clearly Cypriot pottery class into a Cypro-Phoenician amalgamation" and hence diluting the Cypriots' agency and connection to their own product.[53] Even with later reassessments of the local origins of this pottery and the rehabilitation of Cypriot participation in its distribution, the main Phoenician or Levantine role continues to be generally assumed. The difficulty of separating Phoenician and Cypriot agency lies at the heart of the problem, especially as we know historically that they joined forces in mercantile and even colonial ventures launched via or from Cyprus, such as in the foundation of Carthage.[54]

The same dynamics continue and are even better documented in the archaic period (starting around 750 BC). This was a prosperous time for Cyprus, and Levantine influence is manifested in metalwork (e.g., bronze lamp stands), votive deposits at Cypriot sanctuaries (e.g., at Palaipaphos), and in features of the Cypriot production of small terracotta figures. At some point, Greek pottery, mainly Attic style, started to be imported and made locally, but regional pottery styles developed in the south and east were still oriented toward Levantine styles, with pastes and shapes derived from earlier ones and pictorial inspiration imitating Syrian and Phoenician textiles and minor arts (Figure 8.1).[55] In conclusion, within a strongly local history of ceramic production, it is clear that, when Cypriot pottery adopted Near Eastern models (what in other regions we might call "orientalizing"), it engaged with Phoenician pottery production, with which it shared a long partnership.

Metalwork, Jewelry, and the Minor Arts

Cyprus started exporting copper ingots east and west around 1400 BC, although it had produced its own bronze metalwork during the Bronze Age, following local techniques and designs. It is always difficult to know where tin, necessary to create bronze, was obtained. Once the Phoenicians settled in the far west, Iberia or places accessed from there via the Atlantic routes were a likely source. At this time, Iberia and Sardinia were sources of silver, lead, and iron, though these are also found in other areas (e.g., silver from Attica). Cyprus's export of copper "oxhide" ingots is especially well documented, both archaeologically (e.g., Uluburun shipwreck from the late fourteenth century) and textually (Amarna Letters). Toward the end of the Late Bronze Age, new techniques came from the Mycenaean and Near Eastern worlds, and iron entered the metallurgical market. But archaeological evidence shows that there was no deep recession in the production of copper on Cyprus, even as its distribution turned more local, and iron never fully replaced bronze, due to the physical properties of the copper-tin alloy, which made it an essential material throughout antiquity. Given

FIG. 8.1 **Archaeo-Cypriot vase.**
Terracotta jug depicting two figures (perhaps deities) clad in long garments and two stylized birds flanking a central lotus motif, 750–600 BC. The Metropolitan Museum of Art, New York, The Cesnola Collection, Purchased by subscription, 1874–1876.

its ancestral tradition in metallurgy, some scholars believe that Cyprus may have had an important role in the development and dissemination of iron smelting.[56]

Cypriot-style metallurgic production had its own character and can easily be detected. Most characteristic are the bronze D-shaped (or "bow") *fibulae,* found in Palestine, Greece, Sardinia, and Iberia, and bronze bowls with handles decorated with lotus flower, found throughout the Near East, Greece, and Italy, as well as the wheeled stands and rod tripods. In turn, Phoenician immigrants were probably responsible for the bronze lamp stands or incense burners (*thymiateria*) and the decorated bronze bowls or *paterae* generally classified as "Phoenician" or "Cypro-Phoenician," which, as we saw, Glenn Markoe attributed to independent Phoenician workshops on Cyprus (Figure 3.2).[57] Their technique, style, and iconography is paralleled in a whole range of Levantine objects circulating on the island, and their Assyrianizing features reflect the island's orientation toward the Assyrian realm of influence in the seventh century.[58] Karageorghis proposes that the metal bowls are the product of Phoenician artists working for a "royal" clientele, since they are found at Salamis, Amathous, and Kourion.[59] To this type of repertoire belong the bronze harnesses, horse trappings, and vessels from aristocratic Salamis tombs that originated in different parts of the Near East.[60] Among the artifacts from the eighth–seventh centuries are also the first large bronze cauldrons found in the eastern Mediterranean, which Karageorghis sees as an example of an East Mediterranean "*koine* of Phoenician, Egyptian, and even Urartian elements."[61]

Jewelry and luxury fabrics enjoyed long traditions on Cyprus. The island had the resources to produce purple-dyed fabrics locally, from both flax and murex.[62] For gold and silver they depended on trade: gold from Egypt and Syria since the Late Bronze Age, and silver from Anatolia; later, in the classical period, also from Greece. Their jewelry production received multiple inputs, consisting of techniques learned from the Mycenaean Greeks (e.g., D-shaped *fibulae* and granulation—they did not use filigree until the classical period), and other items and techniques adopted from the Near East: these included the gold plaques used for tiaras (*polos*), which flirt with Egyptian style but were likely adopted via Syria-Palestine; beads of various foreign and local origins; and gems used for seal rings from the early sixth century (see below).[63] Decorating furniture with inlaid fake Egyptian hieroglyphs, like the ivory panels on furniture pieces (e.g., in the tombs of Salamis), was a perfect example of Egyptianizing art produced by Phoenician artisans or in Phoenician contexts.[64]

Coins, another medium that reflected the cultural makeup of the island, were minted on Cyprus in silver since the late sixth century to pay tribute to Persia (following the "Persic" standard). Designs and languages in the mints varied by kingdom and reflected the different predominant populations: Cypriot, Greek, and Phoenician, in this case fairly well distinguished epigraphically.[65] Archaic Cypriot seals and gems made of various stones, on the other hand, align more with the tradition of the Levant than of Egypt. Phoenician seals proper also abound on Cyprus, often made of exotic materials brought directly from Egypt or the Levant (lapis lazuli, carnelian, sard, green jasper) (Figure 6.6). It is possible that much of the trade and manufacture of gems and seals was mediated through Phoenicians, and that Greeks learned glyptic technology from Cypriots in the archaic period.[66] Moreover, as Markoe points out, the two main types of Cypro-Phoenician glyptic objects, the "scaraboid" and the "tabloid" types, overlap with the ivories and decorated metal *paterae* ("bowls"), both in style and thematic choices, especially in their distinct Assyrianizing inflections. He thus postulates the existence of a seventh-century workshop on Cyprus, which produced metal bowls, harness trappings, seals, and ivories, in a style that might be termed "Cypro-Phoenician."[67]

Sacred Spaces and Ritual Life

Cypriot architectural remains, including cultic structures, are scarce for this period. But sculpture (discussed below) is a good sign of the existence of a monumentalizing program, and we can imagine that architectural remains have been lost at least in part because they were made of wood. Extra-urban or rural sanctuaries, less visible and traceable, would have been common as well, and their important role in the organization of the emerging city-states or kingdoms has been emphasized more recently, following the model proposed for the Greek city-states.[68]

Despite the scarcity of remains in mainland Phoenicia, there is some evidence that palaces and sanctuaries incorporated Phoenician-inspired elements. Some evidence comes from the motif of the miniature shrine or *naiskos* decorating stelae or small monuments, as well as actual sculptural elements once attached to (wooden?) buildings. For instance, Cyprus has

FIG. 8.2   **Funerary stela from Cyprus.**

Limestone stela (137.1 cm height) topped by volute capital and upward palmette leaves framing the motif of sphinxes and the tree of life in palmette form, prob. from Golgoi or Idalion, fifth century BC. The Metropolitan Museum of Art, New York, The Cesnola Collection, Purchased by subscription, 1874–1876.

produced volute capitals in stone, the so-called Proto-Aeolic capitals, which are a typically Levantine, specifically Phoenician feature. These types of capitals appear replicated in miniature shrines and stelae (Figure 8.2) but they are also documented as doorjambs at Tamassos tombs and in structures at Salamis. The decorations added to some of the Cypriot examples, such as sphinxes, the tree of life, and the use of lotus-shaped capitals, all confirm the Levantine inspiration of these architectural elements. The type known as Cypriot Hathor capitals, sometimes attributed to "eastern and Greek inspiration,"[69] should be unambiguously attributed to Phoenician inspiration, as their symbolic and religious referents lie in the Phoenicians' Egyptianizing iconography.

As already noted, the Phoenicians' prowess as timber traders and wood-workers applied not only to shipbuilding but to temple- and palace build-ing. This industry would also have stimulated Cypriot architecture in this period. Building techniques attested later on (e.g., at Karpasia) show the adoption of Phoenician construction techniques widespread in the central and western Mediterranean, especially the use of pier and rubble walls on ashlar foundations with square blocks at the angles.[70] We know that the Phoenicians were renowned as masons and architects, as attested in ancient Israelite tradition, and Canaanite masons may already have been respon-sible for building a columned hall in one of the Late Bronze Age sanctuaries at Kition in the ninth century (rebuilt after 800 BC). Its freestanding pillars are believed to be a feature of Phoenician temples, introduced also in Solo-mon's temple as the pillars baptized "Jachin and Boaz."[71] Their description as flower-shaped capitals probably evokes the kind of "Proto-Aeolic" or volute capitals often represented in Phoenician art (see Chapter 9).

Even though Cypriot sanctuaries existed during the Late Bronze Age, the first monumental temples appeared in places such as Kition and Palaipaphos toward the end of this period (after ca. 1200 BC), and this de-velopment is associated with Canaanite or "Proto-Phoenician" input. These sanctuaries were close to settlements and at least at Kition next to copper workshops. They follow a Near Eastern type of open court sanctuary, with a small "holy of holies" or other buildings within a sacred precinct or *temenos,* typically enclosed by a wall, and also including an altar topped by bulls' horns or so-called horns of consecration.[72] Other objects found in these sanctuaries include anthropomorphic clay masks and models of kidneys for divination, which reflect traditions from Syria-Palestine. We should note the male horned gods and female "Ashart/Astarte-type" bronze figures (e.g., at Enkomi), standing on copper ingots, which are taken to rep-resent divinities associated with the copper industry.

The same type of cultic space continues through the Iron Age, with the open-air precinct enclosing various cultic installations besides the temples, such as small shrines and altars. The central role of water pools or other water installations, and space for sacred trees or groves (e.g., at Kition), also recall Phoenician practices of this period attested abroad (e.g., at Motya) or in Phoenicia during Persian times, when remains are more abundant (e.g., the Bustan esh-Sheikh sanctuary by Sidon). The older sanctuaries are refounded in the Iron Age (e.g., Temple 1 at Kition). The connection of Iron Age sanctuaries with copper workshops, again, seems to continue or revive a Late Bronze Age pattern (e.g., Tamassos), sometimes near harbor installations (e.g., Kition-Bamboula).[73] Besides these types of urban sanctuaries, there are Iron Age cultic sites outside the urban nuclei, usually called peri-urban (extra-urban) or rural sanctuaries. By contrast, the "standardized" temple of Greek plan appears only much later, under Hellenistic influence, for instance, the temple of Zeus at Salamis from the second century BC.[74]

Models of shrines (mentioned above), were popular since the Late Bronze Age on Cyprus and the Levant, and often represented the divinities worshiped or their symbols. In the Cypriot archaic period, they may represent an anthropomorphic divinity inside the shrine, but at other times the divine entity is represented by a pillar or a betyl, or a symbol, often the disk and crescent or other symbols of Ashtart or her local versions. Betyls and aniconic stelae are a frequent feature of Phoenician shrines and necropoleis around the Mediterranean, as we know not only through archaeological findings but also in depictions of betyls on coins from Phoenicia and Asia Minor and depictions of the temple of Aphrodite at Palaipaphos.[75] Thanks to the datable stratum of the floor leveled by the Persian destruction at Palaipaphos in 498–497 BC (the so-called Persian siege ramp) we have a solid archaeological context for these votive monuments and their Phoenician comparanda throughout the Mediterranean.[76]

The massive quantity of votives deposited throughout the archaic and classical periods (usually discarded in *bothroi*) is still our best clue as to the religious activities of the Cypriots and their interface with other cultures on the island. Archaic-period Cypriot votives come in various sizes and materials, especially in terracotta and limestone (more rarely in bronze), and in all sorts of local modalities, as best represented by the amalgam of deposits at the Ayia Irini sanctuary.[77] The most frequent types include the Egyptianizing male statues, which I discuss below, as well as terracotta and sometimes bronze statuettes that represented male and female worshipers, musicians, horsemen and chariots. Terracotta models or miniatures also show the use of animal masks (mostly bulls) and anthropomorphic masks.

Perfume burners of the Levantine type (*thymiateria*), stelae and small shrines, divination objects (liver models), and other elements found throughout the island also reflect the assimilation of Levantine cultic practices. Besides these material testimonies, two important Phoenician inscriptions, known as the "Kition tariffs," provide insights into temple administration and ritual, in the late fifth–early fourth centuries BC.[78] They mention, for instance, the offering of locks of hair to Ashtart and different types of servants of the temple administration (scholars have seen confirmation of the existence of female and male "sacred prostitution," although the evidence is far from clear).[79]

Finally, burial traditions were resiliently conservative on Cyprus, with an overwhelming and sustained predominance of inhumation, whereas cremation in urns (e.g., outside Amathous) are generally associated with Phoenician communities, among which cremation was widespread in the Iron Age.[80] The usual forms of burial documented for prehistoric times were inhumations under houses or outside in pits, and then (after ca. 2500 BC) mainly in chamber tombs (*hypogea*) cut out of the rock in different formats, some of them with corridors (*dromoi*). This last type, not dissimilar to the *tholos* and chamber tombs of Mycenaean elites, continues with variations until Roman times.[81] Thus, the spread of rock-cut chamber tombs with a *dromos* from the eleventh century onward has often been associated with the Mycenaeans' arrival, but this association has been criticized, as these are only one type of rock-cut tombs among others (some unparalleled outside Cyprus), and local pottery dominates their content. If there is Greek influence, just as in the case of the famous "Homeric-style" *obelos*, we need to consider the idiosyncratic emulation by local elites of Greek culture, as they did with Phoenician culture as well, seeing as there was no Greek dominance over the cultural landscape of the island at this time.[82] In turn, as we have seen in Chapters 4 and 5, chamber tombs and cremations under tumuli also appeared in the orientalizing phases in Iberia (Tartessos) and Etruria, which have been compared with hypogea in the Phoenician colonies and northern Israel. These provide a wider interpretive framework than is usually offered, as in all areas the monumentalization of the funerary world accompanied similar Levantine-inspired cultural transformations.

When monumental tombs start appearing, as at eighth-century Salamis, they incorporated elements that more often than not can be tied to Phoenician models and craftsmanship: the tombs show façades crowned by Egyptian-style cornices and in the interior archaeologists found some of the richest assemblages of the orientalizing kit in the Mediterranean: ivory decoration for furniture, bronze vessels, bronze harnesses and trappings, and more, all appropriate for the elite of a community on the "western fringe of the Assyrian Empire" as Veronica Tatton-Brown puts it. Some of the stone-built tombs ranging from the eighth to the fifth century (e.g., at Tamassos) show Phoenician features. In turn, the use of Egyptianizing sarcophagi has, rather narrowly, been flagged as a sign of Egyptian influence. But this practice aligns with the tradition of anthropoid sarcophagi on the Phoenician mainland, where Tabnit and his son Eshmunazar (kings of Sidon) reused Egyptian sarcophagi in the Persian period. The trend becomes common on classical Cyprus, when the sarcophagi (e.g., at Amathous and Kition) present the same amalgam of Egyptianizing and Aegean features that characterize Phoenician sarcophagi at Sidon, Carthage, and Gadir.[83]

The Gods

Strong lines of continuity in religious beliefs are evident, especially in the manifestations of a female goddess since prehistoric times, a "Cypriot Goddess" who undergoes iconographic transformations through the centuries but maintains a local character, even as she is progressively assimilated to Aphrodite.[84] Otherwise we know little about Eteo-Cypriot religion. Deities of the common Phoenician pantheon, on the other hand, are amply attested, with local peculiarities: Ashtart, Anat, Baal, Eshmoun, Resheph, Mikal, Melqart, Shed; the presence of Anat and Resheph seems to indicate the resilience of the Canaanite legacy on Cyprus, as these gods were part of the Bronze Age Canaanite repertoire but rarely documented in the Iron Age.[85] The Phoenicians introduced their own Egyptianizing repertoire, which became part of the Cypriot religious landscape (see below on the statues). Especially common were Bes, Ptah, Thoeris, and Hathor, who was assimilated to Isis-Ashtart and later to Aphrodite. In contrast, direct manifestations of Egyptian religion are nowhere to be seen during the brief period of Egyptian administration of Cyprus in the sixth century. The evidence of which might be limited to one Isis dedication (see below).

The same Phoenician background explains the appearance of terracotta representations of a seated Baal-Hammon (Zeus Ammon for the Greeks) in the mid- to late sixth century at Meniko-Litharkes, and then distributed widely. These types are paralleled only in Libya and Cyrene, leading Karageorghis to surmise the spread of the cult of Baal-Hammon and Tanit in central Cyprus from Meniko's double sanctuary.[86] The urban sanctuaries dedicated to Ashtart at Kition and Palaipaphos are the best attested. It is more difficult to know which gods were originally worshipped at sanctuaries in places like Golgoi, Pyla, Idalion, whose gods were later identified with Apollo, Aphrodite, and Athena. And it is possible that assimilation between local, Greek, and Phoenician traits also happened at rural sanctuaries, where cults to local deities are archaeologically attested in the seventh–sixth centuries.[87]

Surprising as it may be, on Cyprus Greek gods are not regularly attested before the fourth century, and Greek-style temples even later. Some cults *might* be earlier than their first secure attestations, such as that of Athena at Idalion and Vouni, of Apollo at Idalion, Pyla, and Tamassos-Phrangissa, and perhaps of Zeus at Salamis. The absence of written testimonies from the local or Eteo-Cypriot religion, in turn, poses an unsolvable difficulty, as these gods are only "recognized" to the degree that they were interpreted as equivalents of Greek and Phoenician gods by worshipers and explicitly identified as such in writing, and that is if we are lucky, because cult or votive statues were rarely labeled. The clearest case of a continued local cult is that of the Cypriot Goddess or main fertility goddess mentioned above, who was eventually identified with Ashtart and Aphrodite, but was for most of her history called "the Paphian" in sanctuaries outside Paphos; at Paphos she was called simply "mistress" (*wanassa*), as documented since the fourth century BC.

The popularity of terracotta figurines of pregnant women, which appear as votives to Ashtart in Phoenicia and Cyprus, can be associated with the Cypriot Goddess too. This is probably the background of the special association of Aphrodite and Cyprus by the Greeks from the time of Homer onward: she was "Cypris" in the epic tradition, and Paphos was signaled out as her main "house" or place of cult.[88] The story of her birth in Hesiod's *Theogony* also brings her to Cyprus, and for Herodotos the arrival of Aphrodite's cult to Greece from Syria-Palestine was mediated through Cyprus, as cited in Chapter 7.[89] The Cypriot goddess's aniconic cult in the form of a betyl at Paphos, already mentioned, is particularly Semitic-looking.

The identification of Greek gods with native Cypriot and Phoenician ones becomes more evident in classical times. The Phoenician gods are better represented epigraphically than the Eteo-Cypriot: Zeus, whom the Phoenicians equated with Baal/Baal-Hammon, seems to have been more important now and was the principal god at least at Salamis; Cypriot Hylates was probably identified with Phoenician Resheph, and, as a pestilence god, overlapped with Apollo, whose cults are abundantly attested across Cyprus in classical and Hellenistic times; the Cypriot fertility mistress, easily equated to Phoenician Ashtart, did not fully fall under the rubric of Greek "Aphrodite" until classical times, and at Paphos not until the third century; in turn, we may assume that Anat lies under Athena at Idalion, and perhaps Artemis in some places, whose cult is attested in the fourth century at Kition; finally, Phoenician Eshmoun was subsumed early on under classical Asklepios. Greek gods were increasingly promoted by the kings, especially in Hellenistic times, including Hera and the Demeter-Kore pair, introduced only then.[90]

A Palette of Languages and Scripts

Despite the traditional tendency to place Greek heritage at the center of Cyprus's history, for the period of our interest and from the point of view of writing systems, the two major forces shaping the island's cultural landscape were native Cypriot and Phoenician. The Greek alphabet, adapted from the Phoenician, was used only since the sixth century BC and did not become widespread until the fourth, perhaps thanks to an official move by King Evagoras I of Salamis (late fifth century BC), who used it on his coinage.[91] Before this, what we have is a long tradition of writing uninterrupted since the Late Bronze Age, when the Cypriots adapted the Linear A script of Minoan Crete, known as Cypro-Minoan; they used it throughout the Late Bronze Age (ca. 1550–1050 BC) to write the local, non-Greek language(s) (the Mycenaeans had adapted it to write Greek, what we know as Linear B). In the twelfth century, Greek-speaking groups introduced their language, and, at some point during the Geometric period, they adapted Cypro-Minoan script too, in order to write their Greek dialect (Arcado-Cypriot). This is the origin of what we call Cypro-syllabic script or Cypriot syllabary (e.g., engraved on a metal bowl and a statue in Figures 3.2 and 8.3).

The Cypriots, then, unlike their Greek neighbors in the Aegean, did not lose the technology of writing during the "Dark Ages," although inscriptions of this intermediate phase are scarce.[92] Most Cypro-syllabic documents, used both for Eteo-Cypriot and Greek, date from the sixth century onward, when the Greek language was more widespread. Since much of official writing stemmed from the more organized kingdoms, the majority of inscriptions reflect Greek language, but fewer are preserved for Eteo-Cypriot, largely concentrated in the area of Amathous. The facts that Greek speakers continued using the Cypro-syllabic even when Eteo-Cypriot language(s) had all but disappeared (after the fourth century BC) and that only around 300 BC did inscriptions using the Greek alphabet outnumber those in Cypro-syllabic reflect the strong attachment of the Cypriots to their autochthonous writing system.[93]

Besides Cypro-syllabic, the only other well-attested script on the island in the early first millennium was Phoenician. Hundreds of Phoenician inscriptions have been found on Cyprus, spanning seven centuries (from the ninth to the third centuries BC), with a higher concentration in the fifth–fourth centuries, that is, the Persian period.[94] By contrast, Assyrian or Egyptian texts are scarce, and the rare samples (e.g., the Sargon stela) do not reflect regular use by the population.[95] Phoenician, on the other hand, accompanied the commercial activity and settlement of the Northwest Semitic groups, becoming especially common at Kition and Idalion and generally the southeast of Cyprus, as we might expect. In Kition alone at least 150 Phoenician inscriptions are documented.[96] In turn, eleven Cypro-syllabic inscriptions recovered at Kition and eight Phoenician-Greek bilingual inscriptions on the island are also testimony to the interaction among these communities.[97] Texts from the earlier period are scarce, but we can imagine the information we might have had about these interacting communities if papyrus and other perishable materials had survived. We have a rare window into the complex sociopolitical relations among the kingdoms in the fifth- to fourth-century BC archives of the city of Idalion, of which more than seven hundred texts have been recovered and are under study. They are mostly written in Phoenician (fewer in Cypro-syllabic Greek) with ink over stone fragments and pottery shards, and they illuminate Greek and Phoenician administration and relations during the Persian period.[98]

These languages lived side by side, even though it is difficult to assess the degree to which they intermingled to create bilingual or trilingual families. In Iacovou's view, Cyprus was a trilingual territory, where emerging political boundaries sustained the linguistic plurality and reinforced the divide.[99] In this view, while the material record does not signal clear boundaries between the populations that spoke these three languages, differences became more apparent as the separate Cypriot states consolidated in the archaeo-Cypriot and classical periods.[100] The fact that Greek continued to be written in the Cypro-syllabic script, not switching over to the available Phoenician alphabet, as the Greeks everywhere else did, shows the force of a local Cypriot identity. Perhaps the establishment of Kition on the island (a sort of surrogate outpost of Assyria) explains Cypriot attachment to Cypro-syllabic and rejection of the Phoenician script.[101] But the "Phoenician letters" were used by Greeks elsewhere, so perhaps Cypro-syllabic offered yet another means to express a different, Cypriot-specific modality of Greekness.

The Linchpin: Egyptianizing Cypriot Statues

Cyprus can boast of a long tradition of small-scale sculpture in stone and clay since the Neolithic era. In the second millennium, Cypriot artisans started experimenting with Levantine models, especially in the Late Bronze Age. It is then, for instance, that the "Ashtart/Astarte-type" figure appears: a naked female clay figure holding her breasts, which seems to adopt Syrian prototypes to represent the prehistoric Cypriot fertility goddess.[102] The Cypriots generally shared in the repertoire of Levantine-inspired art, which included winged sphinxes and other hybrids, as well as vegetal motifs (rosettes, palmettes, lotus flowers), always in their own particular variations. Besides the male statues in Egyptian attire (discussed below), male figures appear mostly in terracottas and vase painting portrayed as warriors, carrying large round shields and wearing conical helmets or "bonnets." The traditional female figures, in turn, follow a locally determined typology, with a conical body shape, dressed in long plain robes, and wearing a rectangular crown or *polos*. Other motifs, such as the lyre player, appear across periods and media, underscoring the originality of the Cypriot artistic tradition.[103]

Monumental sculpture, however, was an innovation of the first millennium, starting in the mid-seventh century and arising from the impetus of Cypro-Phoenician interaction. Alongside the ubiquitous small terracotta statuettes, large statues were now dedicated at sanctuaries, made in terracotta, local limestone, and more rarely of clay and bronze (occasionally also imported finished pieces in marble). The large terracotta examples were typically handmade, with different pieces attached together and the faces made by mold, while the backs were generally left flat. Within this corpus of votives, a large group stands out for its Egyptianizing form and holds important clues for our understanding of the Phoenician element in "orientalizing" adaptations in other regions too. These are the standing, male, kilt-wearing figures, many of large, even colossal size made of local limestone, with some smaller bronze statuettes (e.g., at Idalion) and occasional single finds in terracotta and faience. This corpus includes variations such as the warrior with or without helmet, with either quiver and arrow or sword and scabbard, the animal-carrying figure, and more rarely the type with a falcon head holding a stylus and tablet.[104]

Traditional scholarship had squared these votives with direct Egyptian influence, pointing to the reign of Pharaoh Amasis from the Twenty-Sixth Dynasty (569–545 BC), which allegedly marked a phase of Egyptian rule on the island late in the archaic period. Historians follow Herodotos's narrative that this Pharaoh dedicated statues as gifts at various sanctuaries in eastern Greece (Cyrene, Samos, and Rhodes), gifts that are framed as part of inter-elite networks.[105] It is also here that Herodotos says Amasis was the first to "capture" Cyprus (*heile*) and make it tributary. The date and length of this subjugation is uncertain. It was probably overstated by the sources and limited to some cities.[106] A dating for this corpus thus emerged based not on archaeological data but on the Egyptianizing look of the statues and a hypothetical political context for the materials. The same association explains the stylistic category of "Cypro-Egyptian" for these sculptures.[107] Following these superficial clues and assumptions, as with the Greek *kouroi*, the search for the statues' prototypes focused on Naukratis in the Nile Delta, where Cypriot and Greek activity is attested starting in about 625 BC and lasting through the sixth century.[108]

Once more, the Egyptian façade of Levantine-style objects has blocked scholars from looking for alternatives that better fit the historical and cultural context of Cyprus. We owe to Fanni Faegersten the first thorough

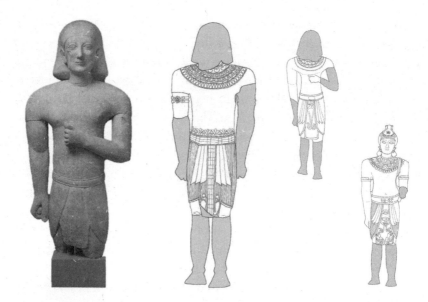

FIG. 8.3   Egyptianizing male statues from Cyprus and Phoenicia.

Left: Over-life size limestone statue from Golgoi (ca. 190 cm original height), with ownership inscription in Cypro-syllabic on one arm; note the Cypriot-style tunic, facial features, and moustache, and the Egyptianizing wig and kilt with cobras; second quarter of the sixth century BC (Faegersten 2003, Cat.24). The Metropolitan Museum of Art, New York, The Cesnola Collection, Purchased by subscription, 1874–1876.

Center: Statue from Sidon, Lebanon (ca. 180 cm original height). National Museum, Beirut; Faegersten 2003, Cat.Ph.22.

Right top: Statue from Tamassos, Cyprus (ca. 50 cm original height). Royal Ontario Museum, Toronto; Faegersten 2003, Cat.44.

Right bottom: Statue from Golgoi, Cyprus (ca. 80 cm original height). The Metropolitan Museum of Art; Faegersten 2003, Cat.30. Drawings courtesy of Fanni Faegersten.

study of this Cypriot group alongside Egyptian, east Greek, and Phoenician statuary (see Figure 8.3). The Phoenician examples have only more recently been recovered at Lebanese sites, with about thirty-eight exemplars so far. First, her study dismantles the narrow chronological and geographical frameworks attached by default to the production of these statues (e.g., Naukratis, mid-sixth century). Her study convincingly traces the Phoenician input behind Cypriot Egyptianizing art, which, by extension, explains other Egyptianizing and Levantine-style art of this period. Indeed, east Greeks (Ionians) and Cypriots interacted with each other and with Egyptians at

Naukratis, and Cypriot workshops were probably operating there at some time. However, the only connection between the Cypriot Egyptianizing statues and the Naukratis context is the appearance there of small-scale Cypriot-style statuettes (called Cypro-Ionian), which are not part of the same kilt-wearing Cypriot type. Only one of the statues found in Naukratis can be said to belong in the kilt-wearing type, but it clearly follows the Cypriot version, not direct Egyptian models.[109] There is no missing link (Egyptian–Cypriot) for our kilt-wearing male statues. Put differently, the connection is circular and does not lead us to an Egyptian prototype, but rather indicates the spread of Cypriot sculpture to sixth-century Naukratis from Cyprus.

Second, Faegersten shows how the dating of votive sculptures on Cyprus is fraught with difficulty. They generally appear in repositories of discarded votives (*bothroi*), which deprives them of a stratified context, obscuring their original position in the sanctuary or in respect to each other. Only at two sites, the sanctuaries at Idalion and Golgoi, do architectural remains provide clues as to the positioning of statues. Based on stylistic grounds, however, most would agree now that the Egyptianizing male statues cover the entire sixth century, and hence do not correspond well to the narrow period of alleged Egyptian rule on Cyprus, which left no material or epigraphic trace to speak of.[110]

In reality, virtually no Egyptian statues were imported to Cyprus that could have been a direct model. Such candidates might be limited to one item, a porphyry statuette of unknown provenance. In turn, the Egyptian statues that appear in other eastern Greek sites, such as Samos and Rhodes (the places that Herodotos mentions as recipients of Egyptian royal gifts), are not possible models, as they belong to different types or a later period.[111] The religious manifestations of the alleged Egyptian period, again, are mute, save a dedication to Isis inscribed on a bronze vessel (a *situla*), which was reused as a votive "to the god" at Kourion, as the added inscription in Greek indicates (the Isis cult was not introduced on Cyprus until Hellenistic times, under Ptolemaic auspices). Egyptianizing, standing male statues that could have served as models are also missing from the record of eastern Greek sites that are otherwise rich in orientalizing art, such as Samos or Rhodes. Instead, what we find in the Aegean sites and at Naukratis are small-scale statuettes categorized as "Cypro-Ionian," namely, nonmonumental, limestone sculptures deemed to be of Cypriot style and characterized by a synthesis of Ionian or Egyptianizing elements, ranging from the seventh to the fifth century, but they are not a precise or indeed valid parallel for the corpus under scrutiny here.[112]

The Phoenician coast provides the only concentration of Egyptianizing statues / statuettes in stone outside Cyprus, with at least thirty-eight statues of this type known from excavations at Phoenician sites, and one example from the western colonies, from Motya in Sicily (the "Stagnone torso").[113] These Phoenician statues are also large, sometimes colossal, and share with the Cypriot ones their stance, kilt, and Egyptian-style headgear. Previous scholars had noted problems with the traditional dating and the assumed direct Egyptian influence in these statues, and had pointed to the possible Phoenician referent, but no thorough systematic study was done to confirm these suspicions. Markoe postulated that the Cypriot statues were votive offerings by Phoenicians settled on Cyprus. Antoine Hermary, on the other hand, discussed the Cypriot statuary's Egyptian influences within the Naukratis context, but stressed that Egyptian influence was already present on Cyprus before this period, and pointed to the statues found in Phoenician sanctuary contexts as a potential point of comparison.[114] Reyes's assessment of Cypro-Archaic monumental sculpture pointed in that direction too: "The Egyptianizing elements of Cypro-Archaic limestone and bronze votive figurines seem largely the result of Phoenician influence," but he drew a contrast with the terracotta sculpture as a truly indigenous art form that sustained its local character even while Phoenician terracottas circulated on the island.[115]

The comparison between the Cypriot and Egyptian statuary requires a great deal of technical expertise, relying on the analysis of decorative details on the individual pieces of the figure's attire, such as the types of garment, the kilt with *devanteau,* belt, broad collar, and headgear (some of the same features appear in Figures 3.1 and 4.4).[116] Faegertsten's scrutiny shows that the "composite whole" of these statues is, in the end, a unique but hybrid Cypriot creation, which draws on modified Egyptian elements. She makes the important chronological point that many of these Egyptian elements had their high point in the New Kingdom, but were current in the adaptations developed in Iron Age Phoenician art. The key to this puzzle is in the close-up comparison with Egyptianizing features in *other* materials present on the island, both prior to and contemporaneously with the development of the limestone statues. These include the range of luxury objects bearing Phoenician Egyptianizing iconography in ivory decoration and metal bowls since the eighth century, and also as sculptural elements preserved in stone, such as sphinxes and Hathor capitals, which appear in the same cultic areas as the statues. In short, "there are not many Egyptian references encountered on Cyprus which are not similarly found within the Phoenician Iron Age iconography known to us."[117]

Details of the statue's clothes or ornaments (collar, belt), had already been altered within Phoenician Egyptianizing art when they entered Cyprus: these include typically Phoenician renditions of the palmette ("cup-palmette," "volute and palmette," "paradise flower"), the Phoenician winged sphinx (here bearded and wearing a helmet), and the four-winged scarab. This shows that the Cypriot artists were drawing on Phoenician (Egyptianizing) and not direct Egyptian models, even when they went on to slightly modify those features. In turn, these statues provide the key to understanding other contemporary Egyptianizing adaptations, such as the so-called Cypro-Ionian statuettes and the Greek *kouroi*. They all share with the Cypriot Egyptianizing and Phoenician male statues a basic rendition of the male body along contemporary Egyptian tastes, in terms of stance, large thumbs, and "archaic smile." On the other hand, the monumentality itself was more prevalent in earlier Egyptian tradition than in this period, and was not a particular tendency in Phoenician art, so it seems to be an Aegean-Cypriot innovation. As argued in Chapter 6, the famous *kouroi* should also be seen against the background of Cypriot–Phoenician–Aegean interaction, not as a straight Egyptian borrowing. They are the Greek counterpart of the Cypriot and Phoenician hieratic male votive, with the stark distinction of their nakedness.[118]

Another key lies in a comparative approach across different materials. Egyptianizing iconography was present on Cyprus since the eighth century if not earlier in the form of various Phoenician imports. In Faegersten's reconstruction, Cypriots transferred this style to stone in order to create a new type of votive, the hieratic male statue, originally painted in color, which joined the existing repertoire of votives in various materials, including limestone, metals, ivory, and wood. It is especially important to insist on the use of wood, as this must have been a basic material for Phoenician (and for that matter Greek) artisans; Egyptianizing art in carved and painted wood was likely arriving on Cyprus with the Phoenicians well before the first stone statues appeared (some of them have traces of paint too). To summarize Faegersten's hypothesis, three distinct craft traditions merged in this statuary: the indigenous Cypriote votive tradition, the east Greek sculptural tradition (from the sixth century BC), and the Phoenician wood and ivory repertoire (from the late eighth century BC). The first (votive tradition) lies behind the Cypriot *use* of the statues, different from the Phoenician one. In Phoenicia they seem to have been deployed mainly to flank a deity or the deity's shrine, while the kilt-wearing statues on Cyprus seem to be exclusively votive (whether they represented a god or a dedicant). Another peculiarity is that these male statues were particularly associated with the Apollo-Resheph cult on Cyprus, or at least with sacred precincts of male deities. As we saw above, the recognition and mutual identification of Phoenician and Greek deities across these groups is attested epigraphically, as well as in the sharing of symbols and probably of sacred spaces, all of which would have opened channels for the adoption of this sort of statue as a votive.[119]

Finally, in the circularity we often find in cultural exchange, this successful Cypriot production fed back into the Phoenician tradition of Egyptianizing statuary. The Phoenicians devoted their craft mainly to smaller formats and other materials, but they started to emulate the Cypriot artists in the use of stone for this type of statue (sometimes in colossal format), absorbing Cypriot adaptations and even importing statues made in Cypriot limestone, which appear in the early sixth century at Amrit and Sidon. All of this indicates "a remarkable coming and going of cultural and technical impulses between Cyprus and the coastal Phoenician cities."[120] These statues show once more the meandering and creative paths that cultural encounters take, and how the local developments in turn feed into international ("global") trends and networks. They also show how much we may be missing by not looking directly at Phoenician evidence or limiting our perspective to monumental art: we have seen time and again how creative adaptations of Levantine models jumped across media (for instance, from metal engraving to pottery, or from ivory and wood to stone), and on Cyprus itself, Phoenician influence is evident in elements of sacred architecture and its miniaturized versions, mentioned above.[121]

Finally, this and other Cypriot adaptations of Levantine art reveal an appreciation and understanding of the Phoenician religious and symbolic universe, at least in the areas that maintained a stronger orientation toward the Levant, such as Salamis, Kition, Amathous, and Palaipaphos. As Fae-gersten concluded, "what we see in the preserved 6th century B.C. Cypriot limestone material is a group of figures which derives from 7th century B.C. Phoenician wooden models, which (originally) had a royal Phoenician ref-erence, but which became a highly 'Cyprified' Phoenician iconography, fully adapted to the Cypriot sanctuary reality with its masses of votive figures and types."[122]

In these Cypriot male statues we have a documented example of the transfer of Phoenician Egyptianizing art onto the Aegean world, anchored in models from the Phoenician mainland and in Phoenician portable arts, and not in those of Egypt or Assyria. To say the least, this case forces us to consider similar processes in areas where we see Levantine-style adapta-tions, likely mediated by or at least involving Phoenicians, including the example of the Greek *kouroi*. In turn, the Cypriot case illustrates how Phoe-nician culture itself absorbed ideas from areas where it settled, and some-times modified versions of its own models, turning the orientalizing kit into a self-feeding carousel of possibilities.

꒰꒰꒱

The case of Iron Age Cyprus bears unique and broadly applicable lessons. First, it brings home the point that cultural influence is never unidirectional or linear: on Cyprus, traits of native, Greek, and Phoenician cultures were entangled since the Early Iron Age. Furthermore, productive trends of "Phoenicianization" need not be constrained by chronological or artistic periodizations: the relationship with the Levantines was constitutive of the island's unique cultural history, and it continued throughout Hellenistic and even Roman times. In turn, Cyprus's emulation of the Levant was highly idiosyncratic, a trait we recognize in responses to the Phoenician stimulus in areas of contact further west: Cypriot artistic and technological adapta-tions of Levantine models were grafted onto a material culture of local char-acter and well-documented prehistoric depth, as in Etruria and Iberia, and the broader Aegean of which Cyprus was also part. The Cypriots also cu-rated their own distinct script during historical times, but in this case set-ting themselves apart from the international wave of alphabetic adaptations during the entire archaic period. At the same time, on Cyprus the Phoe-nicians provided a specific, historically, materially, and linguistically documented tie with the Near East. In the case of Cyprus as in other cases studied in this book, particular disciplinary, ideological, and national inertias lead scholars to be more open or more reluctant to point to the Phoenicians as specific cultural agents.

From the island of Cyprus, we jump in one step to the Levant, where we can see how the beginning of this pan-Mediterranean phenomenon unfolded among the Phoenician centers themselves and their immediate neighbors.

⊰ 9 ⊱

THE LEVANT

From the Ashes: Tyre and the Canaanite Continuum

As we complete our Phoenician-guided circuit throughout the Mediterranean, we return to the Levant, where the Phoenician city-states developed a shared and distinct culture along the coastal territory that crosses the modern frontiers of Syria, Lebanon, and Israel-Palestine (Map 9.1).[1] More than anywhere else, the term "orientalizing" is inapplicable here. And yet, in adjacent regions, the renewed urban culture and elite aesthetics of the Iron Age were directly stimulated by Phoenician commercial and cultural dynamism.

As the Levant recovered from the Late Bronze Age systems collapse, the Phoenician centers offered the fragmented Levantines an inspiring continuity with the lustrous urban world that had once been exemplified by Ugarit, and Tyre in particular was a beacon of exploration and innovation. The Phoenicians' uninterrupted palatial and temple traditions as well as their institutions, preserved since the Bronze Age, served as models for the formation of new city-states, such as in Israel, Judah, and the Aramaean and Neo-Hittite states. Phoenician script was adopted by all surrounding groups in the southern Levant, North Syria, and Cilicia, and used as a sign of international prestige, before it passed on to the Aegean and beyond. Not surprisingly Phoenician art was of the highest value for the Assyrians too, who coveted it, commissioned it, and hoarded it when acquired as tribute, presents, or spoilage.

This situation back "at home" was the matrix behind the spread of orientalizing culture abroad. The orientalizing kit that we have traced as far as Iberia and Sardinia sprang from the Phoenician cities' economic and

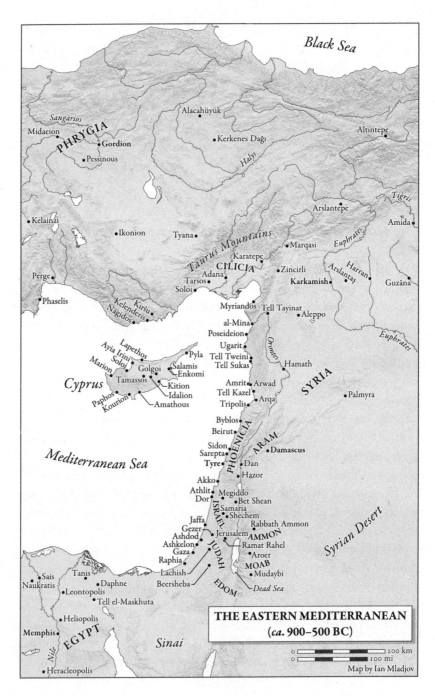

THE EASTERN MEDITERRANEAN
(*ca.* 900–500 BC)

0   200 km
0   100 mi

Map by Ian Mladjov

MAP 9.1

cultural capital back in the Levant itself. As I discuss below, material and textual traces point to Phoenician leadership in fostering and setting standards of the Levantine koine, perhaps most evidently in the regional use of the Phoenician language and script. The final case study of this volume, that of the contested ascription of the "Proto-Aeolic" capitals, in turn, bears directly on our appraisal and definition of orientalizing culture across the Mediterranean.

From Canaanites to Phoenicians

How did the Proto-Phoenician Canaanite cities of the coastal strip become the torchbearers of urban, literate civilization in the Levant? Freed from under the shadow of the Hittites and Egyptians, and somehow unscathed by the waves of destruction suffered by others, these small kingdoms were possibly invigorated by the migration of refugees from devastated interior areas and of displaced Aegean groups (known as "Sea Peoples"). The destruction and abandonment of Ugarit specifically must have contributed to the economic development of the coastal port cities.[2] These surviving states even launched a program of expansion overseas. Indeed, accruing archaeological data seems to confirm what textual evidence already suggested: the Phoenician coastal cities saw no invasion or great disturbance in the transition between the Late Bronze Age and the Early Iron Age.[3] Only some of the northern sites show destruction levels (Tell Sukas, Tell Twieini, Tell Kazel), while none of them were abandoned or show signs of invasion or population replacement. Tyre and the rest may have gone untouched. The resilient legacies in the transition to the Early Iron Age are salient not only in Phoenicia proper but in northern Syria, which was also part of the heartland of Canaanite culture.[4] As Ann Killebrew concludes, "the relatively independent status of city-states located between Arwad and Akko already in the Late Bronze II period and their distance from the Late Bronze Age superpowers, Egypt and the Hittites, appear to have played a pivotal role in their ability to not only survive but also to thrive during the Iron I period."[5]

The fragmented geopolitical configuration after the collapse of the Late Bronze Age systems allowed for the emergence of distinct ethnic groups and political entities, such as the kingdoms of Israel and Judah, or the Neo-Hittite and Aramaean states. In this context, the Phoenicians most of all seem to build on the past cultural homogeneity of the region, what may be called the "Canaanite continuum." In other words, the old harbors at the foot of the Lebanon mountains emerged from the regional ashes with particular buoyancy in the Early Iron Age. Organized around the stronger polities of Arwad, Byblos, Sidon, and Tyre, and parading their continuity with the Canaanite world, Phoenician communities capitalized on their privileged trading relations with new and old partners.[6]

We have a rare witness to the position of the Phoenician states after the Bronze Age collapse in the Egyptian story of Wenamun, which evokes an eleventh-century setting: the text narrates the misadventures of an Egyptian envoy under Ramesses XI, who was sent to Byblos to obtain cedar timber, as it would have been common given the long partnership between these regions. The tale also involves events at Dor, Tyre, and Cyprus, as Wenamun negotiates commercial, diplomatic, and religious rules, and experiences theft, hospitality, and threats to his life. In this story, the Phoenician "trader-kings" whom Wenamun encounters are in total control of the cedar industry and have the upper hand in negotiations with Egypt, a position strengthened by the enduring coexistence and cooperation in the Canaanite cities of royal houses and merchant entrepreneurs. The treatment of this frustrated Egyptian merchant, as he deals with an emboldened trading partner, reveals how the tables of international relations had turned.[7] When he received Wenamun, the story depicts Zakerbaal, king of Byblos, sitting in his reception room, his back to a window open to the sea, the foamy waves crashing against the walls of his palace, saying: "Am I your servant? Am I the servant of he who has sent you? When I cry out towards [Mount] Lebanon, barely has the sky opened when the trees are here, felled by the seashore."[8] The Wenamun story reveals the remarkably "unruffled history" of the Phoenician kingdoms in the Early Iron Age, as Cyprian Broodbank puts it.[9] These coastal Canaanites maintained the basic religious, political, and cultural institutions of their ancestors that were to be a pillar of Phoenician identity in the first millennium.[10] The story also illustrates that diplomatic conventions, including hospitality rules, had not changed much since the time of the Amarna Letters in the New Kingdom, when about sixty letters preserve the correspondence between the Egyptian royal houses of Amenophis III and IV and Canaanite cities in the fourteenth century.[11] The tradition about the collaboration and exchange between King Hiram I of Tyre and King Solomon also assumes trading and diplomatic dynamics rooted in Late Bronze Age palace economies, which included commercial and technological exchanges. It is in the context of these intrastate relations that the biblical tradition portrays Tyre providing timber to its southern neighbor, along with architects and masons to help in the construction of the temple of King Solomon. This picture is supplemented by archaeology, which helps us trace the movement not of trading agents and diplomats but of luxury products from Phoenicia to Israel; these include ivories, textiles, and transportation jars. In exchange, Tyre would have received food supplies from the Israelite lands, such as cereals, oil, perhaps honey and spices.[12] From the biblical coastal Canaanites to the Phoenicians of Homer, these kingdoms had become economic and cultural forces to reckon with.

The tale of Wenamun also conveys another crucial factor that often muddles our understanding of the dissemination of orientalizing materials across the Mediterranean, namely, the special relation between Phoenicia and Egypt, whose culture was grafted onto the Phoenicians' cultural heritage in the second millennium. In fact, the famed cedarwood trade with Egypt started in the third millennium, after which the Phoenician cities became default trading intermediaries between Egypt and Mesopotamia. Centers such as Byblos in the north and Sidon and Tyre in the south maintained an orientation toward Egypt throughout their history.[13] I discuss the artistic aspect of this relation and the success of Phoenician art in the Levant next.

Phoenician Art in Levantine Context

Egyptian royal and religious symbols were part and parcel of Phoenician culture, overlaid with the basic Canaanite streak in Phoenician culture, both components perhaps most evident in funerary and royal self-representation.[14] While Persian and other influences became salient later on, Egyptian and modified Egyptianizing symbols and features characterize the Phoenician artistic output of the eighth to sixth centuries, precisely the art most exported and influential on orientalizing adaptations abroad, as we have seen.[15] But the often-cited apparent eclecticism of Phoenician art did not deprive it of its distinctive personality, as experts on various periods have acknowledged (one may ask, which art is not eclectic?). As Josette Elayi puts it, "despite its detractors, Phoenician art existed and it was original."[16]

S. Rebecca Martin's study shows how later Phoenician communities creatively adopted Persian and Greek artistic modes to "modernize" their traditional art forms (sarcophagi, funerary stelae, architecture, etc.), while never losing their distinct personality or abandoning their symbolic world.[17] The same was true of their earlier art, only with an Egyptianizing and (in the north) Assyrianizing outlook. In Glenn Markoe's words, "The misuse or more properly 'reuse' of foreign motifs (especially Egyptian) has been traditionally identified as a hallmark of Phoenician art."[18] A unique synthesis of local and Egyptianizing traditions marked Phoenician culture, and resilient traits of this synthesis continued through the Persian and Hellenistic periods and also in the Punic world. As Eric Gubel notes regarding the Egyptian streak of Phoenician culture, we are not talking about a superficial emulation, but an influence that penetrated into the realm of religion, which is a notably conservative area of artistic expression and self-definition in the Near East.[19]

The intimate engagement with Egyptian symbols was not limited to the Phoenician elites and the fine arts they consumed. On the contrary, it was a deeply entrenched aspect of Phoenician popular culture, as Hélène Sader has shown. This phenomenon is perhaps best demonstrated in the funerary repertoire, such as on the stelae found in the Tyre al-Bass cemetery and earlier at Byblos. Some of these symbols barely change through the centuries, for instance lotus buds, architectural features in stelae, the ankh symbol and variations of it and other hieroglyphic signs. Others, perhaps precisely due to their mass use and long-lived popularity, have complicated trajectories: for instance, the "Tanit/Tinit symbol" is in all likelihood a popular development from the ankh and pseudo-ankh symbols associated with Isis, life, and the afterlife.[20] The symbol (and the goddess Tanit herself) are scarcely attested in the Levant but become really popular in the Phoenician diaspora, where the symbol becomes a staple of Punic culture throughout the central Mediterranean, and is especially well-attested in the stelae of the tophet sanctuaries. Other Egyptianizing motifs in these stelae include the solar disk and row of uraeus (stylized cobras), such as we see in Figure 5.2.

The predominance of Egyptian models from New Kingdom Egypt (that is, of the Late Bronze Age) in Phoenician art has caused some confusion. These motifs produce an apparent mismatch between first-millennium (i.e., contemporary) Egyptian repertoires and the Phoenician or orientalizing versions. This has already been noted, for instance, regarding the Egyptian-izing statues of Cyprus, but Phoenician metalwork and ivories follow the same pattern, as they especially engage with Late Bronze Age Canaanite themes.[21] The revisiting and re-creation of Late Bronze Age art, including Egyptian art of that period, was not accidental but a deliberate manifesta-tion of the Phoenicians' claim to be the heirs of the golden age of the Ca-naanite continuum. This is not too different conceptually from the evoca-tion of the Late Bronze Age Mycenaean past by the Iron Age communities of Homer through epic poetry and some forms of art, or for that matter early modern and modern appropriations of styles associated with presti-gious pasts, such as in Renaissance or neoclassical art. The difference is in our capacity to recognize these styles more easily for what they are. A sort of "Canaanite renaissance" underpins the artistic Levantine koine of the Early Iron Age, which is adapted according to the backgrounds and char-acter of the different regions surrounding the Phoenician strip, whether the North Syrian-Cilician realm or the southern Levant and Transjordan.

Marian Feldman has stressed that the value of "exotic" Levantine items that were exported or imitated abroad had to stem from *their value in the Levant itself,* on the grounds that art is always "intentionally created and deployed for various strategic ends," including propaganda and diplomacy.[22] Precisely, the Phoenicians' position vis-à-vis neighboring Levantine and Near Eastern cultures in this period must in part explain that value. The Phoe-nicians themselves were not passively absorbing influences from Syria, Cyprus, Assyria, and Egypt, but actively creating a unique culture that acquired great prestige and exerted visible influence on those around them: not only in the southern Levant (including Transjordanian groups), but in the realm of the Neo-Hittite/Luwian and Aramaean states of Cilicia and Syria, which constituted a "Syro-Anatolian culture complex,"[23] and even in Assyria itself farther east. Since the twelfth century, Phoenician polities had already been distinctive in their language and cultural traits, with By-blos and Sidon standing out, judging from external sources. After the mid-tenth century, however, when the literary tradition situates the reign of Hiram I (the traditional dates are 969–936 BC), Tyre emerged as the main Levantine harbor for international trade, possibly the most impor-tant one of the Mediterranean at this point, and it moved to the forefront of the history of Phoenicia.[24] This preeminence of Tyre, along with a re-spite from Assyrian campaigns to the western coast during good part of the eighth century (782–745 BC), facilitated the city's sustained prosperity and investment in colonial networks.[25]

Tyre and Its Networks

After the Bronze Age collapse, small Phoenician settlements stretched from the southern part of the Syrian coast to the north of Israel near Mount Carmel and the Akko plain. These traditional contours of Phoenician settlement were stable by the mid-ninth century under Ittobaal (Ethbaal), when Tyre and Sidon seem to have functioned as a joint polity, just when the Mediterranean-wide colonizing enterprise was at full steam. The political economy of the small coastal communities of this area was profoundly changed with the political expansion and the emerging hegemony of Tyre. This had possibly already happened during the tenth century (hypothetically under Hiram), but certainly under Ittobaal in the ninth. Ongoing excavations at sites in northern Israel, such as Tel Akko, Achziv, and Tel Keisan should shed light on this process in coming years.

Tyre's maritime activity is attested overseas by materials found in Iberia, Euboia, Crete, Cyprus, and North Syria, followed by its more permanent foundations starting in the late ninth century in North Africa and Iberia (Carthage, Utica, Gadir, the Málaga coast, etc.). This process started with Tyre's control of the Akko plain in the tenth century, effectively the first wave of Phoenician expansion beyond their core homeland. Control of this area to the south lasted well into the eighth century, as this was the situation that the Assyrians encountered when they advanced to the west.[26] Based on texts and the trail of pottery it is clear that the Phoenician cities and especially Tyre had already intensified their relations with the rest of the Levant during the second half of the eleventh century, even if it was overseas where they solidified their far-reaching *"emporion."*

The semilegendary narrative of Hiram I's joint naval enterprises with Solomon evokes this period of expansion. The historicity of Solomon and his tenth-century united kingdom is debated and dependent on complicated archaeological dating issues; but the biblical tradition reflects an awareness of the advantageous position of Tyre and its then satellite city of Sidon as hubs of long-distance trade and the potential participation in it of neighboring groups of the southern Levant, among them the Philistines. In short, the Israelite powerhouses of the early Iron Age wanted to join the trading network that Tyre opened up, especially as it tapped into entirely new gold and silver sources, previously a trade monopolized by Egypt, but now flowing through Tyre from Sardinia, Cilicia, and Iberia.[27]

With inwardly looking (if not necessarily weak) Aramaean kingdoms to the north and east, an ambitious and temporarily united Israel to the south, and a vigorous Assyrian Empire still confined to Mesopotamia, Tyre made the best of the geopolitical situation and consolidated itself as "the fore-most naval and commercial power in Asia," a position it held for the first half of the first millennium BC.[28] The "beautiful and perfect" Tyre shat-tered by Ezekiel's verses was at this time built up as a great island fortress whose appearance would strike also Assyrians, Persians, Macedonians, and Romans as "most noteworthy for its size and celebrity among the cities of Syria and Phoenicia."[29] The special treatment granted by the Assyrian Em-pire to the Phoenician cities and particularly to Tyre has already been men-tioned in Chapter 1. According to Josephus, when the Levant fell into Roman hands, Mark Antony retained Tyre and Sidon's freedom out of re-spect for their ancestral independence, while he gave the rest of the Phoe-nician and Levantine coast to Cleopatra.[30] Augustus revoked this special status in 18 BC.[31] Strabo's description, from the time of Augustus, captures the city's preeminence, and is worth enjoying:

> Tyre is wholly an island, built nearly in the same manner as Aradus. [. . .]
> It has two harbors, one enclosed, the other open, which is called the Egyp-tian harbor. The houses here, it is said, consist of many stories, of more even than at Rome; on the occurrence, therefore, of an earthquake, the city was nearly demolished. It sustained great injury when it was taken by siege by Alexander, but it rose above these misfortunes, and recov-ered both by means of the skill of its people in the art of navigation, in which the Phoenicians in general have always excelled all nations, and of their purple-dye industries, the Tyrian purple being held in the highest estimation. [. . .] Their independence was secured to them at a small expense to themselves, not only by the kings of Syria, but also by the Romans, who confirmed what the former had conceded. They pay extra-vagant honors to Herakles. The great number and magnitude of their colonies and cities are proof of their maritime skill and power. Such then are the Tyrians.[32]

Innovative and durable engineering projects that are attributed to this early phase include the city's famous temples, royal palace, high walls, and two harbors (north and south) connected by a canal crossing the island. These two harbors (archaeologically elusive), referred to as "Egyptian" and "Sidonian," respectively, were mirrored in the layout of Tyre's western colony of Gadir. In turn, the territory across the island of Tyre, known as Ushu in Assyrian and Egyptian (and perhaps Hebrew) sources was Tyre's outlet to the continent, providing extensive arable land and freshwater as well as access to murex, wood, and other resources, and functioning also as a buffer for military defense.[33]

With a combination of conservatism and innovative impulse, the Phoenician states followed their coastal Canaanite predecessors' prowess in several industries and trades, which continued to be strong after the Late Bronze Age, most notably timber exploitation, transportation, and construction, as well as weaving and purple dye extraction. (As mentioned in the Introduction, the word for Canaan/Canaanite was used to refer to red/purple dye and dyed textiles in Akkadian texts from Nuzi in the Late Bronze Age.) The Phoenicians also innovated in harbor infrastructure and naval technology, as Strabo and others noted. The use of faster, more powerful ships such as biremes and fifty-oarsmen warships (quinqueremes) was attributed to Phoenicians. Such ships are perhaps depicted in Assyrian reliefs from Nineveh, in a scene capturing the flight of King Luli/Ululaios of Tyre. One of their innovations was also the rudder and the sharp ram, and of the mortise-and-tenon system to join the hull's planks, known as *coagmenta punicana* by the Romans and probably invented by earlier Canaanites. This technology is attested in the Uluburun Canaanite shipwreck, but also in the seventh-century Phoenician haul of Mazarrón in southeast Iberia.[34] Assyrian reliefs also represent the broad merchant ship (like the Greek *gaulos*) and the small boat used for local fishing and transport, called *hippoi* in classical sources for their horse-head prows, depicted carrying wood in the Korshabar reliefs.[35] These naval and harbor innovations, together with those used in metallurgy, urbanization, and the artistic industries typically associated with Phoenicians, spread far and wide mostly through Tyrian networks, with Sidon playing a secondary but important role in closer circles.[36]

As Tyre's networks overseas expended in the ninth–eighth centuries, Phoenician involvement in the surrounding Levant also reached its peak. It is now that Phoenician ivories, the "stars" of Phoenician craftsmanship, become most coveted, their motifs imitated in reliefs in stone and other materials. Levantine elites, in turn, seem to have been less interested in the Phoenicians' decorated metal bowls, or in glass objects and cheap faience amulets than were the Phoenicians' customers in the Aegean and Italy.[37] Just as the orientalizing adaptations abroad are selective and idiosyncratic, Levantine elites would have been equally active in shaping their own "Phoenicianizing" trends (see below). Once again, Phoenician influence cannot be reduced to a select class of luxury products traditionally associated with them in art historical overviews.

As Gunnar Lehmann has noted, the widespread distribution of Phoenician transport jars and commercial containers is also rarely considered in connection with the network of luxury products, which it considerably overlaps with. The prophet Ezekiel, active in the sixth century, although in part evoking an earlier scenario, assumes intensive commercial involvement by Tyre in the southern Levant, Syria, northern Mesopotamia and the Syro-Anatolian realm (oddly not mentioning Egypt). His list of merchandise includes horses and mules, slaves, bronze, textiles, precious stones, wine, timber, grain, honey, balm, and oil, of which only the metals and gems would have left a trace in the archaeological record.[38] Earlier Egyptian accounts, for instance, during the time of Ramesses IX (late twelfth century BC), record the role of Byblos as the main supplier of essential (but perishable) merchandise, such as timber and finished wood, papyrus for writing, ropes (for shipbuilding), linen and leather, and food (vegetables and salted meats); they also mention the more archaeologically friendly precious metals, ivory, and jewelry. As mentioned above, the Phoenicians were a main source of timber for the Assyrians as well, even as represented in their monuments.[39] For instance, Assyrian texts from the reigns of Ashurnasirpal II and Salmaneser III in the ninth century suggest that Phoenician agents were active on the Euphrates as mediators in the trade between the coastal Levant and Assyria, and the flux of Levantine products in Assyria only grew once the Levant was under their grip in the seventh century.[40]

The extraction of purple dye from murex shells or vegetable sources and in general the textile industry is an area where Phoenicians excelled but this has left practically no trace in the archaeological record. The Phoenicians, as we know, became strongly associated with this industry, even if they might have learned it from the Cretans, whose Minoan ancestors extracted purple from at least 1800 BC.[41] We know the Phoenician towns were in-volved in the trade of agricultural and marine products, such as grain, fruits, olive oil, wine, salt, and salted meats and fish (their *garum* sauce would achieve "worldwide" fame). While trade in these staples was by no means a monopoly of Phoenicians, they were at an advantage when it came to sell-ing their stock and acting as intermediaries because of their naval capabili-ties and extensive networks.[42]

In short, the Phoenician cities remained prosperous and independent throughout the early first millennium and constituted themselves into self-fashioned banners of Canaanite prestige culture. They became a point of reference for their southern Levantine neighbors, and held a well-respected position among the Syrian-Anatolian city-states too. In this context, Tyre was the most internationally connected enclave, while later in the millen-nium (during Persian times) Sidon followed its southern neighbor closely in wealth and regional power, possibly with the two forming a political unit led by Tyre from the mid-ninth century and until perhaps the seventh century BC, when the first unequivocally Sidonian king is mentioned in Assyrian sources. No other Phoenician city came close to overshadowing Tyre and none was comparable in its reach overseas.[43] It is against this background that we need to reinterpret the Phoenician cultural position in the Levant and beyond.

A Phoenician Koine for the Levant

When Phoenician polities reached into the west, they already epitomized the admired Levantine urban culture. They were its main representatives, after reformulating several previous traditions, including Egyptian, Ca-naanite, and those of the Syrian-Anatolian cultural continuum to their own liking and that of local consumers. The emulation of Phoenician culture is especially well attested in Israel-Judah, whose higher strata em-braced the international language and elite behavior set by the Phoenician city-states: besides adopting their writing system (see "Aleph-Bet" section below) and general royal symbology expressed in luxury arts, scholars have pointed to choices in dining ware and monumental architecture as ele-ments through which the new elites articulated their latest royal culture and aspirations.[44] This is the effect that the local imitations of Red-Slip Phoenician wares must have aimed for, be it the red burnished pottery, which imitated Phoenician ware in shapes related to banqueting, or the ninth-century "Samaria ware," which (despite the name) was largely imported from Phoenicia.[45] Contrary to the biblical tradition's aggrandizing picture of the united monarchy of David and Solomon in the tenth century, from the archaeological viewpoint the kingdoms forming in Israel were minor players on the international scene, who adopted a "royal assemblage" that dressed them up with the proper outlook of an emergent elite, just like other coalescing groups in the Mediterranean. To quote Alexander Joffe, "the rise of the tenth-century [Israelite] state was largely a function of the northern and central portions of the Southern Levant becoming a periphery of Phoenician city-states and a neighbor or competitor of Aramaean city-states."[46]

While the Phoenicians' pioneering role in architectural design and construction is assumed in the biblical tradition mentioned above, it is difficult to assess the influence of their temple and palace models, given that these sorts of remains from Early Iron Age Phoenicia remain elusive. The best-attested Phoenician type is represented in the ninth century at Kition-Kathari (Ashtart temple, built over Bronze Age Temple 1).[47] Possibly derived from an Egyptian prototype, the type of building was exported to the colonial network as well as to the southern Levant, where it underwent further local modifications. This temple is characterized by rows of pillars inside the cultic room, and is hence sometimes called *Pfeilertempel*, literally "Pillar Temple" (see also the discussion on temple models in Chapter 5).

In turn, public residences began to be monumentalized in the Levant around the late tenth century, perhaps following the so-called *bit-hilani* model, consisting of a broad-room building with porticoed entrance and a long inner hall, rooted in Bronze Age traditions. This type of construction was adopted and developed in the Aramaean and Neo-Hittite realms (e.g., Tell Tayinat). The preserved Phoenician constructions, however, seem to favor the above-mentioned "Pillar Temple" type with flexible iterations, as we see, among other areas of Phoenician settlement in Byblos, Kition, and Motya (Figure 5.3).[48] On the other hand, this is not the pattern of the Solomonic temple, in whose construction the Phoenicians were allegedly involved; its description rather recalls the Syrian temples of the Bronze

Age with no columns inside, such as at Ugarit, Alalakh, and 'Ain Dara'. But evidence for this type in the southern Levant after the tenth century is debated, while the type had some traction in the northern Levant, such as in northern Syria.[49]

Monumentalization of the emerging Levantine states also included fortifications, such as the addition of stone casemate walls and gates to border cities such as Hazor, Megiddo, and Gezer. In Israel and Judah this may have been the result of a centralized monumentalization program in the tenth century BC, as traditional interpretations had it (associating the program with Solomon's reign).[50] But the data remains problematic, and these constructions may belong later in the ninth century (at the time of Omri, Ahab and Ittobaal), as other have proposed, or somewhere within that bracket.[51] What can we make, then, of the biblical statement that "Hiram king of Tyre sent messengers to David, and cedar trees, and carpenters and masons, and they built a house for David"?[52] Whatever the specific case of that relationship, it is safe to say that the states of the southern Levant seem to have snatched up Phoenician models and construction techniques, and employed Phoenician architects and craftspeople.[53] If we can extract anything from the traditional narratives it is the ideas and assumptions that underlie such statements.

Luxury Goods

Particular modalities of Levantine art were cherished and imitated among Mediterranean elites, as we have seen throughout this book. A paradox often noted about Phoenician and orientalizing art is the scarcer attestation of the most famous types of luxury goods at Phoenician sites proper, in part due to the various difficulties of archaeological work there. For instance, only one decorated metal bowl has been excavated in Iron Age Syro-Palestine (from Megiddo, context unclear), in addition to a fragment from Tell Qattina, near Homs, in Syria.[54] But these items were not altogether unwanted by elites in the broader Near East either: only one of these *paterae* has been found in Asia Minor (in a Phrygian tumulus outside Ankara), but other forms of art (e.g., sculpture, metalwork, architecture, and formal inscriptions) indicate a deep engagement by Syro-Anatolian states with Levantine art and their own contribution to the stock of luxury items exported to the Aegean and beyond.[55] Probably following Assyrian channels, a good number of metal bowls arrived in Iran in the seventh century, where a local type developed (only one of known context, from a warrior tomb).[56] In the Near East, the largest groups of metal bowls come from caches of Levantine booty at the Assyrian centers of Nimrud and Khorsabad, which also account for the largest accumulations of Syrian-Phoenician ivories. Whether as gifts, tribute, or loot from subdued Levantine leaders, they added to the Assyrians' imperial wealth and artistic capital diverted from the Levant.[57] We have, therefore, lost these items' possible manufacture or use in the Levant itself before they were transported.

The findings of ivories are also similarly decontextualized in the record. As discussed in Chapter 3, a distinction between two ivory-carving styles has become conventional: an Egyptianizing "Phoenician" style and a North Syrian style more akin to Neo-Hittite and Assyrian aesthetics, although it is far from clear whether the distinction reflects chronological or geographical factors. But these may be substyles within a general Phoenician industry of ivory-carving, which is reinforced by the similarity between the alleged "North Syrian" style and a subset of the Phoenician or Cypro-Phoenician bowls. In Markoe's assessment, both bowls and ivories in this style were simply tailored to North Syrian or Assyrian preferences.[58] Such market-specific versatility agrees with the broader analysis of the orientalizing artistic phenomenon and with the technical and artistic know-how of Phoenician artisans.

Moreover, ivories in the conventionally labeled "Phoenician style" (i.e., more Egyptianizing) are found also in North Syria and Cilicia, that is, in areas where the North Syrian/Neo-Hittite style should have been dominant (e.g., Arslan Tash, Carchemish, Zincirli). Although not everyone agrees on the association of these stylistic categories with Phoenicians, there is no reason that groups of Phoenician artisans could not have operated there, or that North Syrian artisans could not have adopted the Egyptianizing Phoenician style. Equally, both ivories and metal bowls found at Nimrud share stylistic traits (Figures 3.1 and 3.2). In other words, accepting substylistic variants and nuances, a continuum links the ivories found in Syria-Palestine and Assyria to the art represented by metal bowls and ivories in orientalizing settings and connected with Phoenician trade there. Similarly, the influence of the Phoenician style is evident in reliefs from Cilicia, such as those from Karatepe's monumental entrance, which also bears inscriptions in Luwian and Phoenician. Remains of unfinished ivories or sculpted reliefs in situ such as those at Karatepe suggest a degree of mobility of Phoenician artisans.[59] Such movement has been proposed frequently to explain the distribution of Levantine art, but also as a conduit for the transmission and adaptation of stylistic and technological techniques and the creation of local apprenticeships.

Finally, we need to imagine another type of now-invisible Phoenician craftsmanship and merchandise, namely, the valuable wooden artifacts inseparable from the ivories we pay so much attention to: the small ivory plaques we see in museum catalogs and coffee-table books were not intended to stand alone. They were inlaid in jewelry boxes, chests, the backs of chairs and thrones, bed headboards, couches, tables, footstools, and more, beautifully standing out against the darker wood. In some cases the piece of furniture was almost completely inlaid with ivory plaques, as in a chair and a bed frame found in Tomb 79 at Salamis on Cyprus.[60] Images of booty brought to the Assyrian court from the Levant depicted exactly this kind of luxurious furniture, which must account for the abundance of Levantine ivories excavated in Assyrian palaces.[61] To comprehend the pervasiveness of wooden construction and house furnishing (even dominant in our modern houses), we need only turn our gaze to Egypt, where wooden coffins, statues, tools, and furniture are preserved. Wood provided the perfect material to fine-tune carving techniques before they were employed in scarcer and more expensive materials.[62] In fact, Assyrian and Hebrew texts and iconography represent Phoenicians as expert woodworkers and transporters; it was Phoenician woodworkers, masons, smiths, and metal traders who were brought to Israel, not the other way around, as far as we know. The "ghost" use of wood is perhaps an appropriate metaphor for the dismissal of the "ghost" Phoenicians from Mediterranean cultural histories.

Other Circulating Goods

A much less popular subject than ivories are Phoenician transport jars and their distribution. But they penetrated the same markets, more often than fine wares. Phoenician transport jars are especially well attested in the southern Levant but also in North Syria and Assyria. In Israel, for example, they have been found in Ashdod, Ashkelon, and other coastal sites, as well as in the Negev en route to Arabia. They have also been recovered in shipwrecks near Ashkelon, along the route between Egypt and Syria-Palestine, and in northern Israel (the so-called hippo storage jars). All these are inseparable from commerce with Phoenicia.[63] There is also evidence of Phoenician trading activity (possibly posts) in the northern Levant, and it seems increasingly likely that Tyrians collaborated with local Syrians at Al-Mina to channel prized Euboian wares to the region, as discussed in Chapter 2. As mentioned too, in this period the Levantines coveted Greek fine banqueting wares, just as the Greeks coveted Levantine fine products.[64]

Much smaller, portable objects such as seals and gems are often lumped together in the west as "knick-knacks" that pop up in local sanctuaries and elite burials, but they are quite useful for tracing the networks of Phoenician trading elites in the Levant itself. As Gubel notes, "together with ceramics, ivories, bowls, and the diffusion of the alphabetic script, the distribution of these seals mirrors the impact of Phoenician trade on peripheral Levantine regions."[65] The association of Phoenicians with the glyptic arts is evoked in the biblical tradition, where the king of Tyre was famous for his access to precious stones, among other exotic materials, through the famed "ships of Tarshish."[66] Indeed, inscriptions on these seals show their wide use by Northwest Semitic speakers throughout the Levant.[67] Moreover, seals were often carried as amulets but also typically used to seal papyrus scrolls, while in Mesopotamian writing culture rolling cylinder seals were used to mark clay tablets. Seals, in other words, were a by-product of the transactions that accompanied Phoenician commerce, a use that elevates them over the category of random knick-knacks and explains their wide distribution across the Mediterranean. Linking east and west, a group of clay lumps (*bullae*) have been recovered from an oven in a house from eighth-century BC Gadir. On them both the seal mark and the papyrus impression are visible. The clay, a study shows, came from the eastern Mediterranean, not Iberia.[68] The tiny clay lump is an early testimony of the long journeys made by these seals and their carriers (and the documents from the motherland that sometimes were, it seems, intentionally burned).

The Phoenicians' involvement in all stages of metallurgy has been presented in previous chapters. Mining and metalwork had been developing for millennia in the Near East, as Levantines, Anatolians, Egyptians, and Mesopotamians competed for resources and technologies; but smelting technology took off in the second millennium. Late Bronze Age Canaanites and later Phoenicians were at the forefront of tin and silver production and trade (e.g., tin ingots from the Uluburun shipwreck). Starting in the tenth century, Phoenicians played a central role in the intensification of metal production, now including iron; as in Iberia and other areas, they relied on the locals' access, expertise, and workforce, including their transactions with the Israelites, as suggested by the Hebrew Bible. Copper continued to be important for itself as well as for the bronze alloy, and indeed the copper wealth of Cyprus attracted Tyre early on. (A Phoenician coppersmith called Hiram is even mentioned by name in the tradition.[69]) Ultimately it was the Phoenicians who took these Levantine technologies and others, such as writing, to the farthest areas of the Mediterranean and even to the Atlantic coasts.[70]

Aleph-Bet: More Than a Script

Alphabetic writing traveled westward along with the orientalizing kit. I have discussed it alongside other adaptations of the Levantine elite culture in the Aegean, Iberia, and Etruria, which it reached via the earliest Greek adapters.[71] It was not just any "Levantine" alphabet that these groups appropriated, however: it was specifically the Phoenician alphabet, used by Phoenicians and exported by Phoenicians. This is nowhere clearer than in the Levant, where its influence was also transformative and lasting: to put it dramatically, while in the Aegean the alphabet allowed the writing of Homer's *Iliad*, in Israel it provided the medium in which the Hebrew Bible would be written. This trajectory could be extended down to Latin and all western scripts but also to the Qur'an, as the Arabic script too is a great-grandchild of the Phoenician script through its Aramaic and Nabatean intermediaries. Indeed, Phoenician became the basis for writing in Aramaic and Old Hebrew, and from there it was adopted by other emerging ethnic groups and states: Moabite, Ammonite, and Edomite, as well as the Philistines. On the other hand, Phoenician language and script were also used as the international medium of communication and to display prestige in the region, as attested in monumental inscriptions. I briefly sum up the evidence before turning to its broader implications.

Alphabetic Beginnings

Referring to the Semitic alphabet, Christopher Rollston wrote that "the alphabet was invented once, and this occurred during the early-second millennium B.C.E."[72] He was referring to the first attestation of alphabetic script, sometimes called "Sinaitic" or "Protosinaitic." Around the eighteenth century BC, West Semitic speakers created this simplified script departing from knowledge of the acrophonic principle in some Egyptian signs. Put simply, signs represented the first sound of the word associated with the "depicted" thing (using the Hebrew names): the glottal stop *aleph,* the first letter, represented the horned head of an ox (*'alp*), *bet* a square evoking the plan of a house (*bayt*), the sign for "m," which looked like a horizontal zigzag, represented "water" (*mayim*), the roundish letter *'ayin* was an eye (*'ayin*), and so on. This script was not homogeneous and is attested mainly in the Sinai but also in Palestine and Egypt, where groups of West Semites lived.[73] The difference between this new system and the Egyptian and Mesopotamian writing systems is stark: the two great oldest systems in the world used a combination of representational tools, including syllabic signs (1 sign = 1 syllable, e.g., ma, mi, mu), logograms (1 sign = one word), and determinatives (1 sign = a semantic category, e.g., "deity," "person"), besides alphabetic signs (1 sign = 1 sound) in Egyptian. An alphabet, however, comprises only the last type of signs, so it is "a system in which a single grapheme (i.e., letter) is used to signify a single phoneme (i.e., meaningful unit of sound)."[74]

The main leap, therefore, was not among types of alphabets (more or less "consonantal"), as discussed in Chapter 7. The alphabet concept meant a paradigmatic shift away from the old writing systems used since the late fourth millennium: Egyptian hieroglyphic and Mesopotamian cuneiform syllabary used by Babylonians / Assyrians for Sumerian and Akkadian languages. The Semitic alphabet reduced the repertoire of signs from hundreds to twenty few. The question is, why did the alphabet not become generalized sooner? The West Semitic speakers, after all, were flirting with alphabetic writing for centuries, as the Sinaitic inscriptions show, and a formal, regularized version was used at Ugarit for a couple of centuries at the end of the Bronze Age (more below). And yet, during this time the Canaanite city-states of Syria-Palestine, as well as the Hittite state apparatus, chose to follow the Mesopotamian conventions of syllabic writing; in the Hittite case, in addition to the Luwian language and its indigenously developed script, Luwian hieroglyphic, completely different from cuneiform. This means that documents were made mainly in the form of clay tablets (also stone monuments and perhaps some other media) using cuneiform, that is, "wedge-shaped" signs, even for the Ugaritic alphabet. These were state-driven choices, determined by broader dynamics: Babylonian written literature was the backbone of Near Eastern elite culture and education in the second millennium, its belles Lettres.[75] Akkadian had also become the formal language for official records and international correspondence in the Near East (e.g., archives of Ebla, Mari), even between Canaanite cities and Egypt, as exemplified in the Amarna Letters.[76] In turn, the same writing conventions were used in the Late Bronze Age by the Hittites (Indo-European speakers) and the Northwest Semitic speakers of Ugarit to write administrative, royal, and literary texts in their own languages.

Ugarit's linguistic and scribal culture was astonishingly multicultural, with eight languages and five different scripts attested in the brief span of time covered by its preserved texts before the city's destruction circa 1185 BC.[77] Drawing from the traditions attested in the Protosinaitic script, the Ugaritians asserted their cultural uniqueness within this "cuneiform koine" by fitting the cuneiform-and-tablet format to a simplified alphabet script of only thirty signs (hence called "alphabetic cuneiform"). In so doing they created their own alphabetic script, which is the first known standardization of the Northwest Semitic alphabet. This script (also painted in linear form in pottery shards) was used less systematically outside Ugarit too, since a few testimonies have been found in North Syria, Israel, and Lebanon.[78] Moving down the coast, the "proto-Phoenician" cities of this time partook in the international Canaanite-Akkadian correspondence, as shown by letters from the kings of Byblos, Sidon, and Tyre. These states played "a precarious balancing act, maintaining a degree of loyalty to Egypt, on the one hand, while making the right noises to the Hittites on the other."[79] Their historical orientation toward Egypt was reflected also in their writing culture earlier in the second millennium at Sidon and Byblos, where it was not rare for a king of Byblos in the Middle Bronze Age to write his name in Egyptian hieroglyphs.[80]

The Late Bronze Age floruit of alphabetic experimentation, however, died with Ugarit's version. Only after the collapse of the great Bronze Age empires did the second standardized version of the alphabet emerge the in Phoenician cities, this time to stay. This Phoenician version of the North-west Semitic alphabet shed the cuneiform format adopted at Ugarit. The new "linear" (i.e., non-cuneiform) alphabet was used for monumental inscriptions, to mark luxury objects, and most of all for private and busi-ness documents on papyri, the Egyptian general medium, which the Greeks associated with the Phoenicians in particular. The earliest specimens of this distinct alphabet come from a group of royal inscriptions from Byblos dated to the late eleventh and tenth centuries, including the famous funerary in-scriptions of King Ahiram (ca. 1000 BC) and his successors, some of which are written on statues of Egyptian pharaohs (Figure 9.1).[81] Beside this ex-traordinary group of royal inscriptions from Byblos, there is a brief gap in the record, before the Phoenician alphabet resurfaces in the mid-ninth century in its standardized form. This most lasting and influential version hailed from Tyre, now head of the Phoenician *oikoumene*.[82] This is the al-phabet that would persist through the first millennium in the Phoenician realm and it became the *Mutterschrift* of Old Hebrew, Aramaic, Greek, Latin, and other alphabetic scripts.

One Alphabet, Many Peoples

In Israel, the first attestations of the alphabet come from a small group of inscriptions dated to the tenth and ninth centuries. They are virtually iden-tical to those in Phoenician, so much so that scholars scrutinize and debate minor formal details (specifically the length of vertical lines of a few letters) to argue whether they can be classified as "Phoenician," or should instead be labeled "proto-Old Hebrew" or "pre-Hebrew," according to preferences. The most relevant inscriptions for this stage are the Kfar Veradim bowl, the Tel Zayit abecedary, and the Gezer "calendar," besides a few more fragmentary ones.[83] Later in the ninth century, a sufficiently distinct Old Hebrew script is considered a "national script," and the same can be said for the scripts developed by Aramaeans in North Syria and Moabites and Ammonites in the Transjordan region during the ninth–eighth centuries. In fact, the first inscription in what is conventionally called "Old Hebrew" script is the famous Mesha stela from Moab, written in the Moabite lan-guage. Although it is often generally assumed that those other groups fol-lowed the Hebrew initiative in using this alphabet, the idea is based on

FIG. 9.1   Royal reliefs with Phoenician inscriptions from Phoenicia and Cilicia.

Above: Stone relief and Phoenician inscription (detail) on the sarcophagus of King Ahiram (or Ahirom) from Byblos, ca. 1000 BC; the dead king sits on a sphinx throne and holds a downward lotus flower while he receives offerings; note the row of downward open and closed lotuses above, and the Phoenician inscription along the rim of the sarcophagus's lid, identifying the king and issuing a curse against desecrators. National Museum, Beirut. Gianni Dagli Orti/ Shutterstock.

Below: Stone stela depicting King Kulamuwa of Sam'al (Zincirli, Turkey), ninth century BC (partial view); the inscription in Phoenician commemorates his deeds while the king holds a downward lotus flower and points to various religious symbols. Vorderasiatisches Museum, Berlin. agefotostock/Alamy Stock Photo.

assumptions about power dynamics and not on linguistic-epigraphic evidence. There is no reason that the Moabites, for instance, could not have borrowed the script from Damascus or directly from Tyre.[84] As Seth Sanders notes, these first monumental inscriptions present the first "vernacular" versions of royal narratives, meaning texts written in regional languages only now used for official purposes by local rulers, who, in turn aptly borrowed the tropes of imperial propaganda from the Assyrians. These kings "lay out their territories, regimes, and languages at a stroke, on a single iconic monument." At the same time, it is not accidental that these Levantine states departed from the Babylonian-Assyrian–looking cuneiform and chose the dignified Phoenician alphabet at this moment.[85]

The prestige of the Phoenician script and language is nowhere more evident than in its use in official and royal inscriptions in Northern Syria. In the ninth century, King Kulamuwa of Sam'al (Zincirli, southeast Turkey) used the Phoenician language and script to record his exploits on a monumental stela (Figure 9.1). The inscription is written in the standard Tyrian-Sidonian dialect and presents him as a powerful ruler, pointing at religious symbols and invoking local and Phoenician versions of Baal (Baal-Semed, Baal-Hammon) and holding a withering flower, like Ahiram, signaling his death.[86] Testimonies from the same chronological horizon are scattered in the Transjordan (Bar Hadad inscription near Aleppo), Cyprus (the Honeyman stela), and beyond, on Crete (Tekke bowl) and Sardinia (Nora stela).[87] In the late eighth century, other leaders from the Neo-Hittite kingdoms of North Syria and Cilicia displayed their international status in the new alphabet, either in Aramaic or in Phoenician: the most impressive Phoenician inscriptions, besides the above-mentioned one at Kulamuwa, are those flanking the entrance of the fortress at Karatepe, dated to the eighth century; this is the longest Phoenician text found to date. Along the impressive gate blocks (and under a god's statue) the local authority Azatiwada narrated his deeds in both the Phoenician and Luwian languages, written in the local Hittite/Luwian hieroglyphic script and accompanied by Levantine motifs such as guardian winged sphinxes and the tree of life with volutes.[88]

While the prestige and international efficacy of Phoenician inscriptions in the broader Levant is evident, we know little of the inscriptions' audience. We do not know the extent to which Phoenician language was used, if at all, by local elites in these surrounding regions. As James Osborne has suggested for Syria-Cilicia, it is reasonable to think that at least some of the inscriptions' viewers/readers were themselves Phoenician speakers, among them merchants or dignitaries spending time in these communities.[89] Azatiwada presents himself as the "blessed by Baal, servant of Baal," whereas the Luwians have their equivalent Storm God, Tarhun/Tarhuntas.[90] Perhaps these Cilician leaders were not doing anything radically different from the Etruscan king at Caere, who dedicated a local shrine in Pyrgi in both Etruscan and Phoenician, opulently inscribed in gold sheets dedicated to Ashtart and Uni (Figure 5.7). The dual language and identity of the honored goddess also aimed to please and include both a local and a Phoenician audience.

As for the Phoenicians themselves, they stayed the course in their own writing tradition, which was an important part of their cultural identity (no less than for the Israelites and other neighbors, who now had their own "national alphabets"). Indeed, both the Phoenician language and the script remained remarkably consistent across the Mediterranean for over a millennium, a uniformity that Rollston has attributed to "the presence of continued cultural contact and to the nature of the trans-regional Phoenician scribal apparatus."[91]

Even with the development of other Levantine scripts, however, the Phoenician language continued to be a useful tool for interregional commercial relations.[92] It was through these networks, probably, that the Greeks and others encountered the alphabet overseas, and in the mid-eighth century BC the Greek writing system (that other great child of the Phoenician alphabet) spread throughout the Aegean and southern Italy.[93] In other words, the range of adaptations in this early part of the first millennium shows that Phoenician was the culturally hegemonic script of the time. Besides Levantines and Greeks, other local groups adopted this writing system, whether directly from Phoenicians (Tartessic, perhaps late Libyco-Berber, Phrygian?) or through a Greek version (Lycian, Lydian, Etruscan, Phrygian?). In the end, the new literate elites were following transnational trends of self-representation. While the mercantile use of the Phoenician alphabet is more often emphasized, in a sense these locals were doing what the Byblian king in the second millennium was doing when he wrote his name in Egyptian hieroglyphs, or when the Hittite and Canaanite poets and administrators turned to cuneiform tablets.[94]

What did it mean for each emergent independent state in Israel, Judah, Moab, or Sam'al to use an alphabetic writing system in the wake of an era of empires now gone (Egyptian, Hittite) and in the face of the expanding Neo-Assyrian war machine? For Sanders, the use of these regional languages for royal inscriptions by Moabites, Aramaeans, and others exhibits an attempt to talk directly to the people in an unprecedented way.[95] They do so precisely at a time of independence from competing empires and as a way to consolidate their own local languages and literatures. As this happens simultaneously with the emergence and rise of the Neo-Assyrian Empire, the young Levantine written culture became a political statement of independence, even a reaction to the "superposed and prestigious form of pre-existent literature."[96] In fact, among the first attested use of the alphabet in Palestine (twelfth–tenth centuries) are metal arrowheads and a few abecedaries, not exactly the type of inscriptions stemming from centralized authorities (though they might still belong to an elite stratum).[97] At the same time, we should not idealize the alphabet as a tool for the masses. As Rollston has pointed out, Phoenician, Aramaic, Hebrew, and other "national scripts" emerged and were, after all, sustained by a scribal apparatus at the service of the elites.[98]

Broader Implications

The adaptations of the Phoenician script in the broader Levant during the tenth and early ninth centuries BC were part of a specific trend. Even if we declare it a "pan-Levantine" phenomenon, we cannot subsume the Phoenicians into the common mix. Their role and agency in the process was distinct. From the Phoenician coast outward, the picture that emerges is as follows: by the eleventh century, after the withdrawal of the Late Bronze Age great powers from the Levant, Phoenician kings were the first to project an independent and strong royal image. Just as they did through urbanization, trade, and art, in recovering writing the Phoenicians filled the vacuum left by the urban literate states of the Late Bronze Age such as Ugarit. But now they chose the Canaanite, so far unofficial script, not the language of a foreign empire: if anything, it was the language of the expanding *emporion* of Tyre. In other words, the Phoenicians made a statement by formalizing the alphabetic script and using it for royal inscriptions and official

documents. They did not write the name and lineage of their kings in Akkadian cuneiform or in Egyptian hieroglyphs, but in their own renovated
Canaanite script, appropriating and elevating to the international scene this
old Canaanite invention, whose use had hitherto been scattered, inconsistent, and maintained underground but evidently not forgotten.

The other emerging kingdoms followed suit. In writing as in other matters,
the influence of Phoenician models in Syria-Palestine is evident, both archaeologically and in the narratives conveyed in the Hebrew tradition especially reflected in 1–2 Kings. They thought it worth recording that the
Tyrian king Hiram acknowledged David, the king of the new and potentially rival kingdom to the south, by sending an embassy with gifts, including cedarwood, much coveted by Egyptian pharaohs, a gesture that was
repeated when his son Solomon ascended the throne in the mid-tenth
century. This mutually beneficial relationship is celebrated in the Hebrew
Bible and its subsequent antiquarian tradition.[99] It includes not only technical and artistic input but also the concession of fertile lands in Galilee to
Tyre and some kind of Israelite partnership in the Tyrian long-distance trade
routes: the biblical references to the "ships of Tarshish" originated in this
context as a reference to Tyre's long-distance trade and colonies reaching
to the far west (even if the meaning evolved in the later texts).[100] This relationship also included a marriage alliance between King Ittobaal I of Tyre,
whose kingdom had expanded to Beirut (Berytos) and Sidon, and Ahab,
king of the northern kingdom of Israel in the mid-ninth century, who mar-
ried the famous Jezebel of Tyre.[101] In a nutshell, when these kings wrote in
Phoenician script, and even used the Phoenician language, they were emulating the Phoenician states, while making their own statement vis-à-vis
rising empires to the east by going with the Phoenicians' bold rejection of
the supremacy of Mesopotamian and Egyptian writing conventions.

As Madadh Richey and others before her have emphasized, we should
be careful not to rehash narratives of technological determinism, the idea
that the alphabet is a "facile" system fated to spread easily through all levels
of society whenever available.[102] Cultures across the globe have adopted
writing systems that seem cumbersome and extremely difficult to learn to
outsiders, and they stick to them even when alphabets are available, and
indeed the Greek Cypriots used a syllabary derived from the Minoan script
until the classical period. Identities are often more determinative factors
than ease. In this case, the Phoenician alphabet and language were impor-

tant and influential in their own right, not simply as "tools" that spread along with storage jars and trinkets due to some utilitarian value. Nor is the story of this alphabet or the Greek that of "a self-evident miracle," but rather that of "a fascinating technological artifact, whose ups and downs were tied to forces far beyond its inherent faculties and flaws."[103]

The reader might still come across scholarship in which the Phoenician alphabet is "de-alphabetized" and classified as a syllabary, as I pointed out in Chapter 7, or where its consonantal structure is emphasized as an essential quality. The first classification is plainly wrong, the second misleadingly creates a dichotomy between Semitic and Indo-European writing and, by extension, their cultures. Whatever the merits of those or other technicalities, they are beyond the main point: that the emulation of the Phoenician writing system, conventions, and language outside the Phoenician cities should not be demoted to the purely pragmatic or inevitable export of a tool. Neither should it be disassociated from the Phoenicians on the grounds that its use became part of a broader "Levantine" cultural wave. The opposite conclusion can be drawn: that writing systems and conventions are culturally and historically meaningful, and the alphabet's contribution came precisely at a time when Phoenician culture was highly influential, when the economic power and reach of Tyre was at its height, and when doing things "in the Phoenician way" (*phoinikizein*) was not stigmatized but desirable.

Israelite or Phoenician? The Case of "Proto-Aeolic" Capitals

A visitor to the brand-new palaces of Israelite, Judaean, or Moabite kings would note the regular large masonry and beautiful entrances flanked by voluted capitals. Despite their misleading Greek name, the story of the so-called Proto-Aeolic or volute capitals begins in the Levant. Whatever their specific origin, about which there is some debate, they were a staple of Phoenician art and that is how they became easily one of the most widespread shared motifs in the orientalizing Mediterranean.

To date, the earliest archaeologically dated examples concentrate in northern Israel. They were once attributed to the monumentalizing program of the United Kingdom of Israel led by Solomon in the tenth century, but most agree today that they are archaeologically associated with ninth-century

FIG. 9.2   Monumental gate from Iron Age Hazor, Israel.

Entrance to the fortified citadel of Hazor, northern Israel, with large ashlar masonry and volute or "Proto-Aeolic" capitals, ninth century BC. Photo by Amalyah Oren. © The Israel Museum,
Jerusalem.

constructions, which places them within the Omride period of the northern
kingdom of Israel (e.g., Megiddo, Samaria, Hazor) (Figure 9.2).[104] These
capitals, with minor stylistic variations, appear in a broader radius during
the eighth-seventh centuries, in Judah (Jerusalem and nearby Ramat Rachel,
Aroer), Moab (e.g., Mudaybi), and Amon (Rabbath Ammon). So far, over
forty limestone capitals of this type have been found in the Levant.[105]

These capitals were part of royal and elite culture, used and reused in
palatial and fortification gates, usually topping attached pillars, not freestanding columns. Once again, the archaeological gap in Early Iron Age
Phoenicia proper complicates matters. Early stone examples are not found
in Phoenician cities, but that is probably because architecture from this period is largely lacking. Volute capitals of the exact type, however, are reproduced in all sorts of portable media and in architectonic remains in areas
of Phoenician activity throughout the Mediterranean. They are also attested
in northern Syrian palaces (e.g., the column base at Tell Tayinat), another

area of contact with Phoenicia.[106] The volute capital was particularly ubiquitous as a motif in ivories dated between the ninth and eighth centuries.
As we might expect, they also appear on the engraved metal bowls, often
associated with the palmette or the tree of life motifs, sometimes signaling
architectural structures, for instance, framing a religious scene.[107]

Scholars have flagged various artistic precedents for specific elements of
these volute capitals, including Egyptian, Assyrian, Hittite, Minoan, and
Mycenaean. The dissection of features, however, does not say much about
the creation of the specific artistic type as a whole, in its consistent and durable shape. In this sense, the capital itself must have been born in northern
Syria-Palestine (anywhere between Phoenicia and northern Israel). In these
capitals, the decorative and the symbolic go together. The vertical volutes
and a central triangle represent the new offshoots coming off a palm tree
trunk, which symbology fits within popular Near Eastern themes, whether
inspired by the Assyrian tree of life or by Egyptian vegetal motifs. Reinforcing this interpretation, the double volutes appear often with the Phoenician palmette, sometimes stacked on top of each other forming a tree (e.g.,
Figure 3.2, on the gilded bowl from Kourion, Figure 4.3 on the onyx Phoenician ivory). In short, the volute capital is a "Phoenician-Israelite version"
of the tree of life and symbol of Ashtart, a popular ancestral theme in the
Near East and a favorite in Canaanite and Phoenician religion and art.[108]
This symbology, like the lotus flowers and other motifs, is also strongly
associated with royalty. Indeed, we have seen that volute-capital footstools
appear in the context of Etruscan elite or royal tombs and also in Carthage,
and if we look closely enough we can see the feature under the feet of King
Ahiram of Byblos (Figure 9.1).

Filling the gap in the architectural record of Phoenicia, we find the capital in Assyrian reliefs that depict Phoenician palaces or temples, such as
the depiction of Tyre during the flight of its king Luli in the time of Sennach-
erib (705–681). Even if these testimonies are later than the recovered Israelite capitals, they reflect Phoenician monumental architecture that probably preserved traditional features. The volute-capital columns in the high
building above the city walls might be flanking the entrance to the royal
palace or the temple of Melqart,[109] which bring to mind the allusions to
the famous pair of columns flanking the god's temples in Gadir and Tyre
(depicted in coins in later periods).[110] The capitals appear also in "miniaturized," symbolic architectural frames (*naiskoi*) decorating stelae (Figures 5.2

and 8.2) and other media, usually terracotta, ivory, and metal objects.[111] A real-life instance of the type of balustrades with volute capitals, which appears in the theme known as the "woman at the window" in Phoenician ivories (Figure 3.1), was found at Ramat Rachel in Israel, dated between the seventh and the fourth centuries BC.[112]

Later architectural examples are attested throughout the Phoenician-Punic realm. Starting in the west, a small, stone capital comes from Gadir, found out of context and dated between the seventh and the fifth centuries BC. It is presumed to belong to one of the city's sanctuaries.[113] The Gadir capital is four-sided (four volutes), and might have adorned an entrance or topped a freestanding pillar. Such pillars are represented in a terracotta model from Late Bronze Age Lebanon (Kamid el-Loz, in the Bekaa Valley), and were probably made of wood. A signet ring from Cádiz also bears the volute capital as a religious symbol.[114] Moving farther east, a volute capital was found at the Kothon Temple of Baal at Motya, Sicily, dated to the sixth century (Figure 5.3).[115] These "Proto-Aeolic" capitals were adopted in Etruria sometime in the first half of the sixth century, although the motif might have circulated in the portable arts (e.g., ivories) earlier on. Their early use in Italy is similar to that attested on Cyprus (below) and in Syria-Palestine, that is, as an architectonic decorative feature, in this case in Etruscan chamber tombs. But volute capitals were deployed in Etruscan art until the second–first centuries BC, often decorating stone urns, sarcophagi, decorated vases, funerary stelae, and incised in Etruscan bronze mirrors.[116]

In previous chapters I pointed out the connection between the Levantine volute capitals and the appearance of their Aeolic and Ionic counterparts in the eastern Aegean. I also mentioned their popularity on Cyprus, where monumental examples include the entrance to two rock-cut elite tombs from the sixth century, at the end of a stepped corridor (*dromos*). Some of the Cypriot capitals, for instance in funerary stelae, are additionally decorated with typically Phoenician symbolic motifs, such as the downward-facing moon and disk (associated with Ashtart and Tanit) appearing inside the central triangle, or with palmettes framing sphinxes springing from the capital (Figure 8.2).[117] They also mark the entrance of the terracotta shrine model from Idalion, dated to the sixth century BC.[118]

With such a long, wide history of reception, it is difficult to trace the precise eastern prototypes or their trajectories. For instance, Etruscan capitals might be drawing from a variety of eastern Mediterranean sources, at a time when Greek models were highly influential in Italy, and early scholarship often highlights these.[119] In turn, we can see the resilience and adaptability of the volute capital in later western contexts, embedded in Phoenician-Punic networks but less often mentioned in comparative studies. Besides the aforementioned example from Gadir, a few specimens from Iberia belong to a sixth-century horizon—the limestone pillar (probably a portable altar) recovered from the Bajo de la Campana shipwreck (ca. 600 BC); an adobe painted capital flanking the entrance of a sanctuary in Alcudia de Elche (southeast Iberia); and the relief capital carved on the back of a funerary *cippus* / obelisk-statue from Villaricos (Baria)—but they continue to appear in sacred and funerary spaces in the later Iberian-Punic realm.[120] The same can be said of the funerary and votive landscapes of the main areas of Phoenician settlement, where the volute capital is conjured in stelae throughout the Punic period and even overlapping with Roman culture. This is the case across sites on Sardinia and Sicily and in Tunisia and Cyrene, where they are also found in funerary architecture.[121] Sometimes the accompanying elements reinforce the symbology of the volutes, such as human figures (the deceased? a divinity or priest/priestess?) holding a lotus flower or the astral symbol of the disk and crescent, symbols of regeneration and Ashtart or Tanit (Figure 5.2).[122]

The "itinerary" of the volute capital reflects strong ties to Phoenician culture, despite the lack of stone examples in early Iron Age Phoenicia proper. This gap is due to a combination of factors: one is the minimal excavation of those strata in the Lebanon-Syria coastal strip, incommensurable with the archaeological availability and resources of Israel; a second factor is the use of clay/adobe and wood for domestic and early monumental construction as well as sculpture. Once again, it is essential to keep in mind the explanatory potential of lost wooden elements for our reconstruction of ancient life, as we have already seen in the case of the circulation of ivory adornments and the models for early stone constructions and statuary.[123]

The debate about these capitals (like the one about the alphabet), might seem esoteric and inconsequential, but it has broader implications for our cultural history of the Phoenicians. An early line of scholarship framed the volute/"Proto-Aeolic" capitals as an original Israelite type, a hallmark of the Omride dynasty, following Yigal Shiloh's interpretation of the 1970s.[124] In an attempt to rid the capitals of the Hellenocentric classification, Near

Eastern archaeologists proposed renaming them "palmette," "volute," or even "Israelite" capitals, on the grounds that no known Aegean example predates the Syro-Palestinian ones.[125] But classicists remain oblivious. Within the Levant itself, moreover, the claim over these capitals is still contested. Are they originally Israelite or Phoenician? The capitals certainly acquired some significance for regional elite identity in the Iron Age, and even for modern Israeli identity (a volute capital appears on the five-shekel coin). At the same time, it is undeniable that their distribution throughout the Phoenician world challenges the theory of its Iraelite origins. The disassociation of volute capitals from Phoenician culture implies some such scenario: the Phoenicians and other Levantine groups would have imitated this element of northern Israelite palatial architecture, and *only this one;* whence the Phoenicians integrated it in all the attested forms of Phoenician art they developed and exported.

This unlikely scenario, let us not forget, is based on a corpus of *stone* capitals produced in northern Israel (whence the type spread to the south), and on an argument ex silentio: we simply do not have access to this type of material, palatial architecture for Phoenicia in this period. But when and where archaeological evidence is more generous, in places touched by the Phoenician diaspora, we find these volute capitals used as we might expect, in association with sacred and elite art. In the opposite reconstruction, then, the Phoenician model explains why the Israelite capitals appear precisely in northern Israel, which was under the political and cultural influence of Tyre at the turn of the millennium and for centuries thereafter. The topic is of pan-Mediterranean scale, and it deserves further investigation. In the view coherent with my survey in this book, and shared by those who have considered the entire span of the volute capitals, the success of this feature owes to the fact that it evoked yet another unique Phoenician synthesis of older Canaanite motifs of great appeal in the Levant and beyond.[126]

Finishing my journey through the orientalizing Mediterranean in the Levant itself, I problematize the idea of the orientalizing phenomenon as an infinitely fluid and vague process linked loosely with the Near East or the Levant, but dislocated from the Phoenicians specifically.[127] Doing so deprives the process of its principal set of agents and obstructs historical reconstructions of the period, in which art, economy, and sociocultural change need to be considered together. Rarefying the agency here does not advance our knowledge of the process. For instance, when scholars deal with the trend of "Assyrianization" (i.e., emulation of Assyrian cultural models in the same period), they stay away from this sort of vagueness: they speak of a discrete cultural process connected to specific sociopolitical settings and stemming from the prestige of Assyrian imperial elites.[128] Disliked as they are, empires are always easier to talk about, harder to deconstruct. The Phoenicians did not constitute a single polity or an empire, but there is enough evidence to consider them as the prime movers behind the export of the Levantine koine. Parallel to the "Assyrianization" of the region, and in a sense in tension with it, a phenomenon of "Phoenicianization" stimulated, and lent a distinguished and coherent outlook to, the reemerging cultural identities of the Iron Age Levant.

EPILOGUE

And it has always seemed to me that those who are persuaded
that they get a competent view of universal from episodical
history are very like persons who should see the limbs of
some body, which had once been living and beautiful,
scattered and remote. [. . .] For indeed some idea
of a whole may be obtained from a part,
but an accurate knowledge and clear
comprehension cannot.

(POLYB. 1.4.7–9)

We have followed the Phoenicians and their entanglements with local cultures from Iberia to the Levant, sometimes following the trail of trading routes and settlements, and sometimes tracking specific cultural artifacts, including luxury items, sphinxes, the alphabet, or sculptural and architectural models. Polybios is right, however. Our perception of the past is limited and distorted, as we have access only to "episodic history," which is like looking at the scattered limbs of a living being we will never see whole and in motion. This is especially true in the Phoenicians' case, where their written legacy has been lost. The overview presented in this book's chapters, however, will at least help us to appreciate the Phoenician cultural legacy more fully, not simply as circumstantial intermediaries between the greater Near East and the Mediterranean, as they are often presented, but as active fashioners of the Levantine koine that lay behind what we vaguely call "orientalizing" styles and innovations.

In this exploration of the orientalizing phenomenon, we have seen common factors and major variations in regional reactions to the Phoenician enterprise: from contexts where there was colonization but not a full-fledged local adaptation of Levantine elite culture (North Africa), to the opposite, where there was no Phoenician colonization but an eager and creative adaptation of Phoenician models (Etruria, the Aegean), to places where we find both (Iberia, Sardinia, Sicily and Malta, Cyprus). The Phoenicians, however, continue to be problematized in discussions about orientalizing art, due to disciplinary compartmentalization, Classics-centered approaches, and some degree of western-culture bias and national discourses. Some now even doubt their existence.

Each region required true expertise and sensitivity to complex internal dynamics. This makes collaboration and debate crucial as we move forward. Despite the simplifications and flaws that the experts in different areas will see in the details of my synthesis, I hope the picture I have drawn is, on the whole, convincing. Here I identify some ways to topple the methodological, disciplinary, and ideological barriers that my book challenges, as we continue to more fully integrate the Phoenician element into the study of ancient Mediterranean culture:

- **Refocus the marginalized "other":** both fascination and bias mark our view of the Phoenicians vis-à-vis Greece and Rome. They are awkwardly positioned between the classical world and the Near East, and entangled with ancient and modern biases of orientalism. This is further aggravated by the scattered evidence and unfortunate gaps (the fate of the losers of history), and the fragmentation of their study across disciplines that are not bound together by a strong "field" organization (such as classical studies provide for the Greeks and Romans). As a way forward, we need to continue to build bridges between scholarship on the Levant, classics, and the western Mediterranean.

- **Challenge ethnic stereotypes:** we must move past the narrow association of the Phoenicians with trade, metallurgy, the fine arts, and the alphabet. Archaeological studies have broadened their range of expertise to include agriculture, masonry, and naval and architectural technologies. Their cultural expertise in additional areas, too, was admired by the Greeks and Romans, and included their political organization (and Carthaginian empire building), mythology, and philosophy (areas that this book mentions only in passing). Their city-states and institutions flourished earlier than the Greek ones and spread throughout the Mediterranean; Aristotle later even cited them as viable models. They built a commercial empire respected by Assyria and almost brought the Roman Empire to its knees.

• **Look beyond artifacts**: in all the main regions treated here, orientalizing adaptations transcend art historical categories and considerations. For this period, when the Phoenicians' influence was particularly robust, we depend mainly on material culture, having lost the narratives generated by the Phoenician and local communities involved in this process. It is necessary, however, to study Phoenician culture outside the art historical and even archaeological framework. I have incorporated in this book only some of the evidence for the Phoenicians' immaterial or intangible legacies (also mentioned in the previous point). This task of reconstruction requires integrating epigraphical evidence from the Phoenician and Near Eastern side as well as elements from later, Greco-Roman mythographical and historiographical traditions.

• **Move away from strict chronological parceling**: in many cases, the reception of Levantine culture preceded or continued after the "orientalizing period," where locals and Phoenicians continued to be in close contact. Moreover, Phoenician aesthetics evolved through contact with other cultures, for instance, after the sixth century under Persian and then Hellenistic influences, the latter drawing on an Attic cultural koine. This does not mean that their culture ceased to have an influence in the vast areas of their diaspora or through the continuing commercial networks, but artistic exchanges looked different from what we call "orientalizing." While this book has focused mainly on the developments of the eighth–seventh centuries, the parceling of Levantine influence into a rigid period is itself artificial, as we have seen in many examples. We need to continue the diachronic study of interactions between Phoenicians and locals in the Mediterranean. This approach will produce a more complete historical framework that allows full appreciation of the transformative effect of Phoenician culture, including Carthage.

⁂

My title does not propose that the Phoenicians alone "made the Mediterranean," although it was they who first knitted it all together. The Phoenicians were in a position to represent the old prestigious world of the lost Canaanite palace-kingdoms in an evolving Levant of emerging new states. They acted as conduits for both empowering tradition and creating bold innovations; their art and culture were prestigious, valued, and adaptable by those who wanted a piece of that post-Canaanite heritage. Phoenician culture became the backbone of the Levantine koine in the early first millennium, whence it also became a useful tool for the proto-urban communities of the Aegean and beyond.

At the same time, there is nothing deterministic about the process. Its extension happened precisely when geopolitical and economic conditions favored the Phoenicians' capacity to amplify their networks' horizons. The Phoenician westward move was itself a daring innovation, an expansion that was not imperial like those of Egyptians and Hittites, who had fought over Canaan in the previous millennium, or of the Assyrians, doing as much in the Iron Age. The success of a commercial-based expansion required intense collaboration with native groups (including Greeks), proto-urban societies for whom the Phoenicians successfully tailored a customizable cultural package I have called the "orientalizing kit." These encounters had varying results, and it was up to the locals to participate or not, and (if they did) *how* to selectively and creatively adopt aspects of this Levantine koine.

I invite the reader to reflect on how we ourselves construct the history of the Mediterranean, and what room we decide to leave for the diverse cultures involved. The Greeks and Romans certainly wove Phoenicians into their own reconstruction of the past, even in their foundational stories, and the legacies of Phoenician culture continued to be part of the experience of communities in Hellenistic and Roman times, in some cases until late antiquity. As archaeological and epigraphical evidence continues to accrue, and as we refine our interpretive tools, it would be a missed opportunity to brush them off as an ancient or modern construct or to relinquish their study to hyperspecialized domains of scholarship. It is up to us to pull the threads together and move the mainstream narratives about this fascinating period of deep transformation. As recent scholarship and new interests show, we are ready for a cultural history of the Mediterranean that is more inclusive of those who did not get to write it. The *mare nostrum* was as much theirs as "ours."

NOTES

Introduction

1. López-Ruiz and Doak 2019; Vella 2019.

2. Killebrew 2019; Sader 2019, 51–146; Edrey 2019.

3. E.g., Said 1978; Bernal 1987; Huntington 1996; Arvidsson 2006; López-Ruiz 2010, 8–16.

4. Manning 2018, 6, 40–41, 44.

5. Dunbabin 1948a; Boardman 1999a; Lane Fox 2008.

6. S. P. Morris 1992; Burkert 1992; West 1997; and others.

7. Boardman 1999a; Ridgway 1992a; Tsetskhladze and De Angelis 1994; Malkin 1998, 2011; Malkin, Constantakopoulou, and Panagopoulou 2009; Dougherty 2001; Tsetskhladze 2006; Lane Fox 2008; De Angelis 2016; Donnellan, Nizzo, and Burgers 2016a, 2016b.

8. Dietler and López-Ruiz 2009; van Dommelen 2006; Gailledrat, Dietler, and Plana-Mallart 2018; and others.

9. Celestino and Jiménez Ávila 2005; Dietler and López-Ruiz 2009; Celestino and López-Ruiz 2016; Hodos 2020.

10. Nowlin 2021, 55, cf. 2016.

11. E.g., Horden and Purcell 2000; Abulafia 2011; Broodbank 2013; Gosner and Hayne, forthcoming.

12. J. M. Hall and Osborne, 2022.

13. Manning 2018 (with a brief overview of Phoenician trade in 235–237).

14. Leidwanger and Knappett 2018.

15. Hodos 2020 and 2022.

16. I. Morris 2005.

17. Celestino and Jiménez Ávila 2005; Riva and Vella 2006a.

18. Hdt. 1.1.4–1.3.2.

19. Hdt. 1.1.1.

20. Demetriou, forthcoming; Hütwohl 2020.

21. Kaufman 2017, 205.

22. Buck 2019, 56–86; Elayi 2018.

23. Sader 2019, 99–101; Katzenstein 1997, 224.

24. Sader 2019, 142.

25. Álvarez Martí-Aguilar 2019; Aubet 2019.

26. Sader 2019, 125–133; Baaklini 2020.

27. Carthaginian–Roman treaty: Polyb. 3.22.

28. Bonnet 2015; López-Ruiz 2017; Kaldellis 2019; Cruz Andreotti 2019; Machuca Prieto 2019; Lancel 1995, 428–446; Hobson 2019.

29. Richey 2019a; Jongeling 2008; Kerr 2010.

30. Sader 2019, 203–205.

31. Prag 2014.

32. Bourogiannis 2012b, 40.

33. I have treated this topic in more depth in López-Ruiz 2022b and forthcoming.

34. Quinn 2018; cf. Purcell 2006; van Dongen 2010; Feldman 2014; S. R. Martin 2017, 73–96; Porzia 2018.

35. Quinn 2018, 44–63; Woolmer 2017, 4.

36. Vella 2014, 2019, 23–29; Quinn 2018, 22–26. The point of reference is usually Moscati 1988a.

37. Kourou 2012, 34–35.

38. Archaeological data: Aubet 2001, 2008, 2019; Kaufman 2017; Álvarez Martí-Aguilar 2019.

39. *CAD,* vol. K, s.v. *kinaḫḫu; HALOT,* s.v., *knʿn;* Astour 1965; Aubet 2001, 10.

40. Quinn et al. 2014; Quinn 2018, 31–32; López-Ruiz, forthcoming.

41. López-Ruiz, forthcoming.

42. Hdt. 3.19.

43. Quinn 2018; Porzia 2018.

44. Aubet 2001, 9.

45. Arist. *Pol.* 7.7 (1327b30–33).

46. J. M. Hall 1997, 2002.

47. Hdt. 8.144.2.

48. Hodos 2020, 58.

1. Phoenicians Overseas

1. Bhabha 1994; Gosden 2004; Malkin 2002 (middle ground), 2011 (network theory); Knappett 2011; Alberti and Sabatini 2013.

2. J. M. Hall and Osborne 2022.

3. Dietler and López-Ruiz 2009.

4. Gosden 2004, 18–20; Hodos 2020, 68–75; Ashcroft, Griffiths, and Tifflin 1998.

5. Garland 2014, 242.

6. Selective consumption: Dietler 1998, 2009, 2010; hybridity: van Dommelen 2006; Hodos 2006, 2020.

7. Gosden 2004; Garland 2014, 34–56; Domínguez Monedero 2002.

8. Lyons and Papadopoulos 2002; Stein 2005.

9. Gosden 2004, 26, 41–81; Malkin 2011, 3–64.

10. van Dommelen 2012, 398.

11. Hodos 2006, 14–15.

12. I. Morris 1994, 21, quoted in van Dommelen 2015, 42.

13. van Dommelen 2015, 45; I. Morris 1994.

14. Bernal 1987.

15. Díaz-Andreu 2018, 7.

16. Díaz-Andreu 2018, 13; Larsen 1996.

17. Quinn 2018, 3–22; Doumet-Serhal 2019; van Dommelen 2015, 48–50

18. Effros 2018, 201.

19. Fumadó Ortega 2013a; Effros 2018; McCarty 2018; Lafrenz Samuels and van Dommelen 2019.

20. Celestino and López-Ruiz 2016, 147–159.

21. Niemeyer 1993.

22. González de Canales et al. 2008.

23. Plin. *HN* 19.22.63 (Lixus); Vell. Pat. 1.2.3, 1.8.4; Str. 1.3.2; Pompon. 3.39 (Gadir); Sil. 3.241–2; Ps.-Arist. *Mir.* 134 (Utica).

24. Thuc. 1.1–19. Malkin 1998; Finkelberg 2005.

25. López-Castro et al. 2016; Docter et al. 2008; van der Plicht 2009; Aubet 2019; Hodos 2020, 53–54.

26. Philistos of Syracuse (replicated by Appian and others); Lancel 1995, 20–34; Miles 2010, 58–67.

27. Aubet 2008, 179–180, 2001, 256–346; Neville 2007, 1–46 and 83–104 (Gadir); Arruda 2009, 2015, 2019 (Portugal); Guirguis 2019 (Sardinia).

28. Aubet 2008, 180.

29. Thuc. 2.6.

30. Carpenter 1958; Niemeyer 1993, 2000.

31. S. Sherratt 1993; A. Sherratt and S. Sherratt 1993; Gosden 2004, 11–18.

32. Frankenstein 1979; Aubet 2001, 54–60; Ruíz-Gálvez 1998.

33. Aubet 2008; Miles 2010, 38–39; Pappa 2013, 177–188; Fletcher 2012, 213–214; Elayi 2018, 129–182.

34. Aubet 2008, 181.

35. Guirguis 2019, 122.

36. Fletcher 2012, 213–214.

37. González Wagner 2005; Aubet 2006; Arruda 2009, 2015; Monroe 2018, 266.

38. I. Morris 2005, 42, 51.

39. Terpstra 2019. Cf. Demetriou 2012 (Greek networks).

40. E.g., Dietler and López-Ruiz 2009; Celestino and López-Ruiz 2016, 144–145; van Dommelen 2006.

41. Dridi 2019 for discussion and primary sources.

42. Aubet 2019; Álvarez Martí-Aguilar 2019 for discussion and primary sources.

43. Kaufman 2017, 207.

44. Celestino and López-Ruiz 2016, 202–208.

45. S. P. Morris 1992, 148.

46. "Phoenicianized": Kaufman 2017; collision course: Miles 2010, 58–111; Dridi 2019.

47. Hodos 2020, 68–75, 83–93; Sommer 2007.

48. Garnand 2020, 140.

49. Encounter and entanglement: Dietler 2018; cohabitation and interaction: van Dommelen 2018, 226–227; Gailledrat, Dietler, and Plana-Mallart 2018; Bresson and Rouillard 1993.

50. Garnand 2020, 141; cf. Hodos 2020, 73.

51. Garnand 2020, 14, drawing on Fumadó Ortega 2013a.

52. Fumadó Ortega 2013a.

53. van Dommelen 2018; Bresson 2018.

54. Hdt. 4.17, 24, 4.18 (Black Sea), 2.178–79 (Naukratis).

55. Garnand 2020; Demetriou 2011.

56. Hdt. 2.112, 178–79. J. M. Hall 1997, 49–50; Garnand 2020, 150; see Demetriou 2023, for documents of the Hellenistic period.

57. Hdt. 2.154. Lutz 2001; Bonadies 2017.

58. Fantalkin 2006; Hodos 2020, 115; Demetriou 2023.

59. Kestemont 1985, 135; Hodos 2006, 27, 37–40, 45, 50, 55.

60. Aubet 2012; Garnand 2020, 150.

61. Aubet 2006; Docter 2019, 437–438.

62. Aubet 2006; Garnand 2020.

63. de Polignac 1995.

64. Thuc. 6.2.6.

65. Niveau de Villedary 2021; Gener et al. 2014, 36.

66. Arist. *Pol.* 2.1267b.

67. Osborne 2009, 224–230; Boyd and Jameson 1981.

68. Docter 2019, 440; Fumadó Ortega 2013a; cf. Elayi 2018, 19, 91.

69. See Fumadó Ortega 2013a, 2013b for more details; full report in Flügel, Dolenz, and Schmidt, forthcoming.

70. Gener et al. 2014; Aubet 2019, 82, fig. 6.1; Sader 2019, 155–168 for Phoenicia. For construction techniques, see Edrey 2019, 74, fig. 3 1.

71. Kaufman 2017; Aubet 2006, 2019.

72. Miles 2010, 352–373.

73. Quinn 2018, xiii–xiv; Miles 2010, 11–12.

74. S. Sherrat 2010, 135.

75. Sader 2019, 76–96.

76. Lancel 1995, 273–279; Fantar 1998, 114–115.

77. *Rust.* 8.16.9. Celestino and López-Ruiz 2016, 65–66.

78. de Polignac 1995; McHugh 2017.

79. Demetriou 2011; de Angelis 2016, 65–101 (Sicily).

80. Hodos 2006, 91, 158 (North Africa).

81. Gómez-Bellard 2019; Pardo Barrionuevo 2015; van Dommelen and Gómez-Bellard 2008; Celestino and López-Ruiz 2016, 191–194; Delgado 2008, 2012; Delgado and Ferrer 2012.

82. Alvar and González Wagner 1989; González Wagner and Alvar 2003; cf. Neville 2007, 122–123; already suggested by the early archaeologist George Bonsor: Celestino and López-Ruiz 2016, 2, 17, 193–194.

83. Treumann 2009; Johnson and Kaufman 2019.

84. McGovern 2003; Botto 2013; essays in Celestino and Blánquez 2013.

85. Vera and Echevarría 2013.

86. Vella and Anastasi 2019, 564 (Malta); Echevarría Sánchez and Vera Rodríguez 2015 (Iberia); Marlasca Martín and López Garí 2006 (Ibiza).

87. Punic *garum*: Costa and Fernández 2012; purple dye: García Vargas 2020.

88. E.g., Gosden 2004.

89. Domínguez Monedero 2002.

90. Kourou 2012, 40–41; Stampolidis and Kotsonas 2006; Stampolidis 2019; S. P. Morris 1992, esp. 124–149; Papadopoulos 2011.

91. Pratt 2009, 325 about Crete.

92. Bresson 2018, 36–38.

93. Kistler et al. 2015; Kowalzig 2018; R. Osborne 2009, 86–91, 94–96; Gunter 2009, 85–86, 151–154.

94. R. Osborne 2009, 86.

95. A. Sherratt and S. Sherratt 1998, 336; R. Osborne 2009, 83–96; Marinatos and Hägg 1993; Morgan 1994; Pedley 2005; Smith 2009, 251–254; Fourrier 2013; Iacovou 2018, 20–23.

96. Burkert 1992, 20.

97. Gunter 2009, 128–154.

98. Bresson 2018, 35–36; Aubet 2016.

99. Fumadó Ortega 2012.

100. Blakely 2016.

2. From Classicial to Mediterranean Models

1. Dunbabin 1948a, vi.

2. De Angelis 1998; Papadopoulos 2011, 119.

3. Boardman 1999a, 190, 2001a.

4. Boardman 2016, 207–208.

5. Boardman 1999a, 199–200.

6. Boardman 1999a, 215.

7. Boardman 2001a, 33, 37, 2016, 207.

8. Boardman 2016, 209.

9. E.g., Malkin 2011; Garland 2014.

10. S. R. Martin 2017, 78.

11. Lane Fox 2008, 210.

12. Momigliano 1975a, 1975b.

13. López-Ruiz 2019b.

14. Lane Fox 2008, 227.

15. Lane Fox 2008, 227, 242 (case of Adonis).

16. Lane Fox 2008, 67, 128–129.

17. Lane Fox 2008, 99, after Boardman 2005.

18. Hodos 2006, 38.

19. Str. 5.4.9.

20. Boardman 1999a, 39.

21. Boardman 1990, 1999a, 39–54, 1999b, 2001.

22. Hodos 2016, 38; Lane Fox 2008, 100 refutes such biases.

23. Luke 2003; Hodos 2006, 37–40; Lane Fox 2008, 97–107.

24. Waldbaum 1997; Kearsley 1999; Luke 2003; Lehmann 2005; Hodos 2006, 37–40; Papadopoulos 1997, 2011; Kotsonas 2013.

25. Niemeyer 2004, 2005, 2006.

26. Papadopoulos 1997; R. Osborne 2009, 55–60; Broodbank 2013, 500–503.

27. J. M. Hall 2002, 93; S. P. Morris 1992, 101–149; Papadopoulos 1997, 192, 2011, 115–117.

28. Nijboer 2008 comparing Achviz, Lefkandi, and Huelva.

29. Popham and Lemos 1995; Antonaccio 2002, 28–29; Lemos 2002, 168, 219; Luraghi 2006, 34; Kroll 2008, 44.

30. Coldstream 2007, 135, cf. 1998, 356.

31. Crielaard 2016, 61–62.

32. Papadopoulos 2011; Coldstream 1998, 2008; Coldstream and Mazar 2003; Hodos 2006, 37–44.

33. Hodos 2006, 37–40, 61–63.

34. Docter 2014; Boardman 2004.

35. Papadopoulos 1997, 2011.

36. Lemos 2002, 212–217.

37. Lemos 2002, 227.

38. Papadopoulos 2011, 128.

39. Hodos 2020, 21, 108; Dietler 1998, 2010.

40. Str. 5.4.9.

41. Ridgway 1992a, 1994; Boardman 2001a; Hayne 2019; Markoe 1985, 145–146.

42. Buchner and Ridgway 1993; D'Agostino 2011; Hayne 2019, 510.

43. Ridgway 1992a, 114.

44. Ridgway 1992a, 111–120. For the funerary rituals, d'Agostino 2011; Kelley 2012.

45. Ridgeway 1992, 55–57; Boardman 1999, 166.

46. Thuc. 6.2.6; Hayne 2019, 511.

47. Arrington 2015.

48. Papadopoulos 2011, 116 (figs. 2a-b); Kenzelmann Pfyffer, Theurillat, and Verdan 2005, 76–77n66.

49. Papadopoulos 2011, 116.

50. Lane Fox 2008, 58–59, 388; Sossau 2015.

51. Stampolidis 2019, 497, 498, figs. 23.1–23.2; Stampolidis and Kotsonas 2006, 352–353.

52. Stampolidis 1990, 2002, 2004, 2016, 2019, 497; Stampolidis and Kotsonas 2006.

53. S. P. Morris and Papadopoulos 1998, 258–259; S. P. Morris 2019, 90; Ziskowski 2016, 100–101; Ward 2018.

54. J. M. Hall 2002, 95; Röllig 1992, 97.

55. Papadopoulos 2016; Clay, Malkin, and Tzifopoulos 2017; Ilieva 2019; Fletcher 2008.

56. Demetriou 2012, 2023; Stager 2005, 443–445; Quinn 2018, 39–40; Stampolidis 2019, 500–501; Richey 2019a, 229.

57. Diod. Sic. 14.77.

58. Hoyos 2010, 61–62.

59. Demetriou 2023.

60. Wulf 2013, esp. 361; Celestino and López-Ruiz 2016, 1–11.

61. López-Ruiz 2020 2022b, and forthcoming.

62. van Dommelen 2015, 50–55.

63. Nowlin 2016, esp. 54–55.

64. Delgado 2008; Delgado and Ferrer 2012; Gorgues 2016; López-Bertran 2019.

65. Domínguez 2002, 73.

66. Braudel 1972.

67. See http//www.mediterraneanseminar.org.

68. Purcell 2006, 25.

69. Horden and Purcell 2000, 134.

70. Horden and Purcell 2000, 43.

71. Markoe 1985, 1990b, 2000; Sader 2010, 2019; Elayi 2018, 22–24; Gubel 2019.

72. Bell 2016, 101.

73. Broodbank 2013.

74. Broodbank 2013, 602.

75. Broodbank 2013, 27.

76. Broodbank 2013, 603.

77. Broodbank 2013, 20, cf. 602–603.

78. Aruz, Graff, and Rakic 2014 (exhibit catalogue); Aruz and Seymour 2016 (accompanying conference publication).

79. Boardman 2016.

80. Bahrani 2016, 329.

81. Hodos 2020.

82. Hodos 2020, 29–34.

83. Malkin, Constantakopoulou, and Panagopoulou 2009; Malkin 2011; Broodbank 2013; Leidwanger and Knappett 2018; Hodos 2020; J. M. Hall and Osborne 2022; Gosner and Hayne, forthcoming.

84. Broodbank 2013, 603, after Knapp 1993, 342.

85. I. Morris 2005, 51. Cf. Harris 2005; Concannon and Mazurek 2016.

86. I. Morris 2005, 33.

3. The Orientalizing Kit

1. Moscati 1988b, 547.

2. Riva and Vella 2006b, 4–7; Riva 2006, 110; Wengrow 2006, 31; Nowlin 2021.

3. Riva and Vella 2006a.

4. R. Osborne 2006.

5. Gubel 2006, 85.

6. European orientalism: Purcell 2006; Wengrow 2006; R. Osborne 2006. For orientalism, Said 1978; "Phoenician problem": Purcell 2006, 25.

7. S. P. Morris 2006, 80, 2007.

8. Riva and Vella 2006b, 13–14.

9. Purcell 2006; Gunter 2009, 50–79, 2014, 82.

10. Nowlin 2016, 55, 32–36, 2021. For German Philhellenism and Orientalism, Marchand 1996, 2009.

11. Gunter 2009, 70–79; Wengrow 2006, 32.

12. S. P. Morris 2006, 96; Miller 1997.

13. Knapp 2006, 60; Wengrow 2006, 31.

14. Vlassopoulos 2012.

15. Snowden 1983; Isaac 2004; Gruen 2011; Gunter 2014, 94–96.

16. Said 1978, 55–73; E. Hall 1989; S. P. Morris 1989, 40–41, 1992, xxii; Gunter 2009, 55; Gruen 2011, 341–343; cf. López-Ruiz 2017, 2019b.

17. Gordon 1962; Astour 1967; West 1966, 1971; Bernal 1987.

18. Burkert 1992 (German 1984).

19. Burkert 1987, 24, cf. 1983; Grottanelli 1982.

20. Burkert 1992, 2004, 99–124.

21. Burkert 1992, 128.

22. *Od.* 17.383–85.

23. Burkert 1992, 25–40.

24. Burkert 2004, 47–48.

25. Burkert 1992, 33, 2003.

26. Bachvarova 2016, 200–206.

27. I. Morris and Manning 2005.

28. S. P. Morris 1992.

29. S. P. Morris 1997, 1998, 2006.

30. West 1997.

31. West 1966, 1971, 1983, 1994.

32. Haubold 2002–2003, 2.

33. West 2007.

34. West 1997, 626.

35. West 1997, 629.

36. Phoenician literature: López-Ruiz 2016, 2019a; stereotypes of Carthage and Carthaginians: Miles 2010 330–332, 372–373.

37. West 1997, 587, 2011, 3–77; Walcot 1966, 47, 53; Bremmer 2008; Brown 1995, 2000, 2001; Louden 2006, 2011; López-Ruiz 2010.

38. Arvidsson 2006; Vlassopoulos 2007.

39. Brisart 2011.

40. Brisart 2011, 55–56.

41. Gunter 2009; Feldman 2014.

42. Gunter 2009, 124–126; Feldman 2014, 161–170.

43. Feldman 2014, 71; Gunter 2014.

44. Feldman 2014, 139–173.

45. Gunter 2009, 81, 84.

46. Feldman 2014, 181.

47. Gunter 2009, 80.

48. Layard 1853, 182–191; Riva and Vella 2006b, 5; Larsen 1996; Gunter 2014, 83.

49. Helbig 1876, 203; Riva and Vella 2006b, 6.

50. Newton 1880, 289, cited in Riva and Vella 2006b, 7.

51. Riva and Vella 2006b, 9.

52. Celestino and López-Ruiz 2016, 11–16.

53. E.g., *Il.* 23.740–45; *Odyssey* 4.615–19 (= *Od.* 15.115–19). Winter 1995; Gunter 2009, 63, 66, 140; Markoe 1985, 6.

54. Feldman 2014, 111–119.

55. Conze 1870, cited in Nowlin 2016, 29.

56. Newton 1880, 289 (Greco-Phoenician); Collignon and Wright 1886 (Greco-Oriental). Discussed in Nowlin 2016, 32–33 and 2021.

57. S. R. Martin 2017, 27–28; Markoe 1985, 2000, 149–50.

58. Bernal 1987.

59. Sannibale 2016, 311.

60. Maier 1999, 196; Fernández Götz 2007; Celestino and López-Ruiz 2016, 1–23.

61. Celestino and López-Ruiz 2016, 4–13.

62. Purcell 2006, 25.

63. Knapp 2006, 60.

64. Brisart 2011; Riva 2006; Celestino and López-Ruiz 2016; van Dommelen 2006.

65. Dietler 2010, among other works.

66. Knapp 2006, 59.

67. Knapp 2006, 60.

68. Feldman 2014, 2.

69. Hodos 2020, 2022; Broodbank 2013, 518.

70. S. R. Martin 2017, 97–170.

71. Markoe 1985, 7.

72. Markoe 1985, 71.

73. Hodos 2020, 210–211.

74. Manning 2018, 47–48; Liverani 2014, 420–433; Bell 2016; van der Brugge and Kleber 2016.

75. Comaroff and Comaroff 2009.

76. Feldman 2014; S. R. Martin 2017, 88–96.

77. Barnett 1957a.

78. I. Winter 1976a, 1976b, 1981; Suter 2010, 995; Gunter 2009, 95–103; Feldman 2014, 77, 179.

79. Feldman 2014, 197.

80. Gunter 2009, 102.

81. Suter 2015, 43, cf. 2010.

82. Feldman 2014, 179.

83. Feldman 2014, 18–21.

84. Gubel 2019, 356.

85. Vella 2010; Feldman 2014, 111–137, 2016; S. R. Martin 2017, 27–28.

86. Markoe 1985, 149.

87. Markoe 1985, 72–74; Feldman 2014, 111–119.

88. Markoe 1985, 110–112; Gubel 2019, 356–58.

89. Gunter 2009, 102.

90. Markoe 1985, 9–13.

91. S. R. Martin 2017, 96.

92. I. Winter 1995; S. R. Martin 2017, 27, 32, 97.

93. Karageorghis 2005a, 35.

94. *Od.* 4.615–19 (= *Od.* 15.115–19).

95. *Il.* 18.468–608. Burkert 1992, 16; Gunter 2009, 118.

96. *Od.* 7.91; *Il.* 18.416–420. Gunter 2009, 69.

97. Vella 2010, 32.

4. The Far West

1. Broodbank 2013, 316–320, 415–423.

2. Mederos 1999; van Wijngaarden 1999, 28; Bendala 2013.

3. Celestino and López-Ruiz 2016, 182–191.

4. Celestino and López-Ruiz 2016, 64, 191–198; Mederos and Escribano 2015.

5. Mederos 2001; Celestino and López-Ruiz 2016, 4–13.

6. Celestino and López-Ruiz 2016, 16–23.

7. Wulf 2003 for Spanish historiography of antiquity.

8. Mederos 2001, 37.

9. Álvarez Martí-Aguilar 2010; Moret 2011, 244.

10. The bibliography in Spanish is vast. In English, Neville 2007; Dietler and López-Ruiz 2009; Celestino and López-Ruiz 2016.

11. González de Canales, Serrano, and Llompart 2004, 2006, 2008, 633; Gilboa 2013.

12. Nijboer 2005; Nijboer and van der Plicht 2006; Torres 1998, 2008a; Celestino, Rafel, and Armada 2008; Celestino and López-Ruiz 2016, 148–159.

13. *Od.* 13.272–285, Jonah 1,15.

14. Pulak 2008.

15. González de Canales, Serrano, and Llompart 2006, 25–26.

16. One possible Tartessic sign was identified in González de Canales, Serrano, and Llompart 2004, 133–136.

17. González de Canales, Serrano, and Llompart 2006, 22–25.

18. Osuna, Bedia, and Domínguez 2001.

19. Arruda 2019; García Teyssandier and Marzoli 2013.

20. González de Canales, Serrano, and Llompart 2006, 26–27; López-Ruiz 2009a; Celestino and López-Ruiz 2016, 156–159 (Huelva), 111–121 (Tarshish).

21. Eshel et al. 2019; Wood, Bell, and Montero-Ruiz 2020.

22. E.g., González de Canales, Serrano, and Llompart 2008; Gozález de Canales 2018.

23. Barnett 1982, 46.

24. González de Canales, Serrano, and Llompart 2006, 26; Barnett 1982, 15, 46–47.

25. E.g., (in English with further bibliography) Aubet 2001, 2019; Neville 2007, 1–46; Arruda 2009, 2019; Celestino and López-Ruiz 2016, 178–180; López Castro 2019.

26. López-Bertran 2019.

27. Aubet, Núñez, and Tresilló 2004; Aubet 2010; Martín Ruiz 2012.

28. Aubet 2006; Delgado 2017; Celestino and López-Ruiz 2016, 254–256; Martín Ruiz 2018.

29. López Castro 2006; Aubet 2006, 99.

30. Gómez Bellard 2019.

31. Broodbank 2013, 515; González de Canales, Montaño, and Llompart 2020.

32. Celestino and López-Ruiz 2016, 50–95; Machuca Prieto 2019.

33. Arruda 2019, 603; cf. Arruda 2000, 2009, 2011.

34. Celestino and López-Ruiz 2016, 253–266.

35. Celestino 2001; Celestino and López-Ruiz 2016, 159–170.

36. Bendala 1977.

37. Celestino and López-Ruiz 2006.

38. Celestino and López-Ruiz 2016, 253–266.

39. E.g., La Joya (Huelva), Cruz del Negro (Carmona), Setefilla and La Angorrilla (Lora del Río, Seville). Celestino and López-Ruiz 2016, 259–266, fig. 7.13.

40. Celestino and López-Ruiz 2016, 261–263, figs. 7.14, 7.15.

41. Casado 2016; Celestino and López-Ruiz 2016, 270–271, fig. 8.1.

42. Belén Deamos et al. 1997; Belén Deamos 2009, 208; Pachón, Aníbal, and Carrasco 2008; Celestino and López-Ruiz 2016, 271–272, fig. 8.2.

43. Ruiz-Gálvez 1995.

44. Celestino and López-Ruiz 2016, 274–280, figs. 8.4–8.7.

45. Celestino and López-Ruiz 2016, 281–285, figs. 8.8, 8.9.

46. Celestino and López-Ruiz 2016, 285–289, fig. 8.10; Quesada 2014; Torres 2008b; Casado 2014.

47. Escacena and Coto 2010; Le Meaux 2010; Quesada 2014.

48. Celestino and López-Ruiz 2016, 286.

49. Celestino 1997, 364; Celestino and López-Ruiz 2016, 289.

50. Polzer 2014, 232–134.

51. Celestino and López-Ruiz 2016, 232–238.

52. Rodríguez González 2015, 2020; Celestino and López-Ruiz 2016, 244–253, figs. 7.7–7.11.

53. Mierse 2004.

54. Celestino and López-Ruiz 2016, 240–244.

55. Celestino and López-Ruiz 2016, 244–250.

56. Arruda and Celestino 2009; Celestino and López-Ruiz 2016, 236.

57. Celestino and López-Ruiz 2016, 232, 237.

58. Bandera 2002.

59. Marín Ceballos 2006; Gómez Peña 2010; Escacena and Coto 2010.

60. Celestino and López-Ruiz 2016, 238–253 (esp. for the altar 247–249); cf. Belén Deamos 2009, 199–208; Celestino 2009.

61. Bandera and Ferrer 2010.

62. Editions: Solá-Solé 1966; Gibson 1982, 64–66 (n16).

63. de Hoz 2005a.

64. Rodríguez Ramos 2002, 193–198.

65. de Hoz 1991, 2013; Correa 2005; Correia 1996; Celestino and López-Ruiz 2016, 289–300.

66. Main collection in Fuentes Estañol 1986; for an updated overview: Zamora 2019; for Lisbon inscription: Neto et al. 2016.

67. de Hoz 2005a, 375.

68. de Hoz 1991.

69. Lucan, *Pharsalia* 9.40–41, trans. Leigh 2000, 98–99.

70. Leigh 2000.

71. Mela 1.25–40, 1.41–48, 3.100–107; Quinn 2013a; Batty 2000.

72. Mederos 2019; Pappa 2019b.

73. Hodos 2006, 184–188, 198–199, 2020, 203.

74. Manning 2018, 51; Broodbank 2013, 39–40.

75. Hodos 2020, 217.

76. Hdt. 4.183. Quinn 2013a, 266–268.

77. Broodbank 2013, 601.

78. B. Shaw 2003, 93; Quinn 2013a, 261; Manning 2018, 92.

79. Quinn 2013a, 261.

80. Pappa 2019b; Guirguis 2019.

81. An important reassessment is in Stone, forthcoming.

82. Fentress and Docter 2008; Broodbank 2013, 569–572; Gómez Bellard 2019.

83. Justin, *Epitome of Trogus* 18.4–6; Virgil, *Aeneid* 1.326–86. Dridi 2019.

84. Pappa 2019b, 71.

85. Quinn 2013a, 263, 269; Mattingly 2007; Roller 2003; Hoyos 2010, 142–148; Hodos 2006, 175–176, 193.

86. Persistence of Punic culture: Lancel 1995, 430–436; Hobson 2019, 186–188; tophet sanctuaries: Quinn 2013b; Quinn and McCarty 2015; McCarty 2019; linguistic continuity: Hobson 2019, 188–190; Jongeling 2008; Kerr 2010; Ben Younès and Krandel-Ben Younès 2014; Bridoux 2014; Papi 2014, 218; Hodos 2006, 182.

87. Hobson 2019.

88. Hodos 2006, 184–188, 198–199.

89. Aubet 2001, 182–193, esp. 186; Pappa 2019b.

90. Stoddart 2000, 65–68; Broodbank 2013, 334; about gold, Hdt. 4.196, Quinn 2013a, 267; Mederos and Escribano 2015, 375–408.

91. Hodos et al. 2020.

92. Emanuel 2019, 429.

93. Hdt. 4.42. Roller 2006, 22–43, 2019; Mederos and Escribano 2015.

94. Aubet 2001, 193.

5. The Central Mediterranean

1. Bernardini and D'Oriano 2001; Eshel et al. 2019.
2. van Dommelen 2006.
3. Blake 2014a; Russell and Knapp 2017.
4. Botto 2016 and references there.
5. Botto 2017a, 73; Ruiz-Gálvez 2005, 251, 2014; Bernardini and Perra 2012; P. Bartoloni 2017, 37; Bernardini 2017.
6. *KAI* 46. Pilkington 2012; Richey 2019b, 243.
7. P. Bartoloni 2004; Guirguis 2017a, 2019; Mastino 2017, 25.
8. D'Oriano and Oggiano 2005, 177.
9. Roppa 2019a, 529; D'Oriano 2012.
10. Guirguis 2017b, 56; Roppa 2019a, 527; Etruscan trade: Santocchini Gerg 2014.
11. De Rosa, Garau, and Rendeli 2018; Roppa and Madrigali, in press.
12. Quinn 2011, 2013b; McCarty 2019.
13. Roppa 2014; Unali 2017.
14. Torres 2005; Botto 2004–2005, 2017a; Mederos 2006; Guirguis 2019. On the mythology, Celestino and López-Ruiz 2016, 114; Mastino 2017, 24–25.
15. Broodbank 2013, 602.
16. Botto 2017a, 73; Guirguis 2017b, 55.
17. Ruiz-Gálvez 2014, 197.
18. Roppa 2019a.
19. Bernardini 2011; Webster 2015; Roppa 2021.
20. van Dommelen and Roppa 2014; Roppa 2014, 2019a, 529–530; Zucca 2017.
21. González de Canales, Serrano, and Llompart 2004, 183; Bechtold and Docter 2010, 91, 102.
22. Botto 2017a, 74; Guirguis 2017b, 55.
23. Tronchetti 2014.
24. Guiguis 2017b, 56.
25. Bernardini 1992, 2005; van Dommelen 2006; Tronchetti 2014.
26. van Dommelen 2006, 149.
27. van Dommelen 2018, 222–25.
28. van Dommelen 2006, 141; Tronchetti and van Dommelen 2005; Roppa 2019a, 523–526.
29. Guirguis 2017b, 56–59.
30. Lo Schiavo 2008; Bernardini and Botto 2010.
31. Roppa 2019a; Hayne 2010.
32. Rendeli 2018; González de Canales 2018 for Huelva.
33. Oggiano 2000.
34. Frère et al. 2014.
35. Roppa 2019a, 526; cf. Hayne 2010, 155–156; Rendeli 2018, 198–200.
36. Roppa 2019a, 530, 2019b; cf. van Dommelen 2018 (S'Urachi); Perra 2019 (Nuraghe Sirai).
37. Matisoo-Smith et al. 2018.

38. Jeremy Hayne (oral communication).

39. Bedini et al. 2012; Usai et al. 2018.

40. Roppa 2019a; cf. Tronchetti and van Dommelen 2005; Tronchetti 2014.

41. Muscuso 2017, 441; Perra 2019.

42. Garbati 2008.

43. Guirguis and Ibba 2017.

44. Ribichini and Xella 1994, 87–102.

45. Moscati 1988b, 547.

46. Hdt. 1.165–67; Thuc. 1.13.6 (omitting the Etruscans); Diod. Sic. 5.13.4. For the Phokaian foundations, Thuc. 1.13–14; Diod. Sic. 7.11. Bernardini, Spanu, and Zucca 2000.

47. De Vincenzo 2013.

48. Thuc. 6.2.2; Hellanikos of Lesbos, *FGrH* 79a; Philistos of Syracuse, *FGrH* 45. Overviews in Hodos 2006, 92–93; De Angelis 2016, 28–61.

49. Intrieri and Ribichini 2011.

50. Garnand 2020, 160.

51. E.g., Diod. Sic. 13.55.1, 15.24. J. M. Hall 2002, 122; Garnand 2020, 160.

52. Hodos 2006, 89–157; Ampolo 2012; Balco 2012; Spatafora 2013; Öhlinger 2015, 417–418; Blasetti Fantauzzi 2018; Morris 2019, 78, 92–94 (with a criticism of the "middle ground" model); Hodos 2020.

53. Burgersdijk et al. 2015.

54. Thuc. 6.2.6. Pappa 2015, 32.

55. Atack 2015, 39; Burgersdijk et al. 2015.

56. E.g., Hdt. 7.155; Thuc. 1.55, 3.73, 6.4.; Phrynichus, *Satyrs* F47; for Heraclea Pontica, *BNJ* 348 F4; Str. 12.3.4.

57. González Wagner 2007; Celestino and López-Ruiz 2016, 145–47.

58. Orsingher 2016a, 284–285; Nigro and Spagnoli 2017; Tanasi 2020.

59. Thuc. 6.2.6. Nigro 2013, 55.

60. Thuc. 6.2. Blasetti Fantauzzi 2018; Tusa 1990.

61. Phoenician ceramics: Orsingher 2016a, 288; cultic elements: Nigro 2015, 97; Öhlinger 2016, 110.

62. Balco 2012.

63. Blasetti Fantauzzi and De Vincenzo 2012; De Vincenzo 2019; Nigro 2013, 2015.

64. Öhlinger 2016, 108–110; Hodos 2006, 115–116.

65. Diod. Sic. books 9, 13, 14.

66. De Vincenzo 2019; Ward 2017; S. P. Morris 2019.

67. Hodos 2006, 91, 152; Giangiulio 2010; Ampolo 2012; Albanese Procelli 2016; Blasetti Fantauzzi 2018, 9–12.

68. Vasallo 2015, 158, fig. 8.6.

69. Vasallo 2015, 155–156, fig. 8.2.A-B.

70. Hodos 2006, 132–133.

71. Docter 2014.

72. Öhlinger 2016, 111.

73. Öhlinger 2016, 111–114.

74. De Vincenzo 2019, 547–548.
75. Nigro 2015 (Motya); De Vincenzo 2013, 217, 2019, 547–548 (Selinous).
76. On the range of Phoenician sacred architecture, Edrey 2019, 91–120.
77. Ribichini and Xella 1994, 90–91 (Antas, Sardinia); Vella and Anastasi 2019, 561–562, fig. 36.2 (Tas-Silġ, Malta).
78. S. R. Martin 2017.
79. Marconi 2007; R. Osborne 2009, 247–248; cf. Burkert 1992, 85–87.
80. Böhm 2007.
81. Ribichini and Xella 1994, 66–68; Famà and Tusa 2000; Ward 2018; De Vincenzo 2019, 548; S. P. Morris 2019.
82. Diod. 14.77.5. Curbera 1997; van Dommelen and López-Bertran 2013.
83. S. P. Morris 2019, 92.
84. Ribichini and Xella 1994, 64–66; Ruiz Cabrero 2010; Lietz 2012; Brown and Smith 2019, 26–27.
85. Brown and Smith 2019.
86. Ribichini and Xella 1994, 43–85.
87. Hodos 2006, 119, 132–133.
88. López-Ruiz 2015a.
89. Hodos 2006, 147–152, 2020, 202–203.
90. Vella and Anastasi 2019, 553–554; Rossi 2017.
91. Vella and Anastasi 2019, 558.
92. Sagona 2008b, 504.
93. Bonanno 2005; Sagona 2015.
94. Vella 2005; Vella and Anastasi 2019.
95. Naso 2000; Riva 2006, 110–111; Nowlin 2016, 32–50, 2021.
96. Hayne 2019, 505; Nowlin 2016, 7–58, 2021; van Dommelen 2015, 54.
97. Rathje 1979, 147; Haynes 2000, 154–158.
98. Haynes 2000, 116–117; cf. Ammerman 1991; N. A. Winter 2009.
99. Fletcher 2007, esp. 102–109; cf. Botto 2002, 238–239, 2012, 2017b; Ridgway 2002; D'Oriano 2013; Hayne 2019.
100. Hayne 2019, 511; cf. Fletcher 2007, 104–105, 2012.
101. Botto 2010, 2002; Naso 2015; cf. Rathje 1979.
102. Riva 2006, 114.
103. Rathje 1979, 145.
104. Haynes 2000, 74–75, 129–131; Ridgway 2002; Botto 2002, 238–239, 2012, 53; Sannibale 2013, 2016; Markoe 2015; Hayne 2019.
105. Coldstream 1993, 1998, 356–357.
106. Nowlin 2016, 2021.
107. Malkin 2002, 159.
108. Hayne 2019, 505, alluding to Carpenter 1958, 44–45.
109. Hayne 2019, 505.
110. Botto 2005, 68–69, 2008, 2011.
111. Hayne 2019.
112. Fletcher 2007, 41–44; Botto 2008, 2012.
113. Hayne 2019, 507; cf. Fletcher 2007, 41–42.
114. Poole 1993; Nijboer 2006; Botto 2008.
115. Botto 2008, 129–130.

116. Botto 2011, 170–173.
117. Cuozzo 2016; Hayne 2019, 508–511.
118. Docter and Niemeyer 1994.
119. Botto 2008, 129–130; Botto 2010 (Etruria and Latium Vetus).
120. Docter 2014.
121. Hayne 2019, 508; Sciacca 2005; viticulture: Botto 2012.
122. Fletcher 2007, 41–44, 102–109.
123. Haynes 2000, 16–20; cf. Markoe 1985, 128.
124. Haynes 2000, 1–45; Izzet 2007; Riva 2010; Bellelli 2012; G. Bartoloni 2013; Iaia 2013.
125. Sassatelli and Govi 2013 (Adriatic, Po region); Blake 2014b (Bronze Age networks); Riva 2014 (central Italy); Biella and Tabolli 2016 (Falisco-Capenate region); Nowlin 2016 (Adriatic, Abruzzo area).
126. Riva 2006, 111; G. Bartoloni 2013; Sannibale 2013; first stressed by Carpenter 1958, 44.
127. Boardman 1999a, 199–200.
128. DNA studies: Perkins 2017; Lydian-origins hypothesis: Hdt. 1.94; view that they were indigenous to Italy: Dion. Hal., *Ant. Rom.* 1.26.2–1.30.2; Briquel 2013.
129. Bagnasco Gianni 2013; Sannibale 2013; Nowlin 2016, 7–58, 2021.
130. Magness 2001, 93–98.
131. Gunter 2009, 9.
132. Haynes 2000, 38.
133. Nava 2011, 164; Sassatelli and Govi 2013.
134. Overviews in Rathje 1979, 1986a, 1986b; Markoe 1985, 127–148; Botto 2010.
135. Magness 2001, 83.
136. Rathje 1979, 147, 179–81.
137. Rathje 1979, 181.
138. Sannibale 2013.
139. Markoe 1985, 128, 138–139, 146–147; Turfa 2001.
140. Markoe 1985, 129, 92–93.
141. Markoe 1985, 80; Botto 2005, 2008, 2011.
142. Perkins 2015; previously, Ruthje 1979, 157–158.
143. Perkins 2015, 226.
144. Perkins 2015, 227.
145. Perkins 2015, 227; cf. Moscati 1988a, nos. 931–932; Haynes 2000, 59, fig. 43; Brocato and Regoli 2009.
146. Botto 2005, 2013; cf. Magness 2001, 92.
147. Botto 2005, 59; Sassatelli and Govi 2013, 290.
148. Botto 2005, 58–63; cf. Gubel 1996; Xella 2017 (royal self-representation).
149. Haynes 2000, 123, fig. 106.
150. Sciacca 2005.
151. Sciacca 2006–2007, 283, 290; Sannibale 2016, 303–304.
152. Steele 2013a, 231–234.

153. Alexandre 2002; Botto 2017b, 604.

154. Haynes 2000, 161, fig. 142.

155. Bachvarova 2023; cf. Brody 2008; Matthäus 2010; Morstadt 2015.

156. Sciacca 2006–2007, 290; Vella 2010; cf. Gjerstad 1946 (Cypriot workshop?); Rathje 1979, 152–157 (workshop in Levant?); Markoe 1985, 141–145 (workshop in Etruria?).

157. Turfa 2001.

158. Sciacca 2006–2007, 287; Sannibale 2016, 304.

159. Sciacca 2006–2007, 283; Fletcher 2007, 104.

160. Cerasuolo 2016, 30.

161. Magness 2001.

162. Haynes 2000, 74–75, 94; Cerasuolo 2016, 34; Pieraccini and Baughan 2023.

163. Sannibale 2013, 116.

164. Haynes 2000, 129–131.

165. Rask 2011, 98.

166. Decorated Egyptian vases: Haynes 2000, 77–80 (not including the so-called Canopic urns, which probably do not follow Egyptian models, Haynes 2000, 106); elite tombs: López-Castro 2006.

167. Haynes 2000, 71–72; Magness 2001, 85.

168. Magness 2001, 85–90.

169. Celestino and López-Ruiz 2016, 253–266.

170. Aubet 2001, 334–337.

171. Aubet 2010.

172. López-Bertran 2019, 294–295, 302, 305.

173. E. Mazar 2004.

174. Steingräber 2009, 126–127, cf. 1991.

175. Haynes 2000, 35, 45.

176. Steingräber 2009, 127–129.

177. Steingräber 2009, 129–130.

178. Doak 2015, 78–101.

179. Haynes 2000, 35, 91, 95; Riva 2006, 127.

180. Ciasca 1962; Magness 2001, 85.

181. Izzet 2007, 122–23; Riva 2010; Leighton 2013.

182. Sannibale 2013, 115–119.

183. Magness 2001, 90–91; cf. Strøm 1971, 203–212; Rathje 1979, 179; Burkert 1992, 17.

184. Haynes 2000, 126–131; Edlund-Berry 2013.

185. Magness 2001, 81; Prayon 2001, 336–339; Jovino 2010, 168.

186. Rathje 2007; N. A. Winter 2009; cf. Haynes 2000, figs.103–106.

187. Sannibale 2013, 121–122; Tuck 2014, 126.

188. Tuck 2014, 130–135; de Puma 2016; Hodos et al. 2020, 382.

189. Izzet 2007, 222–223; Camporeale 2013, 888–889; Sannibale 2013, 115–116.

190. Livy 1.34; Dion. Hal., *Ant. Rom.* 3.46.3–5; Str. 5.2.2, 8.6.20; Plin., *HN* 35.43.

191. Boardman 1999a, 202; Haynes 2000, 64–65; Demetriou 2012, 64–104; Camporeale 2013.

192. Rask 2011, 92.

193. Ridgway 1992b; Markoe 1992; S. P. Morris and Papadopoulos 1998, 260–261; Magness 2001, 97–98; Camporeale 2013, 890, 896.

194. Leighton 2013, 142.

195. Haynes 2000, 172–176.

196. Serra Ridgway 1990; Baglione et al. 2015; Aubet 2016.

197. Baglione 2008; Ambrosini and Michetti 2013.

198. Ribichini and Xella 1994, 127–136; Cornell 1995, 232, 235–236; Miles 2010, 93, 110n398.

199. Phoenician oil lamps: Michetti 2020.

200. Aubet 2016, 153.

201. Torelli 2000b; Bonfante and Swaddling 2006, 28–33; de Grummond 2006, 209–233; Steingräber and Stockman 2007.

202. Demetriou 2012, 70; cf. Rathje 1990.

203. López-Bertran 2019, 303–304.

204. Rathje 2007, 179; cf. Carter 1997; Nijboer 2013; S. R. Martin 2018.

205. Sannibale 2013, 122–128; Biella and Giovanelli 2016.

206. Malkin 2011, 119–141; Phoenician-Punic perspective: Miles 2010, 108–109; Álvarez Martí-Aguilar 2019; Herakles-Melqart: Bonnet 2015.

207. Cornell 1995, 69, 162.

208. Remedios Sánchez 2010.

209. Miles 2010, 108–110.

210. Agostiniani 2013, 459.

211. Briquel 1991; Bonfante and Bonfante 2002.

212. Ridgway 1992a, 107–120; Wallace 2016; Richey 2019b, 248.

213. van der Meer 2007.

214. Agostiniani 2013; Rask, forthcoming.

215. Examples in Haynes 2000, 271–272, fig. 219.

216. de Grummond 2013.

217. Burkert 1992, 46–48; Turfa 2012, 241–277, 304–313 (brontoscopic tradition).

218. Tuck and Wallace 2013, 16–20.

219. Lancel 1995, 86; Prag 2006, 8; Quinn 2018, 26; Beltrán Lloris et al. 2020, 491.

220. S. P. Morris 2019, 89–90; Beltrán Lloris et al. 2020.

6. The Aegean

Epigraph: Burkert 1992, 129.

1. Whitley 2001, 110.

2. Bonnet 2015, 23–24.

3. Whitley 2001, 100.

4. Gunter 2009, 62.

5. Gunter 2009, 84.

6. Stampolidis 2019, 495.

7. Bernal 1987; S. R. Martin 2017, 73–96.

8. Gunter 2009, 62–64.

9. Snodgrass 1980, 15–48; I. Morris 1987; Langdon 1997; Whitley 2001, 98–101; R. Osborne 2009, 66–130; Murray 2017.

10. Fibiger Bang and Scheidel 2013; Vlassopoulos 2014.

11. Manning 2018, 237.

12. Brisart 2011.

13. Demetriou 2012.

14. Gunter 2009, 129.

15. *Il.* 6. 289–292.

16. Markoe 1985, 43–44.

17. Carter 1997, 86–94.

18. Markoe 1985, 34–38.

19. Markoe 1985, 38–41.

20. Gorgon: Graff 2014, 265–266; Bes: Boardman 2003, 32.

21. Burkert 1992, 20.

22. Markoe 1985, 42–56.

23. Hodos 2020, 2022.

24. Dates according to the chronology of pottery styles in Attica, J. M. Hall 2007, 35.

25. R. Osborne 2009, 79–80, 124–128.

26. Markoe 1985, 119–121.

27. Whitley 2001, 201, fig. 9.4.

28. R. Osborne 2009, 156–59, fig. 39; S. P. Morris 1992, 91–92, figs. 13–15.

29. S. P. Morris 1995, 227.

30. R. Parker 2017, 33–77.

31. Markoe 1985.

32. Markoe 1985, 81.

33. Markoe 1985, 81–82; Stampolidis 2004, 276–280, 2019, 496; S. P. Morris 2006.

34. Gubel 2019, 356.

35. Feldman 2014, 117, pl. 10; cf. Markoe 1985, 81–82 (Cy11).

36. Cremation vessels: Markoe 1985, 81–82; urns in Tartessos: Celestino and López-Ruiz 2016, 263.

37. Markoe 1985, 81, 123.

38. Markoe 1985, 155–156.

39. Stampolidis 2004, 276–282.

40. Markoe 1985, 110–112; Burkert 1992, 16, fig. 1.

41. Markoe 1985, 115.

42. Catling 1977, 12, fig. 27; Coldstream 1982, 271, 2003, 299; Markoe 1985, 117; S. P. Morris 1992, 159.

43. Stampolidis and Kotsonas 2006; Stampolidis 2016, 2019; cf. J. W. Shaw 1989, 1998 and J. W. Shaw and Shaw 2000 (Kommos); Antoniadis 2017 (Knossos).

44. Gunter 2009, 152; Stampolidis 2019, 496.

45. Carter 1998.

46. R. Osborne 2009, 86–88.

47. Kantor 1962.

48. Burkert 1992, 16–18; S. P. Morris 2006, 72–73; Gunter 2009, 124–126; Feldman 2014, 161–70.

49. Feldman 2014, 170–172; cf. S. P. Morris 1992, 134, 1997, 66, 2006, 77.

50. J. M. Hall 2002, 95.

51. Gunter 2009, 149; R. Osborne 2009, 86–87.

52. Tomlinson 1992; Morgan 1994.

53. Morgan 1994, 137–144; Gunter 2009, 149.

54. Gunter 2009, 151–152, after Skon-Jedele 1994, 1778–1780.

55. Gunter 2009, 151.

56. S. P. Morris 2006, 72; Gunter 2009, 142–152.

57. Gunter 2009, 124–127, fig. 42 (equestrian ornament), 175 (scepter).

58. Stampolidis 2004, 286, fig. 378.

59. Culican 1973; Markoe 1985, 92–94, 118, 129; S. P. Morris 1992, 159; Gubel 2019, 358–359.

60. Coldstream 2003, 55–63.

61. Barnett 1982, 56–60; Carter 1985; Feldman 2014, 43–64; Gubel 2019, 359–361; Syro-Phoenician ivories: Markoe 1985, 91, 116–117, 2000, 146–147.

62. Barnett 1982, 60.

63. Dawkins 1929, 248; Barnett 1948, 14; Carter 1985, 1987.

64. Barnett 1982, 60; cf. Carter 1985, 1987.

65. Stampolidis 2019, 496.

66. Markoe 1985, 91–92, 116.

67. Gunter 2009, 140.

68. Carter 1985.

69. Markoe 2000, 165.

70. Markoe 1985, 98–99, 2000, 165; Burkert 1992, 15.

71. Feldman 2014, 32–34, 2019, 377–378; Caubet 2014a; Stucky 2014; Gubel 2019, 363–364.

72. Caubet 2014a, 164.

73. Gubel 2019, 364.

74. Markoe 2000, 165.

75. Gubel 2019, 363, cf. 2015.

76. Hodos et al. 2020.

77. Stampolidis 2003, 499n941, 2019, 500 (Cyclades); Gunter 2009, 140 (Samos).

78. Hodos et al. 2020.

79. López-Bertrán 2019, 302; Costa 2019, 578; Arruda 2019, 608; Le Meaux 2013.

80. Gubel 2019, 363–364.

81. Markoe 2000, 139; López-Bertrán 2019, 302.

82. Savio 2004; Le Meaux 2013.

83. Burkert 1992, 15.

84. Gunter 2009, 140.

85. Gunter 2009, 85–86, 141, 143.

86. Markoe 2000, 22.

87. Markoe 1985, 95–96, 2000, 56–58; Rathje 1976.

88. Markoe 1985, 97.

89. Classical study by Boardman 1968.

90. Markoe 1985, 97–98; Caubet 2014b, 167–168.

91. Caubet 2014b, 167.

92. Boardman 2003; Hölb 2017.

93. Gubel 2019, 362.

94. Markoe 2000, 155–156; Gubel 2019, 361–363.

95. Gubel 2019, 362; Avigad and Sass 1997.

96. James 1962, 461–464; Payne 1962; R. Osborne 2009, 86.

97. Perachora scarabs: Payne 1962, 462–463; Phoenician-Punic scarabs: Boardman 2003.

98. Hodos 2006, 67–70; R. Osborne 2009, 100–101, figs. 27–28.

99. Burkert 1992, 15; Markoe 2000, 154; Gubel 2019, 361.

100. Giovanelli 2016.

101. Boardman 2003.

102. Markoe 1985, 94, 124, 2000, 156.

103. Gubel 2019, 363.

104. Redissi 1999; Kaoukabani 2005; Gener et al. 2012.

105. Markoe 1985, 96.

106. Markoe 1985, 125.

107. *Hom. Hymn Ap.* 391–432; *Od.* 13.272–285, 15.403–484.

108. Pilz 2011; Langdon 2022.

109. Langdon 2022.

110. Sader 2010.

111. Lancel 1995, 339–350; Sader 2010; López-Bertran and Garcia Ventura 2012; S. R. Martin 2017, 30, 94; Gubel 2019, 354–356.

112. Riis 1960–1961; Ammerman 1991; Boardman 1999a, 76–77; Ziskowski 2016, 98–99; Langdon 2022.

113. Ammerman 1991, 208; Boardman 1999a, 76.

114. Langdon 2022; cf. Brøns 2014.

115. Gubel 2019, 353–354.

116. Langdon 2022; cf. Gunter 2009, 149–151.

117. Zimmerman Munn 2003; Fantuzzi et al. 2020.

118. S. P. Morris and Papadopoulos 1998, 254–255.

119. Carter 1987; R. Osborne 2009, 169–170; Orsingher 2018, 51.

120. Graff 2014, 265–266, 270, fig. 142; cf. Burkert 1992, 20; Boardman 1999a, 77.

121. S. P. Morris 1997, 67; J. M. Hall 2002, 95.

122. Carter 1985, 82–91; Langdon 1989; S. P. Morris 1997, 59.

123. Mikrakis 2015, 286.

124. Boardman 1998, 84; cf. Markoe 1985, 120; S. P. Morris and Papadopoulos 1998, 253–254; Whitley 2001, 102–103, 110–111; Gadolou 2014.

125. Ziskowski 2016, 103, 2017, 98; cf. Whitley 2001, 120–124.

126. Ziskowski 2016, 2017.

127. Ziskowski 2016, 99–100; cf. S. P. Morris and Papadopoulos 1998.

128. Coldstream 2003, 360.

129. Whitley 2001, 102–103; Fletcher 2011; cf. Markoe 1985, 117, 125, following Coldstream 1968.

130. Ziskowski 2016, 109, 2017, 99.

131. Markoe 1985, 118–122; S. P. Morris and Papadopoulos 1998, 253–254.

132. Boardman 1998, 83–176.

133. Gadolou 2014, 260.

134. Boardman 1998, 108; Brisart 2011, 115–129.

135. Ziskowski 2017, 103.

136. Gadolou 2014, 260.

137. Gadolou 2014, 258.

138. Whitley 2001, 103, citing Cook 1972, 41; Coldstream 2003, 360.

139. Whitley 2001, 112; Coldstream 2003, 360.

140. Brisart 2011, 198–201.

141. Markoe 1985, 123.

142. E.g., Mazarakis Ainian 1988; Sourvinou-Inwood 1993; Whitley 2001, 134–164; Castleden 2005, 161–182.

143. Marinatos 1993, 229 (emphasis in original).

144. Barletta 2001, 130–137; Whitley 2001, 156–164; Mazarakis Ainian 2016; Scahill 2017.

145. Niemeier 2016, 245; Scahill 2017, 223n9; cf. Burkert 1985, 47, 88–91; West 1997, 37; Jenkins 2006, 10; S. P. Morris 2006, 77.

146. Whitley 2001, 224–225.

147. Gebhard 2001, 50.

148. Jenkins 2006, 16–17.

149. Scahill 2017, 231.

150. Barletta 2001, 21–53; Whitley 2001, 84–87, 156; R. Osborne 2009, 55–58.

151. R. Osborne 2009, 199.

152. Jenkins 2006, 18–19.

153. Rhodes 1987; Scahill 2017.

154. Gebhard 2001, 43.

155. Vitruvius 4.2.1–5. Barletta 2001, 6–7, 125–130.

156. Scahill 2017, 227.

157. Scahill 2017, 223, 226. On shipbuilding techniques, see Edrey 2019, 122–123, fig. 4.1.

158. Scahill 2017, 224–226.

159. Barletta 2001, 101–103.

160. Barletta 2001, 84–124.

161. Barletta 2001, 98–101, 142–144; cf. R. Martin 1955–1956.

162. Jenkins 2006, 19, fig. 8.

163. Hdt. 1.105.3 (Ashtart temple at Ashkelon); Joseph., *Ap.* 1.118 (temples at Tyre); Plin., *HN* 16.216 (cedar beams at one of Utica's temples).

164. 1 Kings 5,18, trans. NRSV. Cf. 1 Kings 5–7, 2 Chronicles 2–4.

165. Mierse 2012.

166. Gebhard 2001, 48–49.

167. *DCPP* s.v., "Sanctuaires."

168. Karageorghis 1976; M. Yon 1986; Caubet 1986; *DCPP* s.v., "Kition" and "Sanctuaires, Chypre;" J. S. Smith 2009, 66–70, 36–48, figs. II.1–7.

169. Nigro 2005, 91–92, 2015, 86; *DCPP* s.v. "Sanctuaires;" Briquel-Chatonet and Gubel 1998, 110–112; Woolmer 2017, 125–130.

170. Marín Ceballos and Jiménez Flores 2004; Álvarez Martí-Aguilar 2019, 618–621.

171. Str. 3.5.3–3.5.6; Mela, *Chor.* 3.6.46; Just. *Epit.* 44.5.2. Mierse 2004.

172. Kronion: Str. 3.5.3; Venus Marina: Avienus, *Ora* 314–317. Remains: Maya et al. 2014; cf. Celestino and López-Ruiz 2016, 233–234.

173. Burkert 1985, 88–89.

174. Lipiński1993; Bergquist 1993; Olmo Lete 2004.

175. Gómez Bellard and Vidal 2000; Marín Ceballos 2010; Gutiérrez et al. 2012; Christian 2013; Vella and Anastasi 2019, 561–564.

176. Vella and Anastasi 2019, 563.

177. Celestino and López-Ruiz 2016, 217, 243 (El Carambolo), cf. 250 (Cyprus).

178. Brodi 2008; Fumadó Ortega 2012; Polzer 2014.

179. Burkert 1992, 20; Bachvarova 2023.

180. Fullerton 2016, 4–9.

181. Carter 1997, 86–95.

182. Fullerton 2016, 68–88.

183. Boardman 2006, 2–12; Fullerton 2016, 4–22.

184. Boardman 2006, 13–24; S. R. Martin 2017, 43–49, 53–59; Fullerton 2016, 24–45.

185. S. R. Martin 2017, 44.

186. Whitley 2001, 213.

187. Boardman 2006, 13.

188. Guralnick 1978; Carter and Steinberg 2010; S. R. Martin 2017, 58.

189. Boardman 2006, 16; S. R. Martin 2017, 55.

190. Boardman 2006, 19–24; Fullerton 2016, 25–26; S. R. Martin 2017, 48.

191. Fullerton, 2016, 25.

192. Boardman 2006, 19.

193. S. R. Martin 2017, 58.

194. Boardman 2006, 4–13, 24; Fullerton 2016, 26–28; S. R. Martin 2017, 58.

195. Carter 1988; Boardman 2006, 26–27; Fullerton 2016, 19–21.

196. Fullerton 2016, 21.

197. Celestino and López-Ruiz 2016, 276–277, fig. 8.5.

198. Celestino and López-Ruiz 2016, 229, 276–277, fig. 7.3; Aubet 2001, 201–204, figs. 43–44.

199. Markoe 2000, 151; Faegersten 2003.

200. E.g., Boston Museum of Art (ca. 675 BC), Delphi (ca. 625–600 BC): Fullerton 2016, 19–20, figs. 1.13–1.14; Etruscan example (early sixth century BC): Haynes 2000, 131, fig. 113.

201. Markoe 2000, 150–151.

202. Gubel 2019, 366.

203. Gubel 2019, 352.

204. Falsone 1970.

205. Gubel 2019, 352.

206. Faegersten 2003, 163–212.

207. Boardman 2006, 25; S. R. Martin 2017, 58.

208. Boardman 2006, 24, on Diod. Sic. 1.98.5–9.

209. Hütwohl 2020.

210. E.g., *Il.* 6. 289–292; *Od.* 4.83–84, 14.199–292; Hdt. 2.112–20. S. Sherratt 2010.

211. Hdt. 2.43–64; cf. Diod. Sic. 1.24.1–4. López-Ruiz 2015b, 370–373.

212. Hdt. 1.105.3.

213. R. Osborne 2009, 197.

214. S. R. Martin 2017, 64.

215. S. R. Martin 2017, 64–65.

216. Brisart 2011; Keesling 2003.

217. Whitley 2001, 106.

218. Whitley 2001, 90–98, 115–127.

219. A lengthier treatment of this topic is in López-Ruiz 2021.

220. OEAANE s.v. "Giza."

221. Hdt. 2.175; Men. *Fr.* p. 411, ed. Meineke.

222. *DCPP* s.v. "Sphinx."

223. Ael., *NA* 12. 38.

224. Pinch 2004, 206; cf. I. Shaw 2003, 87.

225. E.g., Hdt. 4.79.2; Soph., *OT* 391; Eurip., *El.* 471; Apollod. 3.5.8; Paus. 3.18.8, 5. 11.2; Ael., *NA* 12.7. Kourou 2011.

226. OEAANE. s.v. "Tell Halaf," "*Ain Dara*"; Özyar 2016, 139, 143–144, figs. 3, 5a-b.

227. Black and Green 1992, 51, 65.

228. Images in Aruz and Seymour 2016, 22–23, 232, 255, 290–291.

229. Coins: Betlyon 1982, pl. 8, 2019, 394–395; Idalion in Cyprus: Gaber 2008, 54.

230. *DCPP* s.v. "Sphinx."

231. Ziffer 2013, 49.

232. Doak 2015, 109–115.

233. *DCPP* figs. on pp. 50, 159, 160, 163, 313, 339, 341; Lancel 1995, 198. Doak 2015, 59–62, 109–115.

234. Haynes 2000, 296–298.

235. Markoe 2000, 153, fig. 60.

236. Boardman 2003, 62–64.

237. Chapman 2017.

238. A. Mazar 1990, 505–507; Burnett 2016, 37–40n19.

239. Gen. 3,24; Ezq. 21,3–4; 21,10; Ps. 18,11–15. Wyatt 2009, 31; Eichler 2015.

240. Castleden 2005, 127, fig. 5.8, 102–103 (*larnakes*); Kourou 2011, 166–167.

241. Celestino and López-Ruiz 2016, 231, 272, figs. 7.4, 8.2.

242. Sciacca 2013; cf. Haynes 2000, 110, 151–153, 162–164, 296–298.

243. Kourou 2011; Petit 2011.

244. Pensa 1977; Aston 2011; Kourou 2011, 165.

245. Petit 2011, 204–236, 2015.

246. Aston 2011, 293. *LIMC*, s.v. "Oedipous," "Sphinx"; López-Ruiz 2021.

247. Gunter 2022.

248. *Theog.* 326. López-Ruiz 2010, 109–113, 2021 for other origins stories.

249. *Theog.* 304, 306.

250. Soph., *OT* 36., Paus. 9.26.2–4, and Apollod. 3.5.8 gather the main traditions. López-Ruiz 2021.

251. *LSJ* s.v. Σφίγξ, pl. Σφίγγες; Boiotian Φίξ-Φικός (*Theog.* 326). Beekes 2010, s.v. Σφίγξ; Chantraine 1984–1990, s.v. σφίγγω; Ruipérez 2006, 99.

252. Arslan-Tash I, line 4. Demsky 2022.

253. Pardee 1998; Zamora 2003.

254. Bonnet and Xella 1995, 330–331; Ruiz Cabrero 2003; Frendo, de Trafford, and Vella 2005; Amadasi Guzzo 2007; Tribulato 2013; López-Ruiz 2015a.

255. Hdt. 2.49. Astour 1967, 113–124; Berman 2004.

256. Edwards 1979, 58, 60; *DCPP* s.v. "Kadmos"; West 1997, 289–290.

257. Hdt. 2.49, 5.57–61; Paus. 9.25, 6; Str. 9.2,3, 10.1, 8. Latacz 2004, 238–248; Finkelberg 2005, 86–87.

7. Intangible Legacies

1. De Hoz 2005b, 45.

2. Richey 2019b.

3. Amadasi Guzzo 2019; Richey 2019a.

4. E.g., Powell 1991, 71; Malkin 1998, 262; S. R. Martin 2017, 99.

5. E.g., Boardman 2016, 206.

6. Quinn 2018, 71.

7. Powell 1991, 245.

8. Herrenschmidt 2000; R. G. Lehmann 2012. The *abjad* category was introduced by Daniels 1990, 729, in reaction to Gelb 1963.

9. Richey 2019b, 245–247.

10. Rollston 2010, 11; Amadasi Guzzo 2019, 202.

11. McCarter 1975; Janko 2015; Richey 2019b, 248.

12. Pithekoussai and Gabii: Ridgway 1992a, 107–120, 1994; Woodard 2010, 44; Hodos 2020, 193; Eretria: Theurillat 2007; Kommos: Csapo, Johnston, and Geagan 2000; Methone: Tzifopoulos 2013; Janko 2015; Papadopoulos 2016; Clay, Malkin, and Tzifopoulos 2017.

13. Janko 2015, 7.

14. Amadasi Guzzo 1991, 307, 1999; Röllig 1995, 202; Richey 2019b. For the chronological issue, Janko 2015.

15. de Hoz 2005b, 47–48.

16. Richey 2019b, 248.

17. Naveh 1987, 177–178; Bernal 1990; Ruijgh 1997; Waal 2018; counterarguments in Sass 2017.

18. Janko 2015, 23.

19. de Hoz 2005b, 40; Richey 2019b, 245–246.

20. Colvin 2007, 19.
21. Walter Burkert, oral communication at the Ohio State University, April 27, 2006.
22. *Il.* 6.169.
23. Burkert 1992, 30–31; de Hoz 2005b, 48; Janko 2015, 23.
24. Coldstream 1993; S. P. Morris 1997, 67; Bourogiannis 2018a. For bilingualism, J. M. Hall 2002, 111–117; López-Ruiz 2010, 31–32.
25. Bourogiannis 2018a.
26. de Hoz 2005b, 45–47.
27. Pappa 2019a.
28. Lejeune and Pouilloux 1988; Chadwick 1990; Belarte 2009, 104–105; Gorgues 2016.
29. de Hoz 2005b, 49.
30. Powell 1991; cf. Wade-Gery 1952; Janko 1982, 277n3.
31. Mikrakis 2013.
32. West 2011; Montanari, Rengakos, and Tsagalis 2012.
33. Janko 2015, 24.
34. Powell 1991, 24–27, 66–67.
35. Hdt. 5.58–59.
36. Hdt. 5.55–57; cf. Thuc. 6.54–58. S. P. Morris 1992, 378.
37. Other archaic inscriptions: Hdt. 5. 60–61; Tyre: Hdt. 2.44.
38. In a scholion to second-century BC author Dion. Thrax 183.5–9.
39. Stesichoros fr. 213 Page (Palamedes); Aesch., *PV* 460 (Prometheus).
40. E.g., Aristotle and Ephoros (scholia to Dion. Thrax 183.1–5); Diod. Sic. 5.58.3.
41. Phoenician/Kadmean letters: E.g, Str. 9.2,3, 10.1, 8; Diod. Sic. 5.58.3; Paus. 9.25, 6; Chronicle of Lindos (99 BC); inscription from Teos (ca. 470 BC); Thuc. 1.12.3 (Kadmeis as name for Boiotia); Nonnus, *Dion.* 4.259–644, 267–271 (Kadmeian invention of writing); *poinikastas* on Crete: *SEG* XXVII 631; office on Mytilene: *IG* XII.2 96, 97. In a list of inventions, Kritias called the Phoenician letters *alexiloga* (a hapax meaning "speech/thought-averting" or "speech/thought-protecting"), Fr. 2,10 (Diels-Kranz). Jeffery 1967, 153; Powell 1991, 5–6; S. P. Morris 1992, 159–160.
42. Hdt. 2.49; Varro, *Rust.* 3.1.
43. López-Ruiz 2010, 23–37.
44. López-Ruiz 2016, 2019a.
45. Quinn 2018, xxiv; cf. Feeney 2016, 200–209.
46. López-Ruiz 2017, 2019a; cf. Lancel 1995, 351–360; Hoyos 2010, 105–108.
47. Miles 2010, 352–356.
48. Sall., *Iug.* 17.7; Plut. *De fac.* 26–30.
49. August., *Ep.* 17.
50. Joseph., *Ap.* 1.116–119, *AJ* 8.144–149; Philo of Byblos, *FGrH/BNJ* 790 (Kaldellis and López-Ruiz 2009); López-Ruiz 2017, 2019a.
51. Bernal 1987.
52. Astour 1967, xii.

53. S. P. Morris 1989, 1998; Dowden 2001 (review of West 1997); Arvidsson 2006; on Orientalism, Said 1978.

54. Pythagoras: Iambl., *VP* 13 (p. 438); Thales: Hdt. 1.170. O'Meara 1989; S. P. Morris 1992, 378–379; Riedweg 2005, 5–8, 23–26; López-Ruiz 2010, 191–193.

55. Joseph., *AJ* 1.107–108; Tertullian, *Apologeticus* 19. Bowie 1998; López-Ruiz 2017, 2019a; Kaldellis 2019.

56. Zeno and Phoenician philosophers in Athens: J.-B. Yon 2011; Demetriou 2023. Kleitomachos: Diog. Laert., 4.67; Miles 2010, 252–253.

57. Gordon 1962; West 1966, 1971, 1983, 1997; Astour 1967; Bernal 1987; Burkert 1987, 1992, 2003, 2004; Brown 1995–2000–2001.

58. Mesopotamia: Penglase 1994; Currie 2016; Haubold 2013; Anatolia: Bachvarova 2016; Egypt: Marinatos 2010; Moyer 2011; Rutherford 2011; Marinatos and Wyatt 2011; biblical and Northwest Semitic world: Brown 1995–2000–2001; Naiden 2006; Noegel 2007; Bremmer 2008; López-Ruiz 2010; Louden 2011; M. S. Smith 2014; Doak 2019a.

59. López-Ruiz 2010, 2014, 2015b, 2017, 2019a.

60. Hdt. 2.167; Pliny, *HN* 35.151–152; cf. Athenagoras *Leg. pro Crist.* 17.3; shipbuilding: Thuc. 1.13.2–3.

61. Thuc. 1.13.5.

62. Ridgway 1992b; S. P. Morris and Papadopoulos 1998, 260–261.

63. Hdt. 1.18–20, 5.92; Arist. *Pol.* 3.1284a, 5.1311a.

64. Astour 1967, 204–212.

65. For all these possible connections, Dunbabin 1948b; S. P. Morris and Papadopoulos 1998, 257–260; Ziskowski 2016, 99–104, 109, 2017, 103. For prostitution at Akrocorinth, Str. 8.6.21, assumed by scholars for the sanctuary at Eryx and at Motya on Sicily, Kition, and other sanctuaries: Brown and Smith 2019, 22–23; Nigro 2019, 109; Oliveri 2019, 128–130.

66. López-Ruiz 2009b, 2014, 2016, 2022a.

67. López-Ruiz 2010, 130–170, 2015a; West 1983, 1994.

68. West 1997, 626.

69. West 1997, 629, 587–588; Burkert 2004, 47–48.

70. Bachvarova 2016, 299.

71. George 2003 (vol. 1), 56–57, 2007, 458.

72. Hdt. 1.105.3.

73. Hütwohl 2020.

74. West 1971 for early philosophy.

75. S. P. Morris 1992, 180–181.

76. Snodgrass 1980, 32–34; Petit 2019; Garnand 2020, 147.

77. Chantrainne 1984–1990; Beekes 2010, cf. 2004 on Kadmos and Europa.

78. West 1997, 14.

79. Burkert 1992, 33–40; Brown 1995–2000–2001; West 1997, 12–14; Masson 2007; on "wine/vine" words: Gorton 2017.

80. Burkert 1992, 64.

81. Astour 1967, 174–175, 187; Burkert 1985, 163n13.

82. Burkert 1992, 39–40.

83. Dowden 2007, 48; Cyrino 2010, 26; contra West 2000, 135–136; cf. López-Ruiz 2015b, 378–380.

84. Epithets: *Theog.* 185–206; Ourania: Hdt. 1.105.3, Paus. 1.14.7, 3.22.1. Stager 2005, 439–441; Kythereia and Kothar: López-Ruiz 2022a.

85. López-Ruiz 2010, 205–210.

86. Burkert 1992, 37.

87. Burkert 1992, 37.

88. Burkert 1992, 38.

89. Burkert 1983, 1992; Bremmer 2008, 133–151; Bachvarova 2016, 200–206.

90. Silva Jayasuriya 2017, esp. 100–124.

91. Silva Jayasuriya 2017, 191.

92. Silva Jayasuriya 2017, 171–172, 181–187.

93. Burkert 1992, 35–36.

94. West 1997, 630. More skeptical approach, Penglase 1994; Haubold 2013; Kelly 2014, 29–30; Metcalf 2015.

95. West 1966, 31.

96. Graf 2011, 224.

8. Cyprus

1. Leriou 2007.

2. S. Sherratt 2015; Leriou 2007; Iacovou 2014, 117–118, 2018; Petit 2019, 1–2.

3. Rupp 1987 and later works; Petit 2019, 2–3; Körner 2020.

4. Karageorghis 2005a, 45, echoing Bikai 1994, 35.

5. Leriou 2007.

6. S. Sherratt 2015, 73.

7. S. Sherratt 2015, 71–73.

8. Iacovou 2014, 119, 2018; Fourrier 2019.

9. Knapp 2008, 373–389.

10. Petit 2019.

11. Bourogiannis 2018b; Fourrier 2019.

12. S. Sherratt 2015, 79.

13. Names in ancient sources: Knapp 2008, 299–307, 341–343, 2013, 438; trade: Knapp 2008, 335–341; copper: Knapp 2008, 133, 159–160; Broodbank 2013, 367–368.

14. Knapp 2006.

15. Iacovou 2002; cf. Knapp 2008, 293, 372.

16. Georgiou 2018.

17. Steele 2013a, 90–97; Petit 2019, 19.

18. Steele 2019, 56–65; cf. Knapp 2008, 288–289.

19. Knapp 2008, 281–297; cf. Dietler 1998, 295–296.

20. Knapp 2008, 286, 289.

21. Georgiou 2015; Iacovou 2012b; Kourou 2012, 38; Satraki 2012, 268; Mikrakis 2012, 372.

22. Karageorghis 2005b; Petit 2019, 38–40.

23. Petit 2019, 19–44.

24. Steele 2019, 55–75, cf. 2013a.

25. Reyes 1994, 11–21.

26. Cypriot-Geometric koine: Iacovou 2018, 24–25; ceramic production: Georgiadou 2014.

27. Karageorghis 2005a, 32; Knapp 2008, 211–212; cf. Karageorghis and Demas 1985.

28. Karageorghis 1982, 128–129.

29. Boardman 2001b.

30. Karageorghis 2001; Petit 2019, 26.

31. Bourogiannis 2018b.

32. Karageorghis 2005a, 32.

33. Reyes 1994, 69–97; Fourrier 2019, 488.

34. Iacovou 2002, 83, 2018, 27.

35. Radner 2010. For the Assyrian claim, cf. Knapp 2008, 341–347; Reyes 1994, 61–66.

36. Steele 2013a, 233–234; Iacovou 2014, 118; Fourrier 2019, 482–484; for counterarguments, Satraki 2012, 269–270.

37. Amadasi Guzzo and Zamora 2018.

38. S. Sherratt 2003, 238; Fourrier 2019, 483.

39. Knapp 2008, 372, 343–347; Ioannou 2016; cf. Reyes 1994, 49–68.

40. Reyes 1994, 127; Tatton-Brown 1997, 15; Petit 2019.

41. Fourrier 2019.

42. Knapp 2008, 368; cf. Reyes 1994, 18–19.

43. Fourrier 2019, 487–488.

44. Fourrier 2019, 484, 488; J. S. Smith 2009, 250–551.

45. Reyes 1994, 146–147; Fourrier 2019, 488; Orsingher 2016b.

46. Georgiadou 2014.

47. J. S. Smith 2009.

48. Georgiou 2018.

49. Reyes 1994, 127–128, 138–144.

50. Kotsonas 2012.

51. Coldstream 1968.

52. Kotsonas 2012.

53. Coldstream 1968, 381; Bourogiannis 2012a, 190.

54. Bourogiannis 2012a, 193–195.

55. Tatton-Brown 1997, 43–45.

56. Kassianidou 2012, 241–242.

57. Markoe 1985; Matthäus 1985.

58. Markoe 1985, 3, 6–8.

59. Karageorghis 2005a, 43.

60. Tatton-Brown 1997, 33–34.

61. Karageorghis 1982, 133–134.

62. Tatton-Brown 1997, 56; Knapp 2008, 342.

63. Tatton-Brown 1997, 59–60.

64. Karageorghis 1982, 132.

65. Karageorghis 2005a, 44; cf. Tatton-Brown 1997, 76–77.

66. Reyes 1994, 131, 144–145.

67. Markoe 1985, 87–89.

68. Papantoniou 2012.

69. Tatton-Brown 1997, 21; Carbillet 2011.

70. Tatton-Brown 1997, 22; Faegersten 2003, 225–226, 232; Johnston and Kaufman 2019.

71. 1 Kings 7,15–21. Tatton-Brown 1997, 20.

72. Tatton-Brown 1997, 62.

73. Papantoniou 2012, 291–292; Kassianidou 2012, 233–235.

74. Tatton-Brown 1997, 62–63; Karageorghis 1982, 109.

75. Karageorghis 2005a, 43; Doak 2015.

76. Leibundgut Wieland and Tatton-Brown 2019.

77. Lewe 1975; Wriedt Sørensen 1994, 80–82; Tatton-Brown 1997, 50–53; Hermary 2009.

78. *KAI* 37. Gibson 1982, 123–131 (n33: temple tariffs A and B).

79. Tatton-Brown 1997, 66–67; Hermary 2014 for caveats.

80. López-Bertran 2019; Sader 2019, 216–248.

81. Tatton-Brown 1997, 69–71.

82. J. M. Hall 1997, 135–136; Iacovou 2006, 40; Knapp 2008, 284; Kassianidou 2012, 235.

83. Tatton-Brown 1997, 71–74; Hermary 2015.

84. Papantoniou 2011.

85. Fourrier 2019, 485.

86. Karageorghis 1982, 146–149.

87. Karageorghis 2005a, 41–42.

88. *Od.* 8.362–363; *Hom. Hymn Aphr. 58–67.*

89. *Theog.* 190–199.

90. Tatton-Brown 1997, 65–66.

91. Tatton-Brown 1997, 82–83; Steele 2019, 224–225.

92. Iacovou 2006, 36–39.

93. Steele 2013a, 99–172, 2013b; Karageorghis 2005a, 44.

94. Steele 2013a, 178–182, table 9.

95. Steele 2013a, 202n100.

96. Steele 2013a, 173–234, esp. 225–228.

97. Steele 2013a, 202–211, 228–231.

98. Ioannou 2015; Amadasi Guzzo and Zamora 2016; Iacovou 2018, 25–27.

99. Iacovou 2008.

100. Iacovou 2006, 40–44.

101. S. Sherratt 2003, 236; Radner 2010, 444–445.

102. Tatton-Brown 1997, 49–50.

103. Mikrakis 2012.

104. Faegersten 2003, 21–22.

105. Hdt. 2.182.1–2; Diod. Sic. 1.68.6 following Herodotos.

106. Faegersten 2003, 18n50; Asheri, Lloyd, and Corcella 2007, 378.

107. Gjerstad 1948, 103–104; Faegersten 2003, 18, 104–105.

108. Faegersten 2003, 18–19. For recent overview of Cypriot votive sculpture (with focus on the adaptation of Greek iconography), see Ulbrich 2020.

109. Faegersten 2003, 20.

110. Faegersten 2003, 104–105, 142–143, 218.

111. Faegersten 2003, 217–218.

112. Kourou et al. 2002; Faegersten 2003, 146–150; Höckmann 2009; Karageorghis and Kouka 2009.

113. Phoenician sites: Faegersten 2003, 151–163; "Stagnone torso": Falsone 1970.

114. Markoe 1990a; Hermary 2009, 246; cf. Faegersten 2003, 19–21.

115. Reyes 1994, 130–131, 146–147; cf. Bisi 1988.

116. Faegersten 2003, 89–104, 92 for chart.

117. Faegersten 2003, 246.

118. Faegersten 2003, 82.

119. Faegersten 2003, 225–264.

120. Faegersten 2003, 243.

121. Faegersten 2003, 253–257.

122. Faegersten 2003, 261.

9. The Levant

1. Elayi 2018; Edrey 2019; Sader 2019.

2. Killebrew 2019, 43.

3. Sader 2019, 33–49.

4. Sader 2019, 15–17, 37–38, 48; Welton 2019.

5. Killebrew 2019, 50.

6. Aubet 2001, 12; Bondi 2001, 23; Broodbank 2013, 348, 451–472; Cline 2014; Tubb 2016, 88; Elayi 2018, 65, 94–97; Killebrew 2019, 42; Sader 2019, 34–35; Regev 2021, 5–18.

7. Aubet 2001, 30–31; Sass 2002; Broodbank 2013, 470; Elayi 2018, 100–104; Sader 2019, 35–36.

8. Transl. from Elayi 2018, 102; see Goedicke 1975 for the full text; cf. Bunnens 1978; Sader 2019, 35–36.

9. Broodbank 2013, 470.

10. Joffe 2002, 434.

11. Tubb 2016, 90; cf. Liverani 2004, 97–124.

12. Elayi 2018, 104, 119–121; Sader 2019, 263.

13. Elayi 2018, 27–85; cf. Broodbank 2013, 286–303, 362–363.

14. Xella 2017 on royal imagery.

15. S. R. Martin 2017; Gubel 2019.

16. Elayi 2018, 24.

17. S. R. Martin 2017.

18. Markoe 1985, 7; on Phoenician art, Markoe 1990b; Gubel 2019; Hölb 2017.

19. Gubel 2019, 366.

20. Sader 2010; Michelau 2019.

21. Markoe 1985, 7, 15.

22. Feldman 2014, 47, cf. 5–6.

23. J. Osborne 2021.

24. Aubet 2001, 31.

25. Elayi 2018, 116–143; cf. Aubet 2008, 2019.

26. G. Lehmann 2019, 468–470.

27. E.g., Kauff 1991.

28. Aubet 2001, 44, 2019.

29. Ezekiel 27, 3. Great island fortress: Curt. 4.2.2; Str. 16.2.23; Arr., *Anab.* 2.20.10.

30. Joseph., *AJ* 15.4.1.

31. Cassius Dio 54.7.

32. Str. 16.2.23 (trans. George Bell & Sons 1903, slightly modified).

33. Aubet 2001, 31–46.

34. Mederos, Peña, and González Wagner 2004; Negueruela 2004; Knapp and Demesticha 2016; Emanuel 2019, 424–425; Sader 2019, 310.

35. Aubet 2001, 172–182.

36. Fletcher 2004; S. Sherrat 2010.

37. G. Lehmann 2019, 475; cf. Markoe 1985, 94–98.

38. Knapp and Demesticha 2016; G. Lehmann 2019, 471–475.

39. Treumann 2009; Johnston and Kaufman 2019.

40. Kestemont 1985.

41. Sader 2019, 296–300.

42. Johnston and Kaufman 2019, 403, 412–414; Sader 2019, 276–296.

43. Bunnens 2019, 59–60, cf. 1979, 295–299; G. Lehmann 2019, 470.

44. Joffe 2002, 436, 444.

45. Joffe 2002, 448; established by Mazar 1998; for Phoenician Red-Slip ware and its imitations, see Regev 2020, 63–92; for Phoenician pottery production and distribution, see Núñez 2019.

46. Joffe 2002, 446.

47. J. S. Smith 2009, 66–70, 36–48, figs. II.1–7.

48. Overview in Edrey 2019, 91–120.

49. G. Lehmann and Killebrew 2010; Kamlah 2012; Mierse 2012; J. Osborne 2012.

50. E.g., 1 Kings 9,15. Yadin 1958; Dever 1982.

51. Finkelstein and Mazar 2007.

52. 2 Samuel 5,11; 1 Chronicles 14,1.

53. Joffe 2002, 440–442; cf. Shiloh 1979, 82–87.

54. G. Lehmann 2019, 475; cf. Barnett 1957b; Markoe 1985, 99.

55. J. Osborne, forthcoming.

56. Markoe 1985, 83–84, 105–110.

57. G. Lehmann 2019, 473; cf. Markoe 1985, 102–105.

58. Markoe 1985, 90.

59. Markoe 1985, 101; G. Lehmann 2019, 473.

60. Feldman 2014, 155–158, pl. 16 and 18.

61. Faegersten 2003, 226; cf. Barnett 1935, 200, 1939, 5; I. Winter 1976b, figs. 5–6; Uehlinger 1997, 124–128, figs. 45–46.

62. Faegersten 2003, 236–237.

63. G. Lehmann 2019, 472; cf. Joffe 2002, 443; Regev 2020, 19–54.

64. Hodos 2006, 37; Docter 2014.

65. Gubel 2019, 362–363.

66. E.g., 1 Kings 10,10.

67. Gubel 2019, 362; cf. Lemaire 1993; Avigad and Sass 1997.

68. Gener et al. 2012.

69. 1 Kings 7,14.

70. Witte and Diehl 2008; Johnston and Kaufman 2019.

71. Richey 2019b.

72. Rollston 2010, 11.

73. Hamilton 2006; Sanders 2009, 90–102; Rollston 2010, 11–18; Finkelstein and Sass 2013; Sass et al. 2015; Richey 2019b, 241–242.

74. Rollston 2010, 11.

75. Bryce 2002, 56–71; Bachvarova 2016, 54–110.

76. Rainey 2015; Moran 1992.

77. M. Yon 2006, 125–128; Buck 2020.

78. Lam and Pardee 2012, 410–13; Ellison 2014; Horowitz, Oshima, and Sanders 2018.

79. Tubb 2016, 90.

80. Elayi 2018, 50, 59.

81. *KAI* 1. Rollston 2010, 24–27; Sass 2017; Richey 2019b.

82. Alphabet from Tyre: Richey 2019b, 243; Amadasi Guzzo 2014.

83. Sanders 2009, 109; Rollston 2010, 27–35; Pardee 2013.

84. H. Parker 2013.

85. Sanders 2009, 113, 121.

86. *KAI* 24.

87. Rollston 2010, 36–39; Richey 2019b, 243.

88. Yakubovich 2015; G. Lehmann 2019, 472–473.

89. Osborne J. 2021, 211–212.

90. *KAI* 26, Ai, lines 1–2.

91. Rollston 2010, 41; cf. Amadasi Guzzo 2019; Richey 2019a.

92. Lemaire 2013.

93. Röllig 1995; Richey 2019b, 245–249.

94. Rollston 2010, 36–41.

95. Sanders 2009, 113–122; Buck 2019, 75–80.

96. Sanders 2009, 102, quoting Pollock 2006, 328.

97. Sanders 2009, 90–113; Rollston 2010, 27–35; Lemaire 2012; Finkelstein and Sass 2013.

98. Rollston 2010, 41.

99. Joseph., *AJ* 8.50–83.

100. López-Ruiz 2009a.

101. 1 Kings 16,31. Aubet 2001, 43–46; Miles 2010, 31–32; Doak 2019b.

102. Richey 2019b, 251–252; cf. Sanders 2009, 41–57; Rollston 2010, 91–95.

103. Richey 2019b, 252.

104. Lipschits 2011, 204–207. Previously, Ciaska 1961; Shiloh 1979; Stern 1992.

105. Lipschits 2011.

106. J. Osborne 2012; cf. Almagro-Gorbea 2010, 247.

107. Markoe 1985, Cy1, Cy4 (Cyprus), G3 (Olympia); Joffe 2002; Stern and Magen 2002, 50–52; Maya et al. 2014, 162–164.

108. Stern 1995; Stern and Magen 2002, 52–53; illustrations in Kendirci 2012, 35.

109. Maya et al. 2014, 163.

110. Str. 3.5.5–6; Hdt. 2.44.2. Aubet 2001, 275–277, fig. 14; Celestino and López-Ruiz 2016, 233–235.

111. Markoe 2000, 128, fig. 43.

112. I. Winter 2016.

113. Almagro-Gorbea 2010, 250–251; Marín Ceballos and Jiménez Flores 2011; Maya et al. 2014, 162–164; cf. Moscati 1988a, 282.

114. Marín Ceballos and Jiménez Flores 2011, 211, 216–217; Maya et al. 2014, 162.

115. Nigro 2005, 72, fig. 2.96, 2015, 89–90, fig. 9.

116. Ciasca 1962; Moscati 1988a, 744, no. 942.

117. Tanit symbol: Moscati 1988a, 585, no. 6, 1968, 107, fig. 30.

118. Caubet 1979, 95, 110–112; Moscati 1988a, 163. For other terracotta shrines from Cyprus and the Levant with similar features, Betancourt 1971; Culican 1976.

119. Ciasca 1962, 39.

120. Limestone pillar: Polzer 2014, 238–239; other examples: Almagro-Gorbea 2010, 245–253, fig. 212; González Prats 2011, 661, fig. 13; Maya et al. 2014, 164; cf. Ciasca 1962, pl. IX.5.

121. Moscati 1988a, nos. 582, 522, 526, 528 (Sardinia), 310, 313 (Tunisia); Orsingher 2018–2019; Ciasca 1962, pl. VII.1–2 (Cyrene).

122. Moscati 1988a, no. 526.

123. Faegersten 2003, 225–241.

124. Shiloh 1979; Finkelstein 2000; Lipschits 2011.

125. Lipschits 2011, 203–204; Ciasca 1961 had already proposed "volute" capital.

126. Betancourt 1977, 46–49; A. Mazar 1990, 474–475; Stern 1992; Stern and Magen 2002; Almagro-Gorbea 2010; Marín Ceballos and Jiménez Flores 2011; Maya et al. 2014, 162–164.

127. Feldman 2014, 178.

128. Feldman 2014, 95–100; Gunter 2014.

Epilogue

Epigraph: Trans. E. Shirley Shuckburgh and F. Hultsch, 2018 (modified).

BIBLIOGRAPHY

Abbreviations for ancient references (e.g., Hdt. for Herodotos) follow the *Oxford Classical Dictionary*, 4th edition (full name is given for authors or fragments not cited there). Due to space limitations and the international audience of this book, when possible, I have privileged works in English and more recent or comprehensive works that include previous discussions and references.

Abbreviations

BNJ   I. Worthington, ed. Brill's New Jacoby (Fragments of Ancient Historians). Brill Online. http://referenceworks.brillonline.com /entries/brill-s-new-jacoby.

CAD   M. Roth, ed. in chief. 1956–2010. *The Assyrian Dictionary of the Oriental Institute of the University of Chicago.* Chicago.

DCPP   E. Lipiński, ed. 1992. *Dictionnaire de la Civilisation Phénicienne et Punique.* Paris.

Diels-Kranz   H. Diels and W. Kranz, eds. *Die Fragmente der Vorsokratiker* 1934–1937. 5th rev. ed. Berlin.

FGrH   F. Jacoby, ed. 1957–1958. *Die Fragmente der griechischen Historiker.* 2nd ed., commentary, 1954–1962. Leiden.

HALOT   L. Koehler and W. Baumgarten, eds. 1994–2000. *The Hebrew and Aramaic Lexicon of the Old Testament.* Leiden.

IG   *Inscriptiones Graecae.* Berlin 1873–. Ed. minor (IG2), Berlin 1924–. Berlin-Brandenburgische Akademie der Wissenschaften.

KAI   H. Donner and W. Röllig, eds. 1964, 3rd ed. *Kanaanäische und Aramäische Inschriften.* 3 vols. Wiesbaden.

LIMC   *Lexicon Iconographicum Mythologiae Classicae,* 1981–2009. Zurich and Munich. http://www.limc-france.fr

OEAANE   E. Meyers, ed. 1997. *The Oxford Encyclopedia of Archaeology in the Ancient Near East.* New York.

SEG   *Supplementum Epigraphicum Graecum* I–XXV (J. J. E. Hondius et al., eds.) 1923–1971, Leiden; XXVI–XXVII and XXVIII–XIIL (H. W. Pleket et al., ed.) 1978–1979, Alphen; 1980–1995, Amsterdam.

꩜꩜꩜

Abulafia, D. 2011. *The Great Sea.* Oxford.

Agostiniani, L. 2013. "The Etruscan Language." In Turfa, *Etruscan World,* 457–477.

Albanese Procelli, R. M. 2016. "Gli indigeni della Sicilia tra la Prima e la Seconda Età del Ferro: Il contesto locale della 'prima colonizzazione." In Donnellan, Nizzo, and Brugers, *Contexts of Early Colonization,* 199–210.

Alberti, M. E., and S. Sabatini, eds. 2013. *Exchange Networks and Local Transformations: Interaction and Local Change in Europe and the Mediterranean from the Bronze Age to the Iron Age.* Oxford.

Alexandre, Y. 2002. "The Iron Age Assemblage from Cave 3 at Kefar Veradim." *Eretz Zafon:* 52–63.

Almagro-Gorbea, M. 2010. "Estatua-obelisco con capitel protoeólico de Villaricos." In *La escultural fenicia en Hispania,* edited by M. Amlagro-Gorbea and M. Torres Ortiz, 235–263. Madrid.

Alvar, J., and C. González Wagner. 1989. "Fenicios en Occidente: La colonización agrícola." *Rivista di Studi Fenici* 17: 61–102.

Álvarez Martí-Aguilar, M. 2010. "Tartesios: Un etnónimo de la Iberia púnica." *Mainake* 32: 395–406.

Álvarez Martí-Aguilar, M., ed. 2011. *Fenicios en Tartessos: Nuevas perspectivas.* Oxford.

Álvarez Martí-Aguilar, M. 2019. "The Tyre-Gadir Axis." In López-Ruiz and Doak, *Oxford Handbook,* 617–626.

Amadasi Guzzo, M. G. 1991. "'The Shadow Line': Réflexions sur l'introduction de l'alphabet en Grèce." In Baurain, Bonnet, and Krings, *Phoinikeia Grammata,* 293–312.

Amadasi Guzzo, M. G. 1999. "Sulla formazione e diffusione dell'alfabeto." In *Scritture mediterranee tra il IX e il VII secolo a.c.,* edited by G. Bagnasco Gianni and F. Cordano, 27–51. Milan.

Amadasi Guzzo, M. G. 2007. "Une lamelle magique à inscription phénicienne." *Vicino Oriente* 13: 197–206.

Amadasi Guzzo, M. G. 2014. "'Alphabet insaisissable': Quelques notes concernant la diffusion de l'écriture consonantique." *Transeuphratène* 44: 67–86.

Amadasi Guzzo, M. G. 2019. "The Language." In López-Ruiz and Doak, *Oxford Handbook,* 199–221.

Amadasi Guzzo, M. G., and J. A. Zamora. 2016. "L'archivio fenicio di Idalion: Stato delle ricerche." *Semitica et Classica* 9: 187–193.

Amadasi Guzzo, M. G., and J. A. Zamora. 2018. "The Phoenician Name of Cyprus: New Evidence from Early Hellenistic Times." *Journal of Semitic Studies* 63: 77–97.

Ambrosini, L., and L. Michetti. 2013. "L'ultima frequentazione del santuario meridionale: Testimonianze dai contesti." In *Riflessioni su Pyrgi: Scavi e ricerche nelle aree del santuario*, edited by P. Baglione and M. D. Gentili, 123–166. Rome.

Ammerman, R. M. 1991. "The Naked Standing Goddess: A Group of Archaic Terracotta Figurines from Paestum." *American Journal of Archaeology* 95: 203–230.

Ampolo, C. 2012. "Compresenza di ethne e culture diverse nella Sicilia occidentale: Per una nuova prospettiva storica." *Convivenze etniche, scontri e contatti di culture in Sicilia e Magna Grecia*, edited by F. Berlinzani, 15–57. Trento.

Antonaccio, C. 2002. "Warriors, Traders, Ancestors: The 'Heroes' of Lefkandi." *Images of Ancestors*, edited by J. M. Høtje, 13–42. Aarhus.

Antoniadis, V. 2017. *Knossos and the Near East: A Contextual Approach to Imports and Imitations in Early Iron Age Tombs.* Oxford.

Arrington, N. 2015. "Talismanic Practice at Lefkandi: Trinkets, Burials and Belief in the Early Iron Age." *Cambridge Classical Journal:* 1–30.

Arruda, A. M. 2000. *Los fenicios en Portugal: Fenicios y mundo indígena en el centro y sur de Portugal (siglos VIII–V a.C.).* Barcelona.

Arruda, A. M. 2009. "Phoenician Colonization on the Atlantic Coast of the Iberian Peninsula." In Dietler and López-Ruiz, *Colonial Encounters,* 114–130.

Arruda, A. M. 2011. "Indígenas, fenicios y tartésicos en el occidente peninsular: Mucha gente, poca tierra." In Álvarez Martí-Aguilar, *Fenicios en Tartessos,* 151–160.

Arruda, A. M. 2015. "Intercultural Contacts in the Far West at the Beginning of the 1st Millennium BC: Through the Looking-Glass." In Babbi et al., *Mediterranean Mirror,* 263–278.

Arruda, A. M. 2019. "Phoenicians in Portugal." In López-Ruiz and Doak, *Oxford Handbook,* 603–616.

Arruda, A. M., and S. Celestino. 2009. "Arquitectura religiosa en Tartessos." In *Santuarios, oppida y ciudades: La Arquitectura sacra en el origen y desarrollo urbano del Mediterráneo occidental*, edited by P. Mateos, S. Celestino, A. Pizzo, and T. Tortosa, 29–78. Madrid.

Aruz, J. 2016. "Introduction." In Aruz and Seymour, *Assyria to Iberia,* 3–11.

Aruz, J., S. B. Graff, and Y. Rakic, eds. 2014. *Assyria to Iberia at the Dawn of the Classical Age.* New Haven.

Aruz, J., and M. Seymour, eds. 2016. *Assyria to Iberia: Art and Culture in the Iron Age.* New York.

Arvidsson S. 2006. *Aryan Idols: Indo-European Mythology as Ideology and Science.* Chicago.

Ashcroft, B., G. Griffiths, and H. Tiffin. 1998. *Key Concepts in Post-Colonial Studies.* London.

Asheri, D., A. Lloyd, and A. Corcella. 2007. *A Commentary on Herodotus Books I–IV.* Oxford.

Aston, E. 2011. *Mixanthrôpoi: Animal-Human Hybrid Deities in Greek Religion.* Liège.

Astour, M. C. 1965. "The Origin of the Terms 'Canaanite,' 'Phoenician,' and 'Purple.'" *Journal of Near Eastern Studies* 24: 346–350.

Astour, M. C. 1967. *Hellenosemitica: An Ethnic and Cultural Study in West Semitic Impact on Mycenaean Greece.* 2nd ed. Leiden.

Astour, M. C. 1973. "Ugarit and the Aegean." In *Orient and Occident: Essays Presented to Cyrus Gordon on the Occasion of His Sixty-Fifth Birthday,* edited by H. A. Hoffner Jr., 17–27. Kevelaer.

Atack, C. 2015. "The Greeks in Sicily." In Burgersdijk et al., *Sicily and the Sea,* 39–45.

Aubet, M. E. 2001. *The Phoenicians and the West: Politics, Colonies, and Trade.* 2nd ed. Cambridge.

Aubet, M. E. 2006. "The Organization of the Phoenician Colonial System in Iberia." In Riva and Vella, *Debating Orientalization,* 94–109.

Aubet, M. E. 2008. "Political and Economic Implications of the New Phoenician Chronologies." In Sagona, *Beyond the Homeland,* 179–191.

Aubet, M. E. 2010. "The Phoenician Cemetery of Tyre." *Near Eastern Archaeology* 73: 144–155.

Aubet, M. E. 2012. "El barrio comercial fenicio como estrategia colonial." *Rivista di Studi Fenici* 40: 221–235.

Aubet, M. E. 2016. "Phoenician Politics in Colonial Context: Pyrgi Again." In Aruz and Seymour, *Assyria to Iberia,* 147–153.

Aubet, M. E. 2019. "Tyre and Its Colonial Expansion." In López-Ruiz and Doak, *Oxford Handbook,* 75–87.

Aubet, M. E., F. J. Núñez, and L. Tresilló. 2004. "La necrópolis fenicia de Tiro-Al Bass en el contexto funerario fenicio oriental." *Huelva Arqueológica* 20: 41–62.

Avigad, N., and Sass, B. 1997. *Corpus of West Semitic Stamp Seals.* Jerusalem.

Baaklini, A.-A. 2020. "The Presence and Influence of the Neo-Assyrian Empire in Phoenicia: Textual and Archaeological Evidence." In *Imperial Connections: Interactions and Expansion from Assyria to the Roman Period,* edited by K. Gavagnin and R. Palermo, 13–27. Trieste.

Babbi, A., F. Bubenheimer-Erhart, B. Marín-Aguilera, and S. Mühl, eds. 2015. *The Mediterranean Mirror: Cultural Contacts in the Mediterranean Sea between 1200 and 750 BC.* Mainz.

Bachvarova, M. 2016. *From Hittite to Homer: The Anatolian Background of Ancient Greek Epic.* Cambridge.

Bachvarova, M. 2023. "Methodology and Methods of Borrowing in Comparative Greek and Near Eastern Religion: The Case of Incense-Burning." In *The Intellectual Heritage of the Ancient Near East,* edited by R. Rollinger, I. Madreiter, M. Lang, and C. Pappi, 175–189. Vienna.

Baglione, M. P. 2008. "Esame del santuario meridionale di Pyrgi." In *Saturnia Tellus: Definizioni dello spazio consacrato in ambiente etrusco, italico, fenicio-punico, iberico e céltico,* edited by X. Dupré Raventós, S. Ribichini, and S. Verger, 301–318. Rome.

Baglione, M. P., B. B. Marchesini, C. Carlucci, M. D. Gentili, and L. M. Michetti. 2015. "Pyrgi: A Sanctuary in the Middle of the Mediterranean Sea." In Kistler et al., *Sanctuaries,* 221–237.

Bagnasco Gianni, G. 2013. "Massimo Pallotino's 'Origins' in Perspective." In Turfa, *Etruscan World,* 29–35.

Bahrani, Z. 2016. "Assyria to Iberia: Closing Remarks." In Aruz and Seymour, *Assyria to Iberia,* 324–329.

Balco, W. 2012. "Tri-Nodal Social Entanglements in Iron Age Sicily: Material and Social Transformation." *Journal of Collegiate Anthropology* 3: 24–35.

Bandera, M. L. de la. 2002. "Rituales de origen oriental entre las comunidades tartesias: el sacrificio de animales." In *Ex Oriente Lux: Las religiones orientales antiguas en la Península Ibérica,* edited by E. Ferrer, 141–158. Seville.

Bandera, M. L. de la, and E. Ferrer, eds. 2010. *El Carambolo: 50 años de un tesoro.* Seville.

Barletta, B. A. 2001. *The Origins of the Greek Architectural Orders.* Cambridge.

Barnett, R. D. 1935. "The Nimrud Ivories and the Art of the Phoenicians." *Iraq* 2: 179–210.

Barnett, R. D. 1939. "Phoenician and Syrian Ivory Carving I." *Palestine Exploration Quarterly* 1939: 4–19.

Barnett, R. D. 1948. "Early Greek and Oriental Ivories." *Journal of Hellenic Studies* 68: 1–25.

Barnett, R. D. 1957a. *A Catalogue of the Nimrud Ivories in the British Museum,* London.

Barnett, R. D. 1957b. "A Syrian Silver Vase [from Tell Qatine]." *Syria* 34: 243–248.

Barnett, R. D. 1982. *Ancient Ivories in the Middle East and Adjacent Countries.* Jerusalem.

Bartoloni, G. 2013. "The Villanovan Culture: at the Biginning of Etruscan History." In Turfa, *Etruscan World,* 79–98.

Bartoloni, P. 2004. "Per la cronologia dell'area urbana di Sulky." *Quaderni della Soprintendenza archeologica per le province di Cagliari e Oristano* 21: 51–55.

Bartoloni, P. 2017. "I Fenici dal Libano all'Atlantico." In Guirguis, *La Sardegna fenicia,* 31–38.

Batty, R. 2000. "Mela's Phoenician Geography." *Journal of Roman Studies* 90: 70–94.

Baurain, C., C. Bonnet, and V. Krings, eds. 1991. *Phoinikeia Grammata: Lire et écrire en Méditerranée.* Namur.

Bechtold, B., and R. Docter. 2010. "Transport Amphorae from Punic Carthage: An Overview." *Motya and the Phoenician Repertoire between the Levant and the West, 9th–6th Century BC,* edited by L. Nigro, 85–116. Rome.

Bedini, A., C. Tronchetti, G. Ugas, and R. Zucca. 2012. *Giganti di pietra: Monte Prama: L'Heroon che cambia la storia della Sardegna e del Mediterraneo.* Cagliari.

Beekes, R. S. 2004. "Kadmos and Europa, and the Phoenicians." *Kadmos* 43: 167–184.

Beekes, R. S. 2010. *Etymological Dictionary of Greek.* 2 vols. Leiden.

Belarte, M. C. 2009. "Colonial Contacts and Protohistoric Indigenous Urbanism on the Mediterranean Coast of the Iberian Peninsula." In Dietler and López-Ruiz, *Colonial Encounters*, 91–112.

Belén Deamos, M. 2009. "Phoenicians in Tartessos." In Dietler and López-Ruiz, *Colonial Encounters*, 193–228.

Belén Deamos, M., R. Anglada, J. L. Escacena, A. Jiménez, R. Lineros, and I. Rodríguez. 1997. *Arqueología en Carmona (Sevilla): Excavaciones en la Casa-Palacio del Marqués de Saltillo.* Seville.

Bell, C. 2016. "Phoenician Trade: The First 300 Years." In *Dynamics of Production in the Ancient Near East 1300–500 BC,* edited by J. C. Moreno García, 91–105. Oxford.

Bellelli, V. 2012. *Le origini degli Etruschi: Storia, archeologia, antropologia.* Rome.

Beltrán Lloris, F., B. Díaz Ariño, C. Jordán Cólera, and I. Simón Cornago. 2020. "*Tesseram conferre:* Etruscan, Greek, Latin, and Celtiberian *tesserae hospitales.*" *Historia* 69: 482–518.

Bendala, M. 1977. "Notas sobre las estelas decoradas del Suroeste y los orígenes de Tartessos." *Habis* 8: 177–205.

Bendala, M. 2013. "La génesis de Tarteso en la etapa 'precolonial' del segundo milenio: Notas para una discusión." In Campos Carrasco and Alvar Ezquerra, *Tarteso,* 123–135.

Ben Younès, H., and A. Krandel-Ben Younès. 2014. "Punic Identity in North Africa: The Funerary World." In Quinn and Vella, *Punic Mediterranean,* 148–168.

Bergquist, B. 1993. "Bronze Age Sacrificial Koine in the Eastern Mediterranean." In *Ritual and Sacrifice in the Ancient Near East,* edited by J. Quaegebeur, 11–43. Leuven.

Berman, D. W. 2004. "The Double Foundation of Boiotian Thebes." *Transactions of the American Philological Association* 134: 1–22.

Bernal, M. 1987 *Black Athena: The Afroasiatic Roots of Classical Civilisation. Vol. 1: The Fabrication of Ancient Greece 1785–1985.* London.

Bernal, M. 1990. *Cadmean Letters: The Transmission of the Alphabet to the Aegean and Further West before 1400 BC.* Winona Lake.

Bernardini, P. 1992. "La Facies orientalizzante in Sardegna: Problemi di individuazione e di metodologia." In *Sardinia in the Mediterranean: A Footprint in the Sea; Studies in Sardinian Archaeology Presented to Miriam S. Balmuth,* edited by R. H. Tykot and T. K. Andrews, 396–409. Sheffield.

Bernardini, P. 2005. "L'Orientalizzante in Sardegna: Modelli, cifrari, ideologie." In Celestino and Jiménez Ávila, *El Período Orientalizante,* 75–96.

Bernardini, P. 2011. "Necropoli della prima età del Ferro in Sardegna: Una riflessione su alcuni secoli perduti o, meglio, perduti di vista." In *Tharros Felix 4,* edited by A. Mastino, P. G. Spanu, A. Usai and R. Zucca, 351–386. Rome.

Bernardini, P. 2017. "La Sardegna prima dei Fenici: Micenei, Ciprioti e Filistei." In Guirguis, *La Sardegna fenicia,* 39–43.

Bernardini, P., and M. Botto 2010. "I bronzi 'fenici' della Penisola Italiana e della Sardegna." *Rivista di Studi Fenici* 38: 17–117.

Bernardini, P., and R. D'Oriano, eds. 2001. *Argyróphleps nesos: L'isola dalle vene d'argento; esploratori, mercanti e colonie in Sardegna tra il XIV e il VI sec. a.C.* Bondeno.

Bernardini, P., and M. Perra, eds. 2012. *I Nuragici, i Fenici e gli altri: Sardegna e Mediterraneo tra Bronzo Finale e Prima Età del Ferro.* Sassari.

Bernardini, P., P. G. Spanu, R. Zucca, eds. 2000. *La battaglia del Mare Sardonio: Studi e ricerche.* Cagliari.

Betancourt, P. P. 1971. "An Aeolic Shrine in Philadelphia." *American Journal of Archaeology* 75: 427–428.

Betancourt, P. P. 1977. *The Aeolic Style in Architecture: A Survey of Its Development in Palestine, the Halikarnassos Peninsula, and Greece, 1000–500 BC.* Princeton.

Betlyon, J. W. 1982. *The Coinage and Mints of Phoenicia: The Pre-Alexandrine Period.* Chico, CA.

Betlyon, J. W. 2019. "Coins." In López-Ruiz and Doak, *Oxford Handbook*, 385–400.

Bhabha, H. 1994. *The Location of Culture.* New York.

Biella, M. C., and E. Giovanelli. 2016. *Nuovi studi sul bestiario fantastico di età orientalizzante nella penisola italiana.* Trento.

Biella, M. C., and J. Tabolli, eds. 2016. *I Falisci attraverso lo specchio.* Rome.

Bikai, P. 1994. "The Phoenicians and Cyprus." In *Proceedings of the International Symposium: Cyprus in the 11th Century BC,* edited by V. Karageorghis, 31–37. Nicosia.

Bisi, M. 1988. "Terracotta Figures." In Moscati, *Phoenicians,* 328–353.

Black, J., and A. Green. 1992. *Gods, Demons and Symbols of Ancient Mesopotamia.* Austin.

Blake, E. 2014a. "Late Bronze Age Sardinia: Acephalous Cohesion." In *The Cambridge Prehistory of the Bronze and Iron Age Mediterranean,* edited by A. B. Knapp and P. van Dommelen, 96–108. New York.

Blake, E. 2014b. *Social Networks and Regional Identity in Bronze Age Italy.* New York.

Blakely, S. 2016. "Beyond Braudel: Network Models and a Samothracian Seascape." In Concannon and Mazurek, *Across the Corrupting Sea,* 17–38.

Blakely, S. and B. J. Collins, eds. 2019. *Religious Convergence in the Ancient Mediterranean.* Atlanta.

Blasetti Fantauzzi, C. 2018. *Tra Elimi e Greci: La ceramica di età arcaica dai contesti di fondazione della cinta muraria di Erice.* Rome.

Blasetti Fantauzzi, C., and S. De Vincenzo. 2012. "Die phönizischen Neugründungen auf Sizilien und Sardinien und die Problematik der Machtentstehung Karthagos." *Kölner und Bonner Archaeologica* 2: 5–30.

Boardman, J. 1968. *Archaic Greek Gems.* London.

Boardman, J. 1990a. "Al Mina and History." *Oxford Journal of Archaeology* 9: 169–190.

Boardman, J. 1990b. "The Lyre-Player Group of Seals: An Encore." *Archäologischer Anzeiger* 1990: 1–17.

Boardman, J. 1998. *Early Greek Vase Painting: 11th–6th BC: A Handbook.* London.

Boardman, J. 1999a. *The Greeks Overseas: Their Early Colonies and Trade.* 4th ed. London.

Boardman, J. 1999b. "The Excavated History of Al Mina." In Tsetskhladze, *Ancient Greeks West and East,* 135–161.

Boardman, J. 2001a. "Aspects of 'Colonization.'" *Bulletin of the American Schools of Oriental Research* 322: 33–42.

Boardman, J. 2001b. *Cyprus between East and West.* Nicosia.

Boardman, J. 2002. "Al Mina: The Study of a Site." *Ancient West and East* 1: 315–331.

Boardman, J. 2003. *Classical Phoenician Scarabs: A Catalogue and Study.* Oxford.

Boardman, J. 2004. "Copies of Pottery: By and for Whom?" In *Greek Identity in the Western Mediterranean: Papers in Honour of Brian Shefton,* edited by K. Lomas, 149–162. Leiden.

Boardman, J. 2005. "Al Mina: Notes and Queries." *Ancient West and East* 4: 278–291.

Boardman, J. 2006. "Sources and Models." In *Greek Sculpture: Function, Materials, and Techniques in the Archaic and Classical Periods,* edited by O. Palagia, 1–31. Cambridge.

Boardman, J. 2016. "The Ages of Heroes: Greeks and Phoenicians on the Wine-Dark Sea." In Aruz and Seymour, *Assyria to Iberia,* 206–215.

Böhm, S. 2007. *Dädalische Kunst Siziliens.* Würzburg.

Bonadies, L. 2017. "La presenza fenicia in Egitto: Il caso di Naukratis." *Folia Phoenicia* 1: 33–38.

Bonanno, A. 2005. *Malta: Phoenician, Punic and Roman.* Valletta.

Bondi, S. F. 2001. "The Origins in the East." In Moscati, *Phoenicians* (2nd ed., London), 23–29.

Bonnet, C., E. Lipiński, and P. Marchetti, eds. 1986. *Religio Phoenicia.* Namur.

Bonfante, G., and L. Bonfante. 2002. *The Etruscan Language: An Introduction.* 2nd ed. Lancaster.

Bonfante, L., and V. Karageorghis, eds. 2001. *Italy and Cyprus in Antiquity 1500–450 BC.* Nicosia.

Bonfante, L., and J. Swaddling. 2006. *Etruscan Myths.* London.

Bonnet, C. 2015. *Les enfants de Cadmos: Le paysage religieux de la Phénicie hellénistique.* Paris.

Bonnet, C., and P. Xella. 1995. "La religion." In Krings, *La civilisation phénicienne,* 316–333.

Botto, M. 2002. "I contatti fra le colonie fenicie di Sardegna e l'Etruria settentrionale." In Paoletti and Tamagno, *Etruria e Sardegna,* 226–247.

Botto, M. 2004–2005. "Da Sulky a Huelva: Considerazioni sui commerci fenici nel Mediterraneo antico." *AION* 11–12: 9–27.

Botto, M. 2005. "Considerazioni sul periodo orientalizzante nella peninsola italica: La documentazione del *Latium Vetus.*" In Celestino and Jiménez Ávila, *El Período Orientalizante,* 47–74.

Botto, M. 2008. "I primi contatti fra i fenici e le popolazioni dell'Italia Peninsulare." In Celestino and Jiménez Ávila, *El Período Orientalizante,* 123–148.

Botto, M. 2010. "La ceramica fenicia dall'Etruria e dal Latium Vetus." In *Motya and the Phoenician Ceramic Repertoire between the Levant and the West 9th–6th Century BC,* edited by L. Nigro, 152–171. Rome.

Botto, M. 2011. "Le più antiche presenze fenicie nell'Italia meridionale." In *Fenici e Italici, Cartagine e la Magna Grecia: popolo a contatto, cuture a confronto,* edited by M. Intrieri and S. Ribichini, 157–179. Pisa.

Botto, M. 2012. "I Fenici e la formazione delle aristocrazie tirreniche." In Bernardini and Perra, *I nuragici,* 51–80.

Botto, M. 2013. "The Phoenicians and the Spread of Wine in the Central West Mediterranean." In Celestino and Blánquez, *Patrimonio cultural,* 103–131.

Botto, M., ed. 2014. *Los fenicios en la Bahía de Cádiz: Nuevas investigaciones.* Rome.

Botto, M. 2016. "The Phoenicians in the Central-West Mediterranean and Atlantic beteeen 'Precolonization' and the 'First Colonization.'" In Donellan, Nizzo, and Burgers, *Contexts of Early Colonization,* 289–309.

Botto, M. 2017a. "La Sardegna lungo le rotte dell'Occidente fenicio." In Guirguis, *La Sardegna fenicia,* 73–77.

Botto, M. 2017b. "The Diffusion of Near Eastern cultures." In Naso, *Etruscology,* 581–616.

Bourogiannis, G. 2012a. "Pondering the Cypro-Phoenician Conundrum: The Aegean View of a Bewildering Term." In Iacovou, *Cyprus and the Aegean,* 183–206.

Bourogiannis, G. 2012b. "Introduction to the Phoenician Problematic." In *Greeks and Phoenicians at the Mediterranean Crossroads,* edited by P. Adam-Veleni and E. Stefani, 37–41 (Greek 31–36). Thessaloniki.

Bourogiannis, G. 2018a. "The Transmission of the Alphabet to the Aegean." In Niesiołowski-Spanò and Węcowski, *Change, Continuity, and Connectivity,* 235–257.

Bourogiannis, G. 2018b. "The Phoenician Presence in the Aegean during the Early Iron Age: Trade, Settlement, and Cultural Interaction." *Rivista di Studi Fenici* 46: 43–88.

Bourogiannis, G., and C. Mühlenbock, eds. 2016. *Ancient Cyprus Today: Museum Collections and New Research.* Uppsala.

Boyd, T., and M. Jameson. 1981. "Urban and Rural Land Division in Ancient Greece." *Hesperia* 50: 327–342.

Bowie, E. 1998. "Phoenician Games in Heliodorus' *Aithiopika.*" In *Studies in Heliodorus,* edited by R. Hunter, 1–18. Cambridge.

Braudel, F. 1972 (1st ed. French 1949). *The Mediterranean and the Mediterranean World in the Age of Philip II.* London.

Bremmer, J. 2008. *Greek Religion and Culture, the Bible and the Ancient Near East.* Leiden.

Bresson, A. 2018. "Flexible Interfaces of the Ancient Mediterranean World." In Gailledrat, Dietler, and Plana-Mallart, *Emporion,* 35–46.

Bresson, A., and P. Rouillard, eds. 1993. *L'emporion.* Paris.

Bridoux, V. 2014. "Numidia and the Punic World." In Quinn and Vella, *Punic Mediterranean,* 180–201.

Briquel, D. 1991. "L'écriture étrusque d'après les inscriptions du VIIe s. av. J.-C." In Baurain, Bonnet, and Krings, *Phoinikeia Grammata,* 615–632.

Briquel, D. 2013. "Etruscan Origins and the Ancient Authors." In Turfa, *Etruscan World,* 36–55.

Briquel-Chatonnet, F., and E. Gubel. 1998. *Les Phéniciens aux origins du Liban.* Paris.

Brisart, T. 2011. *Un art citoyen: Recherches sur l'orientalization des artisanats en Grèce proto-archaïque.* Brussels.

Brocato, P., and C. Regoli. 2009. "Iconografie orientali nei calici a sostegni in bucchero etruschi." *Rivista di Studi Fenici* 37: 199–212.

Brody, A. J. 2008. "The Specialized Religions of Ancient Mediterranean Seafarers." *Religion Compass* 2: 444–454.

Brøns, C. 2014. "Representation and Realities: Fibulas and Pins in Greek and Near Eastern Iconography." *Greek and Roman Textiles and Dress: An Interdisciplinary Anthology,* edited by M. Harlow and M.-L. Nosch, 60–94. Oxford.

Broodbank, C. 2013. *The Making of the Middle Sea.* Oxford.

Brown, J. P. 1995–2000–2001. *Israel and Hellas.* 3 vols. Berlin.

Brown, A. R. and R. Smith. 2019. "Guardian Goddess of the Surf-Beaten Shore: The Influence of Mariners on Sanctuaries of Aphrodite in Magna Graecia." In Blakely and Collins, *Religious Convergence,* 19–41.

Bryce, T. 2002. *Life and Society in the Hittite World.* Oxford.

Buchner, G., and D. Ridgway. 1993. *Pithekoussai 1: La necropoli; tombe 1–723 scavate dal 1952–1961.* Rome.

Buck, M. E. 2019. *The Canaanites: Their History and Culture from Texts and Artifacts.* Eugene.

Buck, M. E. 2020. *The Amorite Dynasty of Ugarit: Historical Implications of Linguistic and Archaeological Parallels.* Leiden.

Bunnens, G. 1978. "La mission d'Ounamon en Phénicie: Point de vue d'un non-égyptologue." *Rivista di Studi Fenici* 6: 1–16.

Bunnens, G. 1979. *L'expansion phénicienne en Méditerranée: Essai d'interprétation fondé sur une analyse des traditions littéraires.* Brussels.

Bunnens, G. 2019. "Phoenicia in the Later Iron Age: Tenth Century BCE to the Assyrian and Babylonian Periods." In López-Ruiz and Doak, *Oxford Handbook,* 57–73.

Burgersdijk, D., R. Calis, J. Kelder, A. Sofroniew, S. Tusa, and R. van Beek, eds. 2015. *Sicily and the Sea.* Zwolle.

Burkert, W. 1983. "Itinerant Diviners and Magicians: A Neglected Element in Cultural Contacts." In *The Greek Renaissance of the Eighth Century B.C.: Tradition and Innovation,* edited by R. Hägg, 115–119. Stockholm.

Burkert, W. 1985. *Greek Religion.* Cambridge, MA.

Burkert, W. 1987. "Oriental and Greek Mythology: The Meeting of Parallels." In *Interpretations of Greek Mythology,* edited by J. Bremmer, 10–40. London.

Burkert, W. 1992. (German 1984). *The Orientalizng Revolution: Near Eastern Influence on Greek Culture in the Early Archaic Period.* Cambridge, MA.

Burkert, W. 2003. "La via fenicia e la via anatolica: Ideologie e scoperte fra Oriente e Occidente." In *Kleine Schriften II: Orientalia,* edited by M. L. Gemelli Marciano, 252–266. Göttingen.

Burkert, W. 2004. *Babylon, Memphis, Persepolis: Eastern Contexts of Greek Culture*. Cambridge, MA.

Burnett, J. S. 2016. "Ammon, Moab, and Edom: Gods and Kingdoms East of the Jordan." *Biblical Archaeology Review* 42: 26–40.

Campos Carrasco, J., and J. Alvar Ezquerra, eds. 2013. *Tarteso: El emporio del metal*. Córdoba.

Camporeale, G. 2013. "Foreign Artists in Etruria." In Turfa, *Etruscan World*, 885–902.

Carbillet, A. 2011. *La figure hathorique à Chypre (IIe–Ier Mill. Av. J.-C.)*. Münster.

Carpenter, R. 1958. "Phoenicians in the West." *American Journal of Archaeology* 62: 35–53.

Carter, J. B. 1985. *Greek Ivory-Carving in the Orientalizing and Archaic Periods*. New York.

Carter, J. B. 1987. "The Masks of Ortheia." *American Journal of Archaeology* 91: 355–383.

Carter, J. B. 1988. "Isotopic Analysis of Seventh-Century B.C. Perirrhanteria." In *Classical Marble: Geochemistry, Technology, Trade,* edited by N. Herz and M. Waelkens, 419–431. Dordrecht.

Carter, J. B. 1997. "*Thiasos* and *Marzeah*: Ancestor Cult in the Age of Homer." In Langdon, *New Light*, 72–112.

Carter, J. B. 1998. "Egyptian Bronze Jugs from Crete and Lefkandi." *Journal of Hellenic Studies* 118: 172–177.

Carter, J. B., and S. P. Morris, eds. 1995. *The Ages of Homer: A Tribute to Emily Townsend Vermeule*. Austin.

Carter, J. B., and L. J. Steinberg. 2010. "Kouroi and Statistics." *American Journal of Archaeology* 114: 103–128.

Casado, M. 2014. "Los objetos de hueso y marfil." In *La Necrópolis de época tartésica de la Angorrilla: Alcalá del Río: Sevilla,* edited by A. Fernández Flores, A. Rodríguez Azogue, M. Casado, and E. Prados, 481–508. Seville.

Casado, M. 2016. *La cerámica con decoración geométrica del Carambolo*. Seville.

Castleden, R. 2005. *Mycenaeans*. London.

Catling, H. W. 1977. "The Knossos Area, 1974–76." *Archaeological Reports* 23: 3–23.

Caubet, A. 1979. "Las maquettes architecturales d'Idalion." In *Studies Presented in Memory of Porphyrios Dikaios,* edited by V. Karageorghis, 94–118. Nicosia.

Caubet, A. 1986. "Les sanctuaires de Kition à l'epoque de la dynastie phénicienne." In Bonnet, Lipiński, and Marchetti, *Religio Phoenicia*, 153–168.

Caubet, A. 2014a. "Tridacna Shell." In Aruz, Graff, and Rakic, *Assyria to Iberia at the Dawn*, 163–166.

Caubet, A. 2014b. "Phoenician and East Mediterranean Glass." In Aruz, Graff, and Rakic, *Assyria to Iberia at the Dawn*, 167–170.

Celestino, S. 1997. "Santuarios, centros comerciales y paisajes sacros." *Quaderns de prehistòria i arqueologia de Castelló* 18: 359–390.

Celestino, S. 2001. *Estelas de guerrero y estelas diademadas: La precolonización y la formación del mundo tartésico*. Barcelona.

Celestino, S. 2009. "Precolonization and Colonization in the Interior of Tartes-sos." In Dietler and López-Ruiz, *Colonial Encounters,* 229–251.

Celestino, S., and J. Blánquez, eds. 2013. *Patrimonio cultural de la vid y el vino.* Madrid.

Celestino, S., and J. Jiménez Ávila, eds. 2005. *El Período Orientalizante.* Mérida.

Celestino, S., and C. López-Ruiz. 2006. "New Light on the Warrior Stelae from Tartessos (Spain)." *Antiquity* 80: 89–101.

Celestino, S., and C. López-Ruiz. 2016. *Tartessos and the Phoenicians in Iberia.* Oxford.

Celestino, S., N. Rafel, and X. L. Armada, eds. 2008. *Contacto cultural entre el Mediterráneo y el Atlántico (siglos XII–VIII ane): La Precolonización a debate.* Madrid.

Cerasuolo, O. 2016. "The Orientalizing Period: Material and Cultural Connec-tions." In de Grummond and Pieraccini, *Caere,* 27–39.

Chadwick, J. 1990. "The Pech-Maho Lead." *Zeitschrift für Papyrologie und Epigraphik* 82: 161–166.

Chantraine, P. 1984–1990. *Dictionnaire étymologique de la langue grecque: Histoire des mots.* Paris.

Chapman, R. 2017. "Samaria: Capital of Israel." *Biblical Archaeology Review* 43: 24–30, 63.

Christian, M. A. 2013. "Phoenician Maritime Religion: Sailors, Goddess Worship, and the Grotta Regina." *Die Welt des Orients* 43: 179–205.

Ciasca, A. 1961. "I capitelli a volute in Palestina." *Rivista degli studi orientali* 36: 189–197.

Ciasca, A. 1962. *Il capitello detto eolico in Etruria.* Florence.

Clay, J. S., I. Malkin, and Y. Tzifopoulos. 2017. *Panhellenes at Methone: Graphe in Late Geometric and Protoarchaic Methone, Macedonia (ca. 700 BCE).* Berlin.

Cline, E. H. 2014. *1177 BC: The Year Civilization Collapsed.* Princeton.

Coldstream, N. 1968. *Greek Geometric Pottery.* London.

Coldstream, N. 1982. "Greeks and Phoenicians in the Aegean." In *Phönizier im Westen,* edited by H. G. Niemeyer, 261–275. Meinz.

Coldstream, N. 1993. "Mixed Marriages at the Frontiers of the Early Greek World." *Oxford Journal of Archaeology* 12: 89–107.

Coldstream, N. 1998. "The First Exchanges between Euboeans and Phoenicians: Who Took the Initiative?" In Gitin, Mazar, and Stern, *Mediterranean Peoples,* 353–360.

Coldstream, N. 2003 (1st ed. 1977). *Geometric Greece: 900–700 BC.* London.

Coldstream, N. 2007. "Foreigners at Lefkandi?" In Mazarakis Ainian, *Oropos and Euboea,* 135–139.

Coldstream, N. 2008. "Early Greek Exports to Phoenicia and the East Mediter-ranean." In *Networking Patterns of the Bronze and Iron Age Levant: The Lebanon and Its Mediterranean Connections,* edited by C. Doumet-Serhal, 167–188. Beirut.

Coldstream, N., and A. Mazar. 2003. "Greek Pottery from Tel Rehov and Iron Age Chronology." *Israel Exploration Journal* 53: 29–48.

Collignon, M., and J. H. Wright. 1886. *A Manual of Greek Archaeology*. New York.

Colvin, S. 2007. *A Historical Greek Reader: Mycenaean to the Koiné*. Oxford.

Comaroff, J. L., and J. Comaroff. 2009. *Ethnicity, Inc.* Chicago.

Concannon, C., and L. A. Mazurek, eds. 2016. *Across the Corrupting Sea: Post-Braudelian Approaches to the Ancient Eastern Mediterranean*. London.

Conze, A. 1870. *Zur Geschichte der Anfänge griechischer Kunst*. Vienna.

Cook, R. M. 1972. *Greek Painted Pottery*. 2nd ed. London.

Cornell, T. J. 1995. *The Beginnings of Rome: Italy and Rome from the Bronze Age to the Punic Wars (c. 1000–264 BC)*. London.

Correa, J. A. 2005. "Del alfabeto fenicio al semisilabario paleohispánico." *Acta Palaeohispanica* 9 (*Palaeohispanica* 5): 137–154.

Correia, V. H. 1996. *A epigrafía da Idade do Ferro do Sudoeste da Península Ibérica*. Porto.

Costa, B. 2019. "Ibiza." In López-Ruiz and Doak, *Oxford Handbook*, 569–582.

Costa, B., and J. H. Fernández, eds. 2012. *Sal, pesca y salazones fenicios en Occidente*. Ibiza.

Crielaard, J. P. 2016. "Living Heroes: Metal Urn Cremations in Early Iron Age Greece, Cyprus and Italy." In *Omero: Quaestiones disputata*, edited by F. Gallo, 43–78. Milan.

Cruz Andreotti, G. ed. 2019. *Roman Turdetania: Romanization, Identity and Socio-cultural Interaction in the South of the Iberian Peninsula between the 4th and 1st Centuries BCE*. Leiden.

Csapo, E., A. W. Johnston, and D. Geagan. 2000. "The Iron Age Inscriptions." In Shaw and Shaw, *Kommos IV*, 101–134.

Culican, W. 1973. "Phoenician Jewelry in New York and Copenhagen." *Berytus* 22: 31–52.

Culican, W. 1976. "A Terracorra Shrine from Achziv." *Zeitschrift des Deutschen Palästina-Vereins* (1953–) 92: 47–53.

Cuozzo, M. 2016. "Theoretical Issues in the Interpretation of Cemeteries and Case Studies from Etruria to Campania." In *Burial and Social Change in First-Millennium BC Italy: Approaching Social Agents; Gender, Personhood and Marginality*, edited by E. Perego and R. Scopacasa, 3–30. Oxford.

Curbera, J. 1997 "Chthonians in Sicily." *Greek, Roman, and Byzantine Studies* 38: 397–408.

Currie, B. 2016. *Homer's Allusive Art*. Oxford.

Cyrino, M. S. 2010. *Aphrodite: Gods and Heroes of the Ancient World*. London.

D'Agostino, B. 2011. "Pithecusae e Cuma nel quadro della Campania di età arcaica." *Mitteilungen des Deutschen Archäologischen Insituts, Römische abteilung* 177: 35–53.

D'Oriano, R. 2012. "Olbia greca: Il contesto di via Cavour." *Ricerca e confronti 2010: Atti*, 183–199. Cagliari.

D'Oriano, R. 2013. "Phoenician and Punic Sardinia and the Etruscans." In Turfa, *Etruscan World*, 231–243.

D'Oriano, R., and I. Oggiano. 2005. "Iolao ecista di Olbia: Le evidenze archeologiche tra VIII e VI secolo a.C." In *Il Mediterraneo di Herakles: Studi e ricerche*, edited by P. Bernardini and R. Zucca, 169–199. Rome.

Daniels, P. T. 1990. "Fundamentals of Grammatology." *Journal of the American Oriental Society* 110: 727–731.

Dawkins, R. M. 1929. *The Sanctuary of Artemis Ortheia at Sparta*. London.

De Angelis, F. 1998. "Ancient Past, Imperial Present: The British Empire in T. J. Dunbabin's *The Western Greeks*." *Antiquity* 72: 539–549.

De Angelis, F. 2016. *Archaic and Classical Greek Sicily: A Social and Economic History*. Oxford.

de Grummond, N. T. 2006. *Etruscan Myth, Sacred History, and Legend*. Philadelphia.

de Grummond, N. T. 2013. "Haruspicy and Augury: Sources and Procedures." In Turfa, *Etruscan World*, 539–556.

de Grummond, N. T., and L. C. Pieraccini, eds. 2016. *Caere*. Austin.

de Hoz, J. 1991. "The Phoenician Origin of the Early Hispanic Scripts." In Baurain, Bonnet, and Krings, *Phoinikeia Grammata*, 669–682.

de Hoz, J. 2005a. "La recepción de la escritura en Hispania como fenómeno orientalizante." In Celestino and Jiménez Ávila, *El Período Orientalizante*, 363–381.

de Hoz, J. 2005b. "La recepción de la escritura consonántica fenicia en Grecia." In *La escritura y el libro en la Antigüedad*, edited by J. Bartolomé, M. A. González, and M. Quijada, 37–54. Madrid.

de Hoz, J. 2013. "Aristocracia tartesia y escritura." In Campos Carrasco and Alvar Ezquerra, *Tarteso*, 529–539.

De Puma, R. D. 2016. "Gold and Ivory." In de Grummond and Pieraccini, *Caere*, 196–208.

De Rosa, E. Garau, and M. Rendeli. 2018. "Interaction by Design: Relation between Carthage and North Western Sardinia." In *Cartagine fuori da Cartagine: Mobilità nordafricana del Mediterraneo centro-occidentale fra VIII e II sec. A.C.*, edited by A. Chiara Fariselli and R. Secci, 49–78. Ravenna.

De Vincenzo, S. 2013. *Tra Cartagine e Roma: I centri urbani dell'eparchia punica di Sicilia tra VI e I sec. a.C.* Berlin.

De Vincenzo, S. 2019. "Sicily." In López-Ruiz and Doak, *Oxford Handbook*, 537–552.

Delgado, A. 2008. "Alimentos, poder e identidad en las comunidades fenicias occidentales." *Cuadernos de Prehistoria y Arqueología de la Universidad de Granada* 18: 163–188.

Delgado, A. 2012. "Producción artesanal y trabajo femenino en las comunidades fenicias occidentales: Una mirada crítica a la teoría de las esferas separadas." In *Los trabajos de las mujeres en el mundo antiguo: Cuidado y mantenimiento de la vida*, edited by A. Delgado and M. Picazo, 67–161. Tarragona.

Delgado, A. 2017. "'Colonialismos' fenicios en el sur de Iberia: Historias precedentes y modos de contacto." In *De Tartessos a Manila: Siete estudios coloniales y poscoloniales*, edited by G. Cano and A. Delgado, 19–49. Valencia.

Delgado, A., and M. Ferrer. 2012. "Life and Death in Ancient Colonies: Domesticity, Material Culture and Sexual Politics in the Western Phoenician World, Eighth to Sixth Centuries BCE." In *The Archaeology of Colonialism: Intimate*

Encounters and Sexual Effects, edited by B. Voss and E. C. Casella, 195–213. New York.

Demetriou, D. 2011. "What Is an Emporion? A Reasessment." *Historia: Zeitschrift für Alte Geschichte* 60: 255–272.

Demetriou, D. 2012. *Negotiating Identity in the Ancient Mediterranean: The Archaic and Classical Greek Multiethnic Emporia.* Cambridge.

Demetriou, D. Forthcoming. "Phoenicians." In *The Herodotus Encyclopaedia,* edited by C. Baron. Malden.

Demetriou, D. 2023. *Phoenicians Among Others: Why Migrants Mattered in the Ancient Mediterranean.* Oxford and New York.

Demsky, A. 2022. "The First Arslan Tash Incantation and the Sphinx." In *Biblical and Ancient Near Eastern Studies in Honor of P. Kyle McCarter,* edited by C. Rollston, S. Garfein, N. Walls, and R. Byrne, 331–346. Atlanta.

Dever, W. G. 1982. "Monumental Architecture in Ancient Israel in the Period of the United Monarchy." In *Studies in the Period of David and Solomon and Other Essays,* edited by T. Ishida, 269–306. Winona Lake.

Díaz-Andreu, M. 2018. "Archaeology and Imperialism: From Nineteenth-Century New Imperialism to Twentieth-Century Decolonization." In Effros and Lai, *Unmasking Ideology,* 3–28.

Dietler, M. 1998. "Consumption, Agency, and Cultural Entanglement: Theoretical Implications of a Mediterranean Colonial Encounter." In *Studies in Culture Contact: Interactions, Culture, Change, and Archaeology,* edited by J. G. Cusick, 288–315. Carbondale.

Dietler, M. 2009. "Colonial Encounters in Iberia and the Western Mediterranean: An Exploratory Framework." In Dietler and López-Ruiz, *Colonial Encounters,* 3–48.

Dietler, M. 2010. *Archaeologies of Colonialism: Consumption, Entanglement, and Violence in Ancient Mediterranean France.* Berkeley.

Dietler, M. 2018. "Emporia: Spaces of Encounter and Entanglement." In Gailledrat, Dietler, and Plana-Mallart, *Emporion,* 231–242.

Dietler, M., and C. López-Ruiz, eds. 2009. *Colonial Encounters in Ancient Iberia: Phoenician, Greek, and Indigenous Relations.* Chicago.

Doak, B. R. 2015. *Phoenician Aniconism in Its Mediterranean and Near Eastern Contexts.* Atlanta.

Doak, B. R. 2019a. *Heroic Bodies in Ancient Israel.* Oxford.

Doak, B. R. 2019b. "Phoenicians in the Hebrew Bible." In López-Ruiz and Doak, *Oxford Handbook,* 657–670.

Docter, R. F. 2000. "Pottery, Graves and Ritual 1: Phoenicians of the First Generation in Pithekoussai." In *La ceramica Fenicia di Sardegna, dati, problematiche, confronti,* edited by P. Bartoloni and L. Campanella, 135–149. Rome.

Docter, R. F. 2014. "The Phoenician Practice of Adapting Greek Drinking Vessels (Skyphoi and Kotylai)." In *El problema de las "imitaciones" durante la protohistoria en el Mediterráneo centro-occidental: Entre el concepto y el ejemplo,* edited by R. Graells i Fabregat, M. Krueger, S. Sardà, and G. Sciotino, 65–71. Tübingen.

Docter, R. F. 2019. "Residential Architecture." In López-Ruiz and Doak, *Oxford Handbook,* 435–452.

Docter, R. F., F. Chelbi, B. Maraoui Telmini, A. J. Nijboer, J. van der Plicht, W. van Neer, K. Mansel, and S. Garsallah. 2008. "New Radiocarbon Dates from Carthage: Bridging the Gap between History and Archaeology?" In Sagona, *Beyond the Homeland,* 379–422.

Docter, R. F., and Niemeyer, H. G. 1994. "Pithekoussai: The Carthaginian Connection. On the Archaeological Evidence of Euboeo-Phoenician Partnership in the 8th and 7th Centuries BC." In *Apiokia: I piu antichi insediamenti greci in occidente; funzioni e modi dell'organizzazione politica e sociale,* edited by B. D'Agostino, D. Ridgway, and G. Buchner, 101–115. Naples.

Domínguez Monedero, A. 2002. "Greeks in Iberia: Colonialism without Colonization." In Lyons and Papadopoulos, *Archaeology of Colonialism,* 65–95.

Donnellan, L., V. Nizzo, and G.-J. Burgers, eds. 2016a. *Conceptualising Early Colonization.* Turnhout.

Donnellan, L., V. Nizzo, and G.-J. Burgers, eds. 2016b. *Contexts of Early Colonization.* Rome.

Dougherty, C. 2001. *The Raft of Odysseus: The Ethnographic Imagination of Homer's* Odyssey. Oxford.

Doumet-Serhal, C. 2019. "Phoenician Identity in Modern Lebanon." In López-Ruiz and Doak, *Oxford Handbook,* 713–728.

Dowden, K. 2001. "West on East: Martin West's *East Face of Helicon* and Its Forerunners." *Journal of Hellenic Studies* 121: 168–169.

Dowden, K. 2007. "Olympian Gods, Olympian Pantheon." *A Companion to Greek Religion,* edited by D. Ogden, 41–55. Malden.

Dridi, H. 2019. "Early Carthage: From Its Foundation to the Battle of Himera (ca. 814–480 BCE)." In López-Ruiz and Doak, *Oxford Handbook,* 141–154.

Dunbabin, T. J. 1948a. *The Western Greeks: The History of Sicily and South Italy from the Foundation of the Greek Colonies to 480 BCE.* Oxford.

Dunbabin, T. J. 1948b. "The Early History of Corinth." *Journal of Hellenic Studies* 68: 59–69.

Echevarría Sánchez, A., and J. C. Vera Rodríguez. 2015. "Los inicios de la viticultura en la Península Ibérica a partir de las huellas de cultivo." In *Historia y arqueología en la cultura del vino,* edited by R. F. Verde, 57–68. Logroño.

Edlund-Berry, I. 2013. "Religion: The Gods and the Places." In Turfa, *Etruscan World,* 557–565.

Edrey, M. 2019. *Phoenician Identity in Context: Material Cultural Koiné in the Iron Age Levant.* Münster.

Edwards, R. B. 1979. *Kadmos the Phoenician: A Study in Greek Legends and the Mycenaean Age.* Amsterdam.

Effros, B. 2018. "Indigenous Voices at the Margins: Nuancing the History of Frrench Colonial Archaeology in Nineteenth-Century Algeria." In Effros and Lai, *Unmasking Ideology,* 201–225.

Effros, B., and G. Lai., eds. 2018. *Unmasking Ideology in Imperial and Colonial Archaeology.* Los Angeles.

Eichler, R. 2015. "Cherub: A History of Interpretation." *Biblica* 96: 26–38.

Elayi, J. 2018 (French 2013). *The History of Phoenicia.* Atlanta.

Ellison, J. L. 2014. "The Ugaritic Alphabetic Script." In *"An Eye for Form": Epigraphic Essays in Honor of Frank Moore Cross,* edited by J. A. Hackett and W. E. Aufrecht, 56–71. Winona Lake.

Emanuel, J. 2019. "Seafaring and Shipwreck Archaeology." In López-Ruiz and Doak, *Oxford Handbook,* 423–433.

Escacena, J. L., and M. Coto. 2010. "Altares para la eternidad." *SPAL* 19: 149–185.

Eshel, T., Y. Erel, N. Yahalom-Mack, O. Tirosh, and A. Gilboa. 2019. "Lead Isotopes in Silver Reveal Earliest Phoenician Quest for Metals in the West Mediterranean." *PNAS* 116: 6007–6012.

Faegersten, F. 2003. *The Egyptianizing Male Limestone Statuary from Cyprus: A Study of a Cross-Cultural Eastern Mediterranean Votive Type.* Lund.

Falsone, G. 1970. "La statua fenicio-cipriota dello Stagnone." *Sicilia Archaeologica* 10: 54–61.

Famà, M. L., and V. Tusa, eds. 2000. *Le stele del Meilichios di Selinunte.* Padova.

Fantalkin, A. 2006. "Identity in the Making: Greeks in the Eastern Mediterranean during the Iron Age." In *Naukratis,* edited by A. Villing and U. Schlotzhauer, 199–208. London.

Fantar, M. H. 1998. "De l'agriculture à Carthage." *Africa Romana* 12: 113–121.

Fantuzzi, L., E. Kiriatzi, A. M. Sáez Romero, N. S. Müller, and C. K. Williams II. 2020. "Punic Amphorae Found at Corinth: Provenance Analysis and Implications for the Study of Long-Disance Salt Fish Trade in the Classical Period." *Archaeological and Anthropological Sciences* 12: 1–21.

Feeney, D. 2016. *Beyond Greek: The Beginnings of Latin Literature.* Cambridge, MA.

Feldman, M. 2014. *Communities of Style: Portable Luxury Arts, Identity, and Collective Memory in the Iron Age Levant.* Chicago.

Feldman, M. 2016. "Consuming the East: Near Eastern Luxury Goods in Orientalizing Context." In Aruz and Seymour, *Assyria to Iberia,* 227–233.

Feldman, M. 2019. "Levantine Art in the 'Orientalizing' Period." In López-Ruiz and Doak, *Oxford Handbook,* 371–383.

Fentress, E., and R. Docter. 2008. "North Africa: Rural Settlement and Agricultural Production." In van Dommelen and Gómez Bellard, *Rural Landscapes,* 101–128.

Fernández Götz, A. 2007. "¿Celtas en Andalucía? Mirada historiográfica sobre una problemática (casi) olvidada." *SPAL* 16: 173–185.

Fibiger Bang, P., and W. Scheidel, eds. 2013. *Oxford Handbook of the State in the Ancient Near East and Mediterranean.* Oxford.

Finkelberg, M. 2005. *Greeks and Pre-Greeks: Aegean Prehistory and Greek Heroic Tradition.* Cambridge.

Finkelstein, I. 2000. "Omride Architecture." *Zeitschrift des Deutschen Palästina-Vereins* 116: 114–138.

Finkelstein, I., and A. Mazar. 2007. *The Quest for Historical Israel: Archaeology and the History of Early Israel.* Atlanta.

Finkelstein, I., and B. Sass. 2013. "The West Semitic Alphabetic Inscriptions, Late Bronze II to Iron IIA: Archaeological Context, Distribution and Chronology." *Hebrew Bible and Ancient Israel* 2: 149–220.

Fletcher, R. N. 2004. "Sidonians, Tyrians and Greeks in the Mediterranean: The Evidence from Egyptianising Amulets." *Ancient West and East* 3: 51–77.

Fletcher, R. N. 2007. *Patterns of Imports in Iron Age Italy.* Oxford.

Fletcher, R. N. 2008. "Fragments of Levantine Iron Age Pottery in Chalkidike." *Mediterranean Archaeology* 21: 3–7.

Fletcher, R. N. 2011. "Greek-Levantine Cultural Exchange in Orientalising and Archaic Pottery Shapes." *Ancient West and East* 10: 11–42.

Fletcher, R. N. 2012. "Opening the Mediterranean: Assyria, the Levant and the Transformation of Early Iron Age Trade." *Antiquity* 86: 211–220.

Flügel, Ch., H. Dolenz, and K. Schmidt, eds. Forthcoming. *Karthago V. Die Ausgrabungen an der Rue Ibn Chabâat. Frühpunische Besiedlung und mittel-bis spätpunische öffentliche Großbauten mit Hofareal.*

Fourrier, S. 2013. "Constructing the Peripheries: Extra-Urban Sanctuaries and Peer-Polity Interaction in Iron Age Cyprus." *Bulletin of the American Schools of Oriental Research* 370: 103–122.

Fourrier, S. 2019. "Cyprus." In López-Ruiz and Doak, *Oxford Handbook,* 481–491.

Frankenstein, S. 1979. "The Phoenicians in the Far West: A Function of Neo-Assyrian Imperialism." In *Power and Propaganda: A Symposium on Ancient Empires,* edited by M. T. Larsen, 263–294. Copenhagen.

Franklin, J. C. 2015. *Kinyras the Divine Lyre.* Cambridge, MA.

Frendo, A. J., A. de Trafford, and N. C. Vella. 2005. "Water Journeys of the Dead: A Glimpse into Phoenician and Punic Eschatology." In *Atti del V congresso internazionale di studi fenici e punici,* edited by A. Spanò Giammellaro, 427–443. Palermo.

Frère, D., N. Garnier, M. Cygielman, and L. Pagnini. 2014. "Les cruches askoides Sardesen Etrurie: La problématique de leur contenu et de leur fonction." *Studi Etruschi* 77: 253–291.

Fuentes Estañol, M. J. 1986. *Corpus de las inscripciones fenicias, púnicas y neopúnicas de España.* Barcelona.

Fullerton, M. D. 2016. *Greek Sculpture.* Malden.

Fumadó Ortega, I. 2012. "Aspectos marítimos de las divinidades fenicio-púnicas como garantía de la confianza de los mercados." In *La religión del mar: Dioses y ritos de navegación en el Mediterráneo Antiguo,* edited by E. Ferrer, M. C. Marín Ceballos, A. Pereira, 11–36. Seville.

Fumadó Ortega, I. 2013a. "Colonial Representations and Carthaginian Archaeology." *Oxford Journal of Archaeology* 32: 53–72.

Fumadó Ortega, I. 2013b. *Cartago fenicio-púnica. Arqueología de la forma urbana.* Seville.

Gaber, P. 2008. "Excavations at Idalion and the Changing History of a City-Kingdom." *Near Eastern Archaeology* 71: 52–63.

Gadolou, A. 2014. "Near Eastern Imagery in Greek Context: Geometric and Orientalizing Pottery." In Aruz, Graff, and Rakic, *Assyria to Iberia at the Dawn,* 258–262.

Gailledrat, E., M. Dietler, and R. Plana-Mallart, eds. 2018. *The Emporion in the Ancient Western Mediterranean: Trade and Colonial Encounters from the Archaic to the Hellenistic Period*. Montpellier.

Garbati, G. 2008. *Religione votiva: per un'interpretazione storico-religiosa delle terrecotte votive nella Sardegna punica e tardo-punica*. Pisa.

García Teyssandier, E., and D. Marzoli. 2013. "Phönizische Gräber in Ayamonte (Huelva, Spanien): Ein Vorbericht." *Madrider Mitteilungen* 54: 89–158.

García Vargas, E. 2020. "Selfish Purple Production in Iberia and the Balearic Islands in the Pre-Roman Period: Archaelogical Evidence in its Mediterranean Context." In *Interweaving Traditions: Clothing and Textiles in Bronze and Iron Age Iberia,* edited by B. Marín-Aguilera and M. Gleba, 29–46. Valencia.

Garland, R. 2014. *Wandering Greeks: The Ancient Greek Diaspora from the Age of Homer to the Death of Alexander the Great*. Princeton.

Garnand, B. 2020. "Phoenicians and Greeks as Comparable Contemporary Migrant Groups." In *A Companion to Greeks across the Ancient World,* edited by F. De Angelis, 139–162. Hoboken, NJ.

Gebhard, E. 2001. "The Archaic Temple at Isthmia: Techniques of Construction." In *Archaische Griechische Tempel und Altägypten,* edited by M. Bietak, 41–51. Vienna.

Gelb, I. J. 1963. *A Study of Writing*. Chicago.

Gener, J. M., M. A. Navarro, J. M. Pajuelo, M. Torres, and S. Domínguez. 2012. "Las crétulas del siglo VIII a.C. de las excavaciones del solar del Cine Cómico (Cádiz)." *Madrider Mitteilungen* 53: 134–186.

Gener, J. M., M. A. Navarro, J. M. Pajuelo, M. Torres, and E. López. 2014. "Arquitectura y urbanismo de la Gadir fenicia: El yacimiento del Teatro Cómico de Cádiz." In Botto, *Los fenicios*, 14–50.

Gener, J. M., and C. Núñez. 2015. *Gadir: Yacimiento Arqueológico del Teatro de Títeres, Cádiz: El origen fenicio—cómo se hizo*. Cádiz.

George, A. R. 2003. *The Babylonian Gilgamesh Epic: Introduction, Critical Edition, and Cuneiform Texts*. 2 vols. Oxford.

George, A. R. 2007. "Gilgamesh and the Literary Traditions of Ancient Mesopotamia." In *The Babylonian World,* edited by G. Leick, 447–459. London.

Georgiadou, A. 2014. "Productions et styles régionaux dans l'artisanat céramique de Chypre à l'époque géométrique (XIe–VIIIe s. av. J.-C.)." *Bulletin de Correspondance hellénique* 138: 361–385.

Georgiou, A. 2015. "Cyprus during the 'Crisis Years' Revisited." In Babbi et al., *Mediterranean Mirror,* 129–145.

Georgiou, A. 2018. "Ceramic Fluidity and Regional Variations: Elucidating the Transformed Ceramic Industry of Finewares in Cyprus at the Close of the Late Bronze Age." In *Les royaumes chypriotes à l'épreuve de l'histoire,* edited by A. Cannavò and L. Thély, 29–48. Athens.

Giangiulio, M. 2010. "Deconstructing Ethnicities: Multiple Identities in Archaic and Classical Sicily." *BABESCH* 85: 13–23.

Gibson, J. 1982. *Textbook of Syrian Semitic Inscriptions, Vol. III: Phoenician Inscriptions, Including Inscriptions in the Mixed Dialect of Arslan Tash*. Oxford.

Gilboa, A. 2013. "À-propo Huelva: A Reassessment of 'Early' Phoenicians in the West." In Campos Carrasco and Alvar Ezquerra, *Tarteso*, 311–342.

Giovanelli, E. 2016. "Intagli egei nel mondo preromano." In *Dromoi: Studi sul mondo antico offerti a Emanuele Greco, tomo I*, 321–330. Paestum.

Gitin, S., A. Mazar, and E. Stern, eds. *Mediterranean Peoples in Transition: Thirteen to Early Tenth Centuries*. Jerusalem.

Gjerstad, E. 1946. "Decorated Metal Bowls from Cyprus." *OpArch* 4: 1–18.

Gjerstad, E. 1948. *The Swedish Cyprus Expedition*. Vol. 4, part 2. Stockholm.

Goedicke, H. 1975. *The Report of Wenamun*. Baltimore.

Gómez Bellard, C. 2019. "Agriculture." In López-Ruiz and Doak, *Oxford Handbook*, 453–462.

Gómez Bellard, C., and P. Vidal. 2000. "Las cuevas santuario fenicio-púnicas y la navegación en el Mediterráneo." In *Santuarios fenicio-púnicos en Iberia y su influencia en los cultos indígenas*, edited by B. Costa and J. H. Fernández, 103–145. Ibiza.

Gómez Peña, A. 2010. "Así en Oriente como en Occidente: El origen oriental de los altares taurodérmicos de la Península Ibérica." *SPAL* 19: 129–148.

González de Canales, F. 2018. "The City-*Emporion* of Huelva (10th–6th Centuries BC)." In Gailledrat, Dietler, and Plana-Mallart, *Emporion*, 67–78.

González de Canales, F., A. Montaño, and J. Llompart. 2020. "The Beginning of Grape Cultivation in the Iberian Peninsula: A Reappraisal after the Huelva (Southwestern Spain) Archaeological Finds and New Radiocarbon Datings." *Onoba* 8: 35–42.

González de Canales, F., L. Serrano, and J. Llompart. 2004. *El emporio fenicio precolonial de Huelva (ca. 900–770 a.C.)*. Madrid.

González de Canales, F., L. Serrano, and J. Llompart. 2006. "The Pre-Colonial Phoenician Emporium of Huelva, ca. 900–770 BC: A Résumé." *BABESCH* 81: 13–29.

González de Canales, F., L. Serrano, and J. Llompart. 2008. "The Emporium of Huelva and Phoenician Chronology: Present and Future Possibilities." In Sagona, *Beyond the Homeland*, 631–655.

González Prats, A. 2011. "Elementos simbólicos y arquitectónicos: Estelas betiliformes y y cornisas en gola egipcia." In *La Fonteta: Excavaciones de 1996–2002 en la colonia fenicia de la actual desembocadura del río Segura, Gurdamar del Segura (Alicante)*, vol. 1, edited by A. González Prats, 658–672. Alicante.

González Wagner, C. 2005. "Fenicios en el extremo occidente: Conflicto y violencia en el contexto colonial arcaico." *Revista Portuguesa de Arqueologia* 8: 177–192.

González Wagner, C. 2007. "El barco negro en la costa: Reflexiones sobre el miedo y la colonización fenicia en la tierra de Tarsis." *Gerión* 25 (Extra 1): 121–131.

González Wagner, C., and J. Alvar. 2003. "La colonización agrícola en la Península Ibérica: Estado de la cuestión y nuevas perspectivas." In *Ecohistoria del paisaje agrario: La agricultura fenicio-púnica en el Mediterráneo*, edited by C. Gómez Bellard, 187–203. Valencia.

Gordon, C. H. 1962. *Before the Bible: The Common Background of Greek and Hebrew Civilizations.* New York.

Gorgues, A. 2016. "Trade in a Liminal Zone: Commercial Encounter and Transformation in the Iron Age North West Mediterranean." In *Cultural Encounters in Iron Age Europe,* edited by I. Armit, H. Potrebica, M. Črešnar, P. Mason, and L. Büster, 167–210. Budapest.

Gorton, L. 2017. "Revisiting Indo-European 'Wine.'" *Journal of Indo-European Studies* 45: 1–26.

Gosden, C. 2004. *Archaeology and Colonialism: Cultural Contact from 5000 BC to the Present.* Cambridge.

Gosner, L., and J. Hayne, eds. Forthcoming. *Local Experiences of Connectivity and Mobility in the Ancient West-Central Mediterranean.*

Graf, F. 2011. "Myth and Hellenic Identities." In A *Companion to Greek Mythology,* edited by K. Dowden and N. Livingstone, 211–226. Malden, MA.

Graff, S. B. 2014. "Demons, Monsters, and Magic." In Aruz, Graff, and Rakic, *Assyria to Iberia at the Dawn,* 263–271.

Grottanelli, C. 1982. "Healers and Saviours of the Eastern Mediterranean in Pre-Classical Times." In *La soteriologia dei culti orientali nell'impero romano,* edited by U. Bianchi and M. J. Vermaseren, 649–670. Leiden.

Gruen, E. 2011. *Rethinking the Other in Antiquity.* Princeton.

Gubel, E. 1996. "The Influence of Egypt on Western Asiatic Furniture and Evidence from Phoenicia." In *The Furniture of Western Asia: Ancient and Traditional,* edited by G. Herrmann, 139–151. Mainz.

Gubel, E. 2006. "Notes on the Phoenician Component of the Orientalizing Horizon." In Riva and Vella, *Debating Orientalization,* 85–93.

Gubel, E. 2019. "Art and Iconography." In López-Ruiz and Doak, *Oxford Handbook,* 349–369.

Guirguis, M., ed. 2017a. In *La Sardegna fenicia e púnica: Storia e materiali.* Nuoro.

Guirguis, M. 2017b. "Le forme della presenza fenicia in età arcaica (VIII–VI sec. a.C.)." In Guirguis, *La Sardegna fenicia,* 55–61.

Guirguis, M. 2019. "Central North Africa and Sardinian Connections (End of 9th–8th Century BC): The Multi-Ethnic and Multicultural Facies of the Earliest Western Phoenician Communities." In *Archaeology in Africa: Potentials and Perspectives on Laboratory and Fieldwork Research,* edited by S. di Lernia and M. Gallinaro, 111–125. Rome.

Guirguis, M., and A. Ibba. 2017. "Riflessioni sul sufetato tra Tiro, Cartagine e Roma: Nuovi documenti da Sulky (Sardegna) e Thugga (Tunisia)." In *Le forme municipali in Itaia e nelle province occidentali tra i secoli I. A. C. E III D. C.,* edited by S. Evangelisti and C. Ricci, 193–218. Bari.

Gunter, A. C. 2009. *Greek Art and the Orient.* Cambridge.

Gunter, A. C. 2014. "Orientalism and Orientalization in the Iron Age Mediterranean." In *Critical Approaches to Ancient Near Eastern Art,* edited by B. A. Brown and M. H. Feldman, 79–108. Boston.

Gunter, A. C. 2022. "Anatolia, the Aegean, and the Neo-Assyrian Empire: Material Connections." In Hall and Osborne, *Connected Iron Age* 169–193.

Guralnick, E. 1978. "The Proportions of Kouroi." *American Journal of Archaeology* 82: 461–472.

Gutiérrez, J. M., C. Reinoso, F. Giles, C. Finlayson, and A. Sáez. 2012. "La cueva de Gorham (Gibraltar): Un santuario fenicio en el confín occidental del Mediterráneo." In *Confines: El extremo del mundo durante la Antigüedad,* edited by F. Prados, I. García, and G. Bernard, 303–384. Alicante.

Hall, E. 1989. *Inventing the Barbarian: Greek Self-Definition through Tragedy.* Oxford.

Hall, J. M. 1997. *Ethnic Identity in Greek Antiquity.* Cambridge.

Hall, J. M. 2002. *Hellenicity: Between Ethnicity and Culture.* Chicago.

Hall, J. M. 2007. *A History of the Archaic Greek World, ca. 1200–479 BCE.* Malden.

Hall, J. M., and J. Osborne, eds. 2022.*The Connected Iron Age: Interregional Networks in the Eastern Mediterranean 900–600 BCE.* Chicago.

Hamilton, G. J. 2006. *The Origins of the West Semitic Alphabet in Egyptian Scripts.* Washington, DC.

Handberg, S., and A. Gadolou, eds. 2017. *Material Koinai in the Early Greek Iron Age and Archaic Period.* Athens.

Harris, W. V. 2005. "The Mediterranean and Ancient History." In *Rethinking the Mediterranean,* edited by W. V. Harris, 1–38. Oxford.

Haubold, J. 2002–2003. "Greek Epic: A Near Eastern Genre?" *Proceedings of the Cambridge Philological Society* 48: 1–19.

Haubold, J. 2013. *Greece and Mesopotamia.* Cambridge.

Hayne, J. 2010. "Entangled Identities on Iron Age Sardinia?" In *Material Connections in the Ancient Mediterranean: Mobility, Materiality and Identity,* edited by P. van Dommelen and A. B. Knapp, 147–169. London.

Hayne, J. 2019. "The Italian Peninsula." In López-Ruiz and Doak, *Oxford Handbook,* 505–519.

Haynes, S. 2000. *Etruscan Civilization: A Cultural History.* Los Angeles.

Helbig, W. 1876. "Cenni sopra l'arte fenicia. Lettera di W. Helbig al sig. Senatore G. Spano." *Annali dell'Instituto di Correspondenza Archeologica* 48: 197–257.

Hermary, A. 2009. "Ionian Styles in Cypriote Sculpture of the Sixth Century BC." In Karageorghis and Kouka, *Cyprus and the East Aegean,* 244–251.

Hermary, A. 2014. "Les textes antiques ont-ils créé le mythe d'une prostitution sacrée à Chypre?" *Cahiers du Centre d'Études Chypriotes* 44: 239–260.

Hermary, A. 2015. "Un nouveau bilan sur les sarcophages anthropoïdes de Chypre." In *ΠΟΛΥΜΑΘΕΙΑ: Festschrift für Hartmut Matthäus anlässlich seines 65. Geburtstages,* edited by R. Nawracala and S. Nawracala, 201–218. Aegen.

Herrenschmidt, C. J. 2000 (French 1996). "Consonant Alphabets, the Greek Alphabet, and Old Persian Cuneiform." In *Ancestor of the West: Writing, Reasoning, and Religion in Mesopotamia, Elam, and Greece,* edited by J. Bottéro, C. Herrenschmidt, and J-P. Vernant, 3–18. Chicago.

Hobson, M. 2019. "Carthage after the Punic Wars and the Neo-Punic Legacy." In López-Ruiz and Doak, *Oxford Handbook,* 183–196.

Höckmann, U. 2009. "Male Figures Bearing Sacrificial Animals from Cyprus, the Aegean and Naukratis." In Karageorghis and Kouka, *Cyprus and the East Aegean*, 252–262.

Hodos, T. 2006. *Local Responses to Colonization in the Iron Age Mediterranean.* London.

Hodos, T. 2020. *The Archaeology of the Mediterranean Iron Age: A Globalising World c. 1100–600 BCE.* Cambridge.

Hodos, T. 2022. "Globalizing the Mediterranean in the Iron Age." In Hall and Osborne, *Connected Iron Age*, 194–213.

Hodos, T., C. R. Cartwright, J. Montgomery, G. Nowell, K. Crowder, A. C. Fletcher, and Y Gösnter. 2020. "The Origins of Decorated Ostrich Eggs in the Ancient Mediterranean and Middle East." *Antiquity* 94: 381–400.

Hölb, G. 2017. *Aegyptiaca aus Al Mina und Tarsos im Verbande des nordsyrische-sudostanatolischen Raumes.* Vienna.

Horden, P., and N. Purcell. 2000. *The Corrupting Sea: A Study of Mediterranean History.* Oxford.

Horowitz, W., T. Oshima, and S. L. Sanders. 2018. *Cuneiform in Canaan: The Next Generation.* 2nd ed. Winona Lake.

Hoyos, D. 2010. *The Carthaginians.* London.

Hoyos, D. 2019. "Classical Carthage before the Punic Wars (479–265 BCE)." In López-Ruiz and Doak, *Oxford Handbook,* 156–168.

Huntington, S. 1996. *The Clash of Civilizations and the Remaking of World Order.* New York.

Hütwohl, D. 2020. "Herodotus' Phoenicians: Mediators of Cultural Exchange in the Mediterranean." *Rivista di Studi Fenici* 48: 107–120

Iacovou, M. 2002. "From Ten to Naught: Formation, Consolidation and Abolition of Cyprus' Iron Age Polities." *Cahier du Centre d'Études Chypriotes* 32: 73–87.

Iacovou, M. 2006. "'Greeks,' 'Phoenicians,' and 'Eteocypriots': Ethnic Identities in the Cypriot Kingdoms." In *"Sweet Land . . .": Lectures on the History and Culture of Cyprus,* edited by J. Chrysostomides and C. Dendrinos, 27–59. Porphyrogenitus.

Iacovou, M. 2008. "Cultural and Political Configuration in Iron Age Cyprus: The Sequel to a Protohistoric Episode." *American Journal of Archaeology* 112: 625–657.

Iacovou, M., ed. 2012a. *Cyprus and the Aegean in the Early Iron Age: The Legacy of Nicolas Coldstream.* Nicosia.

Iacovou, M. 2012b. "External and Internal Migrations during the 12th Century BC: Setting the Stage for an Economically Successful Early Iron Age in Cyprus." In Iacovou, *Cyprus and the Aegean,* 207–227.

Iacovou, M. 2014. "'Working with the Shadows': In Search of the Myriad Forms of Social Complexity." In *ΑΘΥΡΜΑΤΑ: Critical Essays on the Archaeology of the Eastern Mediterranean in Honor of E. Susan Sherratt,* edited by Y. Galanakis, T. Wilkinson, and J. Bennet, 117–126. Oxford.

Iacovou, M. 2018. "From the Late Cypriot Polities to the Iron Age 'Kingdoms': Understanding the Political Landscape of Cyprus from Within." In *Les royaumes de Chypre à l'épreuve del'histoire: Transitions et ruptures de la fin de l'âge du Bronze au début de l'époque hellénistique,* edited by A. Cannavò and L. Thély, 7–28. Athens.

Iaia, C. 2013. "Metalwork, Rituals and the Making of Elite Identity in Central Italy at the Bronze Age-Iron Age Transition." In Alberti and Sabatini, *Exchange Networks,* 102–116.

Ilieva, P. 2019. "Phoenicians, Cypriots, and Euboeans in the Northern Aegean." *Aura* 2: 65–102.

Intrieri, M., and S. Ribichini, eds. 2011. *Fenici e Italici, Cartagine e la Magna Grecia: Popoli a contatto, culture a confronto.* 2 vols. Rome.

Ioannou, C. 2015. "Cypriotes and Phoenicians." *Kyprios Character: History, Archaeology & Numismatics of Ancient Cyprus.* kyprioscharacter.eie.gr/en/t/ Ac. Accessed September 1, 2015.

Ioannou, C. 2016. "The Political Situation in the Near East during the Cypro-Archaic Period and Its Impact on Cyprus." In Bourogiannis and Mühlenbock, *Ancient Cyprus Today,* 325–332.

Isaac, B. 2004. *The Invention of Racism in Classical Antiquity.* Princeton.

Izzet, V. 2007. *The Archaeology of Etruscan Society.* Cambridge.

James, T. H. G. 1962. "The Egyptian-Type Objects." In Payne, *Perachora,* 461–516.

Janko, R. 1982. *Homer, Hesiod, and the Homeric Hymns: Diachronic Development in Epic Tradition.* Cambridge.

Janko, R. 2015. "From Gabii and Gordion to Eretria and Methone: The Rise of the Greek Alphabet." *Bulletin of the Institute of Classical Studies* 58: 1–32.

Jeffery, L. H. 1967. "Ἀρχαῖα γράμματα: Some Ancient Greek Views." *Europa: Studien zur Geschichte und Epigraphik der frühen Aegaeis, Festschrift für Ernst Grumach,* edited by W. C. Brice, 152–166. Berlin.

Jenkins, I. 2006. *Greek Architecture and Its Sculpture.* Cambridge, MA.

Jiménez Ávila, J., ed. 2015a. *Phoenician Bronzes in Mediterranean.* Madrid.

Joffe, A. H. 2002. "The Rise of Secondary States in the Iron Age Levant." *Journal of the Economic and Social History of the Orient* 45: 425–467.

Johnston, P. A., and B. Kaufman, 2019. "Metallurgy and Other Technologies." In López-Ruiz and Doak, *Oxford Handbook,* 401–422.

Jongeling, K. 2008. *Handbook of Neo-Punic Inscriptions.* Tübingen.

Jovino, M. B. 2010. "The Tarquinia Project: A Summary of 25 Years of Excavation." *American Journal of Archaeology* 114: 161–180.

Kaldellis, A. 2019. "Neo-Phoenician Identities in the Roman Empire." In López-Ruiz and Doak, *Oxford Handbook,* 685–696.

Kaldellis, A., and López-Ruiz, C. 2009. BNJ 790 "Philon of Byblos." *Brill's New Jacoby,* edited by Ian Worthington.

Kamlah, J., ed. 2012. *Temple Building and Temple Cult: Architecture and Cultic Paraphernalia of Temples in the Levant (2.–1. Millennia BCE.).* Wiesbaden.

Kantor, H. 1962. "Oriental Institute Museum Notes, no. 13: A Bronze Plaque with Relief Decoration from Tell Tainat." *Journal of Near Eastern Studies* 21: 93–117.

Kaoukabani, I. 2005. "Les estampilles phéniciennes de Tyr." *Archaeology and History in Lebanon* 21: 3–79.

Karageorghis, V. 1976. *Kition: Mycenaean and Phoenician Discoveries in Cyprus.* London.

Karageorghis, V. 1982. *Cyprus: From the Stone Age to the Romans.* London.

Karageorghis, V. 2001. "The Hellenisation of Cyprus and Crete: Some Similarities and Differences." In *Kreta und Zypern: Religion und Schrift; Von der Frühgeschichte biz zum Ende der archaischen Zeit,* edited by A. Kyriatsoulis, 265–277. Altenburg.

Karageorghis, V. 2005a. "The Phoenicians in Cyprus." In Celestino and Jiménez Ávila, *El Período Orientalizante,* 31–46.

Karageorghis, V. 2005b. *Excavations at Kition: VI. The Phoenician and Later Levels.* Nicosia.

Karageorghis, V., and M. Demas. 1985. *Excavations at Kition V: I. The Pre-Phoenician Levels.* Nicosia.

Karageorghis, V., and O. Kouka, eds. 2009. *Cyprus and the East Aegean: Intercultural Contacts from 3000 to 500 BC.* Nicosia.

Kassianidou, V. 2012. "The Origin and Use of Metals in Iron Age Cyrprus." In Iacovou, *Cyprus and the Aegean,* 229–259.

Katzenstein, J. 1997 (1st ed. 1973). *The History of Tyre: From the Beginning of the Second Millenium BCE until the Fall of the Neo-Babylonian Empire in 539 BCE.* Jerusalem.

Kaufman, B. 2017. "Political Economy of Carthage: The Carthaginian Constitution as Reconstructed through Archaeology, Historical Texts and Epigraphy." In *Bridging Times and Spaces: Papers in Ancient Near Eastern, Mediterranean and Armenian Studies,* edited by P. S. Avetisyan and Y. H. Grekyan, 201–214. Oxford.

Kearsley, R. A. 1999. "Greeks Overseas in the Eighth Century BC: Euboeans, Al Mina and Assyrian Imperialism." In Tsetskhladze, *Ancient Greeks West and East,* 109–134.

Keesling, C. 2003. *The Votive Statues of the Athenian Acropolis.* Cambridge.

Kelley, O. 2012. "Beyond Intermarriage: The Role of the Indigenous Italic Population at Pithekoussai." *Oxford Journal of Archaeology* 31: 245–260.

Kelly, A. 2014. "Homeric Battle Narrative and the Ancient Near East." In *Defining Greek Narrative,* edited by D. Cairns and R. Scodel, 29–54. Edinburgh.

Kendirci, R. 2012. "Iron Age Aeolic Style Capitals in the Israel and Palestine Area." Master's thesis, Upsala University.

Kenzelmann Pfyffer, A., T. Theurillat, and S. Verdan. 2005. "Graffiti d'époque géométrique d'Eretrie VIII: Inscription sémitique." *Zeitschrift für Papyrologie und Epigraphik* 151: 76–77.

Kerr, R. M. 2010. *Latino-Punic Epigraphy: A Descriptive Study of the Inscriptions.* Tübingen.

Kestemont, G. 1985. "Les Phéniciens en Syrie du nord." In *Phoenicia and Its Neighbors,* edited by E. Gubel and E. Lipiński, 135–149. Leuven.

Killebrew, A. E. 2019. "Canaanite Roots, Proto-Phoenicia, and the Early Phoenician Period: Ca. 1300–1000 BCE." In López-Ruiz and Doak, *Oxford Handbook,* 39–55.

Kistler, E., B. Öhlinger, M. Mohr, and M. Hoernes, eds. 2015. *Sanctuaries and the Power of Consumption: Networking and the Formation of Elites in the Archaic Western Mediterranean World.* Wiesbaden.

Knapp, A. B. 1993. "Thalassocracies in Bronze Age Eastern Mediterranean Trade: Making and Breaking a Myth." *World Archaeology* 24: 332–347.

Knapp, A. B. 2006. "Orientalization and Prehistoric Cyprus: The Social Life of Oriental Goods." In Riva and Vella, *Debating Orientalization,* 48–65.

Knapp, A. B. 2008. *Prehistoric and Protohistoric Cyprus: Identity, Insularity, and Connectivity.* Oxford.

Knapp, A. B. 2013. *The Archaeology of Cyprus: From Earliest Prehistory through the Bronze Age.* Cambridge.

Knapp, A. B., and S. Demesticha, eds. 2016. *Mediterranean Connections: Maritime Transport Containers and Seaborne Trade in the Bronze and Early Iron Ages.* London.

Knapp, A. B., and P. van Dommelen, eds. 2014. *The Cambridge Prehistory of the Bronze and Iron Age Mediterranean,* 96–108. New York.

Knappett, C. 2011. *An Archaeology of Interaction: Network Perspectives on Material Culture and Society.* Oxford.

Knauf, E. A. 1991. "King Solomon's Copper Supply." In *Phoenicia and the Bible,* edited by E. Lipiński, 167–187. Leuven.

Kopcke, G., and I. Tokumaru, eds. 1992. *Greece between East and West: 10th–8th centuries BC.* Mainz.

Körner, C. 2020. "Review of Th. Petit. *La naissance des cités-royaumes cypriotes.*" *BMCR* 2020.06.02.

Kotsonas, A. 2012. "'Creto-Cypriot' and 'Cypro-Phoenician' Complexities in the Archaeology of Interaction between Crete and Cyprus." In Iacovou, *Cyprus and the Aegean,* 155–181.

Kotsonas, A. 2013. "Al Mina." In *The Encyclopedia of Ancient History,* 1st ed., edited by R. S. Bagnall, K. Brodersen, C. B. Champion, A. Erskine, and S. R. Huebner, 272–273.

Kourou, N. 2011. "Following the Sphinx: Tradition and Innovation in Early Iron Age Crete." In *Identité culturale, etnicité, processi di transformazione a Creta fra Dark Age e arcaísmo,* edited by G. Rizza, 165–177. Catania.

Kourou, N. 2012. "Phoenicia, Cyprus, and the Aegean." In Iacovou, *Cyprus and the Aegean,* 33–54.

Kourou, N., V. Karageorghis, Y. Maniatis, K. Polikreti, Y. Bassiakos, and C. Xenophontos. 2002. *Limestone Statuettes of Cypriote Type Found in the Aegean: Provenance Studies.* Nicosia.

Kowalzig, B. 2018. "Cults, Cabotage, and Connectivity: Experimenting with Religious and Economic Networks in the Greco-Roman Mediterranean." In *Maritime Networks in the Ancient Mediterranean World,* edited by J. Leidwanger and C. Knappett, 93–131. Cambridge.

Krings, V., ed. *La civilisation phénicienne et punique: Manuel de recherche.* Leiden.

Kroll, J. H. 2008. "Early Iron Age Balance Weights at Lefkandi, Euboea." *Oxford Journal of Archaeology* 27: 37–48.

Lafrenz Samuels, K., and P. van Dommelen. 2019. "Punic Heritage in Tunisia." In López-Ruiz and Doak, *Oxford Handbook,* 729–742.

Lam, J., and D. Pardee. 2012. "Diachrony in Ugaritic." In *Diachrony in Biblical Hebrew,* edited by C. L. Miller-Naudé and Z. Zevit, 407–431. Winona Lake.

Lancel, S. 1995 (French 1992). *Carthage: A History.* Oxford.

Lane Fox, R. 2008. *Travelling Heroes in the Epic Age of Homer.* New York.

Langdon, S. 1989. "The Return of the Horse-Leader." *American Journal of Archaeology* 93: 185–201.

Langdon, S., ed. 1997. *New Light on a Dark Age: Exploring the Culture of Geometric Greece.* Columbia, MO.

Langdon, S. 2022. "Shaping Religious Change: Experimental Modeling in Archaic Corinthian Figurines." In *"Quand on la terre sous l'ongle": Le modelage dans le monde grec antique,* edited by H. Aurigny and L. Rohaut, 305–316. Aix-en-Provence.

Larsen, M. T. 1996. *The Conquest of Assyria: Excavations in an Antique Land.* London.

Latacz, J. 2004 (German 2001). *Troy and Homer: Towards a Solution of an Old Mystery.* Oxford.

Layard, H. 1853. *Discoveries in the Ruins of Niniveh and Babylon with Travels in Armenia, Kurdistan and the Desert: Being the Result of a Second Expedition Undertaken for the Trustees of the British Museum.* London.

Le Meaux, H. 2010. *L'iconographie orientalisante de la péninsule Ibérique: Questions de styles et d'échanges (viiie–vie siècles av. J-C.).* Madrid.

Le Meaux, H. 2013. "Des ivoires et des oeufs: Réflexions sur l'interaction art/technologie dans le contexte orientalisant de la première moitié du Ier millénaire avant J.-C. en péninsule Ibérique." *Mélanges de la Casa de Velázquez* 43: 85–110.

Lehmann, G. 2005. "Al-Mina and the East: A Report on Research in Progress." In *The Greeks in the East,* edited by A. Villing, 61–92. London.

Lehmann, G. 2019. "The Levant." In López-Ruiz and Doak, *Oxford Handbook,* 465–479.

Lehmann, G., and A. E. Killebrew. 2010. "Palace 6000 at Megiddo in Context: Iron Age Central Hall Tetra-Partite Residencies and the Bīt-Ḫilāni Building Tradition in the Levant." *Bulletin of the American Schools of Oriental Research* 359: 13–33.

Lehmann, R. G. 2012. "27–30–22–26: How Many Letters Needs an Alphabet?" In *The Idea of Writing: Writing across Borders,* edited by A. de Voogt and J. F. Quack, 11–52. Leiden.

Leibundgut Wieland, D., and V. Tatton-Brown, 2019. *Nordost-Tor und persische Belagerungsrampe in Alt-Paphos IV.* Wiesbaden.

Leidwanger, J., and C. Knappett, eds. 2018. *Maritime Networks in the Ancient Mediterranean World.* Cambridge.

Leigh, M. 2000. "Lucan and the Libyan Tale." *Journal of Roman Studies* 90: 95–109.

Leighton, R. 2013. "Urbanization in Southern Etruria from the Tenth to the Sixth Century BC: The Origins and Growth of Major Centers." In Turfa, *Etruscan World,* 134–150.

Lejeune, M., and J. Pouilloux. 1988. "Une transaction commerciale ionienne au-Ve siècle à Pech-Maho." *Comptes Rendus de l'Académie des Inscriptions et Belles-Lettres* 1988: 526–535.

Lemaire, A. 1993. "Les critères non-iconographiques de la classification des sceaux nord-ouest sémitiques inscrits." In *Studies in the Iconography of Northwest Semitic Inscribed Seals,* edited by B. Sass and C. Uehlinger, 1–26. Fribourg.

Lemaire, A. 2012. "From the Origin of the Alphabet to the Tenth Century BCE: New Documents and New Directions." In *New Inscriptions and Seals Relating to the Biblical World,* edited by M. Lubetski and E. Lubetski, 1–20. Atlanta.

Lemaire, A. 2013. "Remarques sur les inscriptions phéniciennes de Kuntillet 'Ajrud." *Semitica* 55: 83–99.

Lemos, I. S. 2002. *The Protogeometric Aegean: The Archaeology of the Late Eleventh and Tenth Centuries BC.* Oxford.

Leriou, A. 2007. "The Hellenisation of Cyprus: Tracing Its Beginnings (an Updated Version)." In *Patrimonies culturels en Méditerranée orientale: Recherche scientifique et enjeux identitaires,* edited by S. Müller Celka and J.-C. David, 1–33. Lyon.

Lewe, B. 1975. *Studien zur archaischen kyprischen Plastik.* Dortmund.

Lietz, B. 2012. *La dea di Erice e la sua diffusione nel Mediterraneo: Un culto tra Fenici, Greci e Romani.* Pisa.

Lipiński, E. 1993. "Rites et sacrifices dans la tradition phénico-punique." *Ritual and Sacrifice in the Ancient Near East,* edited by J. Quaegebeur, 257–281. Leuven.

Lipschits, O. 2011. "The Origin and Date of the Proto-Aeolic Capitals from the Levant." In *The Fire Signals of Lachish: Studies in the Archaeology and History of Israel in the Late Bronze Age, Iron Age, and Persian Period in Honor of David Ussishkin,* edited by I. Finkelstein and N. Na'aman, 203–225. Winona Lake.

Liverani, M. 2004. *Myth and Politics in Ancient Near Eastern Historiography.* Ithaca, NY.

Liverani, M. 2014. *The Ancient Near East: History, Society, and Economy.* London.

Lo Schiavo, F. 2008. "La metallurgia sarda: relazioni fra Cipro, Italia e la Penisola Iberica; Un modello interpretativo." In Celestino, Rafel, and Armada, *Contacto cultural,* 417–436.

López-Bertran, M. 2019. "Funerary Ritual." In López-Ruiz and Doak, *Oxford Handbook,* 293–309.

López-Bertran, M., and A. Garcia-Ventura. 2012. "Music, Gender and Rituals in the Ancient Mediterranean: Revisiting the Punic Evidence." *World Archaeology* 44: 393–408.

López Castro, J. L. 2006. "Colonials, Merchants and Alabaster Vases: The Western Phoenician Aristocracy." *Antiquity* 80: 74–88.

López Castro, J. L. 2019. "The Iberian Peninsula." In López-Ruiz and Doak, *Oxford Handbook,* 585–602.

López Castro, J. L., A. Ferjaoui, A. Mederos Martín, V. Martínez Hahnmüller, and I. Ben Jerbania. 2016. "La colonización fenicia inicial en el Mediterráneo

Central: nuevas excavaciones arqueológicas en Utica (Túnez)." *Trabajos de Prehistoria* 73: 68–89.

López-Ruiz, C. 2009a. "Tarshish and Tartessos Revisited: Textual Problems and Historical Implications." In Dietler and López-Ruiz, *Colonial Encounters*, 255–280.

López-Ruiz, C. 2009b. "Mopsos and Cultural Exchange between Greeks and Locals in Cilicia." In *Antike Mythen: Medien, Transformationen, Konstruktionen; Fritz Graf Festschrift*, edited by U. Dill and C. Walde, 382–396. Berlin.

López-Ruiz, C. 2010. *When the Gods Were Born: Greek Cosmogonies and the Near East*. Cambridge, MA.

López-Ruiz, C. 2014. "Greek and Near Eastern Mythology: A Story of Mediterranean Encounters." *Approaches to Greek Mythology*, 2nd rev. ed., edited by L. Edmunds, 154–199. Baltimore.

López-Ruiz, C. 2015a. "Near Eastern Precedents of the 'Orphic' Gold Tablets: The Phoenician Missing Link." *Journal of Near Eastern Religions* 15: 52–91.

López-Ruiz, C. 2015b. "Gods: Origins." In *Oxford Handbook of Greek Religion*, edited by E. Eidinow and J. Kindt, 369–382. Oxford.

López-Ruiz, C. 2016. "Greek Literature and the Lost Legacy of Canaan." In Aruz and Seymour, *Assyria to Iberia*, 316–321.

López-Ruiz, C. 2017. "'Not That Which Can Be Found among the Greeks': Philo of Byblos and Phoenician Cultural Identity in the Roman East." *Religion in the Roman Empire* 3: 366–392.

López-Ruiz, C. 2019a. "Phoenician Literature." In López-Ruiz and Doak, *Oxford Handbook*, 257–269.

López-Ruiz, C. 2019b. "Alien o alienable? Notas sobre la relación entre fenicios y griegos." In *Tras los pasos de Momigliano: Centralidad y alteridad en el mundo greco-romano*, edited by G. Cruz Andreotti, 43–55. Barcelona.

López-Ruiz, C. 2020. "Reificar o no reificar? Fenicios, tartesios, y el problema de las identidades sin voz." In *Un viaje entre el Oriente y el Occidente del Mediterráneo*, edited by S. Celestino and E. Rodríguez, 51–56. Mérida.

López-Ruiz, C. 2021. "The Sphinx: A Greco-Phoenician Hybrid." In *Text and Intertext in Greek Epic and Drama: Essays in Honor of Margalit Finkelberg*, edited by R. Zelnick-Abramovitz and J. Price, 292–310. Oxon.

López-Ruiz, C. 2022a. "From Kothar to Kythereia: Exploring the Northwest Semitic Past of Aphrodite." In *"Like 'Ilu Are You Wise": Studies in Northwest Semitic Languages and Literatures in Honor of Dennis G. Pardee*, edited by H. H. Hardy II, J. Lam, and E. D. Reymond, 355–375. Chicago.

López-Ruiz, C. 2022b. "Phoenicians and the Iron Age Mediterranean: A Response to Phoenicoskepticism." In Hall and Osborne, *Connected Iron Age*, 27–48.

López-Ruiz, C. Forthcoming. "The Resilience of a 'Non-People': The Case for a Reconstructed Phoenician Identity." In *Identities in Antiquity*, edited by V. Manolopoulou, J. Skinner, and C. Tsouparopoulou. London.

López-Ruiz, C., and B. R. Doak, eds. 2019. *Oxford Handbook of the Phoenician and Punic Mediterranean*. Oxford.

Louden, B. 2006. *The* Iliad: *Structure, Myth, and Meaning*. Baltimore.

Louden, B. 2011. *Homer's* Odyssey *and the Near East*. Cambridge.

Luke, J. 2003. *Ports of Trade, Al Mina and Geometric Greek Pottery in the Levant.* Oxford.

Luraghi, N. 2006. "Traders, Pirates, Warriors: The Proto-History of Greek Mercenary Soldiers in the Eastern Mediterranean." *Phoenix* 60: 21–47.

Lutz, R. T. 2001. "Phoenician Inscriptions from Tell el-Maskhuta." In *The World of the Aramaeans,* edited by P. M. M. Daviau, J. W. Wevers, and M. Weigl, 190–212. Sheffield.

Lyons, C. L., and J. Papadopoulos, eds. 2002. *The Archaeology of Colonialism.* Los Angeles.

Machuca Prieto, F. 2019. *Una forma fenicia de ser romano: identidad e integración de las comunidades fenicias de la Peneinsula Ibérica bajo poder de Roma.* Seville.

Magness, J. 2001. "A Near Eastern Ethnic Element Among the Etruscan Elite?" *Etruscan Studies* 8: 79–117.

Maier, J. 1999. *Jorge Bonsor (1855–1930): Un académico correspondiente de la Real Academia de la Historia y la Arqueología española.* Madrid.

Malkin, I. 1998. *The Returns of Odysseus: Colonization and Ethnicity.* Berkeley.

Malkin, I. 2002. "A Colonial Middle Ground: Greek, Etruscan, and Local Elites in the Bay of Naples." In Lyons and Papadopoulos, *Archaeology of Colonialism,* 151–181.

Malkin, I. 2011. *A Small Greek World: Networks in the Ancient Mediterranean.* Oxford.

Malkin, I., C. Constantakopoulou, and K. Panagopoulou, eds. 2009. *Greek and Roman Networks in the Mediterranean.* London.

Manning, J. G. 2018. *The Open Sea: The Economic Life of the Ancient Mediterranean World from the Iron Age to the Rise of Rome.* Princeton.

Marchand, S. 1996. *Down from Olympus: Archaeology and Philhellenism in Germany, 1750–1970.* Princeton.

Marchand, S. 2009. *German Orientalism in the Age of Empire: Religion, Race and Scholarship.* New York.

Marconi, C. 2007. *Temple Decoration and Cultural Identity in the Archaic Greek World: The Metopes of Selinus.* Cambridge.

Marín Ceballos, M. C. 2006. "De dioses, pieles y lingotes." *Habis* 37: 35–54.

Marín Ceballos, M. C. 2010. "Santuarios prerromanos de la costa atlántica andaluza." In *Debate en torno a la religiosidad protohistórica,* edited by T. Tortosa and S. Celestino, 219–243. Madrid.

Marín Ceballos, M. C., and A. M. Jiménez Flores. 2004. "Los santuarios feniciopúnicos como centros de sabiduría: el templo de Melqart en Gadir." *Huelva Arqueológica* 20: 215–240.

Marín Ceballos, M. C., and A. M. Jiménez Flores. 2011. "El capitel protoeólico de Cádiz." In *Cultos y ritos de la Gadir fenicia,* edited by M. C. Marín Ceballos, 207–220. Seville.

Marinatos, N. 1993. "What Were Greek Sanctuaries? A Synthesis." In Marinatos and Hägg, *Greek Sanctuaries,* 228–233.

Marinatos, N. 2010. *Minoan Kingship and the Solar Goddess: A Near Eastern Koine.* Urbana.

Marinatos, N., and R. Hägg, eds. 1993. *Greek Sanctuaries: New Approaches.* London.

Marinatos, N., and N. Wyatt. 2011. "Levantine, Egyptian, and Greek Mythological Conceptions of the Beyond." In *A Companion to Greek Mythology,* edited by K. Dowden and N. Livingstone, 383–410. Malden.

Markoe, G. E. 1985. *Phoenician Bronze and Silver Bowls from Cyprus and the Mediterranean.* Berkeley.

Markoe, G. E. 1990a. "Egyptianizing Male Votive Statuary from Cyprus: A Re-examination." *Levant* 22: 111–122.

Markoe, G. E. 1990b. "The Emergence of Phoenician Art." *Bulletin of the American Schools of Oriental Research* 279: 13–26.

Markoe, G. E. 1992. "In Pursuit of Metal: Phoenicians and Greeks in Italy." In Kopcke and Tokumaru, *Greece between East and West,* 61–84.

Markoe, G. E. 2000. *Phoenicians.* London.

Markoe, G. E. 2015. "Current Assessment of the Phoenicians in the Tyrrhenian Basin: Levantine Trade with Sicily, Sardinia, and Western Coastal Italy." In Babbi et al., *Mediterranean Mirror,* 245–260.

Marlasca Martín, R., and J. López Garí. 2006. "Eivissa, la isla recortada: Las zanjas y recortes de cultivo deépoca púnico romana." In *The Archaeology of Cropfields and Gardens,* edited by J. Morel, J. Tresserras, and J. Carlos Matamala, 87–99. Bari.

Martin, R. 1955–1956. "Problème des origins des orders à volutes." *Études d'arquéologie classique* 1: 119–132.

Martin, S. R. 2017. *The Art of Contact: Comparative Approaches to Greek and Phoenician Art.* Philadelphia.

Martin, S. R. 2018. "Eastern Mediterranean Feasts: What Do We Really Know about the Marzeah?" In Niesiołowski-Spanò and Węcowski, *Change, Continuity, and Connectivity,* 294–307.

Martín Ruiz, J. A. 2012. "Las necrópolis tartésicas de la provincia de Málaga." *Mainake* 33: 327–342.

Martín Ruiz, J. A. 2018. "The Phoenician Population in Málaga Bay (Spain)." In *De Huelva a Malaka: Los fenicios en Andalucía a la luz de los descubrimientos mas recientes,* edited by M. Botto, 285–303. Rome.

Masson, E. 2007. "Greek and Semitic Languages: Early Contacts." In *A History of Ancient Greek: From the Beginnings to Late Antiquity,* edited by A.-F. Christidis, 733–737. Cambridge.

Mastino, A. 2017. "La Sardegna arcaica tra mito e storiografia: gli eroi e le fonti." In Guirguis, *La Sardegna fenicia,* 19–29.

Matisoo-Smith, E., A. L. Gosling, D. Platt, O. Kardailsky, S. Prost, S. Cameron-Christie, C. J. Collins, J. Boocock, Y. Kurumilian, M. Guirguis, R. Pla Orquín, W. Khalil, H. Genz, G. Abou Diwan, J. Nassar, and P. Zalloua. 2018. "Ancient Mitogenomes of Phoenicians from Sardinia and Lebanon: A Story of Settlement, Integration, and Female Mobility." *PLoS ONE* 13: e0190169.

Matthäus, H. 1985. *Metallgefässe und Gefassuntersätze der Bronzezeit, der geometrischen un archaischen Periode auf Cypern.* Munich.

Matthäus, H. 2010. "Spätbronzezeitliche und früheisenzeitliche Thymiateria in der Levante und auf der Insel Zypern: Formgeschichtliche Untersuchungen." *Cahiers du Centre d'Études Chypriotes* 40: 205–230.

Mattingly, D. J. 2007. "The African Way of Death: Burial Rituals Beyond the Roman Empire." In *Mortuary Landscapes of North Africa,* edited by D. L. Stone and L. M. Stirling, 138–163. Toronto.

Maya, R., G. Jurado, J. M. Gener, E. López, M. Torres, and J. A. Zamora. 2014. "Nuevos datos sobre la posible ubicación del Kronion de Gadir: Las evidencias de época fenicia arcaica." In Botto, *Los fenicios,* 156–180.

Mazar, A. 1990. *Archaeology of the Land of the Bible: 10,000–586 BCE.*

Mazar, A. 1998. "On the Appearance of Red Slip in the Iron Age I Period in Israel." In Gitin, Mazar, and Stern, *Mediterranean Peoples,* 368–378.

Mazar, E. 2004. *The Phoenician Family Tomb n. 1 at the Northern Cemetery of Achziv (10th–6th Centuries BCE).* Barcelona.

Mazarakis Ainian, A. J. 1988. "Early Greek Temples: Their Origin and Function." In *Early Greek Cult Practice,* edited by R. Hägg, N. Marinatos, and G. Nordquist, 105–119. Stockholm.

Mazarakis Ainian, A. J., ed. 2007. *Oropos and Euboea in the Early Iron Age.* Volos.

Mazarakis Ainian, A. J. 2016. "Early Greek Temples." In *A Companion to Greek Architecture,* edited by M. Miles, 15–30. Malden.

McCarter, P. K. 1975. *The Antiquity of the Greek Alphabet and the Early Phoenician Scripts.* Missoula.

McCarty, M. 2018. "French Archaeology and History in the Colonial Maghreb: Inheritance, Presence, and Absence." In Effros and Lai, *Unmasking Ideology,* 59–82.

McCarty, M. 2019. "The Tophet and Infant Sacrifice." In López-Ruiz and Doak, *Oxford Handbook,* 311–325.

McGovern, P. 2003. *Ancient Wine: The Search for the Origin of Wine.* Princeton.

McHugh, M. 2017. *The Ancient Greek Farmstead.* Oxford.

Mederos, A. 1999. "Ex Occidente Lux. El comercio micénico en el Mediterráneo Central y Occidental (1625–1100 AC)." *Complutum* 10: 229–266.

Mederos, A. 2001. "Fenicios evanescentes: Nacimiento, muerte y redescubrimiento de los fenicios en la Península Ibérica. I. (1780–1935)." *SAGUNTUM* 33: 37–48.

Mederos, A. 2006. "Fenicios en Huelva, en el siglo X a.C. durante el reinado de Hîrãm I de Tiro." *SPAL* 15: 167–188.

Mederos, A. 2019. "North Africa: From the Atlantic to Algeria." In López-Ruiz and Doak, *Oxford Handbook,* 627–643.

Mederos, A., and G. Escribano. 2015. *Oceanus Gaditanus: Oro, púrpura y pesca en el litoral Atlántico Norteafricano y las Islas Canarias en época fenicia, cartaginesa y romana republicana.* Las Palmas.

Mederos, A., V. Peña, and C. González Wagner, eds. 2004. *La navegación fenicia: tecnología naval y derroteros: encuentro entre marinos, arqueólogos e historiadores.* Madrid.

Metcalf, C. 2015. *The Gods Rich in Praise.* Oxford.

Michelau, H. 2019. "Das Ankh und das sogenannte 'Tinnit'-Symbol im Kontext einiger phönizischer Grabstelen." *CARTHAGE STUDIES* 11: 51–66.

Michetti, L. M. 2020. "Cinque lucerne fenicie dal Quartiere "pubblico-cerimoniale" di Pyrgi." In Guirguis, *La Sardegna fenicia,* 105–119.

Mierse, W. E. 2004. "The Architecture of the Lost Temple of Hercules Gaditanus and Its Levantine Associations." *American Journal of Archaeology* 108: 545–576.

Mierse, W. E. 2012. *Temples and Sanctuaries from the Early Iron Age Levant.* Winona Lake.

Mikrakis, M. 2012. "The 'Originality of Ancient Cypriot Art' and the Individuality of Performing Practices in Protohistoric Cyprus." In Iacovou, *Cyprus and the Aegean,* 371–393.

Mikrakis, M. 2013. "The Destruction of the Mycenaean Palaces and the Construction of the Epic World (Performative Perspectives)." In *Destruction: Archaeological, Philological, and Historical Perspectives,* edited by J. Driessen, 221–242. Louvain-La-Neuve.

Mikrakis, M. 2015. "Pots, Early Iron Age Athenian Society, and the Near East: The Evidence from the Rattle Group." In *Pots, Workshops and Early Iron Age Society: Function and Role of Ceramics in Early Greece,* edited by V. Vlachou, 277–289. Brussels.

Miles, R. 2010. *Carthage Must Be Destroyed: The Rise and Fall of an Ancient Civilization.* London.

Miller, M. 1997. *Athens and Persia in the Fifth Century BC: A Study of Receptivity.* Cambridge.

Momigliano, A. 1975a. *Alien Wisdom: The Limits of Hellenisation.* Cambridge.

Momigliano, A. 1975b. "The Fault of the Greeks." *Daedalus* 104: 9–19.

Monroe, C. 2018. "Marginalizing Civilization: The Phoenician redefinition of Power ca. 1300–800 BCE." In *Trade and Civilisation: Economic Networks and Cultural Ties, from Prehistory to the Early Modern Era,* edited by K. Kristiansen, T. Lindkvist, and J. Myrdal, 231–287. Cambridge.

Montanari, F., A. Rengakos, and C. Tsagalis, eds. 2012. *Homeric Contexts: Neoanalysis and the Interpretation of Oral Poetry.* Berlin.

Moran, W. L. 1992. *The Amarna Letters.* Baltimore.

Moret, P. 2011. "¿Dónde estaban los Turdetani? Recovecos y metamorfosis de un nombre, de Catón a Estrabón." In Álvarez Martí-Aguilar, *Fenicios en Tartessos,* 235–248.

Morgan, C. 1994. "The Evolution of Sacral 'Landscape': Isthmia, Perachora, and the Early Corinthian State." In *Placing the Gods: Sanctuaries and Sacred Space in Ancient Greece,* edited by S. E. Alcock and R. Osborne, 105–142. New York.

Morris, I. 1987. *Burial and Ancient Society.* Cambridge.

Morris, I. 1994. "Archaeologies of Greece." In *Classical Greece: Ancient Histories and Modern Archaeologies,* edited by I. Morris, 8–47. Cambridge.

Morris, I. 2005. "Mediterraneanization." In *Mediterranean Paradigms and Classical Antiquity,* edited by I. Malkin, 30–55. London.

Morris, I., and J. G. Manning. 2005. "Introduction." In *The Ancient Economy: Evidence and Models,* edited by J. G. Manning and I. Morris, 1–44. Stanford.

Morris, S. P. 1989. "Daidalos and Kadmos: Classicism and Orientalism." *Arethusa* 1989: 39–54.

Morris, S. P. 1992. *Daidalos and the Origins of Greek Art.* Princeton.

Morris, S. P. 1995. "The Sacrifice of Astyanax: Near Eastern Contributions to the Siege of Troy." In Carter and Morris, *Ages of Homer,* 221–245.

Morris, S. P. 1997. "Greek and Near Eastern Art in the Age of Homer." In Langdon, *New Light,* 56–71.

Morris, S. P. 1998. "Daidalos and Kothar: The Future of a Relationship." In *The Aegean and the Orient in the Second Millennium,* edited by E. H. Cline and D. Harris-Cline, 281–289. Liège.

Morris, S. P. 2006. "The View from East Greece: Miletus, Samos and Ephesus." In Riva and Vella, *Debating Orientalization,* 66–84.

Morris, S. P. 2007. "Linking with a Wider World: Greeks and 'Barbarians.'" In *Blackwell Guides in Global Archaeology: Classical Archaeology,* edited by S. Alcock and R. Osborne, 383–400. Malden.

Morris, S. P. 2019. "Close Encounters on Sicily: Molech, Meilichios, and Religious Convergence at Selinous." In Blakely and Collins, *Religious Convergence,* 77–99.

Morris, S. P., and Papadopoulos, J. 1998. "Phoenicians and the Corinthian Pottery Industry." In *Archäologische Studien in Kontaktzonen der antiken Welt,* edited by R. Rolle and K. Schmidt, 251–263. Göttingen.

Morstadt, B. 2015. "Phoenician Bronze Candelabra and Incense Burners." In Jiménez Ávila, *Phoenician Bronzes,* 147–181.

Moscati, S., ed. 1968. *The World of the Phoenicians.* London.

Moscati, S., ed. 1988a. *The Phoenicians.* Milan.

Moscati, S. 1988b. "Orientalizing Art." In Moscati, *Phoenicians,* 542–547.

Moyer, I. 2011. *Egypt and the Limits of Hellenism.* Cambridge.

Murray, S. 2017. *Collapse of the Mycenaean Economy: Imports, Trade and Institutions 1300–700 BCE.* Cambridge.

Muscuso, S. 2017. "I vetri e l'ambra." In Guirguis, *La Sardegna fenicia,* 439–441.

Naiden, F. 2006. "Rejected Sacrifice in Greek and Hebrew Religion." *Journal of Ancient Near Eastern Religions* 6: 189–223.

Naso, A. 2000. "The Etruscan Aristocracy in the Orientalizing Period: Culture, Economy, Relations." In Torelli, *Etruscans,* 111–139.

Naso, A. 2015. "Bronzi fenici e bronzi etruschi." In Jiménez Ávila, *Phoenician Bronzes,* 375–393.

Naso, A., ed. 2017. *Etruscology.* Boston.

Nava, M. L. 2011. "La tradizione millenaria dell'ambra." In *Le grandi vie delle civiltà: Relazioni e scambi fra Mediterraneo e il Centro Europa della prehistoria alla Romanità,* edited by F. Marzatico, R. Gebhard, and P. Gleirscher, 159–167. Trento.

Naveh, J. 1987. *Early History of the Alphabet: An Introduction to West Semitic Epigraphy and Palaeography.* 2nd ed. Jerusalem.

Negueruela, I. 2004. "Hacia la comprensión de la construcción naval fenicia según el barco 'Mazarrón 2' del siglo VII a.C." In Mederos, Peña, and González Wagner, *La navegación fenicia,* 227–278.

Neto, N., P. M. Rebelo, R. A. Ribeiro, M. Rocha, and J. A. Zamora López. 2016.

"Uma inscrição lapidar fenícia em Lisboa." *Revista Portuguesa de Arqueologia* 19: 123–128.

Neville, A. 2007. *Mountains of Silver and Rivers of Gold: The Phoenicians in Iberia*. Oxford.

Newton, C. T. 1880. *Essays on Art and Archaeology*. London.

Niemeier, W.-D. 2016. "Greek Sanctuaries and the Orient." In Aruz and Seymour, *Assyria to Iberia*, 234–250.

Niemeyer, H. G. 1993. "Trade before the Flag? On the Principles of Phoenician Expansion in the Mediterranean." In *Biblical Archaeology Today, 1990*, edited by A. Biran and J. Aviram, 335–344. Jerusalem.

Niemeyer, H. G. 2000. "The Early Phoenician City-States on the Mediterranean." In *A Comparative Study of Thirty City-State Cultures*, edited by M. H. Hansen, 89–115. Copenhagen.

Niemeyer, H. G. 2004. "Phoenician or Greek: Is There a Reasonable Way Out of the Al Mina Debate?" *Ancient West and East* 3: 38–50.

Niemeyer, H. G. 2005. "There Is No Way Out of the Al Mina Debate." *Ancient West and East* 4: 292–295.

Niemeyer, H. G. 2006. "The Phoenicians in the Mediterranean, between Expansion and Colonization." In Tsetskhladze, *Greek Colonisation*, 143–168.

Niesiołowski-Spanò, Ł., and M. Węcowski, eds. 2018. *Change, Continuity, and Connectivity: North-Eastern Mediterranean at the Turn of the Bronze Age and in the Early Iron Age*. Wiesbaden.

Nigro, L. 2005. *Mozia XI. Zona C. Il Tempio del Cothon*. Rome.

Nigro, L. 2013. "Before the Greeks: The Earliest Phoenician Settlement in Motya—Recent Discoveries by Rome 'La Sapienza' Expedition." *Vicino Oriente* 17: 39–74.

Nigro, L. 2015 "Temples in Motya and Their Levantine Prototypes: Phoenician Religious Architectural Tradition." In *Cult and Ritual on the Levantine Coast and Its Impact on the Eastern Mediterranean Realm*, edited by C. Doumet-Serhal and A. M. Maila-Afeiche, 83–108. Beirut.

Nigro, L. 2019. "The Temple of Astarte 'Aglaia' at Motya and Its Cultural Significance in the Mediterranean Realm." In Blakely and Collins, *Religious Convergence*, 101–125.

Nigro, L., and F. Spagnoli. 2017. *Landing on Motya: The Earliest Phoenician Settlement of the 8th Century BC and the Creation of a West Phoenician Cultural Identity in the Excavations of Sapienza University of Rome, 2012–2016*. Rome.

Nijboer, A. J. 2005. "La cronologia assoluta dell'età del Ferro nel Mediterraneo, dibattito sui metodi e sui risultati." In *Oriente e Occidente: metodi e discipline a confronto: Riflessioni sulla cronologia dell'età del ferro in Italia*, edited by G. Bartoloni and F. Delpino, 527–556. Pisa.

Nijboer, A. J. 2006. "*Coppe di tipo Peroni* and the Beginning of the Orientalizing Phenomenon in Italy during the Late 9th Century BC." In *Studi di protostoria in onore di Renato Peroni*, 288–304. Florence.

Nijboer, A. J. 2008. "A Phoenician Family Tomb, Lefkandi, Huelva, and the Tenth Century BC in the Mediterranean." In Sagona, *Beyond the Homeland*, 365–377.

Nijboer, A. J. 2013. "Banquet, Marzeah, Symposion and Symposium during the Iron Age: Disparity and Mimicry." In *Regionalism and Globalism in Antiquity: Exploring Their Limits,* edited by F. de Angelis, 95–125. Leuven.

Nijboer, A. J., and J. van der Plicht. 2006. "An Interpretation of the Radiocarbon Determinations of the Oldest Indigenous-Phoenician Stratum Thus Far, Excavated at Huelva, Tartessos (South-West Spain)." *BABESCH* 81: 31–36.

Niveau de Villedary y Mariñas, A. M. 2021. "La Gadir arcaica: cronología, topografía y morfología urbana." In *Entre Útica y Gadir: Navegación y colonización fenicia en el Mediterráneo occidental a comienzos del I milenio AC,* edited by J. L. López Castro, 315–352. Granada.

Noegel, S. 2007. "Greek Religion and the Ancient Near East." In *A Companion to Greek Religion,* edited by D. Ogden, 21–37. Malden.

Nowlin, J. 2016. "Reorienting Orientalization: Intrasite Networks of Value and Consumption in Central Italy." PhD diss., Brown University.

Nowlin, J. 2021. *Etruscan Orientalization.* Leiden.

Núñez, F. J. 2019. "Pottery and Trade." In López-Ruiz and Doak, *Oxford Handbook,* 329–348.

Oggiano, I. 2000. "La ceramica fenicia di Sant'Imbenia (Alghero, SS)." In *La cerámica fenicia di Sardegna: Dati, problematiche, confronti,* edited by P. Bartoloni and L. Campanella, 236–258. Rome.

Öhlinger, B. 2015 "Indigenous Cult Places of Local and Interregional Scale in Archaic Sicily: A Sociological Approach to Religion." In Kistler et al., *Sanctuaries,* 417–434.

Öhlinger, B. 2016. "Ritual and Religion in Archaic Sicily: Indigenous Material Cultures between Tradition and Innovation." In *Material Culture and Identity between the Mediterranean World and Central Europe,* edited by H. Baitinger, 107–120. Mainz.

Oliveri, F. 2019. "Venere del Mare: Testimonianze del culto nel trapanese." In Blakely and and Collins, *Religious Convergence,* 127–145.

Olmo Lete, G. del. 2004. "Sacrifice, Offerings, and Votives: Syria-Canaan." In *Religions of the Ancient World: A Guide,* edited by S. I. Johnston, 332–333. Cambridge, MA.

O'Meara, D. J. 1989. *Pythagoras Revived: Mathematics and Philosophy in Late Antiquity.* Oxford.

Orsingher, A. 2016a. "The Ceramic Repertoire of Motya: Origins and Development between the 8th and 6th Centuries BC." In *Karthago Dialogue: Karthago und der punische Mittelmeerraum—Kulturkontakte und Kulturtransfers im 1. Jahrtausend vor Christus,* edited by F. Schön and H. Töpfer, 283–312. Tübingen.

Orsingher, A. 2016b. "Reconsidering the Necropoleis of Ayia Irini: A Glimpse of the Iron Age Evidence." In Bourogiannis and Mühlenbock, *Ancient Cyprus Today,* 313–324.

Orsingher, A. 2018. "Across the Middle Sea: The Long Journey of Phoenician and Punic Masks." In *"La medesima cosa sono Ade e Dioniso" (Eraclito, fr. 15. D-K): maschere, teatro e rituali funerari nel mondo antico,* edited by M. Barbanera, 51–68. Rome.

Orsingher, A. 2018–2019. "Stelae, Graves and Eastern Mediterranean Connections and Carthage: A Fresh Look at Tomb 324 OF P Gauckler's Excavation." *Karthago* 31: 1–25.

Osborne, J. 2012. "Communicating Power in the Bit Hilani Palace." *Bulletin of the American Schools of Oriental Research* 368: 29–66.

Osborne, J. 2021. *The Syro-Anatolian City-States: An Iron Age Culture.* Oxford.

Osborne, J. Forthcoming. "Interregional Relations between the Aegean and Syro-Anatolian Worlds during the Early First Millennium BCE." In *The Cambridge Companion to the Early Greek Iron Age,* edited by J. Carter and C. Antonaccio. Cambridge.

Osborne, R. 2006. "W(h)ither Orientalization?" In Riva and Vella, *Debating Orientalization,* 153–158.

Osborne, R. 2009 (1st ed. 1996). *Greece in the Making: 1200–479 BC.* 2nd ed. London.

Osuna, M., J. Bedia, and A. M. Domínguez. 2001. "El santuario protohistórico hallado en la calle Méndez Núñez (Huelva)." In *Ceràmiques jònies d'època arcaica: Centres de producció i comercialització al Mediterrani Occidental,* edited by P. Cabrera and M. Santos, 177–188. Barcelona.

Özyar, A. 2016. "Phoenicians and Greeks in Cilicia? Coining Elite Identity in Iron Age Anatolia." In Aruz and Seymour, *Assyria to Iberia,* 136–146.

Pachón, J. A., C. Aníbal, and J. Carrasco. 2008. "El conjunto orientalizante de Cerro Alcalá (Torres, Jaén): Cuestiones de cronología, contexto e interpretación." *Archivo de Prehistoria Levantina* 27: 115–159.

Paoletti, O., and P. L. Tamagno, eds. *Etruria e Sardegna centro-settentrionale tra l'età del bronzo finale e l'arcaismo.* Pisa.

Papadopoulos, J. K. 1997. "Phantom Euboians." *Journal of Mediterranean Archaeology* 10: 191–219.

Papadopoulos, J. K. 2011. "'Phantom Euboians': A Decade On." *Euboia and Athens,* 113–133. Athens.

Papadopoulos, J. K. 2016. "The Early History of the Greek Alphabet: New Evidence from Eretria and Methone." *Antiquity* 90: 1238–1254.

Papantoniou, G. 2011. "'Hellenising' the 'Cypriot Goddess': Reading the Amathousian Terracotta Figures." In *From Pella to Gandhara: Hybridisation and Identity in the Art and Architecture of the Hellenistic East,* edited by A. Kouremenos, S. Chandrasekaran, and R. Rossi, 35–48. Oxford.

Papantoniou, G. 2012. "Cypriot Sanctuaries and Religion in the Early Iron Age: Views from Before and After." In Iacovou, *Cyprus and the Aegean,* 285–320.

Papi, E. 2014. "Punic Mauretania?" In Quinn and Vella, *Punic Mediterranean,* 202–218.

Pappa, E. 2013. *Early Iron Age Exchange in the West: Phoenicians in the Mediterranean and the Atlantic.* Leuven.

Pappa, E. 2015. "Phoenicians in Sicily." In Burgersdijk et al., *Sicily and the Sea,* 32–37.

Pappa, E. 2019a. "The Poster Boys of Antiquity's 'Capitalism' Shunning Money? The Spread of the Alphabet in the Mediterranean as a Function of a Credit-based, Maritime Trade." *Revista do Museu de Arqueologia e Etnologia* 33: 91–138.

Pappa, E. 2019b. "Near Eastern Colonies and Cultural Influences from Morocco to Algeria before the Carthaginian Expansion: A Survey of the Archaeological Evidence." *Hélade* 5: 57–82.

Pardee, D. 1998. "Les documents d'Arslan Tash: authentiques ou faux?" *Syria* 75: 15–54.

Pardee, D. 2013. "A Brief Case for Phoenician as the Language of the 'Gezer Calendar.'" In *Linguistic Studies in Phoenician: In Memory of J. Brian Peckham,* edited by R. D. Holmstedt and A. Schade, 226–246. Winona Lake.

Pardo Barrionuevo, C. A. 2015. *Economía y sociedad rural fenicia en el Mediterráneo Occidental.* Seville.

Parker, H. 2013. "The Levant Comes of Age: The Ninth Century BCE through Script Traditions." PhD diss., Johns Hopkins University.

Parker, R. 2017. *Greek Gods Abroad: Names, Natures, and Transformations.* Oakland.

Payne, H. 1962. *Perachora: The Sanctuaries of Hera Akraia and Limenia: Excavations of the British School of Archaeology at Athens, 1930–1933. Vol II: Pottery, Ivories, Scarabs, and Other Objects from the Votive Deposits of Hera Limenia,* edited by T. J. Dunbabin. Oxford.

Pedley, J. 2005. *Sanctuaries and the Sacred in the Ancient Greek World.* Cambridge.

Penglase 1994. *Greek Myths and Mesopotamia: Parallels and Influence in the Homeric Hymns and Hesiod.* London.

Pensa, M. 1977. *Rappresentazioni dell'Oltretomba nella ceramica apula.* Rome.

Perkins, P. 2015. "Bucchero in Context." In *A Companion to the Etruscans,* edited by S. Bell and A. A. Carpino, 224–236. Malden.

Perkins, P. 2017. "DNA and Etruscan Identity." In Naso, *Etruscology,* 109–118.

Perra, C. 2019. *La Fortezza Sardo Fenicia del Nuraghe Sirai (Carbonia): Il Ferro II di Sardegna.* Rome.

Petit, T. 2011. *Oedipe et le Chérubin. Les sphinx levantins, cypriotes et grecs comme symvole d'Immortalité.* Fribourg.

Petit, T. 2015. "Sphinx, Chérubins et 'Gardiens' Orphiques." *Museum Helveticum* 72: 142–170.

Petit, T. 2019. *La naissance des cités-royaumes cypriotes.* Oxford.

Pieraccini, L., and E. Baughan. 2023. *Etruria and Anatolia: Material Connections and Artistic Exchange.* New York.

Pilkington, N. 2012. "A Note on Nora and the Nora Stone." *Bulletin of the American Schools of Oriental Research* 365: 45–51.

Pilz, O. 2011. *Frühe matrizengeformte Terrakotten auf Kreta.* Möhnesee.

Pinch, G. 2004. *Egyptian Mythology: A Guide to the Gods, Goddesses, and Traditions of Ancient Egypt.* Oxford.

Polignac, F. de. 1995 (French 1984). *Cults, Territory, and the Origins of the Greek City-State.* Chicago.

Pollock, S. 2006. *The Language of the Gods in the World of Men: Sanskrit, Culture, and Power in Premodern India.* Berkeley.

Polzer, M. E. 2014. "The Bajo de la Campana Shipwreck and Colonial Trade in Phoenician Spain." In Aruz, Graff, and Rakic, *Assyria to Iberia at the Dawn,* 230–242.

Poole, F. 1993. "Scarabs from the Necropolis of Pontecagnano." In *Sesto Congresso internazzionale di egittologia*, edited by G. M. Zaccone and T. Ricardi di Netro, 407–414. Turin.

Popham, M. R., and I. S. Lemos 1995. "A Euboean Warrior Trader." *Oxford Journal of Archaeology* 14: 151–157.

Porzia, F. 2018. "'Imagine There's No Peoples': A Claim against the Identity Approach in Phoenician Studies through Comparison with the Israelite Field." *Rivista di Studi Fenici* 46: 11–27.

Powell, B. B. 1991. *Homer and the Origin of the Greek Alphabet*. Cambridge.

Prag, J. 2006. "*Poenus plane est*—but Who Were the 'Punickes?'" *Papers of the British School at Rome* 74: 1–37.

Prag, J. 2014. "*Phoinix* and *Poenus:* Usage in Antiquity." In Quinn and Vella, *Punic Mediterranean*, 11–23.

Pratt, C. E. 2009. "Minor Transnationalism in the Prehistoric Aegean? The Case of Phoenicians on Crete in the Early Iron Age." *Diaspora* 18: 305–335.

Prayon, F. 2001. "Near Eastern Influences on Early Etruscan Architecture?" In Bonfante and Karageorghis, *Italy and Cyprus*, 335–350.

Pulak, C. 2008. "The Uluburun Shipwreck and Late Bronze Age Trade." In *Beyond Babylon: Art, Trade, and Diplomacy in the Second Millennium BC,* edited by J. Aruz, K. Benzel, and J. M. Evans, 288–310. New York.

Purcell, N. 2006. "Orientalizing: Five Historical Questions." In Riva and Vella, *Debating Orientalization*, 21–30.

Quesada, F. 2014. "Phoenician Ivories and Orientalizing 'Ivories' in the Iberian Peninsula." In Aruz, Graff, and Rakic, *Assyria to Iberia at the Dawn*, 228–229.

Quinn, J. C. 2011. "The Cultures of the Tophet: Identification and Identity in the Phoenician Diaspora." In *Cultural Identity in the Ancient Mediterranean*, edited by E. S. Gruen, 388–413. Los Angeles.

Quinn, J. C. 2013a. "North Africa." In *A Companion to Ancient History,* edited by A. Erskine, 260–272. Malden.

Quinn, J. C. 2013b. "Tophets in the 'Punic World.'" In *The* Tophet *in the Phoenician Mediterranean,* edited by P. Xella, 23–48. Verona.

Quinn, J. C. 2018. *In Search of the Phoenicians*. Princeton.

Quinn, J. C., and M. M. McCarty. 2015. "Echos puniques: langue, culte, et gouvernement en Numidie hellénistique." In *Massinissa au cœur de la consécration d'un premier Etat numide, 20 et 21 septembre 2014, El Khroub (Constantine), Algérie,* edited by D. Badi, 167–199. Algiers.

Quinn, J. C., N. McLynn, R. M. Kerr, and D. Hadas. 2014. "Augustine's Canaanites." *Papers of the British School at Rome* 82: 175–197.

Quinn, J. C., and N. Vella, eds. 2014. *The Punic Mediterranean: Identities and Identification from Phoenician Settlement to Roman Rule.* Cambridge.

Radner, K. 2010. "The Stele of Sargon II of Assyria at Kition: A Focus for an Emerging Cypriot Identity?" In Rollinger et al., *Interkulturalität in der Alten Welt,* 429–449.

Rainey, A. F. 2015. *The El-Amarna Correspondence*. 2 vols. Leiden.

Rask, K. 2011. "New Approaches to the Archaeology of Etruscan Cult Images."

In *The Archaeology of Sanctuaries and Ritual in Etruria,* edited by N. T. de Grummond and I. Edlund-Berry, 89–112. Portsmouth, RI.

Rask, K. Forthcoming. "Animal Sacrifice in Parts: Theorizing Bodily Division in Greek and Etruscan Ritual Killing." In *From Snout to Tail: Exploring the Greek Sacrificial Animal from the Literary, Epigraphical, Iconographical, and Zooarchaeological Evidence,* edited by G. Ekroth and M. Carbon. Athens.

Rathje, A. 1976. "A Group of 'Phoenician' Faience Anthropomorphic Perfume Flasks." *Levant* 8: 96–106.

Rathje, A. 1979. "Oriental Imports in Etruria in the Eighth and Seventh Centuries BC: Their Origins and Implications." In *Italy before the Romans: The Iron Age, Orientalizing and Etruscan Periods,* edited by D. Ridgway and F. Ridgeway, 145–183. London.

Rathje, A. 1986a. "A Tridacna Squamosa Shell." In Swaddling, *Italian Iron Age,* 393–396.

Rathje, A. 1986b. "Five Ostrich Eggs from Vulci." In Swaddling, *Italian Iron Age,* 397–404.

Rathje, A. 1990. "The Adoption of the Homeric Banquet in Central Italy in the Orientalizing Period." In *Sympotica: A Symposium on the Symposion,* edited by O. Murray, 279–288. Oxford.

Rathje, A. 2007. "Murlo, Images and Archaeology." *Etruscan Studies* 10: 175–184.

Redissi, T. 1999. "Etude des empreintes de sceaux de Carthage." In *Karthago III: Die deutschen Ausgrabungen in Karthago,* edited by A. von den Driesch, J. Holst, and F. Rakob, 4–92. Mainz.

Regev, D. 2020. *New Light on Canaanite-Phoenician Pottery.* Sheffield.

Regev, D. 2021. *Painting the Mediterranean Phoenician: On Canaanite-Phoenician Trade-Nets.* Sheffield.

Remedios Sánchez, S. 2010. "Apuntes sobre la presencia púnica en la Roma arcaica." *SPAL* 19: 187–196.

Rendeli, M. 2018. "Sant'Imbeina and the Topic of the Emporia in Sardinia." In Gailledrat, Dietler, and Plana-Mallart, *Emporion,* 191–204.

Reyes, A. T. 1994. *Archaic Cyprus: A Study of the Textual and Archaeological Evidence.* Oxford.

Rhodes, R. F. 1987. "Early Corinthian Architecture and the Origins of the Doric Order." *American Journal of Archaeology* 91: 477–480.

Ribichini, S., and P. Xella. 1994. *La religione fenicia e punica in Italia.* Rome.

Richey, M. 2019a. "Inscriptions." In López-Ruiz and Doak, *Oxford Handbook,* 223–240.

Richey, M. 2019b. "The Alphabet and Its Legacy." In López-Ruiz and Doak, *Oxford Handbook,* 241–255.

Ridgway, D. 1992a. *The First Western Greeks.* Cambridge.

Ridgway, D. 1992b. "Demaratus and His Predecessors." In Kopcke and Tokumaru, *Greece between East and West,* 93–102.

Ridgway, D. 1994. "Phoenicians and Greeks in the West: A View from Pithekoussai." In *The Archaeology of Greek Colonisation: Essays Dedicated to Sir John Boardman,* edited by G. Tsetskhladze and F. de Angelis, 35–46. Oxford.

Ridgway, D. 2002. "Rapporti dell'Etruria con l'Egeo e il Levante: Prolegomena sarda." In Paoletti and Tamagno, *Etruria e Sardegna*, 215–223.

Riedweg, C. 2005. *Pythagoras: His Life, Teaching, and Influence*. Ithaca, NY.

Riis, P. J. 1960–1961. "Plaquettes syriennes d'Astarte dans les milieux grecs." *Mélanges de l'Université Saint-Joseph* 37: 194–198.

Riva, C. 2006. "The Orientalizing Period in Etruria: Sophisticated Comunities." In Riva and Vella, *Debating Orientalization*, 110–134.

Riva, C. 2010. *The Urbanization of Etruria: Funerary Practices and Social Change, 700–600 BC*. Cambridge.

Riva, C. 2014. "Connectivity Beyond the Urban Centre in Central Italy." In Knapp and van Dommelen, *Cambridge Prehistory*, 437–453.

Riva, C., and N. Vella, eds. 2006a. *Debating Orientalization: Multidisciplinary Approaches to Processes of Change in the Ancient Mediterranean*. London.

Riva, C., and N. Vella. 2006b. "Introduction." In Riva and Vella, *Debating Orientalization*, 1–20.

Rodríguez González, E. 2015. "Southwestern Iberian Peninsula Archaeology: Latest Developments in Final Bronze Age–Early Iron Age." In Babbi et al., *Mediterranean Mirror*, 293–304.

Rodríguez González, E. 2020. "Tarteso y lo orientalizante. Una revisión historiográfica de una confusión terminológica y su aplicación a la cuenca media del Guadiana." *Lucentum* 39: 113–129.

Rodríguez Ramos, J. 2002. "El origen de la escritura sudlusitano-tartesia y la formación de alfabetos a partir de alefatos." *Rivista di Studi Fenici* 30: 187–222.

Roller, D. W. 2003. *The World of Juba II and Kleopatra Selene: Roman Scholarship on Rome's African Frontier*. New York.

Roller, D. W. 2006. *Through the Pillars of Herakles: Greco-Roman Exploration of the Atlantic*. London.

Roller, D. W. 2019. "Phoenician Exploration." In López-Ruiz and Doak, *Oxford Handbook*, 645–653.

Röllig, W. 1992. "Asia Minor as a Bridge between East and West: The Role of Phoenicians and Aramaeans in the Transfer of Culture." In Kopcke and Tokumaru, *Greece between East and West*, 93–102.

Röllig, W. 1995. "L'alphabet." In Krings, *La civilisation phénicienne*, 191–214.

Rollinger, R., B. Gufler, M. Lang, and I. Madreiter, eds. 2010. *Interkulturalität in der Alten Welt: Vorderasien, Hellas, Ägypten und die vielfältigen Ebenen des Kontakts*. Wiesbaden.

Rollston, C. A. 2010. *Writing and Literacy in the World of Ancient Israel: Epigraphic Evidence from the Iron Age*. Atlanta.

Roppa, A. 2014. "Identifying Punic Sardinia: Local Communities and Cultural Identities." In Quinn and Vella, *Punic Mediterranean*, 257–281.

Roppa, A. 2019a. "Sardinia." In López-Ruiz and Doak, *Oxford Handbook*, 521–536.

Roppa, A. 2019b. "Colonial Encounters and Artisanal Practices in the Western Phoenician World: Ceramic Evidence from Sardinia." *Rivista di Studi Fenici* 47: 53–66.

Roppa, A. 2021. "Nuraghi and the Rural Landscapes of Punic Sardinia (5th–2nd c. BC)." In *Transformations and Crisis in the Mediterranean—III: "Identity" and Interculturality in the Levant and Phoenician West during the 5th–2nd Centuries BCE*, edited by G. Garbati and T. Pedrazzi, 245–258. Rome.

Roppa, A., and E. Madrigali. In press. "Colonial Production and Urbanization in Iron Age to early Punic Sardinia (8th–5th c. BC)." In *Making Cities: Economies of Production and Urbanisation in Mediterranean Europe 1000–500 BCE*, edited by M. Gleba and B. Marín-Aguilera. Cambridge.

Rossi, A. M. 2017. "Archaeology and Archaeological Discourse in Pre-Independence Malta." *Malta Archaeological Review* 11: 51–59.

Ruijgh, C. J. 1997. "La date de la création de l'alphabet grec et celle de l'épopée homérique." *Bibliotheca Orientalis* 54: 533–603.

Ruipérez, M. S. 2006. *El mito de Edipo: Lingüística, psicoanálisis y folklore.* Madrid.

Ruiz Cabrero, L. A. 2003. "El estuche con banda mágica de Moraleda de Zafayona (Granada): una nueva inscripción fenicia." *Byrsa* 1: 85–106.

Ruiz Cabrero, L. A. 2010. "La devoción de los navegantes: El culto de Astarté Ericina en el Mediterráneo." In *La devozione dei naviganti: Il culto di Afrodite Ericina nel Mediterraneo*, edited by E. Acquaro, A. Filippi, and S. Medas, 97–135. Lugano.

Ruiz-Gálvez, M. L., ed. 1995. *Ritos de paso y puntos de paso: La ría de Huelva en el mundo del Bronce Final europeo.* Madrid.

Ruiz-Gálvez, M. L. 2005. "Der Fliegende Mittlemeermann: Piratas y héroes en los albores de la edad del hierro." In Celestino and Jiménez Ávila, *El Período Orientalizante*, 251–275.

Ruiz-Gálvez, M. L. 2014. "Before the 'Gates of Tartessos': Indigenous Knowledge and Exchange Networks in the Late Bronze Age Far West." In Knapp and van Dommelen, *Cambridge Prehistory*, 196–214.

Rupp, D. W. 1987. "'Vive le Roi': Emergence of the State in Iron Age Cyprus." In *Western Cyprus: Connections*, edited by D. W. Rupp, 147–168. Götteborg.

Russell, A., and A. B. Knapp. 2017. "Sardinia and Cyprus: An Alternative View on Cypriotes in the Central Mediterranean." *Papers of the British School at Rome* 85: 1–35.

Rutherford, I. 2011. "Mythology of the Black Land: Greek Myths and Egyptian Origins." In *A Companion to Greek Mythology*, edited by K. Dowden and N. Livingstone, 459–470. Malden.

Sader, H. 2010. "Phoenician 'Popular Art': Transmission, Transformation, and Adaptation of Foreign Motifs in the Light of Recent Archaeological Evidence from Lebanon." In Rollinger et al., *Interkulturalität in der Alten Welt*, 23–40.

Sader, H. 2019. *The History and Archaeology of Phoenicia.* Atlanta.

Sagona, C., ed. 2008a. *Beyond the Homeland: Markers in Phoenician Chronology.* Leuven.

Sagona, C. 2008b. "Malta: Between a Rock and a Hard Place." In Sagona, *Beyond the Homeland*, 487–536.

Sagona, C. 2015. *The Archaeology of Malta: From the Neolithic through the Roman Period.* New York.

Said, E. 1978. *Orientalism.* New York.

Sanders, S. 2009. *The Invention of Hebrew.* Urbana.

Sannibale, M. 2013. "Orientalizing Etruria." In Turfa, *Etruscan World*, 99–133.

Sannibale, M. 2016. "The Etruscan Orientalizing: The View from the Regolini-Galassi Tomb." In Aruz and Seymour, *Assyria to Iberia*, 296–315.

Santocchini Gerg, S. 2014. "'Mercato sardo' e 'mercato fenicio': materiali etruschi e interazioni culturali nella Sardegna arcaica." In *Materiali e contesti nell'età del Ferro sarda*, edited by P. van Dommelen and A. Roppa, 75–86. Rome.

Sass, B. 2002. "Wenamun and His Levant: 1075 BC or 925 BC?" *Ägypten und Levante/Egypt and the Levant* 12: 247–255.

Sass, B. 2017. "The Emergence of Monumental West Semitic Alphabetic Writing, with an Emphasis on Byblos." *Semitica* 59: 109–145.

Sass, B., Y. Garfinkel, M. G. Hasel, and M. G. Klingbail. 2015. "The Lachish Jar Sherd: An Early Alphabetic Inscription Discovered in 2014." *Bulletin of the American Schools of Oriental Research* 374: 233–245.

Sassatelli, G., and E. Govi. 2013. "Etruria on the Po and the Adriatic Sea." In Turfa, *Etruscan World*, 281–300.

Satraki, A. 2012. "Cypriot Polities in the Early Iron Age." In Iacovou, *Cyprus and the Aegean*, 261–281.

Savio, G. 2004. *Le uova di struzzo dipinte nella cultura punica.* Madrid.

Scahill, D. 2017. "Craftsmen and Technologies in the Corinthia: The Development of the Doric Order." In Handberg and Gadolou, *Material Koinai*, 221–244.

Sciacca, F. 2005. *Patere braccellatte in bronzo: Oriente, Grecia, Italia in età orientalizzante.* Rome.

Sciacca, F. 2006–2007. "La circolazione dei doni nell'aristocrazia tirrenica: esempi dall'archeologia." *Revista d'Arqueologia de Ponent* 16–17: 281–292.

Sciacca, F. 2013. "Le prime sfingi in Etruria: iconografie e contesti." In *Il bestiario fantastico di età orientalizzante nella penisola italiana*, edited by M. C. Biella, E. Giovanelli, L. G. Perego, 239–285. Trento.

Serra Ridgway, F. 1990. "Etruscans, Greeks, Carthaginians: The Sanctuary at Pyrgi." In *Greek Colonists and Native Populations*, edited by J.-P. Descoeudres, 511–530. Oxford.

Shaw, B. 2003. "A Peculiar Island: Maghrib and Mediterranean." *Mediterranean Historical Review* 18: 93–125.

Shaw, I. 2003. *The Oxford History of Ancient Egypt.* Oxford.

Shaw, J. W. 1989. "Phoenicians in Southern Crete." *American Journal of Aarchaeology* 93: 165–183.

Shaw, J. W. 1998 "Kommos in Southern Crete: An Aegean Barometer for East-West Interconnections." In *Eastern Mediterranean: Cyprus-Dodecanese-Crete, 16th–6th Century BC*, edited by V. Karageorghis and N. C. Stampolidis, 13–27. Athens.

Shaw, J. W., and M. C. Shaw, eds. 2000. *Kommos IV: The Greek Sanctuary.* Woodstock.

Sherratt, A., and S. Sherratt. 1993. "The Growth of the Mediterranean Economy in the Early First Millennium BC." *World Archaeology* 24: 361–378.

Sherratt, A., and S. Sherratt. 1998. "Small Worlds: Interaction and Identity in the Ancient Mediterranean." In *The Aegean and the Orient in the Second Millennium BC*, edited by E. Cline and D. Harris-Cline, 329–343. Liège.

Sherratt, S. 1993. "Who Are You Calling Peripheral? Dependence and Independence in European Prehistory." In *Trade and Exchange in Prehistoric Europe,* edited by C. Scarre and F. Healy, 245–255. Bloomington.

Sherratt, S. 2003. "Visible Writing: Questions of Script and Identity in Early Iron Age Greece and Cyprus." *Oxford Journal of Archaeology* 22: 225–242.

Sherratt, S. 2010. "Greeks and Phoenicians: Perceptions of Trade and Traders in the Early First Millennium BC." In *Trade as Social Interaction: New Archaeological Approaches,* edited by A. Bauer and A. Agbe-Davies, 119–142. Walnut Creek.

Sherratt, S. 2015. "Cyprus and the Near East: Cultural Contacts 1200–750 BC." In Babbi et al., *Mediterranean Mirror,* 71–83.

Shiloh, Y. 1976. "New Proto-Aeolic Capitals Found in Israel." *Bulletin of the American Schools of Oriental Research* 222: 67–77.

Shiloh, Y. 1979. *The Proto Aeolic Capital and Israelite Ashlar Masonry.* Jerusalem.

Silva Jayasuriya, S. de. 2017. *The Portuguese in the East: A Cultural History of a Maritime Empire.* London.

Skon-Jedele, N. J. 1994. "*Aigyptiaka:* A Catalogue of Egyptian and Egyptianizing Objects Excavated from Greek Archaeological Sites, ca. 1100–525 BC, with Historical Commentary." PhD diss., University of Pennsylvania.

Smith, J. S. 2009. *Art and Society in Cyprus from the Bronze Age into the Iron Age.* Cambridge.

Smith, M. S. 2014. *Poetic Heroes: The Literary Commemorations of Warriors and Warrior Culture in the Early Biblical World.* Grand Rapids.

Snodgrass, A. 1980. *Archaic Greece: The Age of Experiment.* Berkeley.

Snowden, F. M. 1983. *Before Color Prejudice.* Cambridge, MA.

Solá-Solé, J. M. 1966. "Nueva inscripción fenicia de España (Hispania 14)." *Rivista degli Studi Orientali* 41: 97–108.

Sommer, M. 2007. "Networks of Commerce and Knowledge in the Iron Age: The Case of the Phoenicians." *Mediterranean Historical Review* 22: 97–111.

Sossau, V. 2015. "The Cultic Fingerprint of the Phoenicians in the Early Iron Age West?" In Kistler et al., *Sanctuaries,* 21–41.

Sourvinou-Inwood, C. 1993. "Early Sanctuaries, the Eighth Century and Ritual Space: Fragments of a Discourse." In Marinatos and Hägg, *Greek Sanctuaries,* 1–17.

Spatafora, F. 2013. "Ethnic Identity in Sicily: Greeks and Non-Greeks." In *Sicily: Art and Invention between Greece and Rome,* edited by C. L. Lyons, M. J. Bennett, C. Marconi, and A. Sofroniew, 37–47. Los Angeles.

Stager, J. M. 2005. "'Let No One Wonder at This Image': A Phoenician Funerary Stele in Athens." *Hesperia* 74: 427–449.

Stampolidis, N. C. 1990. "A Funerary Cippus at Eleutherna: Evidence of Phoenician Presence?" *Bulletin of the Institute of Classical Studies* 37: 99–106.

Stampolidis, N. C., ed. 2003. *Sea Routes: From Sidon to Huelva: Interconnections in the Mediterranean, 16th–6th c. BC.* Athens.

Stampolidis, N. C., ed. 2004. ΕΛΕΥΘΕΡΝΑ. Πόλη - Ακρόπολη—Νεκρόπολη. Athens.

Stampolidis, N. C. 2016. "Eleutherna on Crete: The Wider Horizon." In Aruz and Seymour, *Assyria to Iberia,* 283–295.

Stampolidis, N. C. 2019. "The Aegean." In López-Ruiz and Doak, *Oxford Handbook*, 493–503.

Stampolidis, N. C., and A. Kotsonas. 2006. "Phoenicians in Crete." In *Ancient Greece from the Mycenaean Palaces to the Age of Homer*, edited by S. Deger-Jalkotzy and I. S. Lemos, 337–360. Edinburgh.

Steele, P. M. 2013a. *A Linguistic History of Ancient Cyprus: The Non-Greek Languages and Their Relations with Greek, c. 1600–300 BC*. Cambridge.

Steele, P. M., ed. 2013b. *Syllabic Writing on Cyprus and Its Context*. Cambridge.

Steele, P. M. 2019. *Writing and Society in Ancient Cyprus*. Cambridge.

Stein, G., ed. 2005. *The Archaeology of Colonial Encounters: Comparative Perspectives*. Santa Fe.

Steingräber, S. 1991. "Etruskische Monumentalcippi." *Archeologia Classica* 43: 1079–1102.

Steingräber, S. 2009. "The Cima Tumulus at San Giuliano: An Aristocratic Tomb and Monument for the Cult of the Ancestors of the Late Orientalizing Period." In *Votives, Places and Rituals in Etruscan Religion: Studies in Honor of Jean Macintosh Turfa*, edited by M. Gleba and H. Becker, 123–133. Leiden.

Steingräber, S., and R. Stockman. 2007. *Abundance of Life: Etruscan Wall Painting*. Los Angeles.

Stern, E. 1992. "The Phoenician Architectural Elements in Palestine during the Late Iron Age and the Persian Period." In *The Architecture of Ancient Israel from the Prehistoric to the Persian Periods*, edited by A. Kempinski and R. Reich, 302–310. Jerusalem (Hebrew).

Stern, E. 1995. "Four Phoenician Finds from Israel." In *Immigration and Emigration within the Ancient Near East (Festschrift E. Lipiński)*, edited by K. von Lerberghe and A. Schoors, 319–334. Leuven.

Stern, E., and Y. Magen. 2002. "Archaeological Evidence for the First Stage of the Samaritan Temple in Mount Gerizim." *Israel Exploration Journal* 52: 49–57.

Stoddart, S. K. 2000. "Contrasting Political Strategies in the Islands of the Southern-Central Mediterranean." *Accordia Research Papers* 7 (1997–1998): 59–73.

Stone, D. Forthcoming. "Isolation and Connectivity: The Maghrib and the Mediterranean in the First Millennium BC." In Gosner and Hayne, *Local Experiences*.

Strøm, I. 1971. *Problems Concerning the Origin and Early Development of the Etruscan Orientalizing Style*. Odense.

Stucky, R. 2014. "Tridacnamuschel." In *Reallexikon der Assyriologie und Vorderasiatischen Archäologie* vol. 14, edited by M. P. Streck, 134–136. Berlin.

Suter, C. 2010. "Luxury Goods in Ancient Israel: Questions of Consumption and Production." In *Proceedings of the 6th International Congress on the Archaeology of the Ancient Near East, Vol. 1: Near Eastern Archaeology in the Past, Present and Future: Heritage and Identity*, edited by P. Matthiae, F. Pinnock, L. Nigro, and N. Marchetti, with L. Romano, 993–1002. Wiesbaden.

Suter, C. 2015. "Classifying Iron Age Levantine Ivories: Impracticalities and a New Approach." *Altorientalische Forschungen* 41: 31–45.

Swaddling, J. ed. 1986. *Italian Iron Age Artefacts in the British Museum.* London.

Tanasi, D. 2020. "Sicily before the Greeks: The Interaction with Aegean and the Levant in the Pre-colonial Era." *Open Archaeology* 6: 172–205.

Tatton-Brown, V. 1997. *Ancient Cyprus.* 2nd ed. London.

Terpstra, T. 2019. *Trade in the Ancient Mediterranean: Private Order and Public Institutions.* Princeton.

Theurillat, T. 2007. "Early Iron Age Graffiti from the Sanctuary of Apollo at Eretria." In Mazarakis Ainian, *Oropos and Euboea,* 331–344.

Tomlinson, R. A. 1992. "Perachora." In *Le sanctuaire grec: huit exposés suivis de discussions,* edited by A. Schachter and J. Bingen, 321–351. Geneva.

Torelli, M. 2000a. "Etruscan Religion." In Torelli, *The Etruscans,* 273–289.

Torelli, M., ed. 2000b. *The Etruscans.* New York.

Torres, M. 1998. "La cronología absoluta europea y el inicio de la colonización fenicia en Occidente: implicaciones cronológicas en Chipre y el Próximo Oriente." *Complutum* 9: 49–60.

Torres, M. 2005. "Tartesios, fenicios y griegos en el Sudoeste de la Península Ibérica: algunas reflexiones sobre los recientes hallazgos de Huelva." *Complutum* 16: 292–304.

Torres, M. 2008a. "Los tiempos del la precolonización." In Celestino, Rafel, and Armada, *Contacto cultural,* 59–92.

Torres, M. 2008b. "Los marfiles hispano-fenicios de Medellín." In *La Necrópolis de Medellín II: Estudio de los hallazgos,* edited by M. Almagro-Gorbea, 401–512. Madrid.

Treumann, B. 2009. "Lumbermen and Shipwrights: Phoenicians on the Mediterranean Coast of Southern Spain." In Dietler and López-Ruiz, *Colonial Encounters,* 169–190.

Tribulato, O. 2013. "Phoenician Lions: The Funerary Stele of the Phoenician Shem/Antipatros." *Hesperia* 82: 459–486.

Tronchetti, C. 2014. "Cultural Interactions in Iron Age Sardinia." In Knapp and van Dommelen, *Cambridge Prehistory,* 266–284.

Tronchetti, C., and P. van Dommelen. 2005. "Entangled Objects and Hybrid Practices: Colonial Contacts and Elite Connections at Monte Prama, Sardinia." *Journal of Mediterranean Archaeology* 18: 183–208.

Tsetskhladze, G. R., ed. 1999. *Ancient Greeks West and East.* Leiden.

Tsetskhladze, G. R., ed. 2006. *Greek Colonisation: An Account of Greek Colonies and Other Settlements Overseas.* Vol. 1. Leiden.

Tsetskhladze, G. R., and F. De Angelis, eds. 1994. *The Archaeology of Greek Colonization: Essays Dedicated to Sir John Boardman.* Oxford.

Tubb, J. 2016. "A New Millennium–A New Order: Philistines, Phoenicians, Aramaeans, and the Kingdom of Israel." In Aruz and Seymour, *Assyria to Iberia,* 88–103.

Tuck, A. 2014. "Manufacturing at Poggio Civitate: Elite Consumption and Social Organization in the Etruscan Seventh Century." *Etruscan and Italic Studies* 17: 121–139.

Tuck, A., and R. Wallace, 2013. *First Words: The Archaeology of Language at Poggio Civitate.* Amherst.

Turfa, J. M. 2001. "The Role of the Phoenicians and Cypro-Phoenicians in Connections between Cyprus and the Cities of Etruria." In Bonfante and Karageorghis, *Italy and Cyprus,* 271–290.

Turfa, J. M. 2012. *Divining the Etruscan World: The Brontoscopic Calendar and Religious Practice.* Cambridge.

Turfa, J. M., ed. 2013. *The Etruscan World.* London.

Tusa, S. 1990. "Preistoria e protostoria nel territorio degli Elimi: la genesi di un ethnos e di una cultura." In *Gli Elimi e l'area elima fino all'inizio della prima guerra punica,* edited by G. Nenci, S. Tusa, and V. Tusa, 31–54. Palermo.

Tzifopoulos, Y. 2013. *Letters from the 'Underground': Writing in Methone, Pieria, Late 8th–Early 7th Century BC.* Thessaloniki.

Uehlinger, C. 1997. "Anthropomorphic Cult Statuary in Iron Age Palestine and the Search for Yahweh's Cult Images." In *The Image and the Book: Iconic Cults, Aniconism, and the Rise of Book Religion in Israel and the Ancient Near East,* edited by K. van der Toorn, 97–155. Leuven.

Ulbrich, A. 2020. "Adoption and Adaptation of Greek Iconography in Cypriot Votive Sculpture of the Late Archaic and Classical Periods." In *Classical Cyprus,* edited by M. Christidis, A. Hermary, G. Koiner, and A. Ulbrich, 221–244. Vienna.

Ulf, C. 2009. "Rethinking Cultural Contacts." *Ancient West and East* 8: 81–132.

Unali, A. 2017. "L'eredità della cultura punica in età romana." In Guirguis, *La Sardegna fenicia,* 111–119.

Usai, A., S. Vidili, C. Del Vais, and A. Carannante. 2018. "Nuovi dati e nuove osservazioni sul complesso di Mont'e Prama (Scavi 2015–2016)." *Quaderni: Rivista di Archeologia* 29: 81–140.

van der Brugge, C., and K. Kleber. 2016. "The Empire of Trade and the Empires of Force: Tyre in the Neo-Assyrian and Neo-Babylonian Periods." In *Dynamics of Production in the Ancient Near East 1300–500 BC,* edited by J. C. Moreno, 187–222. Oxford.

van der Meer, L. B. 2007. *Liber linteus zagrabiensis. The Linen Book of Zagreb: A Comment on the Longest Etruscan Text.* Louvain.

van der Plicht, J., H. J Bruins, and A. J Nijboer. 2009. "The Iron Age around the Mediterranean: A High Chronology Perspective from the Groningen Radio-carbon Database." *Radiocarbon* 51: 213–242.

van Dommelen, P. 2006. "The Orientalizing Phenomenon: Hybridity and Material Culture in the Western Mediterranean." In Riva and Vella, *Debating Orientalization,* 135–152.

van Dommelen, P. 2012. "Colonialism and Migration in the Ancient Mediterranean." *Annual Review of Anthropology* 41: 343–409.

van Dommelen, P. 2015. "Punic Identities and Modern Perceptions in the Western Mediterranean." In Quinn and Vella, *Punic Mediterranean,* 42–57.

van Dommelen, P. 2018. "Trading Places? Sites of Mobility and Migration in the Iron Age West Mediterranean." In Gailledrat, Dietler, and Plana-Mallart, *Emporion,* 219–229.

van Dommelen, P., and C. Gómez Bellard. 2008. *Rural Landscapes of the Punic World.* London.

van Dommelen, P., and M. López-Bertran. 2013. "Hellenism as Subaltern

Practice: Rural Cults in the Punic World." In *The Hellenistic West: Rethinking the Ancient Mediterranean,* edited by J. Prag and J. C. Quinn, 273–299. Cambridge.

van Dommelen, P., and A. Roppa. 2014. *Materiali e contesti dell'età del ferro sarda.* Rome.

van Dongen, E. 2010. "'Phoenicia': Naming and Defining and Region in Syria-Palestine." In *Interkulturalität in der Alten Welt Vorderasien, Hellas, Ägypten und die vielfältigen Ebenen des Kontakts,* edited by R. Rollinger, B. Gufler, M. Lang, and I. Madreiter, 471–488. Wiesbaden.

van Wijngaarden, G. J. 1999. "Mycenaean Pottery in the Central Mediterranean: Imports and Local Production in their Contexts." In *The Complex Past of Pottery: Production, Circulation and Consumption of Mycenaean and Greek Pottery (Sixteenth to Early Fifth Centuries BC),* edited by J. P. Crielaard, V. Stissi, and G. J. van Wijngaarden, 21–47. Amsterdam.

Vasallo, S. 2015. "Ogetti in movimento in età arcaica e clasica ad Himera, porto sicuro per uomini, merci, idee." In Kistler et al., *Sanctuaries,* 153–167.

Vella, N. 2005. "Phoenician and Punic Malta (review article)." *Journal of Roman Archaeology* 18: 436–450.

Vella, N. 2010. "'Phoenician' Metal Bowls: Boundary Objects in the Archaic Period." *Bolletino di archeologia on line* 1: 22–37.

Vella, N. 2014. "The Invention of the Phoenicians: On Object Definition, Decontextualization and Display." In Quinn and Vella, *The Punic Mediterranean,* 24–41.

Vella, N. 2019. "Birth and Prospects of a Discipline." In López-Ruiz and Doak, *Oxford Handbook,* 23–35.

Vella, N., and M. Anastasi. 2019. "Malta and Gozo." In López-Ruiz and Doak, *Oxford Handbook,* 553–568.

Vera, J. C., and A. Echevarría. 2013. "Sistemas agrícolas del I milenio a.C. en el yacimiento de la Orden-Seminario de Huelva." In Celestino and Blánquez, *Patrimonio cultural,* 95–106.

Vlassopoulos, K. 2007. *Unthinking the Greek Polis: Ancient Greek History beyond Eurocentrism.* Cambridge.

Vlassopoulos, K. 2012. "The Barbarian Repertoire in Greek Culture." Αριάδνη 18: 53–88.

Vlassopoulos, K. 2014. "Which Comparative Histories for Ancient Historians?" *Synthesis* 21: 31–47.

Waal, W. 2018. "'On the Phoenician Letters': A Case for an Early Transmission of the Greek Alphabet from an Archaeological, Epigraphic, and Linguistic Evidence." *Aegean Studies* 1: 83–125.

Wade-Gery, H. 1952. *The Poet of the* Iliad. Cambridge.

Walcot, P. 1966. *Hesiod and the Near East.* Cardiff.

Waldbaum, J. C. 1997. "Greeks *in* the East or Greeks *and* the East? Problems in the Definition and Recognition of Presence." *Bulletin of the American Schools of Oriental Research* 305: 1–17.

Wallace, R. E. 2016. "Language, Alphabet, and Linguistic Affiliation." In *A Companion to the Etruscans,* edited by S. Bell and A. Carpino, 203–223. Chichester.

Ward, A. F. 2017. "Post-409 Selinus and the Dangers of Cultural Periodization."

Annual meeting of the Archaeological Institute of America, Toronto, January 5–8 (abstract).

Ward, A. F. 2018. "The Stelai Shrines of Greek Corinth: New Approaches and Evidence." Annual meeting of the Archaeological Institute of America, Boston, January 4–7 (poster abstract).

Webster, G. S. 2015. *The Archaeology of Nuragic Sardinia*. London.

Welton, L. 2019. "Shifting Networks and Community Identity at Tell Tayinat in the Iron I (ca. 12th to mid-10th cent. BCE)." *American Journal of Archaeology* 123: 291–333.

Wengrow, D. 2006. "Approaching Ancient Orientalization *via* Modern Europe." In Riva and Vella, *Debating Orientalization*, 31–47.

West, M. L. 1966. *Hesiod:* Theogony; *Edited with Prolegomena and Commentary*. Oxford.

West, M. L. 1971. *Early Greek Philosophy and the Orient*. Oxford.

West, M. L. 1983. *The Orphic Poems*. Oxford.

West, M. L. 1994. "*Ab Ovo:* Orpheus, Sanchuniaton, and the Origins of the Ionian World Model." *Classical Quarterly* 44: 289–307.

West, M. L. 1997. *The East Face of Helicon: West Asiatic Elements in Greek Poetry and Myth*. Oxford.

West, M. L. 2000. "The Name of Aphrodite." *Glotta* 76: 133–138.

West, M. L. 2007. *Indo-European Poetry and Myth*. Oxford.

West, M. L. 2011. *The Making of the* Iliad: *Disquisition and Analytical Commentary*. Oxford.

Whitley, J. 2001. *The Archaeology of Ancient Greece*. Cambridge.

Winter, I. 1976a. "Phoenician and North Syrian Ivory Carving in Historical Context: Questions of Style and Distribution." *Iraq* 38: 1–22. Republished in *OAANE* 1: 187–224 (2010).

Winter, I. 1976b. "Carved Ivory Furniture Panels from Nimrud: A Coherent Subgroup of the North Syrian Style." *Metropolitan Museum Journal* 11: 25–54.

Winter, I. 1981. "Is There a South Syrian Style of Ivory Carving in the Early First Millennium BC?" *Iraq* 43: 101–130.

Winter, I. 1995. "Homer's Phoenicians: History, Ethnography, or Literary Trope? [A Perspective on Early Orientalism]." In Carter and Morris, *Ages of Homer*, 247–271.

Winter, I. 2016. "The 'Woman at the Window'": Iconography and Inferences of a Motif in First-Millennium BC Levantine Ivory Carving." In Aruz and Seymour, *Assyria to Iberia*, 180–193.

Winter, N. A. 2009. *Symbols of Wealth and Power: Architectural Terracotta Decoration in Etruria and Central Italy, 640–510 BC*. Ann Arbor.

Witte, I. J., and J. F. Diehl, eds. 2008. *Israeliten und Phönizier: Ihre Beziehungen im Spiegel der Archäologie und der Literatur des Alten Testaments und seiner Umwelt*. Fribourg.

Wood, J. R., C. Bell, and I. Montero-Ruiz. 2020. "The Origin of Tel Dor Hacksilver and the Westward Expansion of the Phoenicians in the Early Iron Age: The Cypriot Connection." *Journal of Eastern Mediterranean Archaeology and Heritage Studies* 8: 1–21.

Woodard, R. D. 2010. "*Phoinikēia Grammata:* An Alphabet for the Greek

Language." In *A Companion to the Ancient Greek Language,* edited by E. J. Bakker, 25–46. Malden, MA.

Woolmer, M. 2017. *A Short History of the Phoenicians.* London.

Wriedt Sørensen, L. 1994. "The Divine Image?" In *Cypriote Stone Sculpture,* edited by F. Vandenabeele and R. Laffineur, 79–89. Brussels.

Wulf, F. A. 2003. *Las esencias patrias: Historiografía e historia antigua en la construcción de la identidad española* (siglos xvi–xx). Barcelona.

Wulf, F. A. 2013. "Tarteso en la historiografía española: notas sobre un (relativo) desinterés." In Campos Carrasco and Alvar Ezquerra, *Tarteso,* 631–639.

Wyatt, N. 2009. "Grasping the Griffin: Identifying and Characterizing the Griffin in Egyptian and West Semitic Tradition." *Journal of Ancient Egyptian Interconnections* 1: 29–39.

Xella, P. 2017. "Self-Depiction and Legitimation: Aspects of Phoenician Royal Ideology." In *Herrschaftslegitimation in vorderorientalischen Reichen der Eisenzeit herausgegeben,* edited by C. Levin and R. Müller, 97–110. Tübingen.

Yadin, Y. 1958. "Solomon's Wall and Gate at Gezer." *Israel Exploration Journal* 8: 8–86.

Yakubovich, I. 2015. "Phoenician and Luwian in Early Iron Age Cilicia." *Anatolian Studies* 65: 35–53.

Yon, J.-B. 2011. "Les Tyriens dans le monde méditerranéen à l'époque hellénistique." In *Sources de l'histoire de Tyr: Textes de l'antiquité et du Moyen Âge,* edited by P.-L. Gatier, J. Aliquot, and L. Nordiguian, 33–61. Beirut.

Yon, M. 1986. "Cultes phéniciennes à Chypre: l'interpetation chypriote." In Bonnet, Lipiński, and Marchetti, *Religio Phoenicia,* 127–152.

Yon, M. 2006. *The City of Ugarit at Tell Ras Shamra.* Winona Lake.

Zamora, J. A. 2003. "Textos mágicos y trasfondo mitológico: Arslan Tash." In *Epigrafia e storia delle religioni: del documento epigrafico al problema storico-religioso,* edited by P. Xella and J. A. Zamora, 9–23. Rome.

Zamora, J. A. 2019. "Phoenician Epigraphy." In *Palaeohispanic Languages and Epigraphy,* edited by A. Sinner and J. Velaza, 1–32. Oxford.

Ziffer, I. 2013. "Portraits of Ancient Israelite Kings?" *Biblical Archaeology Review* 39: 41–51.

Zimmerman Munn, M. L. 2003. "Corinthian Trade with the Punic West in the Classical Period." In *Corinth: The Centenary 1896–1996,* edited by C. K. Williams and N. Bookidis, 195–217. Princeton.

Ziskowski, A. 2016. "Networks of Influence: Reconsidering Braudel in Archaic Corinth." In Concannon and Mazurek, *Across the Corrupting Sea,* 91–110.

Ziskowski, A. 2017. "Material Koine: Constructing and Narrative of Identity in Archaic Corinth." In Handberg and Gadolou, *Material Koinai,* 91–108.

Zucca, R. 2017. "Rapporti di interazione tra Fenici e Nuragici." In Guirguis, *La Sardegna fenicia,* 45–53.

ACKNOWLEDGMENTS

This book has been five years in the writing but about twenty in the making. My research has benefited from conversations with more audiences, colleagues, and students than I can remember. Important books on the Phoenicians have appeared while my project was already well underway. While this book is not a response to them, my intellectual engagement with their premises has sharpened and reinforced my argument and the sense of urgency to publish it. Several relevant works were available only when my book was finished or in production, and I have been unable to engage with them as fully as I would have liked (especially Edrey 2019, published in late 2020, and Regev 2021; thanks to access to proofs of Hodos 2020, I could incorporate more references to it, for which I am truly grateful).

It is an honor to publish this book with Harvard University Press, not the least since Walter Burkert's *The Orientalizing Revolution* (1992) was a great inspiration for my early pursuit of Greek–Near Eastern contacts. I want to thank Sharmila Sen, editorial director at the Press for the faith that she showed in this project from the start and her wise advice; her associate editor, Heather Hughes, for her attentive guidance throughout the preparation of the manuscript; Stephanie Vyce for her assistance with matters of intellectual property; and Cheryl Hirsch for her phenomenal job as production editor. Therese Malhame did the smoothest copyediting I have seen. Finally, I greatly benefited from the comments of the anonymous readers appointed by the Press. My discussion of the sphinx in Chapter 6 summarizes a longer essay on the topic (López-Ruiz 2021), and my response to Phoenikoscepticism in the Introduction stems from discussions I developed more fully in two recent essays (López-Ruiz 2022b and forthcoming). The input of peer reviewers and editors of those publications must be acknowledged here, too.

I owe much to my department chairs at Ohio State University over these years, Benjamin Acosta-Hughes, Nathan Rosenstein, and Scott Levi, for supporting my research in ways both material (for instance, with funds for image acquisition and indexing) and immaterial, not the least with flexibility and encouragement. For their administrative support, I thank Khalid Jama and Adam Bacus, who patiently helped navigate bureaucratic hurdles. The College of Arts and Humanities at Ohio State has funded initial research for this book through the Virginia Hull Research Award (2008) and the Arts and Humanities Larger Grants (2014–2015). The Melton Center for Jewish Studies has provided a wonderfully interdisciplinary community and supported my research over the years, besides generously helping with the cost of the images for this book.

A handful of devoted colleagues read the entire manuscript before submission and gave detailed comments: Denise Demetriou, Tamar Hodos, Anthony Kaldellis, and Sarah Morris. My father, Rafael López Pintor, did so, too, and his historical and sociological perspective (and the love for antiquity we share) was, as always, precious, instructive, and inspiring. In turn, many colleagues with expertise in different fields have read sections of my book, answered specific questions, and shared published or forthcoming research. This was especially appreciated as I was finishing the writing during the months of lockdown in the spring and summer of 2020. These include Sebastián Celestino, Salvatore De Vincenzo, Bonnie Effros, Fanni Faegersten, Sabine Fourrier, Iván Fumadó, Fritz Graf, Jeremy Hayne, Maria Iacovou, Sarah Johnston, Susan Langdon, Gunnar Lehmann, Tim McNiven, Jessica Nowlin, James Osborne, John Papadopoulos, Katherine Rask, Madadh Richey, Esther Rodríguez González, Andrea Roppa, David Schloen, Omer Sergi, Peter van Dommelen, Nicholas Vella, Andrew Ward, José-Ángel Zamora, and Angela Ziskowski. For insightful conversations on the argument of the book, I should especially mention Yiorgos Anagnostou, Alain Bresson, Jesús García de la Morena, Dannu Hütwohl, Gregory Jusdanis, Pedro Pereira, Andrea Rotstein, Tina Sessa, Sofía Torallas Tovar, Brigitte Treumann, and Marcus Ziemann.

Ian Mladjov and Esther Rodríguez have been my miracle workers, respectively, for the maps and the image compositions made for this book, and Ayla Çevik did meticulous work with the index. I cannot praise enough their skill, knowledge, and patience. I thank the many friends and scholars who helped with image information or acquisition (not all of which made it to the final cut for the book): Yael Barschak, María Belén Deamos, Luis Calero, Sebastián Celestino, Brian Doak, Fanni Faegersten, John Franklin, José María Gener, Michele Guirguis, Tamar Hodos, Hélène Le Meaux, Lorenzo Nigro, Bengt Pettersson, Nikos Stampolidis, Gemma Storti, Mariano Torres, Carlo Tronchetti, Lita Tzortzopoulou, and Peter van Dommelen. Besides the institutions and agencies involved in providing images and licenses, separate thanks go to several colleagues who courteously facilitated my use of images or gave permissions: Felipa Díaz (National Archaeological Museum, Madrid), Eirini Galli (Archaeological Museum of Heraklion), Guillermo Kurtz (Archaeological Museum of Badajoz), Ricado Lineros (Museum of the City of Carmona), Isabel López Delgado (Junta de Andalucía), Sharon Sultana (National Museum of Archaeology, Malta), and the staff at the British Museum.

Finally, the initial writing phase of this book was funded by the National Endowment for the Humanities, with a Fellowship (2016–2017) granted under the initiative "The Common Good: The Humanities in the Public Square." I am deeply grateful for the Endowment's support for "research, education, preservation, and public programs in the Humanities," which resists current trends to divest from these essential disciplines of human self-knowledge.

ACKNOWLEDGMENTS

I dedicate this book with much love to my life partner, friend, and colleague, Anthony Kaldellis (Antonis). Besides his unconditional support in all my academic and (sometimes outlandish) personal pursuits, our conversations have made me a sharper thinker and writer, for the benefit of my readers.

INDEX

Page numbers in *italics* refer to illustrations.